THE OPPOSITE SEX

The OPPOSITE SEX

Edited by Anne Campbell

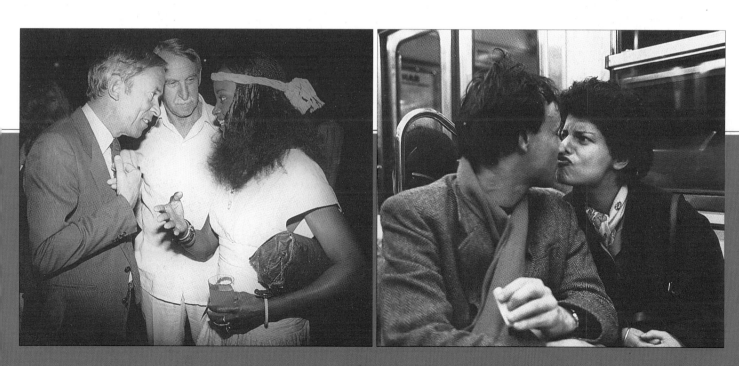

Salem House Publishers
Topsfield, Massachusetts

CONTENTS

Part One: Girls and Boys

CONTRIBUTORS

AC Dr Anne Campbell
Associate Professor of Psychology,
Rutgers University, New Jersey, USA

ACl Dr Anne Colby
Director, The Henry A Murray
Research Center, Radcliffe College,
Cambridge, Massachusetts, USA

BG Professor Bernard Gorman
Professor of Psychology, Nassau
Community College, New York, USA

BL Dr Barbara Lloyd
Reader in Psychology, University of
Sussex, UK

CE Dr Caroline Edwards
Associate Professor of Education,
University of Massachusetts, USA

CJ Professor Carol N Jacklin
Professor, Program for the Study of
Women and Men in Society,
University of Southern California, USA

CJC Dr C Jan Carpenter
Assistant Professor of Human
Development and Family Ecology,
School of Human Resources and
Family Studies, University of Illinois,
USA

CL Dr Charles N Lewis
Lecturer in Developmental
Psychology, University of Reading,
UK

CR Dr Colin Rogers
Lecturer in Education, University of
Lancaster, UK

CTH Professor Charles T Hill
Professor of Psychology, Whittier
College, California, USA

DJH Dr David Hargreaves
Lecturer in Psychology, University
of Leicester, UK

EC Dr Eva Conrad
Associate Professor of Psychology,
San Bernardino Valley College,
California, USA

EL Dr Ellen Lenney
Associate Professor of Psychology,
University of Maine, USA

ES Dr Evan Stark
Assistant Professor of Public
Administration, Rutgers University,
New Jersey, USA

FJC Professor Faye J Crosby
Professor of Psychology, Smith
College, Northampton,
Massachusetts, USA

HDS Professor Horst D Steklis
Professor of Anthropology, Rutgers
University, New Jersey, USA

JBG Dr J Brooks-Gunn
Senior Research Scientist,
Educational Testing Service,
Princeton, USA

JW Dr Jane E Wilson
Staff Research Associate in
Psychiatry, University of California,
Los Angeles, USA

**KAC-S Professor Kathleen Alison
Clark-Stewart**
Professor of Psychology, University
of California, Irvine, USA

KS Dr Karin Sandqvist
Research Scientist, Stockholm
Institute of Education, Sweden

MH Dr Melissa Hines
Assistant Biobehavioral Scientist,
Department of Psychiatry, University
of California, Los Angeles, USA

First published in the United States
by Salem House Publishers, 1989,
462 Boston Street,
Topsfield, MA 01983

Devised and produced by
Andromeda Oxford Ltd
Dorchester-on-Thames
Oxford OX9 8JU, UK

Copyright © Andromeda Oxford Ltd
1989

Library of Congress
Cataloging-in-Publication Data

The opposite sex: the complete
illustrated guide to differences
between the sexes / edited by Anne
Campbell.
1. Sex Differences (Psychology)
I. Campbell, Anne, 1951-
BF692.2.O77 1989   155.3′3–dc19
87-35603 CIP

ISBN 0-88162-369-5

Originated by Scantrans,
Singapore

Printed by G Canale Co, Italy

CONTENTS
Part Two: Men and Women

PW   Dr Pamela Wells
Senior Lecturer in Psychology,
Goldsmiths' College, London, UK

RE   Dr Richard Epro
Assistant Professor of Psychology,
Nassau Community College, New
York, USA

SJM   Dr Steven J Muncer
Assistant Professor of Psychology,
Nassau Community College, New
York, USA

VOL   Dr Virginia O'Leary
Special Assistant to the President,
Radcliffe College, Cambridge,
Massachusetts, USA

WD   Professor William Damon
Professor of Psychology and
Education, Clark University,
Worcester, Massachusetts, USA

WW   Dr Wendy Wood
Associate Professor of Psychology,
Texas A and M University, USA

THE OPPOSITE SEX VOLUME EDITOR

Dr Anne Campbell
Associate Professor of Psychology,
Rutgers University, New Jersey, USA

DISTINGUISHED CONSULTANTS

Professor Carol N Jacklin
Professor, Program for the Study of
Women and Men in Society,
University of Southern California,
USA

Professor Carol Anne Tavris
Professor of Psychology, University
of California, Los Angeles, USA

ADVISORY EDITORS

Dr Peter K Smith
Reader in Psychology and Head of
Department, University of Sheffield,
UK

Dr Michael S Kimmel
Assistant Professor of Sociology,
State University of New York at Stony
Brook, USA

PROJECT EDITOR
Stuart McCready

TEXT

Editorial consultant
David Blomfield

Copy editors
Nancy Duin
Shirley McCready
Mirilee Pearl
Avril Price-Budgen

Indexer
Dr J Gibson

Word-processing
Reina Foster-de Wit
Sue Flanders
Louisa Tillier
Regina Barakauskas

PICTURES

Research coordinator
Thérèse Maitland

Researchers
Suzanne Williams
Sue Williams
Celia Dearing

ART

Art editor and layout design
Chris Munday

Additional layout design
Michael Grendon
Barry Cooper

Art assistants
Martin Anderson
Mary Ann Le May

Artwork
Simon Driver
Oxford Illustrators Ltd
Taurus Graphics

INTRODUCTION

D O YOU VALUE and look forward to good relationships with the opposite sex? If so, you will need no
convincing that a world in which men and women
understood each other better would be a better world. Why
then do men and women so often find it difficult to communicate with each other, even when the will is there? And
when the will is lacking, what fuels the so-called "battle of
the sexes?" The answer, research suggests, is basically this:
most of us still take our conventional assumptions about
sex differences too much for granted.

That men and women *are* different in certain obvious
ways is undoubted. But what differences are we talking
about? As soon as we finish with sexual anatomy and move
on to questions about behavior, abilities and social roles,
"obvious" differences turn out to be not nearly as obvious
as we may have thought at first.

A growing appreciation of this has, in recent years, led
to a surge of interest in the study of sex differences and sex
roles; and increasingly social scientists are emphasizing

that it is as much society as nature that turns boys into
men and girls into women. The transformation is by no
means foretold in the genes alone.

Women in particular have come to see themselves as
unnecessarily disadvantaged by the way unquestioned –
and often false – assumptions about sex differences are
enshrined in social customs and attitudes. A general feeling of dissatisfaction with their traditional lot is sweeping
through their ranks. Some women think their best course
is to try to compete more on men's terms: to become more
assertive, postpone or reject motherhood and deny the
relevance of their biology to their destiny. Others believe
as strongly that equality does not mean similarity – that
society should assign motherhood its true value and give
full recognition to a woman's characteristic sensitivity and
capacity for nurture.

Many men too have begun to reappraise their masculine
role. For some, male dominance is rediscovered as an
irresistible outcome of evolution. Others doubt whether
the evolutionary evidence in fact supports this – or is of
sufficient relevance for modern humanity. Some men are
beginning to see advantage in relinquishing masculine
"privileges" such as ulcers, heart attacks, decreased long-
evity and other effects of the stress associated with their
roles. Why, they ask, should men be excluded from the joy
of day-to-day interaction with their children? Why should
the burden of war be borne by them alone? Could not men,
like women, learn to express their aggression less destruc-
tively? In the United States, a "Men's Liberation" movement
is demanding equality with women: freedom from the onus
of being the sole provider for the family; and the right to
stay home with the children.

So central is our gender to our experience of the world
that we all – especially if provoked – have an opinion on
the subject of sex differences. And the debates can be
heated. Let a man mention emotional instability and men-

strual cycles in the same breath and some woman will instantly voice her indignation. Let a woman complain of sexism in the workplace and some man will argue that reverse discrimination now penalizes male job applicants.

What then are the facts of the matter? To begin with, some often-confused concepts need defining: underlying sex *differences* need to be distinguished from differences in sex *roles*. Studies of the former aim to uncover differences in ability or competence between the sexes: Are men more intelligent? Are women better at fine manual tasks? Are the sexes equally accomplished in verbal and spatial abilities? Studies of sex roles, on the other hand, address questions about the customary parts that men and women play in society: Do men "bond" with their infants as strongly as women? Why do so few women achieve power in the corporate structure? It is also important to separate studies which describe differences from those that aim to explain how such differences arise. In the main, the latter concentrate on childhood development and the whole process of becoming socialized, as well as on comparisons between various cultures around the world.

As this book amply demonstrates, obtaining and interpreting the evidence has been a multi-disciplinary effort – everyone from biologists to anthropologists has had something to contribute. Although much remains to be clarified, and controversies still abound, a consistent picture is perhaps slowly beginning to appear – a picture that progressively emerges in the pages ahead. It is not, however, the aim of this book to grind an axe for any standpoint other than that of science.

But what of the practical implications of scientific study? The men and women, leaders in their areas of research, who have contributed to this book will occasionally draw your attention to ways in which they think human potential might be increased and the sexes might interact more fairly and with less prejudice. But this brings us to the threshold of a debate in which current scientific thinking is not the sole consideration. Changes in social policy, whether achieved through legislation or custom or childrearing, come from society, not from scientists. How in the future sex differences and sex-role differences are interpreted by society lies in the hands of us all. We can, if we choose, minimize or even eliminate many apparent differences – by the way we raise our children, by the way we respond as individuals and corporately to inequality of role and opportunity, by the way we respond to the media, and by the way we vote at election time. In the thick of the debate there are men and women who feel that both sexes should work toward some sort of consensus about their roles, their strengths and their weaknesses, not just as a society but as individuals who will together conceive and raise a new generation of girls and boys. In theory this should not be too hard – our similarities are more marked than our sex differences. After all, how much difference can a Y chromosome make? Turn to Chapter One and find out.

SUBJECT GUIDE TO PART 1
Childhood: Girls and Boys

USE this alphabetical guide to find the main subjects in Part One of *The Opposite Sex* - Childhood: Girls and Boys. A single reference is given for each, indicating the page or beginning page of its fullest treatment. For a guide to Part Two see page 10. For a wider reference to a subject and for a more extensive list of subjects, see the index at the end of the book.

9

LEADING QUESTIONS
Childhood: Girls and Boys

What determines whether a baby will be a girl or a boy? — SEE PAGE 18

Do sex hormones affect our behavior? SEE PAGE 20

Why are more boys born than girls? SEE PAGE 24

Do newborn girls behave differently from newborn boys? — SEE PAGE 26

How does the sex of a baby affect the way we behave with it? — SEE PAGE 28

Do parents teach girls to be girls and boys to be boys? — SEE PAGE 32

Is there really an "Oedipus complex" in boys, an "Electra complex" in girls? — SEE PAGE 42

Does the sex of a brother or sister make a difference to a child's personality? — SEE PAGE 48

Is it harder for boys than for girls when mother goes to work? — SEE PAGE 54

Are boys "naturally" more aggressive than girls? — SEE PAGE 64

Do parents punish sons and daughters in the same way? — SEE PAGE 66

Does television make children aggressive? SEE PAGE 68

LEADING QUESTIONS
Adulthood: Men and Women

1

CHILDHOOD
GIRLS AND BOYS

THE OPPOSITE SEX PART ONE

Before Birth

IS IT a girl or a boy? This is usually the first question we ask a new parent, and we think the answer should be obvious. However, sex is not a single physical certainty arising from one deciding factor. Many biological characteristics are involved. They begin to appear at the moment of conception and continue throughout development, regulated by genes controlling sex hormones and by the environment. A particularly crucial stage is a baby's development in the womb. While parents wait and wonder, embryos that are remarkably alike for the first few months of pregnancy gradually change into boys and girls. The resulting differences in visible sex organs are obvious, but internal differences are not. Hormones that shape microscopic areas of the brain before birth may help to create differences in the behavior of boys and girls and men and women.

How do we become male or female?

A person's "genetic sex" is determined at the moment of conception, by the chromosome combination that occurs when an egg from the mother is fertilized by a sperm from the father. Each egg and each sperm has 23 chromosomes containing genetic information for the development of a unique human being. One chromosome from each parent, designated by geneticists as number 23, determines the genetic sex of a child. The mother's contribution is always an X chromosome, while the father's contribution can be either an X or a Y. It is the father's sperm that determines the child's genetic sex, for the XX combination is female and the XY combination is male.

At this stage, the determination of sex has only begun. Before weeks 7 to 10 of pregnancy, the embryonic sex organs are the same for both males and females. If the fetus is a genetic male, with an XY chromosome makeup, the "primordial gonads" develop as testes in about week 7. In the case of an XX makeup – in a developing female – these gonads develop as ovaries in about week 10.

Soon after a boy's gonads have developed as testes, they produce large amounts of male sex hormones – chemicals, especially one called "testosterone," that circulate in the body fluids and affect specific kinds of cells, giving them distinctively male functions. The other reproductive organs develop as male organs only if these hormones reach them. If instead the gonads develop as ovaries, they produce little or no masculinizing hormones, and the rest of the reproductive organs develop in the female way.

All fetuses have the potential to look either male or female. Because hormones determine physical development, anything that alters their levels – or the ability of developing organs to recognize them – can lead to a mismatch between genetic sex and apparent physical sex. Some females (about one in 10,000) have "congenital adrenal hyperplasia," a genetic defect that causes their adrenal glands to make large amounts of hormones similar to those produced by the testes. As a result, these babies look ambiguous or – in very severe cases – male, even though they are genetic females with normal ovaries. About one in 2,500 girls is born with "Turner's syndrome." One X chromosome is absent or imperfect. As a consequence, the ovaries do not develop and so do not ever produce hormones. However, because it is the absence of male hormones that determines female development in the womb, these girls are born with normal external sex organs.

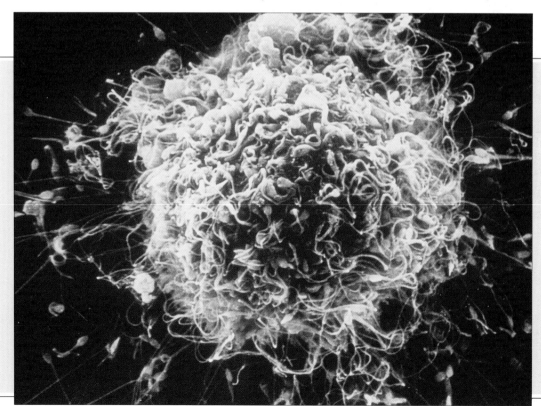

► **Moments before conception**, *sperm cells from a human male almost totally obscure an egg – whose outer membrane only one will succeed in piercing. Depending on whether it carries an "X" or a "Y" chromosome, the one sperm cell successfully fertilizing the egg will determine whether the child who develops from it is an XX (genetically female) or an XY (genetically male) offspring.*

Although cultural pressures may often create or exaggerate differences between boys' and girls' behavior and skills, some of these differences may be a natural development of physical differences that appear, before birth, in the womb.

Normally, hormones affecting sexual development are controlled by the baby's genes, but hormones present in the mother's bloodstream can also have an effect. Some women who were prescribed synthetic forms of the hormone progesterone during pregnancy gave birth to girls with normal ovaries, but with external sex organs that appeared male. The reason for this was that the synthetic hormone had unexpected similarities to male sex hormones.

What happens to male children if they have low levels of testosterone during development? If the testes produce lower than normal amounts of this male hormone, and the deficiency begins during pregnancy, these children can be born with female-looking external sex organs.

Perhaps the most dramatic illustration of the importance of hormones for sexual development comes from studies of people with a syndrome called "testicular feminization." Genetically normal males who have testes that produce normal amounts of male hormones may nevertheless be born with female-looking external sex organs. Their appearance can be so similar to that of females that, in some cases, they are not discovered to be males until they fail to menstruate at puberty. The cause of the problem in these children is usually that, during development in the womb, key cells in the sex organs are not able to recognize testosterone. The result is the same as if the hormones were not there – development follows the female pattern.

Male and female brains?

The prenatal changes that researchers suspect of having the greatest influence on later behavior do not appear to the naked eye. Women may have more connections between

19

▲ **Is it a girl or a boy**? *The question tantalizes all pregnant women whose baby's sex is unknown. Most of the approximately 150 million women worldwide now expecting babies have a preference. Those hoping for boys will have a slightly better chance of seeing their wishes fulfilled than those hoping for girls (see p24).*

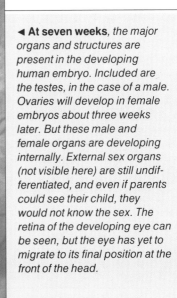

◄ **At seven weeks**, *the major organs and structures are present in the developing human embryo. Included are the testes, in the case of a male. Ovaries will develop in female embryos about three weeks later. But these male and female organs are developing internally. External sex organs (not visible here) are still undifferentiated, and even if parents could see their child, they would not know the sex. The retina of the developing eye can be seen, but the eye has yet to migrate to its final position at the front of the head.*

In a sense, a baby's sex is decided at conception, but this aspect of its physical identity, like all the others, needs to develop. An embryo develops in an essentially female way, except when male hormones make the difference.

the left and right halves of the brain (see p90). Also experiments have shown that certain areas of the brain contain cells that recognize and interact with testosterone and other sex hormones. In some brain areas, these cells differ for the two sexes, and differences seem to be controlled by male hormones during development.

A group of cells in the part of the brain that regulates male sexual behavior (part of the "preoptic" area in the hypothalamus) is normally larger in males than in females. However, in experimental animals, when testosterone is given to a genetic female just before and after birth, this group of cells is as large as in the male. In females there is a group of cells in a different part of the hypothalamus that is normally larger than in males. Early treatment with testosterone reduces the size of that brain region, and makes it resemble a male's.

Treatment with sex hormones can also affect behavior. Normal female animals given testosterone during early development show more male sexual behavior, including attempts at copulation with normal females and resistance of sexual overtures of normal males, and less female sexual behavior. Testosterone treatment also changes behavior that is not related in obvious ways to reproduction, but nonetheless differs for females and males.

For instance, young males typically show more rough and tumble play than do females. Treating young female animals with testosterone increases this type of play. Hormone treatment can also alter the level of activity and induce changes in certain types of learning, eating patterns, posture and movement.

During normal male brain development, testosterone converts to the female sex hormone, estrogen. In fact, estrogen itself, or synthetic estrogen (DES – diethylstilbestrol), influences male-type brain development more strongly

than testosterone, perhaps because the brain cells do not have to convert it before they can use it. The fact that DES promotes male-type brain development in animals is particularly interesting because this synthetic hormone has been prescribed for millions of pregnant women. Estimates suggest that, in the United States alone, between 1 and 5 million pregnant women took DES over three decades – in the 1940s, 1950s and 1960s.

Do sex hormones affect behavior?

Differences in the behavior of girls and boys, men and women, are much smaller than differences in their physical appearance. In addition, the influence of early learning on behavioral differences between the sexes complicates any study of the effects of hormones. Even such a large sex difference as preference in sexual partner is far from absolute. Approximately 20 percent of men and 7 percent of women between the ages of 20 and 35 have had at least as much homosexual as heterosexual experience.

Sex differences in intellectual and personality traits are even smaller. Individual differences are sometimes greater than those between the average of each sex. However, solid evidence for different averages appears in three nonsexual areas: play behavior, physical aggression and thinking and reasoning. The play behavior of boys is typically rougher and more active than that of girls, and boys and girls prefer different toys. Boys gravitate toward toys like cars and trucks, while girls prefer dolls (see *Ch 8*). Other studies have shown that aggressive behavior is different in girls and boys. In most cultures, at all ages, males are more physically aggressive than females (see *Ch 7*).

FROM IDENTICAL TO OPPOSITE

■ "*Primordial gonads*" *are identical in both male and female embryos until the Y chromosome in boys instructs them to become testes and to produce androgens – male hormones, including testosterone. They become ovaries in girls. Originally identical structures become the clitoris or – stimulated by androgens – the penis. In girls, labia and the lower part of the vagina form, while in boys the same structures become the scrotum, into which the testes descend before birth. In girls, the "Wolffian ducts" disappear. In boys, they are stimulated by androgens and develop as vas deferens, one day to channel*

sperm in the mature male. The epididymus, including a mass of tiny tubes at the back of each testis, develops at one end of the vas deferens, and a seminal vesicle for storage develops at the other, where sperm will gather before mixing with fluid from the prostate gland. The "Müllerian ducts" disappear in boys but in girls the upper parts become fallopian tubes, and middle and lower parts fuse to form the the womb and the upper part of the vagina. In the mature female, sperm released in the vagina will pass through the womb into the fallopian tubes – where a single egg from an ovary may be fertilized.

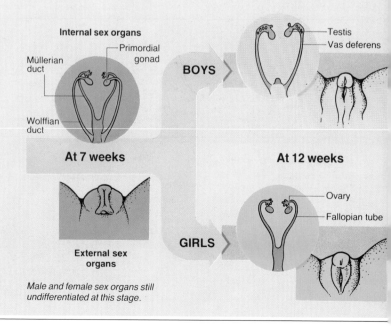

Internal sex organs

Müllerian duct
Primordial gonad
Wolffian duct

BOYS
Testis
Vas deferens

At 7 weeks

At 12 weeks

External sex organs

GIRLS
Ovary
Fallopian tube

Male and female sex organs still undifferentiated at this stage.

21

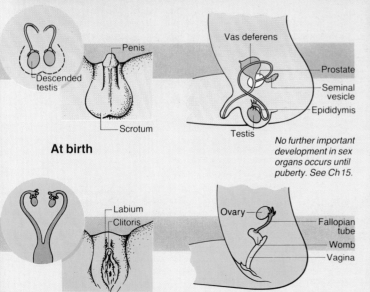

At birth

Penis
Descended testis
Scrotum

Vas deferens
Prostate
Seminal vesicle
Epididymis
Testis

No further important development in sex organs occurs until puberty. See Ch 15.

Labium
Clitoris

Ovary
Fallopian tube
Womb
Vagina

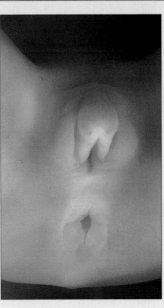

DEVELOPING SEX ORGANS

▲ **At about five months,** *the external sex organs are well enough developed to differentiate this girl from a boy.*

◄ **At 17 weeks** *a boy's penis begins to take its distinctive shape, but an opening still appears where the two halves of the scrotal sac will eventually meet. In the girl, these structures do not meet, but instead become labia.*

The overall intelligence of girls and boys is similar, but certain specific differences exist in the way they think and reason. Research has demonstrated that while men excel at tasks involving visual-spatial ability such as the imaginary rotation of three-dimensional objects in space, women are better at verbal tasks, particularly those requiring the fluent production of words.

Other studies suggest that these thinking and reasoning differences may relate to the way language is organized in the left and right sides of the brain in men and women. For example, in males, language seems to depend more exclusively on the left side of the brain, while women seem to rely more on the left *and* right sides of the brain (see *Ch10*).

Studies suggest that hormone-controlled prenatal development affects all these sex differences. Two reports suggest that women accidentally exposed to high levels of male sex hormones before birth have more homosexual fantasies and experiences. In one study, women had been exposed before birth to male hormones that produced external sex organs with a male appearance, and it is possible that the psychological consequences of their physical development may have contributed to their fantasies and experiences. However, in the second study women had been exposed to high levels of synthetic estrogen (DES) before birth. In this case, homosexual fantasy and experience cannot be attributed to the influence of masculine physical development. Other studies suggest that girls and

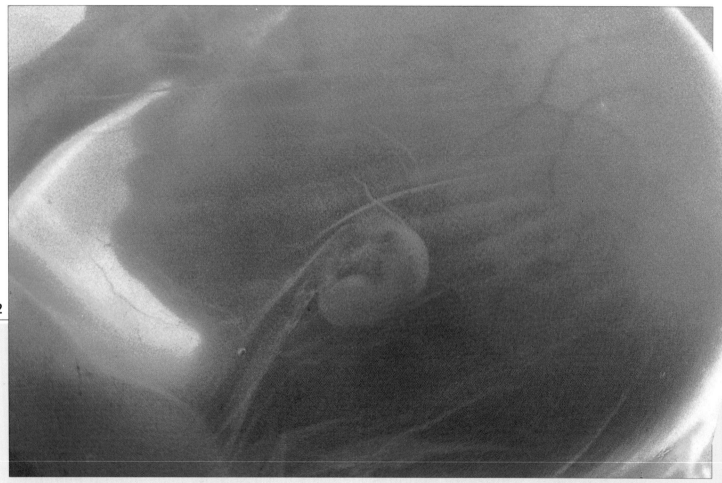

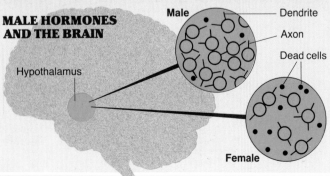

MALE HORMONES AND THE BRAIN

Hypothalamus

Male

Dendrite

Axon

Dead cells

Female

◀ **Unequal development** of the "sexually dimorphic nucleus" in the "preoptic area" of the hypothalamus, which throughout our life regulates hormones affecting behavior. Evidence from experiments with animals suggests that the nucleus stimulates male sexual behavior. During fetal development it becomes less dense in females as cells die for lack of the hormonal stimulation that they receive in males. Axons (threads that send nervous impulses) and dendrites (threads that receive them) fail to meet between the few remaining cells, and this microscopic area of the hypothalamus becomes underactive.

In-the-womb developments in the nervous system probably help to shape adult sexual behavior. Other types of behavior may also be affected: boys, for example, are more physically aggressive than girls, and their play is rougher.

women exposed before birth to high levels of sex hormones show higher levels of aggression, are more likely to prefer toys usually chosen by boys, take part in more rough-and-tumble play and rely more exclusively on the left side of the brain for tasks related to language and have visual-spatial abilities more like males. In the study, linking exposure to DES with increased tendency toward homosexual fantasy and experience, it was clear that this outcome was not inevitable. Half the women exposed to DES in the womb (aged between 17 and 30 by the time of the study) were exclusively heterosexual. In a comparison group of women who had not been exposed to DES in the womb, 75 percent were exclusively heterosexual. This kind of result is typical of studies reporting relationships between hormones and behavior – they suggest that, although hormones contribute to the development of sex differences in human behavior, other factors, such as the social and cultural environment, are important as well.

In visual-spatial ability, females exposed to male sex hormones score part way between normal males and normal females. On the other hand, normal girls who prefer to play with toys usually chosen by boys are better at tasks involving visual-spatial ability than are other girls who prefer girls' toys. Similarly, normal girls who are encouraged to play with boys' toys increase their visual-spatial ability. It is therefore possible that females exposed before birth to male sex hormones develop better visual-spatial ability partly through changes in their childhood play behavior.

Investigations of hormonal influences on human behavior are not truly experimental because people cannot be experimented upon and studies of people exposed to

hormones accidentally can be very difficult to interpret. Although special methods have gone some way toward making studies of hormonal influences more informative, conclusions drawn so far are still tentative. Most of the evidence gathered suggests, however, that hormones do influence the development of human behavior, although these influences, like the sex differences they affect, are smaller than those on physical development. In addition it is clear that social factors exert a strong influence on sex differences, as we will see in other chapters of this book. However, hormones, because they can operate from conception onward, may play a role in setting the stage for these social influences by determining the physical framework in which social factors have their influence. **MH**

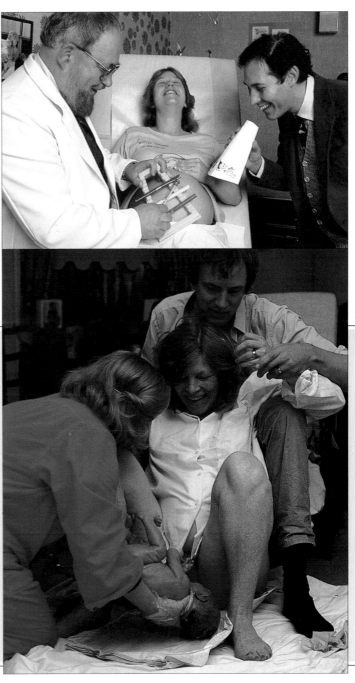

◄ Neural development. *External sex organs are now fully female in this five-month fetus, but she continues to become different from a boy in more subtle ways – ones that experts do not fully understand – particularly in the organization of the nervous system that is centered in her developing brain. She now weighs between 250 and 500g (0.5-1lb) and is about 18cm (7in) long. The mother will be able to feel movement as the fetus flexes newly formed limbs.*

► First communication. *TOP An obstetrician plays the xylophone to an unborn child, while the father makes an attempt to communicate by megaphone. They hope by such stimulation to accelerate language development and parent-infant bonding. Kicks from the child may be a form of interactive response – if this is true, it is the only time in the child's life when others' knowledge of its sex will not be a factor coloring its interactions (see Chs 2, 27). BOTTOM Already, within seconds of birth, the sex of the newborn is crystallizing the attitudes, expectations and behavior of others present.*

23

WHY ARE MORE BOYS BORN THAN GIRLS?

■ *A man necessarily produces the same number of male and female sperm. We might expect, therefore, that equal numbers of boys and girls would be born. Yet this is not the case. In Europe, for example, 105-107 males are delivered for every 100 females – a "birth sex ratio" of 106:100. Why is this? And is there any way that you can influence what happens in the case of the baby that you are yourself trying to conceive?*

The tendency to have more boys is stronger in some populations; so perhaps something that people do differently in different cultures and societies has an effect.

Both Caribbean and American blacks, for example, have a lower proportion of male births than Europeans, while Asians have higher proportions. Korean women bear 115 sons per 100 daughters. On the island of Fiji, the native Fijians have more sons than their countrymen of Indian origin.

Of course, it might be that these populations are simply different genetically – and that nothing in their behavior or environment affects the ratio. Genetic factors have indeed been found at the individual level: mothers with blood group AB have more sons. In studies of domestic animals, including one that examined the 150,000 offspring of 107 bulls, an inherited tendency to produce more male and more female offspring has been detected.

But behavioral and environmental factors seem also to have a bearing – for example, the age at which a couple have children. In 16th-century Venice and in Illinois folklore over the past 100 years, it has been said that "Boys are had more frequently by youthful than by elderly parents." This belief is now supported by considerable scientific evidence, except that, for

reasons unknown, there is a dramatic increase of boys born to women over the age of 45.

Having children very close to each other in age slightly increases the likelihood that they will both be girls or both be boys. In Australia more boys are born 11 months after the onset of the rainy season, perhaps as a result of an increase in trace elements in the drinking water. During major wars a slight but definite rise in male births has been recorded. Strangely, men who fly high-speed military aircraft and women who take LSD near conception have more daughters. It is difficult to say how such influences work, because our understanding of biology is still so imperfect. We have certainly made progress. In Europe alone before the mid-nineteenth century, there were an estimated 500 "scientific" theories of sex determination. A popular one stemming from Aristotle was that eggs which develop on the right side of the body are male, on the left, female. To have a son it was advised that a woman get out of bed with the right foot. Today's knowledge, however, probably raises just as many questions about sex-determination as it supplies answers.

Immediately after production in equal numbers in the testes, X-bearing and Y-bearing sperm are stored in the scrotum. They are viable for 21 days in rats, for 35 days in rabbits and for an unknown period in humans. Some aspects of diet might favor the survival of stored Y-bearing sperm or stored X-bearing sperm, but there is only speculation.

When sperm are ejaculated into a woman's reproductive tract they encounter a surprisingly hostile environment. On average, more than 175 million sperm are released, but only about 2,000 reach the area of

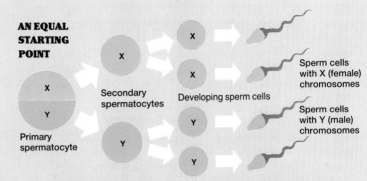

AN EQUAL STARTING POINT

Primary spermatocyte — Secondary spermatocytes — Developing sperm cells

Sperm cells with X (female) chromosomes

Sperm cells with Y (male) chromosomes

the fallopian tube where an egg awaits fertilization. A sperm has to swim from the point in the vagina or womb where the ejaculation leaves it, and vaginal mucus contains antibodies that attack such foreign objects as sperm. It has been speculated that something about Y-bearing sperm gives them a slight advantage over X-bearing sperm in surviving the journey.

Secretions in the fallopian tube act chemically on sperm to make them ready to penetrate the egg. It is possible that

▲ **The production of sperm.** *Each primary sperm-producing cell (spermatocyte) in the testes includes the male XY chromosome pair. The cell divides into two secondary ones, each with an unpaired X or an unpaired Y. Cells from a second division develop into two X-bearing sperm, which can give the man daughters, and two Y-bearing sperm, which can give him sons.*

DISCOVERING THE SEX OF UNBORN CHILDREN

■ *If you have a test to reassure you that your child is free of genetic defects, you can also learn its sex by asking to see its "karyotype" – its chromosome pattern. A magnified picture is made of the chromosomes from a single fetal cell* RIGHT. *Chromosome images are cut out and mounted on a card in pairs to display the karyotype* BOTTOM. *The 23rd pair, here highlighted, reveals sex: XX for a girl and XY, as here, for a boy.*

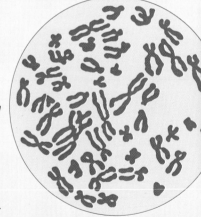

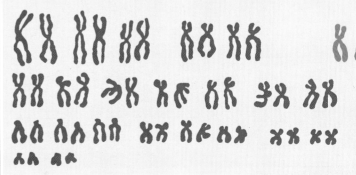

Your environment and your behavior – from rainfall patterns in Australia to frequency of sexual intercourse – can influence the many complex biological processes that determine whether your child will be male or female.

women help Y- more than X-bearing sperm at the final stage.

Recent evidence suggests that the time within the woman's monthly cycle when sperm enter her reproductive tract has a considerable influence. Hormones influencing her cycle are present in lower quantities early and late in her fertile period. At this time the chances of conceiving a male seem to be high. During the middle of the fertile period a girl is more likely to be conceived. Evidence for this pattern comes from a diversity of sources. Studies of women receiving hormone treatment in order to conceive reveal that the number of males born is reduced to 85 per 100 females, presumably because the level of hormones is so high.

By contrast, women who have intercourse six or more days before the slight temperature rise which indicates that they are ovulating are twice as likely to produce boys as girls. This might indicate that "male" sperm survive longer.

That males are more often conceived late in the woman's fertile period is suggested in the example of the practices of Orthodox Jews, who have a male-biased birth sex ratio. The Talmud lays down that a woman should abstain from intercourse until the 12th day of the menstrual cycle, or seven days after the end of her period. This is marked by the "mikveh" ritual bath. As a result of this period of abstinence the chances of conception may be restricted to the middle and latter part of the woman's fertile time.

These fertility patterns point to a possibility that the birth ratio is related to the frequency of intercourse. This would explain why more girls are born to older couples and those married for longer – it is known that frequency of intercourse in marriage declines with time, and may well occur only when the woman is most receptive.

That more boys are born in wartime might also be explained by patterns of sexual intercourse. These change during wars, with greater sexual promiscuity and with men home on short bursts of leave. With couples being less selective about when they have intercourse, sperm are more likely to be available early and late in the woman's cycle.

After conception there are still nine months of events that might affect the birth sex ratio; and it is not known precisely how they do. Early researchers believed that many more boys are miscarried than girls, and that therefore the sex ratio at conception might be as high as 120:100 in European populations. However, this calculation was based on counts of fetuses aborted after three months, when the sex can be seen from anatomical development. Sexing of samples of earlier abortions using modern genetic techniques suggests that more girls are miscarried than boys before three months. It is not known what would cause a higher female failure rate in early fetuses. The later male failure rate may be related to the fact that from six weeks the male fetus becomes dissimilar to his mother in ways that a female fetus does not: his fluids, for example, begin to carry male sex hormones. After six weeks, boys are especially more susceptible to miscarriage if the mother smokes.

Worldwide, there is a preference for sons, largely because in most cultures families are patrilineal – they need a male heir to survive as socially recognized entities from one generation to the next. Does this preference have a psychological influence on body chemistry affecting sperm storage, conception and fetal survival?

A tiny amount of research gives fuel to this speculation. A study in which expectant mothers were interviewed at length on their feelings about their unborn children found that 29 out of 50 had a definite preference for one sex (16 for males and 13 for females). Surprisingly 21 of these 29 women got the child they had hoped for. It may be of interest to watch the birth sex ratio for changes. In industrial countries, interviews with expectant fathers reveal that many more of them than before now prefer a daughter as their first child. **CL**

25

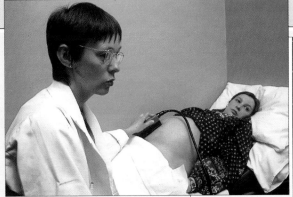

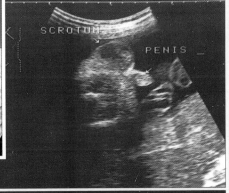

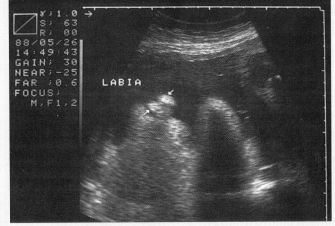

■ A common part of prenatal care is the "ultrasound scan," creating an image that an expert and the mother TOP can observe on a screen. It will reveal the position and rate of growth of the baby. In about 50 percent of scans, the expert may also spot whether the fetus is a boy TOP RIGHT or a girl BOTTOM, but the danger of making a wrong prediction will usually prevent her from mentioning this.

Early Infancy

PARENTS and researchers often suggest that babies react to their parents in ways revealing basic biological differences between boys and girls. Others regard the parents' behavior at this time as crucial in shaping the child's sex-role development. Both views are plausible. There *are* differences in the behavior of newborn girls and boys. At the same time, parents react in predictably different ways to their sons and to their daughters – particularly firstborn sons and daughters – and these parental reactions do exert an effect. Researchers have become increasingly aware that child and parent influence *each other* in a complex way.

The earliest behavior of infants

In the past 30 years there has been a massive shift in our understanding of the newborn child. As recently as the 1960s many specialists still imagined that newborn babies do not distinguish shapes, sounds and smells. New research techniques have revealed, however, that they are well able to do so. For example, they can easily tell two sounds apart and they have a rudimentary ability to imitate such facial gestures as tongue protrusion.

Innate abilities enable the child to distinguish its own caregivers from strangers, soon after birth. Within two days of delivery, boys and girls alike can learn to switch on the sound of a woman reading a story, by sucking on an automated pacifier (or dummy). Even infants reared in hospital nurseries will vary their suck to produce the sound of their mother's voice in preference to a stranger's. The sense of smell also quickly attunes itself. Week-old babies will turn toward the scent of their mother's milk in preference to that of another woman.

While many parents believe that their babies recognize them by sight early in life, the evidence is not conclusive. All we can be certain of is that three-month-olds look longer at pictures or videorecordings of their mothers and fathers than of other men and women. Babies are born with sophisticated perceptual abilities, but their understanding of the world around them develops only gradually.

Early sex differences in infants' social behavior are limited. Such differences as there are can only be discerned by comparing groups of girls and boys and finding the average tendency for each. The babies and toddlers you know may not conform to the patterns described here, but they are more likely to than not.

Newborn boys, being more muscular, move more and have a stronger handgrip than girls. About half of the reported studies find them more irritable, showing more intense crying and fussing. Girls in the early days of life are more attentive to an experimenter's eyes and to different sounds. They also appear to be more "oral," having a

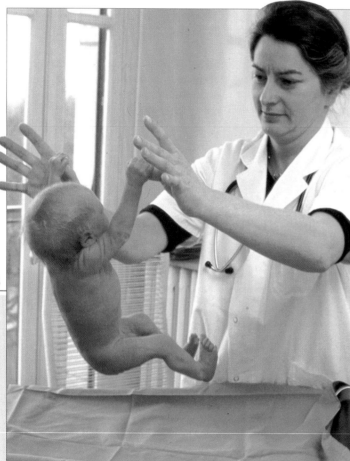

▲ **Surprisingly tenacious**, the handgrip of newborn babies of either sex is strong enough to lift the whole body. Newborn boys, however, are already more muscular and measurably stronger than girls. By the time adulthood is reached, the handgrip of the average male will be nearly twice as strong as the average female's.

▶ **Girl babies** are more attentive to sounds than boy babies are – and mothers talk to them more. They are also more stimulated by eye contact and reward social interaction with their mothers more generously.

Newborn infants are very much more aware of their parents than was once supposed. Slowly emerging differences in boys' and girls' behavior are not clear-cut but appear surprisingly early – even before children are conscious of sex roles.

stronger preference for sweet foods and smiling more than boys do.

Most of these earliest behavioral differences between boys and girls become less apparent over the first few months of life. Other sex-typed characteristics, however, emerge around the end of the first year, as babies become socially more active.

By the end of the first year, boys are more likely to play independently. They seem to have an urge to explore the workings of objects, particularly transportation toys and other mechanical novelties. Indeed, they seem to have a general desire to control their immediate surroundings. When confronted by a noisy toy which they cannot turn off, one-year-old boys will often dissolve immediately into tears. Girls are much less likely to mind.

One-year-old girls tend to be more sociable. During free play they are more likely to stay close to their mothers and to initiate more games and conversation. In turn, they are also more responsive to the requests of their parents.

While these very early and later sex differences in interaction are of interest, we cannot infer that either is the result of simple biological influences; nor is there sufficient evidence to suggest that the early patterns influence later ones. The typical patterns of masculine and feminine interaction that emerge at the end of the first year may well arise simply because boys and girls are treated differently.

DIFFERENCES IN REACTING TO STRESS

■ *Once a child can walk or crawl, watch how it reacts to a stressful event like a loud noise. Boys tend to freeze for a short period. Most girls seem to be relatively unaffected and will crawl calmly to their mothers. If a barrier is placed between toddlers and their mothers, girls will tend to appeal to their mothers for help. The vast majority of 10-month-old boys will attempt to climb over or round the barrier.*

▶ **Frustrated and upset** *by his inability to achieve a desired end, a toddler reacts to stress by dissolving into tears. One-year-old boys generally seem to attach much greater import-ance to having their immediate surroundings under their con-trol than girls do.*

27

How parents tend to react

From the moment of birth, children enter a social world that is organized along lines of gender. Sex-role stereotypes appear to influence parents even in the delivery room. Audiotapes of conversations in the 20 minutes after birth reveal that as many as 82 percent of parental comments refer to the child's sex. Within hours of delivery, mothers and fathers tend to depict their daughters as "softer" and "finer-featured." Sons in contrast are more often labeled as "firmer," more "alert" and "stronger."

Such stereotyping continues unceasingly. It can be measured in the laboratory when adults are asked to play with a baby – dressed in sex-neutral clothing – who is labeled either as a boy or a girl. Such experiments reveal that adults tend to see babies labeled "male" as more active than babies labeled "female," regardless of their actual sex. They also tend to offer "males" typically masculine toys. Children labeled as "girls" receive more social stimulation. These patterns occur even when the child shows behavior that is more typical of its true sex – for example, when a girl labeled as a boy stays closer to her mother than boys usually do.

After parents' and strangers' first meetings with young children, similar sex-typed patterns of interaction continue to occur, but they are less marked and vary according to other factors such as the age of the child. In the first three months, males have been found to receive more attention, but this may well be a reaction to their greater irritability. Parents have been found to talk more to their daughters than to their sons, although only in studies of firstborns is this result consistently found. Perhaps mothers and fathers continue to act in stereotyped ways with first children but less consistently with later ones.

After the early weeks, parents' handling of the baby changes in subtle ways. In the first place, they are less likely to differentiate between boys and girls during everyday activities until the child becomes mobile. The evidence suggests that mothers and fathers learn much from each other about how to relate to their new baby. As a result most one-year-olds display similar patterns of affection or "attachment" to each parent (see Ch12).

However, when the numerous studies on early interaction are examined it becomes clear that fathers are more likely than mothers to treat their boys and girls differently. After the delivery, fathers appear to be more stereotyped in their perceptions than their partners and they also act differently. Fathers of sons talk about and hold their children more than fathers with daughters. They also stay longer in the delivery room. In many cultures there is some support for the belief that men show a preference for sons. A study of Israeli kibbutzim, for example, found that men visited their four-month-old sons more than daughters in the nursery.

As the baby's routine is becoming established fathers are far more restricted or selective in the tasks they perform with their children and their involvement may vary according to the sex of their child. In everyday interactions throughout the first two years British and American fathers are more likely to engage in intensive physical play with their sons, while, like their wives, they have a tendency to talk more to their daughters.

Such differences between mothers and fathers are interesting but we should be cautious when assessing their significance. They might arise simply because mothers are more used to acting as nurturant parents in a variety of settings. In contrast, the presence of a researcher might prompt men into stereotyped interaction styles simply

28

◀ **The father of a son** tends to hold him and talk about him more than does the father of a daughter. Less cuddlesome styles of holding a son are much more likely to be adopted by fathers than by mothers.

▶ **Watching mother.** A daughter closely observes her mother's distinctively feminine style of paddling at the water's edge. One-year-old girls usually stay closer to mother and initiate more games and conversation than one-year-old boys do. They are generally more sociable than boys and as a result receive more social stimulation.

Most parents develop a "parental style" that is in line with their society's usual stereotypes: they treat boys "like boys" and girls "like girls." There are further differences in maternal and paternal behavior toward sons and daughters.

because such "public" displays are unusual for them – particularly if the researcher is a woman. Research in Sweden, where sexual equality is a governmental priority, reveals no such differences in the behavioral styles of mothers and fathers toward their sons and daughters. Similarly, in Fiji, fathers rarely relate to their babies in a distinctively masculine style. So, culture seems to play an important part in influencing parents' interaction styles. Yet children in Sweden and Fiji still develop clearly defined gender roles.

Two-way traffic

We are becoming increasingly aware that early interactions are "transactional" – that is, they change both parent and child. Sex differences in babies' behavior provoke apparently unconscious reactions in mothers and fathers that may influence the development of boyishness and girlishness. Two examples from research on breast-feeding illustrate this.

In an Israeli study on two-day-olds, it was discovered that boys and girls act differently during breast-feeding. So, too, do their mothers in response. When boys fall asleep at the breast they usually continue to suck. Mothers talk to and touch their sleeping boys, but pay little attention to them when awake and alert. In contrast, when girls fall asleep they are more likely to refuse the breast. Mothers tend to jiggle sleeping daughters in an attempt to persuade them to continue feeding. When awake, girls tend to suck more than boys and to gaze more at their mothers, who reciprocate by smiling and cooing.

Just why such differences occur in the interaction between boys and girls with their mothers is hard to specify.

▲ **Paternal style.** *A Soviet father joyfully tosses his baby son into the air and catches him – a spectacular instance (not as alarming as the camera makes it look here) of a tendency of fathers to engage in intensive physical play with their young sons. Distinctive masculine and feminine parental styles emerge in most countries – in Britain* and the United States, for example – but not everywhere. In Sweden mothers and fathers apparently play with their children in much the same style.

HOW A BABY'S SEX CAN AFFECT ADULTS

■ *Playing with a baby may well influence the way you feel about yourself. For example, in one study, adults played in a laboratory with babies they did not know. Afterwards, the sex-role identification of the adults was found to be affected by whether they had just been playing with a girl or with a boy. Those who had interacted with a girl identified themselves with more of the typically masculine characteristics mentioned in Ch19. Adults who had played with a boy identified themselves with more of the feminine characteristics. This effect was* *found even when the sex of the child had been misrepresented.*

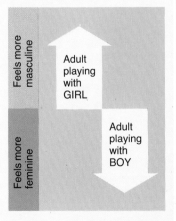

Feels more masculine

Feels more feminine

Adult playing with GIRL

Adult playing with BOY

Yet this example of contact between newborns and their main caregivers reveals the unconscious meshing of the infant's and mother's behavior. Further research is needed to establish whether such patterns influence later ones. Mothers may unknowingly encourage daughters to develop their sociability.

Research on older children reveals the existence of similar patterns in some types of interaction. For instance, girls of about three months develop mature breast-feeding patterns earlier than boys, having larger feeds in the evening to enable unbroken sleep through the night. Males tend to continue feeding voraciously during the day until they are slightly older.

At the same time, mothers' impressions of boys' and girls' hunger differ. Their estimates of how hungry their daughters are match the amount that they take in during a feed. Fewer than half the mothers of sons are accurate at estimating how much breast milk they take. Such findings give support to a popular belief that males are generally more difficult to care for – a view usually dismissed by health professionals.

We have recently realized that such transactions do not simply influence parent and child at particular times of the

HOW BABIES PROMPT PARENTS TO TREAT THEM DIFFERENTLY

■ *Some gender-different patterns of behavior in babies are present at birth. And some of these seem to prompt parents to treat their girl and boy babies differently. The mother's response to a newborn while breast-feeding is a case in point. One study of two-day-old babies showed that when they fell asleep at the breast the*

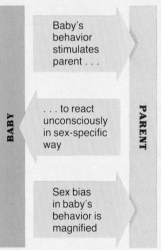

Baby's behavior stimulates parent . . .

. . . to react unconsciously in sex-specific way

BABY PARENT

Sex bias in baby's behavior is magnified

30

mothers' responses depended on whether they were boys, who continued suckling, or girls, who stopped. Mothers tried to coax sleeping girls to feed. (See main text p 29). The greater rapidity with which girls' breastfeeding patterns mature and the greater irritability of boy babies (they sleep less and cry more) are other factors which incline mothers to treat their boys and girls differently. How these early patterns affect later behavior is not yet well understood.

Just as parents are biologically programmed to respond protectively to the sight of their baby, so, up to a point, babies may be programmed to stimulate behavior in their parents that helps to reinforce their own sexual identity.

baby's development. How you react to your son or daughter now may influence his or her self-confidence and personality in the future. We are far from understanding the nature of long-term influences of parental style on sex-role development, but they have been found to exist.

A series of recent experiments indicates that maternal style in reaction to the demands of ten-month-olds is related to the later independence of sons and daughters. Boys whose mothers are highly responsive to them are more likely to show greater independence and sociability, up to two years later. In contrast, self-confidence in three-year-old girls is predicted in families where the mothers are slightly less attentive to their demands before they are one.

Other evidence of gender differences

The social sex-role system involves more people than mother, father and baby. Indeed, those less familiar with the child may rely more upon sex-role stereotypes when in play. Grandparents, uncles, aunts, friends of the family, almost invariably resort to sex-stereotyped interactions with the child. We tend to assume that differences between boys and girls will be significant, and we rely more on general assumptions when interacting with someone we do not know very well.

Observations of infant play in the home suggest that even two-year-old brothers and sisters form relationships with the new baby which differ according to the baby's sex. Around the youngest child's first birthday, same-sex pairs appear to play more cooperatively and to imitate one another more often than mixed-sex pairs.

The way that infants themselves respond to sex differences is probably also an ingredient in the interactions that affect their development. Their awareness of sex differences is evident in their choice of playmates.

Children as young as 10 months prefer other infants of the same sex. They look slightly longer at photographs of same-sex children. In studies using film, they show the same preference. Looking at videorecordings of other toddlers dressed randomly in same-sex or opposite-sex clothing, one-year-olds are not put off by appearances. They prefer to watch toddlers who are genuinely of their own sex. Indeed, children will tend to look longer at videorecordings of same-sex children walking even when the only information available to them is 12 patch-light displays attached to the walker's major joints. **CL**

WHO CHOOSES THE TOYS?

■ *It is difficult to tell who controls parent-infant interaction. Research shows that parents often provide sex-appropriate toys for their babies to play with, even when given a choice that includes those appropriate to the opposite sex. We have tended to assume that such patterns are caused by the parents selecting the toys they think correct. Yet research shows that when presented with toys appropriate to the opposite sex, children play with them less. Year-old boys, for example, often lay aside dolls that are handed to them. The knowledge that your child is more likely to play with sex-typed toys may well encourage you to start a game with one, particularly if you are being observed by a researcher.*

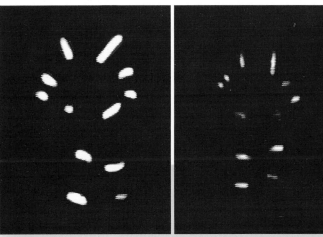
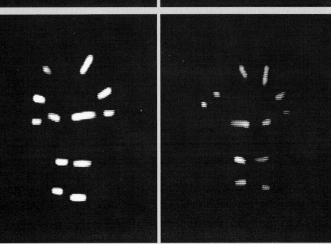

▶ **Different walking styles**. *These stills from videorecordings show the effect of patch-light displays attached to a boy and a girl walking in a darkened room.* TOP LEFT *A child walks toward the camera.* TOP RIGHT *The same child, farther away, walks away from the camera.* BOTTOM LEFT *A second child walks away, and then* BOTTOM RIGHT *back. Even without the cues of movement, male and female walking styles can be guessed by adults from stills such as these (the top child is the boy). Infants, as well, even before they are consciously aware of themselves as individuals with a sex-role identity, seem able to recognize others of their own sex and of similar age. Laboratory experiments reveal that minimal information about the way another child walks is enough to tell an infant whether the walker is of the same or the opposite sex.*

Adopting a Sex Role

PARENTS who are not conscious of teaching their sons to be boys and their daughters to be girls are often surprised by how early and how strikingly their children develop distinctively masculine and feminine styles. The surprise greets even parents who have consciously tried to shield little boys from the aggressive images so common in children's television, and girls from images that restrict females to being pretty and coy. When these patterns emerge anyway, it is easy to draw the conclusions that there must be a very strong biological factor in children's behavior. In fact, there may be. However, even if none is at work, or it is very slight, the familiar contrasts can be explained. Contrary to the impression that sex roles appear from nowhere, a subtle and pervasive learning process definitely is at work. We act unconsciously during much of the conditioning that we give to boys and girls. Children are themselves motivated, as well, to conform to the concepts they have of their roles – if I am a boy, I will want to act like one. And it is society at large, not only parents but peer-group friends and media images, that in the end defines what this will mean.

Learning how to be a boy or girl

Part of the story of how children take on sex roles can be explained by "social learning theory." This is a general theory about how we learn a wide range of behavior, not just to be feminine or masculine. And it is a theory not just about humans, but about any animal that can learn. The basis of the theory is that our behavior develops from what is known as "operant conditioning."

Training animals is a good example of operant conditioning. When teaching animals a new trick, such as leaping through a hoop, the trainer will reward them with food immediately after they do what is wanted. Operant conditioning was first studied by E L Thorndike, who observed that once a cat had accidentally found how to escape from a box to reach food (it lifted a latch) it became more and more adept at escaping in the same way. The cat was conditioned to operate on the environment in a particular way (lifting the latch) by the reinforcement it received in the form of food which then became available. B F Skinner elaborated on this principle. The central point to be gleaned from both Thorndike's and Skinner's work is that positive consequences following an action increase the probability of that action's being repeated.

Other scientists also elaborated on the theory. They found, for example, that animals and humans learn through

▲ **Strong identification with her mother,** *who has just given birth, is both rewarded and reinforced as a girl shares in a womanly experience. Her father looks on supportively and very approvingly, lending positive recognition to the role modeling that his daughter encounters.*

▶ **Identification with women at large** *is reinforced by a visit to the hairdressing salon. There is pleasure in the faces of the other customers as they in turn identify with the new entrant into their world.*

If I am a girl, then I will want to act like one. Very early on, I will be motivated by a desire for consistency with my own concept of myself. Parents, friends and society at large will also impose subtle pressures on me to act in role.

observation as well as experience. By observing how others behave and by observing the consequences of their actions, we learn to imitate or avoid those actions. Thus, according to social learning theory, the most important components of learning are observation, imitation and reinforcement.

How then do these principles apply to the way children learn sex roles? In essence, they say that children are rewarded for certain actions and criticized or punished for others, and they are thus conditioned to choose the actions that bring rewards. Some of the actions are rewarded or criticized depending on whether you are a girl or a boy, and so girls and boys receive different conditionings. As with Thorndike's cat, reinforcement is crucial. For example, if a boy is punished for crying or clinging but is rewarded for doing things independently, he is more likely to develop an independent attitude than a sister who is discouraged from being self-reliant.

Children develop an awareness of sex roles very early, starting in the first years of life and using their own and their friends' experiences as a guide to how they should behave. Then, as we all tend to imitate those most similar to us, children will begin to shape themselves on same-sex models, especially their mothers, if they are girls, and their fathers, if they are boys. As early as three years of age, children of both sexes begin to imitate same-sex models more than those of the opposite sex. From then on, through-

out childhood, children are continuously exposed to models of sex-appropriate attitudes – in the home, at school, on television. By watching how adults and their own friends behave they accumulate sex-appropriate skills.

For example, a boy sees his father lifting weights. He decides to try to do the same. As he does so, he is rewarded by his father with a smile and a proud nod of the head. The boy is also encouraged by his friends, who admire his new strength. He turns on the television to see the world weight-lifting championships. Huge men are performing. They are the focus of everyone's admiration and attention. The boy also notices how his sister and mother are unable to take part in such activities and he is thus drawn closer to his father and enjoys his father's praise. As he continues to receive his father's support, and the approval of his friends and society, the boy will probably continue to lift weights.

33

■ **Defenders and providers**. *A small boy ABOVE learns the values of a male-dominated warrior society. LEFT Equally dressed for his part, after the manner of his own culture, another boy carefully studies and assimilates the rituals of a conventionally male pastime.*

Understanding that I am a boy or girl

Only extreme versions of social learning theory hold that all learning results from conditioning. Unlike those trained animals jumping through hoops, even a very young child is a thinking being, and the way that it organizes its thinking has important consequences for how it behaves. Research findings support this view. For example, although both boys and girls tend to model themselves on others of the same sex, boys have been found to do so even more than girls. It has been suggested that this is not only in spite of but because of the father usually spending less time at home than the mother. Boys have a more difficult time than girls in establishing a male identity, something they are motivated to do from the time their concept of themselves as a male begins to form. They have to rely far more on their friends to define what is and what is not appropriate male conduct. This starts very early in life.

The pressure to conform to the male role has been seen in toddlers as young as 21 to 25 months. A recent study using this age range found that both boys and girls received more positive feedback from their playmates when they played with members of their own sex, but the messages

◄ **Carers, not curers**. *Two girls imitate sex-role models by playing nurse. Their mothers might be doctors, but the majority of examples they meet will suggest that nursing, not medical practice, is for girls. The sons of male nurses will play at being doctors, imitating those adults whom they assume to impose the most important changes upon the world.*

▲ **Cinderella's story** *tells girls that they will be rewarded for being pretty and ornamental, in spite of having to perform household duties that no one will admire them for. Unlike boys, girls do not learn that a capacity for getting things done will make them desirable.*

Children hardly ever base their image of a sex type on a single model, such as their mother or father. A girl whose mother is an engineer, for example, may still accept social stereotypes viewing women as unsuitable for such careers.

were slightly different. The boys' message was clear: play with others like you, and there are certain girls' things, such as playing with dolls, that you must never do. The girls' groups gave the message to girls to play with others like them, but there was no such limit on their activities. The effect of this group pressure was that within a few months any actions that did not conform to the male role dropped out of the boys' repertoire.

Another example of the power of the child's role-concept is provided by the daughters of working mothers. Research evidence suggests that children whose mothers work outside the home see the sexes as more similar than do children of homemaker mothers. The effect, however, is muted and, interestingly, children raised in a home where the parents make a conscious effort not to sex-type their children often still behave in sex-typed ways. A child whose mother is an engineer, for example, may still believe that she herself cannot be an engineer. Initially puzzled by such apparent contradictions, researchers now realize that children hardly ever base their identification on their observation of a single model. The engineer's daughter, for example, learns through observation (of television, friends, story books, etc) that not very many women are engineers; therefore it is exceptional for a woman to be an engineer; therefore she does not herself expect to become an engineer. Hence, a child may imitate a parent, but only where the parent's conduct is seen to be representative of the other

members of the child's sex. The parents are most immediately placed to offer rewards for the behavior they prefer in their children. However, it is society at large that teaches concepts, and the children's internalization of these concepts is a powerful influence on their behavior.

Power versus sex in social learning

Sex roles reflect to some degree the balance of power between the sexes. We know that children model themselves mostly on those of the same sex, but when females modeled the "male" attribute of power in an experiment conducted with nursery-school children, boys readily imitated them in preference to male models. This again seems to point to the motivating force of a child's role-concept during learning. One group of children was shown a film depicting three dominant girls and three subordinate boys. A second group watched a film where three boys held power and three girls were subordinate. The two films the children saw were otherwise identical. In the films, the powerful children owned a playroom with a large collection of toys. The subordinate children had to ask to play with them, and were only grudgingly allowed to do so.

At the end of the film, all the children were put into a room with toys, while the researchers observed them through a one-way mirror to see what patterns of imitative behavior would emerge. Girls imitated the female models whether or not they had power, while the boys were influenced only by the power of the models: when the powerful models were girls, they were imitated by the boys to the same degree as the powerful male models.

◄ **Adulation for masculine prowess** *shines in young eyes as supporters mob a masked wrestler on his way to the ring in Juárez, Mexico. In developing a mental picture of the sex role that they are growing into, children are influenced partly by their parents, partly by mass media and other forms of entertainment, partly by the attitudes of their peers.*

This finding appears to go against the view that boys more rigidly imitate males than girls do females. The explanation seems to be that boys are happy to imitate any models whose actions are consistent with their concept of the male role, regardless of the model's sex. Similar cross-sex patterning might well have been seen with the girls if the film had portrayed nursing, which is more consistent with the female sex-role stereotype than is the exercise of power.

Cognitive development

Social learning theory would predict increasing strength of children's sex stereotypes with age, because there would be increasing exposure to observable stereotypes to imitate.

Research on age patterns, however, does not bear out this prediction. In fact, sex-role stereotyping is most pronounced around five or six years. This has been explained in terms of the child's cognitive development. At very young ages, children have the tendency to see the world in terms of absolute categories.

An especially influential approach to these questions was taken by Lawrence Kohlberg, who argued that children's understanding of gender is dependent on the level of their intellectual growth. Kohlberg built his theories on those of Jean Piaget, the Swiss psychologist who suggested that the human ability to think logically unfolds by stages, in a strictly sequential fashion. The child's understanding of its sex

ONE GIRL'S SEX-ROLE DEVELOPMENT

6 months – gender differentiation: there are two kinds of people.

18 months – gender identity: "I am a girl."

2¹/₂ years – gender stability: "I will grow up to be a woman."

4 years – gender constancy: "People's sex does not change."

▲ **Stages of a developing sex-role understanding**. *Ages of development vary. Gender constancy, often understood by the age of four, is still not understood by many at age six.*

▶ **The pleasure of winning an advantage** *unites members of a New York Little League team, as the umpire decides in their favor. Competition has deepseated male associations, and belonging to a group that wins against others earns a boy high prestige. Team sports are organized by adults for boys on a much more extensive basis than for girls.*

36

Children seem to be happy to imitate any models whose actions are consistent with the sex-roles they are trying to adopt. Boys will even imitate girls, if the girls are acting out roles involving power and influence.

role, Kohlberg said, is just one product of its intellectual, or cognitive, development. It depends on the child's ability to classify males and females into two distinct groups and to identify behavior that is associated more with one group than the other. This approach to sex-role development is called "cognitive developmental theory."

Our sex-role development begins with a complete lack of consciousness of sex differences. However, within a few months of birth, infants seem to enter a first stage of sex differentiation. We know that, even from the moment of birth, infants are capable of some types of classification. In the early months they are able to recognize special sounds, and they prefer human faces drawn with eyes, noses and mouths to faces drawn without human physical characteristics. By five to six months of age, they are able to distinguish infant faces from adult faces and can even tell male faces from female ones.

Our ability to classify information increases with age, and well before the age of four children begin to distinguish between objects they think appropriate to their sex. There is certainly evidence that girls by their second birthday prefer to play with soft toys and dolls, like to dress up and dance. At the same age, boys are more likely to prefer transportation toys and blocks, and to play more often with toys and household items forbidden by their parents.

In one study, two-year-olds accurately sorted out pictures of toys, articles of clothing and tools according to whether they belonged to girls or boys. In another study, nursery-school children were read a story with a male and a female character in it. When they were asked which character they liked better, 90 percent of them chose the character of their own sex. When asked why, the children usually indicated that they identified with that character in some way.

A child's level of understanding the distinctions between girls and boys may be reflected in its choice of playthings. Investigators asked children to say whether they were boys or girls and to identify a series of cut-out figures as boy or girl, man or woman. Boys who did not answer these kinds of question correctly spent more time with girls' toys, such as dolls, than did boys who answered the questions correctly. Among the girls, however, there was no appreciable difference in the choice of toys.

Kohlberg referred to "gender identity" as the stage when children recognize that they are boys or girls. "Gender stability" occurs when children realize that their sex will always be the same and that they will grow up to be men and women. For example, a little boy who states that he is going to be a daddy when he grows up is showing that he has not

37

▲ Introduction to a male ritual. *Wonder and concentration fill a baby's face as he observes and absorbs. Parallel moments with his mother will give the world an enduring duality long before he identifies his own sex.*

■ What friends regard as appropriate *helps children to define their sex roles. Other girls will tend to show you that pretending to care for dolls and other soft toys is what should give you pleasure. Other boys will introduce you to play that encourages mastery of things mechanical and offers sensation as a reward.*

only developed a male identity, but that he has also learned that becoming a daddy is part of being a boy.

The child's grasp of "gender constancy" – the ability to understand that an individual's sex will stay the same even though there may be changes in that person's external appearance – is a key stage in sex-role development. It normally appears between four and six years. If a boy puts on his sister's clothes, very young children who have not reached a high enough level of understanding will believe that the boy is now a girl. Once the permanence of their own sex is grasped at the gender-stability stage, however, children can move on to seeing their friends as being irrevocably either boys or girls.

From then on, sex difference becomes central to their behavior, as they begin to value same-sex behavior and attitudes and devalue other-sex behavior. Typically, when one researcher asked if a girl could be changed into a boy, or vice versa, children who had reached the level of gender constancy answered negatively and explained that "she was born a girl," or "he cannot change without an operation." Many objected vehemently to any change.

An essential feature of cognitive developmental theory is that it claims that sex-typed behavior is motivated by the child's own desire to behave in a way consistent with his or her sex label, and that once children have a clear conception of themselves as a boy or girl they value and strive to behave in ways appropriate to their sex. The young child will develop both a concept of itself as a girl or boy and a value system that it considers appropriate to its sex, even in the absence of external pressure to do so. As the child

CLOTHES MAKE THE BOY, OR THE GIRL

■ Parents do not have to say continually "It's a girl (or a boy") to the people who stop to admire their baby. Rather, the child's sex is usually conveyed by the way it is dressed. This includes color coding (ie blue for a boy, pink for a girl) and also the type of clothes (soft and frilly for girls, hard with no frills for boys). Differences in dress have three important consequences. First, they label the child and guide the behavior of adults and other children toward the child. For example, boys are treated more roughly. The lesson for the child is that boys are tough, since they receive such rough treatment.

Second, merely wearing soft clothes teaches that girls are softer than boys. Third, soft clothes like dresses make it more difficult to engage in activities like climbing a tree.

Thus another indirect lesson is that adventure and strenuous physical activity are for boys.

◄ A dressing-up drawer stocked with mother's cast-offs provides opportunities for exaggerated role-model imitation. Strings of beads that become over-long in this use and out-sized petticoats and boots allow little girls to lend greater emphasis to the role signals of the model they are imitating. Father's old clothes have not been put in the drawer.

▲ A girl's bedroom, clearly labeled with cuddly toys both on the bed and in the wall-paper, and with appropriate frills, has been furnished as well with a hard and masculine-looking computer giving a better advantage in the male world of numbers and mathematics.

38

Although increasingly exposed to sex stereotypes as they grow older, children tend not to perceive the world in such rigid categories after the age of about six. With growth in sophistication, their behavior too becomes more flexible.

develops greater conceptual sophistication, however, it distinguishes boys and girls less rigidly, and its own behavior becomes less stereotyped. Choice of playmate on the basis of sex, however, becomes more pronounced and peaks between the ages of 10 and 14 (see *Ch9*).

Seeing the world through boy or girl glasses

Like social learning theory, "gender schema theory," developed by Sandra Bem, stresses the importance of cultural factors: it is by observing the distinctions made between females and males that children learn their sex roles and also that sex and distinctions made by sex are important in their culture. Like cognitive developmental theory, gender schema theory stresses that the child's internalization of concepts motivates its learning. It is as though society makes, and the child puts on, a pair of girl-tinted or boy-tinted glasses that pick out the clothing styles, toys, games and possible careers that the child will focus on as its own.

The following brain-teaser illustrates the problems explored by this theory:

A father and his son were involved in a car accident. The father was killed and the son seriously injured. The father was pronounced dead at the scene of the accident and his body was taken to a local mortuary. The son was taken by ambulance to a hospital and was immediately wheeled into an operating room. A surgeon was called. Upon seeing the patient, the surgeon exclaimed, "Oh my God, it's my son!"

The solution to the puzzle is, of course, that the surgeon is the boy's mother. But why is it that most of us fail to associate the concept of mother with the concept of surgeon? According to Bem, it is because we too readily process information on the basis of associations with sex roles, allied to our culture's beliefs. If we were more accustomed to finding women in the role of surgeon, the brain-teaser would not have been a brain-teaser at all.

To understand gender schema theory, it is important to

39

LEARNING FROM SURROUNDINGS

■ *Young children's surroundings structure the world they explore and the ways in which we interact with them. Parents, relatives and friends tend to provide boys with materials that encourage active exploration and girls with objects that develop sociability and language skills. Such sex-typing is apparent even in the nursery. Boys' rooms often have superhero or space-adventurer motifs on the wallpaper and bedspread. These rooms are equipped with toy vehicles, sports equipment, toy zoo animals, military toys and such spatial-manipulation toys as blocks and clocks.*

Girls' bedrooms more usually promote symbolic play and communicative skills. The feminine toys that are there will include dolls and cuddly toys to talk to and to care for and dolls' houses to keep in order. The decor is often pink, with floral wallpaper and bedspreads with ruffles. **CL**

▲ **A boy's bedroom**, *dominated by a bed in the shape of a powerful racing car and by wallpaper in the same motif, has been made the setting for extra work in reading, a subject in which girls lead boys by up to 18 months (see Ch11).*

understand the concept of a schema. The term "schema" was derived from the branch of psychology that studies how people organize, process and remember information. A schema is a network of information that people have about a certain subject. The schema serves to guide and organize information about the topic. For example, when we are talking or thinking about professional basketball players, the picture that immediately comes to mind for most people is that of a tall athletic male. This picture makes it easy to recall information about them.

The schema you use is never the *only* possible way of organizing information. It just happens to be the one that you unconsciously employ. For example, if you are especially interested in tennis, then your "self schema" includes a tendency to think of yourself when you think of

tennis, or to think of tennis when trying to define yourself. The schema profoundly affects your behavior – if someone mentions the word "tennis," your interest is spontaneously aroused. Schemas can be very beneficial because they help us to organize information efficiently. If our minds did not have the capacity to group together relevant information about a subject, we would have a lot of trouble in everyday situations.

Schemas in general are essential because they help us to remember and process information. However, not everyone believes that schemas that relate most concepts to sex roles are desirable.

PUTTING A LIMIT ON SOCIAL INFLUENCES

■ *Sandra Bem, the psychologist who developed gender schema theory (see main text) also developed a list of suggestions for parents who want to raise their children to be "gender aschematic" (nonreliant on sex-typing in organizing their concept of the world). Parents who want to do this might prefer simply to ignore sex roles in their child-rearing. However, society at large is gender schematic, and parents must therefore, according to Bem, positively "inoculate" their children against sex-typed categories. Bem offers the following strategies.*

1 At an early stage, emphasize the biological differences between males and females. Most children do not learn to define sex in terms of biological differences until relatively late in their development. This contributes to an emphasis on the cultural correlates of sex (eg personality traits, toys and activities, clothing, etc) as the defining characteristics of maleness and femaleness.

2 Reduce sex-stereotyping in your child's home environment. The mother and father should participate equally in household work and child care. They can make sure that their child is provided with both male and female toys: cooking sets and tool sets, dolls and trucks. They can also arrange for their child-

ren to see women and men involved in nontraditional occupations.

3 Censor your very young child's exposure to books and television programs that draw attention to definitions of sex differences along cultural rather than biological lines. To fill any gaps created by this censorship, parents can seek out and create materials that do not teach sex stereotypes. Bem suggests parental alteration of available materials by, for example, changing the sex of a story's main character. She advises, however, that you avoid stories that seek to overcome sex stereotypes by explicitly inveighing against them. For example, a story arguing that little girls should be allowed to play with trucks implicitly teaches that little girls and trucks do not normally go together.

4 Provide children with alternatives to society's established gender schema. Regardless of how successfully parents follow the first three strategies, their children will inevitably learn that their culture does associate many nonbiological attributes with sex. Parents must therefore teach the child to take account of individual differences, pointing out the wide variations that exist within each sex as compared to the relatively small average differ-

ences between sexes. The parent, for instance, should counter any sweeping generalization the child makes about a sex difference by listing specific examples of people who

are exceptions to this generalization. (Bem suggests a great deal of preparation here, so that the parent is ready in advance with a long list of counterexamples.) Second,

Studies show wide variations in how extensively we have learned to organize our thinking around sex roles. Variations are reflected even in how much we rely on sex-role associations when we try to remember everyday objects.

Bem believes that associations with sex roles play a primary role in our thinking, but this is only because of the emphasis society places on these roles. Developing children are taught many sex-related associations, which then come to serve as a schema and to guide their behavior. They see that their clothing, their toys, their games, adult occupations, the chores and activities in which adults participate in the home, all vary according to sex. To have a schema, however, in which we perceive the world in male and female categories can be very limiting for both sexes. It disregards the tremendous differences in personality within each sex. Thus, as wider social acceptance is received for the values of personal self-realization and role versatility, it is possible that we will see a decline in the sex-typing of so many aspects of the world that children encounter. Research already reveals wide variations in the degree to which people organize their concepts around sex roles. We vary from the "gender-schematic" (people who are very reliant on sex-role associations when using their memory) to the gender "aschematic" (nonreliant on sex-role associations). **CJ JW**

■ **Breaking the stereotype** *of the girl who watches while boys do, Heather Newhouse* FAR LEFT, *a seven-year-old stunt motorcyclist from Yorkshire in England, glances with interest at men's motorcycle magazines from mid-air.*

◄ **Cooking lessons** *are traditionally for girls, but* TOP *a boy, with his female partner, makes an early start at demystifying the world of women.*

■ **Greater understanding by a girl of her father** BOTTOM LEFT *and of the roles that men can play may result from his participation in child care and housework.*

◄ **Early awareness of biological sex-differences** BOTTOM RIGHT *may help a child to avoid basing categories too rigidly on contingent differences such as style of clothes and type of work.*

parents can teach the child to take account of cultural relativism, emphasizing that different people believe different things. Knowing that opposing beliefs frequently coexist in society will help children as they come face to face with the contradiction between their beliefs about sex roles and those of many of their peers, and of much of literature and the mass media. This leads to Bem's third suggestion, that parents point out the historical causes and current effects of sex discrimination. The goal here is twofold: to help the children understand why the sexes appear to be so different in our society; and to help the children perceive – and resist – limitations on their own behavior. **EL**

41

The Freudian View

WHAT DOES our unconscious mind have to do with the development of our masculinity or femininity? Everything, according to Sigmund Freud. Freud (1856-1939) produced the first comprehensive theory of how male and female identity develops in children. Most psychologists are now critical of it, and Freud himself noted that all of his theories were tentative. His ideas have had a tremendous impact, however, on European and American culture. They continue to stimulate present-day thinking about the development of sex roles and are an essential piece of background to the topic of child development.

Before sexual identity

Freud believed that much of our behavior and many of our feelings are motivated by unconscious forces – drives of which we are unaware. Prominent among these are sexual thoughts and fantasies. He taught that the nature of such unconscious drives is profoundly affected by our experiences at five distinct stages. He called those our "psychosexual development." Each stage is concerned with a major biological function, and each influences the development of our personality. These are the oral, anal, phallic, latency and genital stages.

Until about the age of four, as they pass first through the oral and then the anal stages of development, boys and girls are, he believed, alike in failing clearly to distinguish themselves by sex.

In the oral stage, infants are completely dependent on others for their survival. Because the mouth is associated with nourishment and gratifies basic instinctual urges, infants become emotionally attached to their mothers, as the mothers are the ones most likely to provide oral gratification by feeding them. Conflict arises between mother and infant because of the infant's high demands for oral gratifi-

cation and eventually because of weaning. "Fixation" on the oral drive can result from sudden weaning, producing adults who are prone, for example, to overeating, drinking too much and smoking.

During the anal stage – around the second and third years of life – the central focus of pleasure, according to Freud, moves from the mouth to the anal region. The infant's central concern at this time is the elimination and retention of feces. Freud believed that toilet training has important consequences for later personality development. Over-severe training may lead to an anal fixation – for example, an obsession with cleanliness and tidiness. The mother again is believed to be the primary object of the child's emotions and attention since she is probably the person most involved with toilet training.

Beginning in the fourth year and continuing until about the fifth year of life, the psychological development of boys and girls begins to diverge as children enter into the phallic stage. Here they face the task of overcoming a sense of conflict with the same-sex parent. Freud believed that this is a crucial phase in the young child's life, vital to the healthy development of sexual identity. He called these developmental conflicts the Oedipal complex for the boy, and the Electra complex for the girl.

The Oedipal complex

Freud derived the term "Oedipal complex" from the Greek legend of Oedipus, the man who unknowingly killed his father and then later, still unknowingly, married his mother. Freud believed that every boy unconsciously desires his mother and wishes to kill his father. The boy, however, begins to fear his father and to believe that he may discover his incestuous feelings for his mother, and punish him by castration. Since, at this stage, his genitals are his

■ **Oral and anal gratification** combined RIGHT. *Freud saw conflict between child and parent at every stage in the developmental sequence he described. Conflict arises between mother and infant because of the baby's drive for oral gratification through feeding. Next the child comes into conflict with her over toilet training. Freud believed that oral and anal fixations could develop if these conflicts were not successfully resolved.* LEFT *A pacifier gives babies security during underwater swimming.*

Freud believed that unconscious sexual thoughts and fantasies determine how, in identifying with our same-sex parent, we acquire a sexual identity, and that unconscious attitudes toward our bodily functions color our sexual personality.

chief concern, castration would be the worst type of punishment the child could imagine. The child's castration anxiety is greatly increased when he observes that girls lack external genitals. He believes that girls have already lost their penis and that he too could lose his. At this time he reasons that, since girls do not have a penis, they are inferior to him. This belief of female inferiority then persists throughout later stages of development.

Chiefly as a result of his fear of castration, the boy then represses his desire for his mother and his fear and hostility toward his father. He no longer sees himself as his father's rival. Instead he begins to identify with him. Then he begins to adopt his father's morals and values.

These morals and values supply him with his "superego," or conscience – the learned social rules that teach him how to control his natural drives – and the boy's masculine identity begins to emerge. This identification with the father is the normal resolution of the Oedipal complex. If, however, the boy is unable to resolve the conflict with his father, he may instead adopt a homosexual orientation.

The Electra complex

For the girl, the events of this phallic stage of development begin when she discovers that she does not have a penis like her brother or father. This leads her to feel cheated, and envious of males. She blames her mother, because she too does not have a penis. Freud believed that the mother and all other girls then become greatly devalued in the girl's eyes. Freud named this female version of the phallic stage after Electra, the woman in Greek mythology who plotted to kill her mother to avenge her father. Motivated by what Freud termed "penis envy," the girl renounces her love for her mother and vies with her mother for her father's attention and love. Freud believed that the girl's

desire for her father stems from her desire to possess his penis. She also comes to equate having a penis with having a baby. She views her father as someone who could symbolically provide her with a penis by giving her a child. The original wish for a penis is then transferred to her wish for a baby, which leads her to love men because they are the agents through which she can acquire a child. Because it is through the vagina that the girl may obtain her father's penis, she comes to view her vagina as more important to her than her clitoris.

The phallic period comes to an end for the girl when she

◀ **Entering the phallic stage,** a toddler starts to be fascinated by his genitals. According to Freud, the boy will become concerned about losing his penis, as a punishment for rivaling his father. His possession of a penis will also give him a lasting sense of superiority over girls, while they will suffer from "penis envy."

▲ **Rivaling father for the attention of mother.** From the age of four, said Freud, boys experience an unconscious sexual desire for their mothers and become jealous of their fathers. Cross-cultural studies suggest that a father's imposition of authority, rather than his possession of the mother, is what is really at the heart of father-son conflict.

In Freud's view, castration anxiety leads a boy to resolve feelings of rivalry with his father by adopting masculine values. Girls adopt their mother's feminine values, but they are never quite able to overcome their penis envy.

realizes that she cannot have her father for a lover. She then identifies with her mother and adopts the behavior and attitudes of the female role. It is through this process that the girl acquires her superego – in her case, a set of moral values acquired through her mother.

The girl's resolution of the phallic stage is never complete, Freud thought, and she can never fully develop a mature superego like a boy, because she never fully overcomes her penis envy. Thus, the female is not as open to growth and change as the male, and is morally and ethically undeveloped compared to men. Additionally, the rewards and satisfactions a woman experiences in her life are of a "masochistic" nature – she feels a need to fulfill herself through suffering. Freud believed that what the woman really desires in sexual intercourse is rape and violence, and, in the mental realm, humiliation. The process of childbirth gives her an unconscious masochistic satisfaction. Freud believed that the mother's relationship with her children is also of a masochistic nature – she is their willing victim. Women must forever live with jealousy and shame.

The phallic period ends with each sex identifying with their same-sex parent. Basic to Freudian theory is the belief that the phallic period is not only important in the development of sexual identity, but it is also the beginning of heterosexual attraction.

When children reach about seven years of age, until the onset of puberty, they enter the latency stage of psychosexual development. Freud wrote very little about this stage, but essentially the children move away from the intense attachment they had to their parents, and same-sex peers become the central focus for the children. The child's

sexuality is largely repressed during this time. The last stage of development in Freudian theory is the genital stage. The girl's erotic focus is now on the vagina, and the male's is on his penis. In this final stage, both boys and girls become oriented toward heterosexual relationships.

Criticisms of Freud

It has never been proved that sexual motives, as Freud suggests, are the primary motives of behavior. There are virtually no scientific studies concerning the universality of penis envy in girls or castration anxiety in boys. It is not

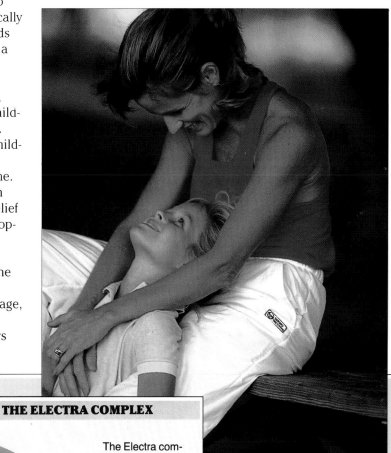

▲ **Identifying with her mother** – *and a code of feminine behavior. As a girl does this she learns, according to Freud, to renounce the impossible dream of rivaling her mother for her father's affections; but because her penis envy remains, she will continue to devalue herself – and women in general. Mature self-estimation which boys can in principle achieve as men, will always elude her.*

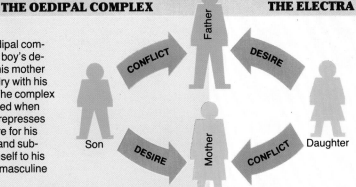

THE OEDIPAL COMPLEX

THE ELECTRA COMPLEX

Father

The Oedipal complex is a boy's desire for his mother and rivalry with his father. The complex is resolved when the boy represses his desire for his mother and submits himself to his father's masculine values.

CONFLICT

DESIRE

Son

DESIRE

CONFLICT

Mother

Daughter

The Electra complex is a girl's desire for her father and rivalry with her mother. The complex is resolved when the girl represses her desire for her father and identifies with her mother's feminine values.

▲ **Conflict and desire** *in sexrole development. Freud based his theories of the Oedipus and Electra complexes on personal introspection and on reflection* about the dreams and childhood memories of his patients. However, none said directly that they wished they had a penis or feared their father's power to castrate them. Many authorities regard Freud's theories as untestable. Others consider them testable and disproved.

known what the reaction is of the little girl who discovers she has no penis, nor whether or not the little boy is fearful that his father will castrate him.

Freud's theories were largely based on adults who came to him for treatment of psychological disorders. None of his patients revealed that they wished they had a penis or were afraid they would be castrated. Freud simply inferred the childhood conflicts, on which his theories are based, from his patients' dreams and memories.

Freud commented that the mental life of women was impossible to understand, and once remarked that "if you want to know more about femininity you must interrogate your own experience or turn to the poets, or else wait until science can give you more coherent information." His theories, however, remain central to the psychoanalytic tradition in psychology, even though there is no research evidence to support them.

Studies of children in different cultures specifically contradict the notion of penis envy. The anthropologist, Margaret Mead, found that in cultures that were very open about menstruation, pregnancy and penile erection, envy of

a woman's reproductive capacity was more common. This supports Freud's critic, Karen Horney (see box).

In societies where the mother's brother is the main disciplinarian, anthropologists have also noted a particularly relaxed relationship between the father and the four- to five-year-old son. Hostility of small boys to their fathers in Freud's Vienna may have reflected not from sexual rivalry but a dislike of discipline.

Downtrodden motherhood

Nancy Chodorow, a contemporary psychoanalytic theorist, has developed a very different theory from Freud's in her book, *The Reproduction of Mothering*.

The central argument of this theory is that the nature of our relationships and the roles we play in society result from our being mothered by women. As the primary carer, the mother produces daughters who want to mother sons and sons who devalue and dominate women.

Because infants have their needs satisfied totally by their mothers, they assume that mothers have no other interests beside themselves, and from then on both girls and boys continue to expect women to be sacrificial. As children get older, these attitudes subconsciously harden. In the case of little girls, because mothers are the same sex as their daughters, their close attachment is never completely broken, and through this attachment the daughter will learn how to mother, will want to mother, and will learn how to get gratification from mothering.

Boys begin with the same attachment to their mothers as do little girls. But because he must develop a masculine identity, the boy represses his attachment to his mother. Thus, the boy finds his identity in opposition and rebellion. Masculinity comes to be defined as nonfemininity, includ-

46

◀ **For mother and daughter alike,** *Freud saw a manifestation of penis envy in the desire to be mothers. An empty cradle symbolizes the female sense of being incomplete in one's self.*

▶ **Fulfillment by suffering** *was considered by Freud an unconscious, masochistic urge of women. Even in their emotional relationship with their children, he thought that mothers were willing victims. This self-punishment was seen as arising out of a sense of shame for their envy of men.*

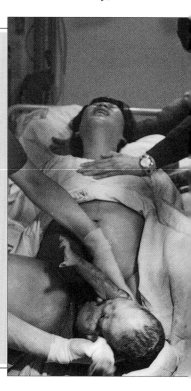

WOMB ENVY

■ *Among Freud's critics was Karen Horney, who worked closely with him but later became skeptical of his theories. She believed that girls do not necessarily envy the male's genitals, but rather the male's superior status in society. She also believed that female masochism resulted from a woman's dependence on men for economic security, the restriction to domestic spheres*

of life, and the prevailing cultural belief regarding the inferiority of women. She argued that it was males who suffered from envy – of the fact that women can bear children. She called this, appropriately enough, womb envy. Horney also suggested that male achievement is actually an overcompensation for feelings of anatomical inferiority.

An alternative view to Freud's finds the origins of sex-roles in the reaction of children to mothers. They produce daughters who want to mother sons and sons who devalue all women in order to work out a separate masculine identity.

ing the denial of feminine maternal attachment. All women then come to be devalued in the eyes of the male, because of his need to separate himself from his mother and other women in order to work out a masculine identity.

Boys then begin to identify with their fathers. While a girl's identification with her mother takes place in a close relationship with her, a boy's with his father is much less personal. Because fathers are away from home much of the time, the boy develops an idealized view of the male role, and his notion of masculine superiority increases.

Chodorow believes that the adult man's needs for interpersonal closeness are satisfied by a relationship with a woman, where they can recapture the feelings of warmth and security they experienced from their mother when they were infants. A woman, however, has greater needs for closeness, which cannot be filled completely by her husband. So women have babies, their needs for closeness are satisfied, and the cycle repeats itself.

According to Chodorow, this cycle of female inferiority and male superiority is not inevitable. Because women's mothering perpetuates the whole division of labor by gender, and because women's mothering creates the devaluation of women, men must participate equally in child care. If they did so, this would create a wholly different pattern of family dynamics, which would provide boys with a masculine role model there at home with whom to identify, a model of a nurturant father. The cycle would thus be broken. **CJ JW**

▲ **Mothers as servants to their male children**. *On a feminist reinterpretation of Freud, the early experience of children is a reaction to the self-sacrifice of the female role. By identifying with their mothers, girls learn how to achieve gratification from mothering. Boys recognize the female role as lacking status, however, and they learn to devalue and dominate women, rejecting female qualities as models for their own.*

Brothers and Sisters

DO YOU have a sibling – that is, a brother or a sister? Would you be surprised to hear that the sex of your sibling has influenced your own sense of masculinity or femininity? Researchers have discovered a probability that it has, especially if you are younger, but not much younger. The sex of your sibling and your place in the birth-order rank also combine to influence other personality differences – whether you are the responsible, serious one in your family or the bold, outspoken and rebellious one; whether you are more like your father in personality or you are more like your mother. However, the effect of our brothers and sisters on our personalities is not a simple one to predict. Younger siblings show a tendency to model themselves on older ones, but we also have a tendency to develop traits that distinguish us from our siblings, so as not to compete with them directly.

Why are firstborns more prominent?

Social scientists first became concerned with sibling effects as early as 100 years ago. In the latter part of the 19th century, Sir Francis Galton, the pioneering British geneticist, statistician and psychologist, observed that firstborn and only children were more likely to be prominent in the arts, sciences and literature than later-born children, and consequently, more were to be found in such registers of eminent people as *Who's Who* than could be expected by pure chance. Since Galton's time, many things have changed, but his findings have been consistently supported. However, knowing that firstborn and only children are more likely to be successful in important spheres of life does not tell us why this should be the case.

Alfred Adler, the famous psychoanalyst who broke away from the Freudian school in 1912, was one of the first to consider the dynamics behind sibling differences. Unlike Sigmund Freud, who believed that most human behavior is fueled by attempts to satisfy sexual and aggressive needs (see *Ch 4*), Adler thought that the main drive in our lives is the need to become more competent and superior.

According to Adler, humans are, by their very nature, born inferior. The human infant is far less capable of caring for itself – and for a much longer time – than nearly any other member of the animal kingdom, and children have to learn a variety of strategies to make up for this helplessness and become superior. Adler called these strategies, collectively, the "life style" or "life plan," but these terms are really synonyms for "personality." He was aware that human life is always social, and that children's personalities, particularly in infancy and early childhood, are constantly being shaped as they interact with other people, until they eventually form ones that are unique to them. Everything that we do – from gestures to daydreams, from our choice of career to the way we handle social relationships – reflects our personalities.

48

► **Sister and brothers.** *All of these children will be influenced by their position in the birth order and the resulting nature of their relationship with each other. The girl, as eldest, is likely to model her behavior most closely on her parents'. We may expect that she will be the most conforming of the three. The boys, however, will tend to identify not only with parents, and their father in particular, but with their older sister as well. They may develop less exclusively masculine styles of behavior than peers who do not have older sisters.*

Depending on its position in the birth order, each child in a family encounters a different social environment. Where do you come in your family? Do you have a brother or a sister? How might this have affected your personality?

Although Adler believed that the personality of every one of us is unique, he also accepted that there are some common themes running through many human lives. One influence in general that can be observed is that of "birth order." He observed that the oldest children in a family often grow up to be serious, proper, responsible, conservative people who are concerned with their power and authority. Later-borns, such as Adler himself, are competitive, lively and rebellious.

Adler tried to explain why this should be. At first, the oldest child is in the advantageous position of having the complete love and attention of the parents – they are truly "Number One" with a special status of power and affection within the family. Then the second child arrives. Although firstborns may crave the friendship of a younger brother or sister, they often feel threatened or displaced by the new baby. In fact, it is not uncommon for parents to notice that, during the first few months after the birth of a second child, their older children regress back into their own babyhood, demanding more cuddling, wanting constant reassurances at night, wanting to be spoon- or bottle-fed, and/or wetting the bed. Later, to regain their sense of personal superiority and the love and security they fear that they may have lost

to the newcomer, firstborns try to please their parents by becoming the "good ones," of whom the parents can be genuinely proud.

Paradoxically, while the older child feels displaced and in some way "swindled" by the turn of events, so does the younger child. According to Adler, younger children often think their parents ignore them, and they see their older siblings as much more capable, more likely to be able to communicate with their parents, and more likely to have

▲ **Sibling rivalry** *is competition between brothers and sisters for family resources. In this case, the contest is for the mother's attention. Usually, the firstborn shows more jealousy than later children. This is because firstborns have experienced a time when they had parental love all to themselves.*

▶ **Sibling support**. *Older children, who most closely identify with their parents, often adopt part of the parental role and express it in caretaking behavior toward younger siblings. Encouraging this is one way of ensuring that the older child feels important and, consequently less jealous.*

privileges and better toys, clothing and bedrooms. Because of this, younger children may feel compelled to adapt by becoming competitive and socially charming.

The sex roles of siblings

However, these effects of birth order can be modified if, for example, the children in a family are widely spaced in age; then several children may reap the benefits of being in what is to all intents and purposes the position of a firstborn and only child. In addition, Adler was well aware of the possibility that children in different positions in the birth order might adopt different sex roles.

Take, for instance, the only boy in a family of girls. Adler felt that he would be in a special position: if he were a younger child, he may become the pet of his older sisters and grow up to be more feminine in his interests than other boys; alternatively, because of his "different" position within the family, he may enjoy his uniqueness and so develop a

An older child is more likely to influence a younger sibling than the other way around. But when there is a wide difference in their ages the younger may also reap the benefits associated with being a firstborn or only child.

heightened sense of masculinity. In recent decades, studies attempting to explain the differences in the personalities and abilities of siblings have continued to ask how siblings affect each other's developing sex roles (the attitudes and socially defined forms of behavior associated with being male or female – see *Ch3*). For example, in 1958, Orville Brim, an American social psychologist, analyzed data on siblings and found that, in general, when they are of the opposite sex, there will be more behavior associated with the opposite sex than there would be if the siblings were of the same sex. He reported that boys with older sisters were more likely to show some feminine traits than other boys, while girls with older brothers were more likely to show masculine characteristics than other girls. However, these are not simple, uncomplicated relationships, for it also

seems that this effect is much more common in younger than in older siblings – that is, older children are more likely to influence younger children than vice versa.

Your "sibling status"

Alfred Adler was a skilled psychotherapist and clinician, but by modern standards his research left much to be desired. Today, social scientists devise theories that are based on statistical evidence that has been gathered from well-designed surveys and controlled laboratory experiments. They also believe that since the complex interactions of a whole family need to be studied in order to understand personality development, Adler's simple notion of "birth order" needs to give way to a more precise one – "sibling status." Sibling status includes the interplay of birth order, the gender of siblings, the ages of children and their parents, family size, and social trends and beliefs about childrearing. Therefore, rather than just labeling someone

as a "firstborn," it is much more accurate (even if more long-winded) to describe them in terms that will more fully reveal their sibling status – eg "a firstborn, Norwegian, middle-class girl with two younger brothers and one younger sister."

Psychologists have developed a useful notation scheme to keep track of three key elements in sibling status. It involves a sequence of Ms, Fs and numbers to denote genders, birth orders and numbers of siblings. In a family of two boys, the sequence of letters is MM; in a family with a boy followed by a girl, MF; girl followed by a boy, FM; and two girls, FF.

To focus on one of the children in a sequence, a number is inserted next to the letter for the child's gender. For example, in two-children families a boy with an older sister would have the code FM2; a girl who has a younger brother, F1M; a boy with a younger sister, M1F; and so on. In all, there are eight codes for two-children families, and for a five-children family, there are a possible 32 codes.

Patterns in two-children families

Research has discovered the following, sometimes conflicting, patterns in two-children families. Each sibling status is represented by one of the codes described above.

MM2 These secondborn boys seem to model themselves after their older brothers. Of all the sibling-status groups studied, these boys are the most masculine and least feminine, least anxious and most nonconforming children. They are very athletic and more likely than others to engage in high-risk sports and choose entrepreneurial careers in sales, production management or banking.

FF2 In some studies, these secondborn girls with older sisters show a prevalence of such traditional feminine characteristics as dependency, belonging and conformity.

51

SAME-SEX SIBLINGS

■ *Two brothers and two sisters* FAR LEFT *and* LEFT. *The elder brother may be conforming and more anxious. The younger will take his brother as a model, and both will be highly masculine, but the younger will feel surer of* *his role. Her caring role will tend to give the elder sister a very feminine personality. The younger may model herself on this or seek a distinctive identity with a more masculine outlook.*

SIBLING STATUS CODES

◄ *The eight possible sibling status codes for two-children families, grouped into the four possible combinations, including the two same-sex combinations shown on these pages. "M" stands for "male," "F" for "female." The number following a letter is the birth order of the particular child coded.*

M1M
MM2

F1F
FF2

M1F
MF2

F1M
FM2

This finding would fit a theory such as Orville Brim's (see above), in which a conforming older sister would serve as a model of conformity for the younger sister. However, other studies have found these girls to be highly masculine in their behavior, which would fit Adler's theory (see above) that younger children are rebellious and independent.

M1M These firstborn boys with younger brothers seem to be highly masculine, but also anxious, conforming and above average in terms of dominance, at least in their early years. M1Ms were among those tested in a social psychology laboratory experiment in which they were influenced to accept judgments that, in fact, were wrong. Researchers found that the M1M boys were the ones most likely to agree with the wrong judgments when it was made to seem that peers would agree. These traits would fit the Adlerian notion that firstborns are likely to be conforming and concerned with maintaining power.

F1F These firstborn girls with younger sisters can be called "caretakers." They are sensitive, feminine and have good relationships with younger siblings but usually prefer to play with other girls of the same age. In an experiment involving fear arousal, young F1F women were more likely to want to stay with and be comforted by other people, whereas in the same situations, later-born young women most commonly wanted to stay by themselves.

FM2 Some studies find these boys with older sisters the most feminine of all male groups – perhaps because they model themselves on their sisters to some degree. However, not all studies have found this. While these boys may be more feminine or dependent when they are quite young, by the time they reach the age of 18, they may show a shift toward high masculinity.

GROWING UP AS ONE FAMILY

■ In the Israeli kibbutz system, children grow up in communal groups, supervised mainly by just one adult. They have much less contact with parents than children in Europe and the United States, and they take on the primary nurturing roles for each other. Researchers find them happier than children raised in families, but exhibiting a less profound range of emotions, with fewer ups and downs.

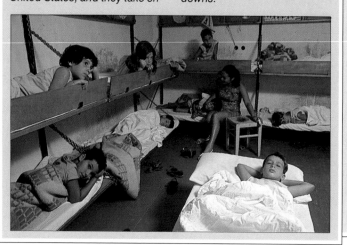

MIXED-SEX SIBLINGS

■ Firstborn girls with younger brothers TOP are often more curious, original and tenacious than other girls. They can be competitive and jealous, and they may like to show off. The brother may develop a highly feminine personality but with a strong shift toward masculinity in late adolescence. Firstborn boys who have a younger sister ABOVE tend to feel secure in their male role. The sister is more likely than other girls to be tomboyish, athletic and assertive. When there are three children, the pattern of relationships becomes more complex. In interactions with the baby of the family, both the middle sister ABOVE and the middle brother RIGHT will be influenced by the standards that a firstborn sibling creates.

In general, when siblings are of the opposite sex, brothers show more femininity than other boys do and sisters show more masculine traits than other girls. However, sibling rivalry and identification with parents complicate these patterns.

MF2 These girls with older brothers display several masculine traits and interests – they are tomboyish, athletic, assertive and dominant. It has also been found that a disproportionate number of girls who major in physical education at university fit this pattern.

F1M These firstborn girls with younger brothers have been described as curious, original and tenacious, and they are also noted for being competitive, jealous and likely to show off. They are friendly toward teachers, and are known for their leadership. Perhaps one way to summarize the personality patterns of these girls is to describe them as competent women who are concerned with loss of power.

M1F This group of firstborn boys with younger sisters seems to be highly masculine. They have a special status of being the only boy and are secure in their male role.

The de-identification factor

Whether female or male, older siblings tend to become responsible, conforming, sociable people who model themselves on the traditional adult role for their own sex. Secondborn children with siblings of the opposite sex, however, seem to model themselves to some extent on their siblings – that is, a boy with an older sister is likely to develop some feminine traits, while a girl with an older brother may seem more masculine. However, some studies find secondborn boys with older sisters (FM2) to be highly masculine. Secondborn children with siblings of the same sex tend to mimic the sex roles of their older siblings. But some studies find girls with older sisters (FF2) to be more masculine, rebellious and assertive. One attempt to explain these apparent inconsistencies is the theory of *sibling de-identification*. Even though at some stage younger children model themselves on their older siblings, this theory notes – as Adler did before in the past – that children often see themselves in intense competition with their siblings and may try to become as unlike them as possible, in order to avoid the stress of competition. Each child becomes specialized in different sectors of life, thus avoiding the pain of losing to a brother or sister.

In surveys, university students have been asked to report on their experiences as siblings, and mothers have been asked to describe their children's personalities. These surveys have found that de-identification is a very strong possibility when the first two children in a family are the same sex, but later pairs of siblings, and siblings who are widely spaced in terms of age, do not show this effect to any great degree.

A complicating factor is *split-parent identification*. According to this concept, one sibling may become like the mother while the other is likely to become like the father. As with de-identification, this effect is more likely to occur in closely spaced, first- and second-sibling pairs. Boys do not necessarily identify automatically with their fathers and girls with their mothers, but an only boy in a family with two or more older sisters is very likely to identify with his father.

While it is clear that siblings influence each other's development, the relationships between birth orders and sex roles are extremely complicated. Newer, more sophisticated theories – and the research to back them up – are still needed to understand fully the effects of brotherhood and sisterhood on masculinity and femininity. **BG**

When Mother Goes to Work

IN THE traditional image of the family, the mother stays at home with her children all day – baking bread, mending clothes, doing the laundry, tending to scraped knees, bruised egos and emotional needs. However, over the last few decades, that picture has changed. Gradually, more and more mothers have found themselves in the role of employee, until today mothers are just as likely to spend their days in full-time jobs outside the home as they are to be full-time homemakers. When children are born, employed women – often already committed to a job or career – continue to work; or, at most, they take time off for a year or two while their children are very young. Concern about the effect on children of having their mother only part time has led to much research. Are there any differences between boys and girls in their ability to adjust when their mother works? The differences are usually small, and they do not crop up in all studies. When they do appear, it is daughters who manage best, and often positively benefit. Sons are more likely to suffer from their mothers taking jobs outside the home.

Spending time together

One thing that clearly changes when a mother has a job is the amount of time a family has to be together. Full-time employed mothers spend, on average, 40 hours a week at their place of work, and this does not take into account the time taken up by traveling to and fro and preparing for work. Would this time otherwise have been spent with the children? Surprisingly, perhaps, researchers have found that the answer is no.

Employed mothers spend less time than nonemployed ones doing housework – washing dishes, cleaning, shopping, tidying – and they seldom bake bread. They also devote fewer hours to personal pursuits – reading, gardening, knitting, doing volunteer work, visiting, entertaining, or just doing nothing. And they spend less time supervising and feeding their children.

However, most childrearing chores do not simply go away just because the mother has a job. Employed mothers continue to carry out these tasks – bathing, dressing, and

▲ **Mother's goodbye.** The quality of interaction between child and mother is much more important than the quantity. Research suggests that the children of mothers who go out to work – even children as young as three months – do not show signs of maternal deprivation if adequate daycare arrangements are made for them. If parents are under stress, however, sons may fare worse than daughters.

Although the sons and the daughters of career mothers usually adjust to the resulting pattern of family life with equal facility, there may be significant shifts in their sex-role expectations, some of positive benefit, others perhaps less so.

transporting their children, teaching and talking to them and putting them to bed. In an average week, employed mothers spend only about five hours less on child care than non-employed ones, and there is no difference in the amount of time they spend actually interacting with their children. To achieve this, employed mothers deliberately set aside time to be with their children after work, on weekends and during holidays.

Basically, employed mothers have *two* full-time jobs – not only do they spend about 40 hours a week on work, they also spend almost the same amount (36 hours on average) on housework and child care. Even if they have hired help to assist with these tasks – a cleaning person, someone to look after the children's needs, housekeeper, laundry service – it is still the mother's responsibility to arrange for and supervise such assistance.

Is there any difference in the time that working mothers spend with sons and daughters? When they are toddlers, and if they are in daycare centers and their parents are under stress, it is boys who, being more noncompliant and aggressive than girls to begin with, may become unpleasantly so; this leads to their parents having more negative reactions toward them and interacting with them less. Preschool girls, who gain from the independence and assertiveness that daycare centers can foster, are viewed more positively by parents, who interact with them more as a result.

Children's experiences

The lives of employed mothers are clearly different from those of homemaker mothers, but how different are the lives of their children? Researchers have tried to answer this question by observing, interviewing, and comparing hundreds of children and parents in families with employed and nonemployed mothers. As one might expect, there *are* differences for the children – both obvious and subtle.

One major one is that children whose mothers are employed have more varied experiences than children with homemaker mothers. They are taken care of by more adults and interact with a wider range of children, often because of the sort of daycare they are given. In particular, daycare centers offer children not only exposure to more people but also to many different types of toys, materials, activities, and field trips. The kinds of interactions children experience in daycare settings also differ in terms of quality from those with parents and siblings. Daycare providers are more dispassionate and instructive, and are more likely to encourage children to follow their own paths of learning, while relationships with other children are more casual and transitory than those with brothers and sisters.

◄ **Father's goodbye**. *In the traditional ideal family, father is the daily-absent breadwinner, mother the ever-present homemaker, chiefly responsible for the nurture of the children. Affirming this arrangement or altering it will subtly affect a child's sense of sexual identity.*

► **A mother entertains her son**. *Although sufficient maternal attention and warmth are vital to the development of a confident, loving personality, a homemaker mother can sometimes be too much of a good thing if she monopolizes her child, limiting other opportunities for emotional and intellectual growth.*

In addition to these experiences *outside* the home, children of employed mothers have different experiences *within* it. Where mothers have outside jobs, households tend to be more structured and tightly organized, and there are more clear rules and regulations. Children are given more responsibilities and chores at an earlier age, and they are encouraged to be more independent by being taught important skills at the earliest opportunity – toilet training, dressing themselves, fending for themselves after school.

Children whose mothers are employed are also more likely to be given formal lessons – eg ballet, tennis, piano, computers. In part, this is because these occupy their time when parents cannot be there, and in part, because their parents have higher educational aspirations for them. They may also have more material resources at their disposal, because of their mother's income.

One final difference in the experiences of children with employed mothers is that fathers usually participate a little more actively in housework and child care, especially if the mother is pursuing a career and not just holding down a job. Although the absolute amount of time a father contributes in this way is not much – the best predictor of how much housework he does is *his* work schedule, not the mother's – he will contribute proportionately more to these tasks simply because the mother spends less time on them. Consequently, in such families, children are likely to be

exposed to more egalitarian gender roles, with both mothers and fathers cleaning the home and paying the bills, and to have relatively more direct interaction with their fathers than children whose mothers stay at home.

There are, however, many ways in which the experiences of children whose mothers are employed are *not* any different from those whose mothers stay at home. Overall, their home environments are as equally likely to be clean, safe

◄ If father is responsible for the housework, while mother pursues her career, a daughter's confidence in her own sex role may gain, a son's may suffer. If both parents go out to work, egalitarian role expectations are more likely to prevail.

▲ In two-career families, father helps more, but mother is unlikely to relinquish the role of chief homemaker. And the time father is prepared to devote to domestic duties is still likely to be dictated – and curtailed! – by the demands of his career rather than mother's.

The children of families in which both parents go out to work may often benefit from a richer and more varied pattern of interaction and activity – inside as well as outside the home – than they would if mother simply stayed at home.

and stimulating. In addition, the emotional climate at home is unlikely to be related to the mother's work status. Although employed mothers are not at home as much as homemakers, and although they may be under greater stress because they have, in effect, two full-time jobs, the quality of employed mothers' interactions with their children when they *are* at home is just as physical, responsive, sensitive, supportive, helpful, stimulating, emotional and affectionate – or just as rejecting, punitive and disciplinary. Employed mothers simply spend less time playing and watching television with their children.

How much insecurity do children suffer?

The lives of mothers, fathers and children in households where the woman is either a homemaker or employed are basically very similar, but there are differences. Will these differences affect a child's development, or will the experiences that are common to children with both types of mother have a greater influence on them? There is a widely held belief – even among experts in child development and among employed mothers themselves – that children's development suffers if mothers are employed. Is this belief grounded in fact or in fear?

One way that a child's development might suffer is if maternal employment leads to his or her being less emotionally secure than one whose mother is more available. The fear that children might suffer in this way because they are separated from their mothers originates from observations of children raised in institutions – infants who were "deprived of a mother's love." It cannot be argued that these children, without the continuous and consistent care of a nurturing adult, were greatly damaged emotionally. However, an infant whose mother is employed is *not* deprived of her love – the infant is simply deprived of some of her time. In almost all cases, such a child will be nurtured by another adult in the mother's absence, and the mother will reliably be with her child at least at the beginning and end of every day.

In the normal course of development during the first year of life, home-reared infants develop a passionate love relationship with their mothers because of their repeated, pleasurable interactions with her. They come to prefer their mothers over all others, wanting to be held by them and to stay close to them, especially when the infants are tired or sick. Does this occur in infants whose mothers are employed? According to a number of studies, it does. The infants of employed mothers are no less likely to become attached to their mothers than are the infants of homemaker mothers.

◄ **A career mother** *is likely to feel more confident than a homemaker mother about coping with intellectually exacting homework problems, as her child's formal education progresses. She is less likely to rely on the traditional fallback: "You had better ask your father."*

▲ **Responsibility** *for household chores and child care features earlier and more extensively in the lives of most children whose parents both go out to work. In many such families, as a result, the children are encouraged to become more independent and resourceful.*

Recently, however, there has been concern that the *quality* of this relationship may be less secure for the infants of employed mothers. This is based on observations made during the assessment of infant-mother relationships. In a standard situation, mothers leave their infants in an unfamiliar room with an unfamiliar woman, and the infants' reactions to their mothers' departure and return are recorded. Children with a secure relationship with their mother – and this would account for the vast majority – let their mothers leave without protest and, when they return, greet them happily or go to them. However, some 10 percent of infants whose mothers are in full-time employment have been observed to be rather more likely to ignore or avoid their mothers when they return. Boys are a slightly greater proportion of this group than girls are.

Some psychologists claim that this shows infants of fully employed mothers to be at risk of emotional insecurity. They say the children are avoiding their mothers because they do not trust them or want to be with them. However, the majority of psychologists are more optimistic, believing that infants of employed mothers are more used to being left, and therefore they are less likely to make a big fuss after only a brief separation. Besides, even if a difference does exist, that does not prove that maternal employment has caused it; the relatively small proportion of infants who ignore their mothers may do so for any number of reasons. And this is the only difference in infant development that has been found.

Development in early childhood

Another concern about maternal employment that has been expressed by some experts and parents is that

There is little evidence that daycare children of working mothers form less strong mother-child bonds than children of homemaker mothers. Among the few who show signs of emotional insecurity, boys may be more susceptible than girls.

mothers' employment will detrimentally affect the intellectual and social development of their preschool children. If mothers are not there to respond to children's questions, demands and quests for knowledge, how will the children get the attention and stimulation they need to develop their full intellectual potential? In a daycare center or a childminder's home with only one adult and many children, will the children get lost in the shuffle? Or will children in this

ing until you find a mature, responsible, kindly person who has some experience, training and education and shares your opinions on child rearing values and practices. Then you can arrange for the children to have supplementary social and educational experiences.

▲ **Momentary anxiety** crosses the face of this young girl as her mother departs for work, leaving her in the care of a day-babysitter. How successful the arrangement is will depend on how appropriate the babysitter's personal qualities happen to be, and whether her charge's day is sufficiently stimulating and varied.

DAYCARE AT HOME – WHAT TO LOOK FOR

■ *Having a babysitter, nanny or housekeeper in your own home is the ultimate in child-care convenience. There is no need for the children to travel; they remain in a familiar, safe place; hours are flexible and under the parents' control. The children receive individualized attention; siblings can remain together; and the mother gets to know the caregiver well and can instruct her daily and in detail. You will not have to take time off from work when illness keeps your child at home.*

If the caregiver is a relative and provides her services free or for a very little charge, if there are several children in the family or if other services – eg

laundry, housekeeping – are included, this sort of arrangement can be relatively economical. However, if the caregiver is given a true salary, especially if she has had some training, this is the most expensive form of child care. It is also usually difficult to find a suitable person, one who will provide the kind of love and stimulation the parents want; and if someone is found, she may not stay with the family very long. However, even the best in-home caregiver is unlikely to provide formal educational activities or arrange for her charges to be with other children.

The key to finding good at-home care is extensive search-

CHILDMINDERS — WHAT TO LOOK FOR

■ *This child-care arrange-ment – the most economical – has the advantages of usually being located nearby in a familiar neighborhood, and of offering children new and varied experiences and inter-action with different adults and children, in a homely, comfor-table setting. Many towns and cities license or register care-givers once their homes have passed inspection for safety. Being licensed or registered usually means that the care-giver can only look after a limited number of children.*

However, not all childminders and providers of daycare homes are licensed or regis-tered. Most are not trained in child care, and many take in so many children that they can *offer each only minimal atten-tion. Few have the education of the children as their goal or offer focused learning activities. There is also little flexibility in hours; it can be difficult to leave work and travel home in time to pick up the children at the appointed time. You will have to take time off from work when your child has to stay at home with an illness.*

The key to finding a good daycare home or childminder is to look for an educated and licensed or registered person caring for a small number of children. She should also make an effort to provide educational activities and not just leave the children to play by themselves all day while she does the housework.

▲ A need for reassuring body contact *with a mother figure is evident in these young children who spend their parents' work-ing day at a childminder's home. Even though she may spend more time with them than they do with their actual mothers, the childminder is highly unlikely to displace a mother in her child's affections.*

▶ Mothers who feel "guilty" *about being "just" housewives and not "self-actualizing" careerists may suffer emotional stress to a degree that can ad-versely affect their competence as homemakers. When this happens, their sons are more likely to show signs of disturbed behavior than their daughters.*

kind of daycare arrangement spend so much time with others that they will become too dependent on and too subject to the influence of their peers?

Researchers have carried out many studies in an attempt to answer these questions, and their results have been quite consistent. Overall, the intellectual and social development of preschool children whose mothers are employed is no different from that of children with homemaker mothers.

There may, however, be differences between children in

Children whose mothers work away from home may react in different ways. Daughters tend to be achievers at school and more ambitious. Middle-class sons may do less well. Working-class sons may come into conflict with their fathers.

daycare centers and those who are spend their days in somebody's home, either a childminder's or their own with their own mothers or a babysitter/nanny. Among the many studies that have compared children in these two different settings, only one showed that children in daycare centers develop more slowly than children at home – and this was

DAYCARE CENTERS – WHAT TO LOOK FOR

■ *Daycare centers (or crêches) are stable (ie they do not close when the caregiver is sick). They have predictable hours, and they are open for public inspection. The environment, equipment and programs are designed for children, and caregivers usually have at least some training in child development.*

The best daycare centers are also expensive (unless their cost is subsidized by government or your employer). They have eligibility criteria and waiting lists and do not provide care for children when they are sick.

The quality of daycare centers runs the gamut from custodial to enriching. The things to look out for are a trained and capable director and an adequate number of well-educated and committed staff so that the ratios between caregivers and children are low; organized activities that are appropriate for the children's developmental level, and are interspersed with periods of free play; and a calm, clean, safe, attractive environment, well stocked with toys and materials. Look also for staff who are happy, responsive, accepting, warm, calm and playful with the children. Check the staff turnover for stability.

a study of a less-than-adequate center where the adult-child ratio was about 1 to 20 and care was custodial at best.

All other studies have shown that, on tests of intellectual and social development, children in daycare centers do at least as well as children in a home, and they often do better (especially children from poor families who are in model daycare centers). On intelligence tests, these children may score 20 to 30 points higher than children not in daycare, and on tests of fluency, complexity and comprehension of language, problem solving, bead stringing, writing and drawing, daycare-center children are more advanced. In one study assessing the intellectual skills of middle-class children, two- to four-year-olds in daycare centers were six to nine months ahead of children who spent their days in someone's home.

Research has also revealed that preschool children at daycare centers are more advanced socially. They are more comfortable in new situations, more cooperative and interactive, outgoing, self-confident, assertive, self-sufficient and independent. At the same time, they tend to be more demanding, boisterous, competitive and aggressive – a pattern that may or may not indicate advanced social development.

All these differences in social and intellectual competence are, however, only temporary. When children who have been at home with their mothers, babysitters, nannies or childminders start nursery or primary school, they quickly catch up with daycare peers.

Achievement in school

These research findings have been virtually duplicated when applied to children whose mothers work or stay home during the school years. In general, there are no differences between these children in intelligence, social maturity, problem behavior, emotional adjustment, academic performance or achievement motivation. In fact, only two differences have been observed – children whose mothers are employed tend to have somewhat higher self-esteem; and in some professional-class and lower-class families, but not others, children of employed mothers know more and achieve more in school.

There is some difference between boys and girls. During the school years, the increased independence, assertiveness and self-confidence, and the positive view of women they have gained from having employed mothers, stands the daughters in good stead, contributing to higher levels of achievement and aspiration. The sons, although as sociable and psychologically well adjusted as those of homemaker mothers, may be more aggressive, do less well at school (this is observed only in middle-class families) or have a strained relationship with their fathers (this is observed only in working-class families).

It may be that the increased independence training or lack of supervision that is the experience of children of employed mothers is too much for these boys. However, for the daughters, it is developmentally valuable because, in

61

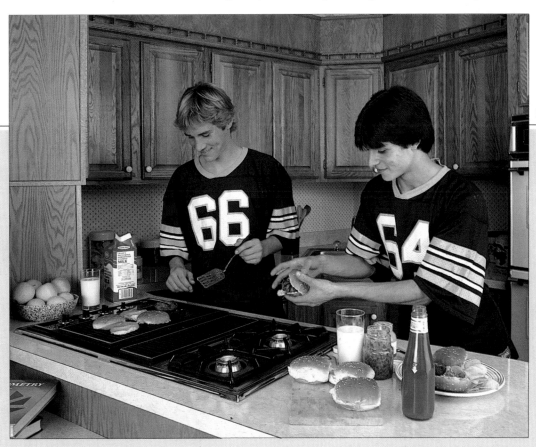

◄ **Daycare-center activities** provide preschool boys and girls with a new range of social contexts and experiences. These are usually more varied and often more instructive or challenging than those normally available to them at home.

► **Teenagers** whose mothers go out to work tend to behave in less gender-stereotyped ways. For example, the are more likely than others to perceive women as competent and men as warm.

general, they receive less of it than boys and so are otherwise in danger of being overprotected and dependent. It may also be that the high-status, competent role model that an employed mother provides is of value to these girls, who identify with their mothers, while if this model takes away from the male role model, it is detrimental to boys who identify with their fathers.

Teenagers with employed mothers continue to have higher self-esteem and to achieve more. There is also a tendency for these young people to behave in less gender-stereotyped ways, to perceive men and women as being more similar – for example, women as competent and men as warm – and to favor and aspire to more egalitarian gender roles for themselves – careers for women, parental participation for men.

However, the lack of evidence for differences is more noteworthy than any differences that have been found. In addition, because it is very difficult to separate the effects of maternal employment from other conditions with which

it may be associated (divorce, level of education, family size, career motivation, etc), it can be difficult to interpret the small differences that have been observed.

When employment can harm

There are few differences in children's development when mothers are employed, and what differences there are tend to be generally positive. However, maternal employment is not *always* a good thing – sometimes people's fears about its effects are well founded. When this is so, the consequences tend to fall as heavily on girls as as on boys.

Occasionally, maternal employment places too much stress on parents and children, and in such cases, the latter's development may indeed suffer. The issue is not simply whether mothers are employed are not, but how much, how long, and how happily they work, and what their situation is at home.

All work is not created equal, and when mothers are in stressful jobs – when they are given little independence, work long hours (more than 40 a week) with little flexibility or time off, find their work schedule conflicts with their family's, are dissatisfied with their jobs and conditions at work – they become fatigued, distressed and driven, anxious and depressed. Their interest in their children declines, and when they interact with them, their behavior is less involved, affectionate, playful, and stimulating, and more authoritarian and strict. As a consequence, the children are likely to become less attached to their mothers and, later, do less well at school.

The mother's reasons for having a job also make a difference. Children are more likely to suffer if the mother is just working for the money she earns – not pursuing a career. The mother's attitude toward work in the home and outside matters, too. She may want to work and may think that it will

UNDERSTIMULATED CHILDREN

■ *For homemaker and career mothers alike what counts is the quality of their attention when they are with their children and the quality of the care arrangements when they are at work. Children are in danger of being understimulated and socially and intellectually impoverished if, for example, a homemaker mother confines them too long to cot or playpen, or a mother who takes her infant to the office works most of the day with her back turned, or a returning schoolchild spends most afternoons alone at home.*

Whether mother goes to work or stays at home, what really matters is how the family works out its own way of caring for the children. Under some circumstances, however, mother's going out to work could affect her children adversely.

benefit her children, but she cannot find a suitable job or is unable to work for some other reason. Alternatively, she may not want to work and thinks that, if she does, it will harm her children, but she finds she has to, and subsequently feels guilty and anxious about it. In both cases, the children's development is in danger of being negatively affected.

It is not only the job itself and the mother's attitude toward employment that counts – the attitudes of her husband and of the community at large are also important. If neither the husband nor the community provide support and help, the employed mother will feel guilty and not get the assistance she needs to run the household and care for the children. If the mother's employment reflects negatively on the husband by suggesting that he is a failure – if, for example, he is unemployed himself – or if the community is not one

in which women have jobs, her employment then becomes a stigma, and there may be negative effects on the children.

If she has *no* husband and/or no help from the community, an employed mother faces even more serious challenges. This is also the case if the family set-up already involves stress – for instance, the presence of twins, a handicapped child, more than five children. If the mother's employment adds even more stress, the effect on the children will probably be deleterious.

Finally, the importance of child-care arrangements cannot be overemphasized. If stable and satisfactory arrangements cannot be made, this can have both direct and indirect negative effects on children. It can directly hold back their development by preventing them from enjoying the varying experiences that good child care can provide. Indirectly, it can affect their relationship with their mother, because if she is not assured that her children are safe in her absence, she cannot concentrate on her work or feel that she is doing the right thing. **KAC-S**

WHAT REALLY MATTERS

■ *The most important thing in children's development is not whether the mother is employed or at home, nor whether they are boys or girls. What really matters is how the family works out its own way of caring for the children, and the nature of the children's day-to-day experiences. Children thrive when their parents:*

● *balance warmth and affection with control and discipline.*

● *are consistent in their demands and realistic in their expectations.*

● *are sensitive, responsive, and easy to know and understand.*

● *provide stimulation and educational experiences.*

● *encourage both independence and social responsibility.*

● *monitor homework, encourage friendships, and show interest in their activities.*

● *participate together in child rearing.*

● *feel good about themselves and support each other.*

These conditions can apply whether mother is employed or not. All parents must strive to

provide their children with such experiences and seek for themselves a comfortable balance between meaningful work and fulfilling family life.

▲ **A few minutes daily** *in which a career mother interacts warmly with her child and responds with total concentration – not easy if work is very stressful –*

can compensate for hours of absence at the office.

63

The Roots of Aggression

THE SCENE is familiar: eight-year-old John is play-fighting with one of his friends. Nearby, his sister Jill, two years older, is scrambling up a tree. And looking on is their teenage sister Jane, already behaving in every way "like a grown woman."

How is it that John as a type is permitted, even encouraged, to stay the way he is, but "tomboy" Jill must eventually turn into a Jane? It seems that while a rough-and-tumble style is considered "unwomanly," masculinity and a measure of violence go hand in hand. They are expected in the developing man.

Sex differences in the level of aggressive behavior have now been systematically observed in children from over a hundred societies around the world, documented in laboratories, seen on school playgrounds, and reported by teachers, parents and the children themselves. That the male *is* the more violent sex is beyond dispute. Even in apparently nonviolent males, laboratory tests reveal subconscious aggressive impulses. There is also the inescapable statistic that of all those arrested for violence in any year the great majority (for the United States the figure is around 90 percent) are male.

But where does this aggression come from? Does every society in the world encourage boys to fight and girls to "play nicely"? Or is there something about masculinity, something genetic perhaps, that pushes boys on from anger to attack?

Are boys naturally aggressive?

Does male body chemistry provide the answer? If the male-determining Y chromosome is present at conception (see *Ch1*), testes instead of ovaries will appear in the developing embryo. The testes then secrete into the bloodstream male hormones that will affect the unborn child's physical and neurological development as a boy.

The influence of male hormones on the brain before or just after birth has been closely studied in animals, where scientists can alter the hormone levels in order to observe

▲ **Sex-role influences** probably best explain the behavior of these boys and girls, all guests at a child's birthday party. The presence of girls – and the photographer – prompts typical "show-off" behavior among the boys. Two immediately indulge in "manly" play-fighting, while a third – identifying himself with a strongly masculine role model by wearing an English policeman's helmet – tries to upstage them. Meanwhile the girls hang back diffidently; they have learned that such antics are unfeminine and not expected of them. And no doubt the little girl in the foreground is unconsciously registering the photographer's interest in and acquiescent "approval" of the scene.

Why are boys characteristically more aggressive than girls? The presence of male sex hormones seems to have much to do with it – but this is not the whole story. Our social environment plays a part – and also affects our hormone levels.

long-term effects, and the results are striking. Female mice and monkeys injected with the male hormone testosterone, for example, develop a masculine level and style of fighting in later life.

Conversely, male mice injected with female hormones show much lower rates of fighting than expected. It seems as if the brain can be permanently affected by sex hormones if they reach it at the crucial early period when brain functions are being differentiated.

Sadly, nature provides a way of examining a similar phenomenon in humans. Some little girls before birth are exposed to abnormally high levels of male hormones either because of a genetic defect or because of a drug that was unwittingly given to the pregnant mother before its side

effects were known. By following their development we can gain some insight into the early impact of male hormones on human females. These girls do show masculine levels of rough-and-tumble play and prefer male companions, but they do *not* show significantly higher levels of aggressive fighting than their normal sisters.

Aggression itself, however, can *affect* testosterone levels, as well as the other way around. When male monkeys that are low in dominance are separated from their more aggressive peers and put in a cage with low-status females whom they can dominate and mate with, their testosterone level increases greatly. But as soon as they are taken back to the cut-and-thrust world of other, more successful males, their testosterone level falls again. So the environment plays a part in body chemistry.

Moreover, testosterone does not have an effect only on aggression. It may produce more generalized changes in behavior, and of a kind where the increase in aggression is only a by-product. One example may be the male-hormone girls, with their higher levels of rough-and-tumble play. Some psychologists believe that both aggression and physical play result from an underlying effect of testosterone – the general increase in vigor and activity it brings. Boys expend energy at a higher rate than girls, particularly in social situations. They tend to prefer larger playmate groups, and to wrestle and make rough physical contact more than girls do. Perhaps their physical aggression – the pushing and hitting – is just an extension of their general enjoyment of active physical pursuits. And perhaps only extreme aggressiveness, such as is found in violent criminals, can be linked directly to testosterone as its cause.

Even those who argue that biology has a strong role in sex differences stress the importance of social learning of sex roles. Genetic predispositions to aggression can be

THE SOURCE OF MALE AGGRESSION?

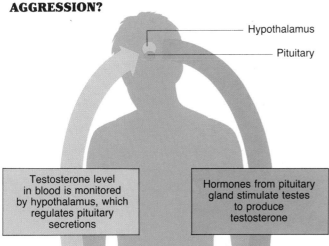

Hypothalamus

Pituitary

Testosterone level in blood is monitored by hypothalamus, which regulates pituitary secretions

Hormones from pituitary gland stimulate testes to produce testosterone

Testes

65

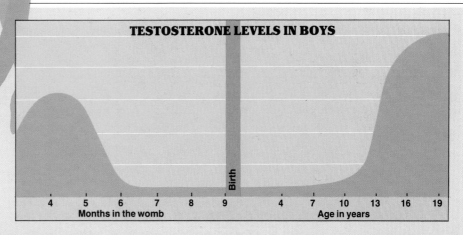

TESTOSTERONE LEVELS IN BOYS

4 5 6 7 8 9
Months in the womb

Birth

4 7 10 13 16 19
Age in years

■ **The physical development of a boy** and, later, of the man depend crucially on the presence of the male sex hormone testosterone and its level of concentration in the blood.

Because testosterone levels in the unborn male child as it develops in the womb are similar to those at the height of puberty, when very evident sex-specific changes in physique

and behavior are occurring, it has been a prime suspect in the search for an explanation of greater male aggression. The picture turns out to be far from straightforward, however, even

though an increase in testosterone does seem to be linked to an increase in rough-and-tumble behavior in children of both sexes.

accentuated or suppressed by the social environment: a girl raised in a violent family is likely to become far more aggressive than a boy whose parents encourage self-control and negotiation rather than hostility. The social experience can create sex differences in two ways. It either increases a boy's aggressiveness or decreases a girl's; and either makes aggression more attractive or makes self-control more difficult. In each case it probably does a bit of both.

Folk wisdom tells us that parents punish aggression in girls but not in boys. For a father to say "I hope you hit him back" to the son who has come home in tears after his first fist-fight is a common reaction. We discourage any sign of cowardice in boys because, while a tomboy daughter may be cute, an "effeminate" son is not.

Punishment as a model for aggression

However, studies have largely failed to support the idea that girls are more often punished for aggression. In fact, the opposite appears to be true. Aggression is discouraged in both sexes, but parents and teachers alike discipline boys more often than girls. It has also been shown that, after misbehaving, boys are twice as likely to be smacked by their

6 Models herself on the stereotype of femininity

5 Tends not to play with boys

1 Young girl identifies with brothers, plays with boys

4 Avoids rough play

3 Receives nonphysical discouragement

2 Indulges in tomboyish rough play

BEHAVING "LIKE A GIRL"

▲ *The postures and actions of the girls photographed above contrast sharply with those of the boys illustrated on the opposite page and elsewhere in this chapter. The hand thrown back and the kneeling and bending postures are all unmistakably feminine – examples of a precocious feminine grace that shows the influence of female role models. If it appears at all, tomboyish behavior in a girl is usually a passing phase. Where it persists, it is sometimes associated with a slight increase in the small amount of testosterone normally present in girls.*

Although aggressive behavior is discouraged in boys and girls alike, the way parents, especially fathers, discipline their sons seems to lie at the root of much boyish aggression and later violence. For daughters, the parental style is more gentle.

parents than are girls, for whom the punishment is more often threats of withdrawal of love or loss of special treats. Boys it seems must learn more painfully than girls that aggression is naughty.

What do boys learn from being hit as a punishment for hitting? They learn that being hit is something to do with being a boy, because sisters are not hit as much and because fathers, not mothers, do the really important spanking. They learn to "take it like a man" and learn that physical pain is brief and tolerable. They also see a successful demonstration of the very principle that parents

should be trying to teach them to reject: that physical force is a legitimate way to impose your will on others. They learn not from what parents say but from what they do. And it is the fathers whose behavior is watched most closely in this.

Fathers, even more than mothers, tend to treat infants and toddlers in sex-appropriate ways. They describe their sons at birth as firmer, more alert and stronger than their daughters. From three months on, they encourage independence and prefer rough-and-tumble games with their sons to the more sedate "peekaboo" play that mothers offer. Mother deals with the humdrum business of diaper-changing and feeding. It is Father who provides the novelty, excitement and fun.

But if fathers hold such a special place in family life, why do daughters not imitate them just as much as sons do? The answer hinges on the child's understanding of roles. Between the ages of three and six, the child can identify his or her own sex, and learns that being a boy or a girl is something that lasts forever and cannot be changed by

BEHAVING "LIKE A BOY"

5 Physical punishment (especially by father) reinforces male-aggressive stereotype

4 Rough play becomes aggressive

3 Receives encouragement

2 Indulges in rough play

1 Young boy identifies with male-aggressive stereotype

■ **Boys being boys.**
The interests and pursuits of these boys, encouraged by parents, teachers, school-friends, national institutions and the media, are all associated in one way or another with acts of explosive aggression and distinctively masculine display or adventure.

cutting one's hair or dressing differently. It is during this time that boys and girls start to show greater divergence in their choices of toys and activities in terms of masculinity and femininity. This is also the time when boys begin to prefer male role models and like to copy the behavior of their own sex.

But there is an important distinction between acquisition and performance. We acquire a vast amount of information through watching the behavior of other people, yet that does not necessarily mean that we will ever put what we know into practice. That depends upon whether we are likely to be rewarded or punished for it.

A highly significant study conducted in the United States by Albert Bandura and his colleagues showed that both boys and girls will imitate aggressive behavior, but under rather different circumstances. Such changes in the children's behavior are due to what is known as "observational learning." Children model their actions on those of the important other people around them, and (for boys in particular) experiencing violence arouses their own violence potential.

The difference between the boys and girls shown in this Bobo-doll study (see box) might suggest that females are less inclined simply to imitate the behavior of other people than boys are. However, its conclusion indicates that girls know how to be aggressive, as much as boys do, but that they do not choose to display it unless there is some real point in doing so. For boys, being aggressive and macho brings rewards in itself. Girls, however, need to see some further benefit before they will act in the same manner.

The implications of this are quite important. They suggest that aggression in the home is likely to lead to imitative behavior among the children, especially the boys. If adults are seen to get their way by being aggressive – to get rewards other than those resulting from the aggression itself – then girls will also tend to adopt this "instrumental" approach in their own lives.

Other role models and the media

From here it is a short step back to punishment and its effects. But what about parents who never use physical punishment and fathers who never strike anyone? Can children be insulated from the stereotype that links masculinity to aggression? Bear in mind that while an American study found that fathers on average spend 12 minutes a day with their sons, children can average six hours a day watching television. Television programs depict male violence much more frequently than they show female aggression, and many studies have indicated a link between violence on TV and the aggressive behavior of children who

The media – especially television – foster stereotypes about sex differences in violent behavior. Studies suggest that boys are particularly influenced by those programs which represent violence as "manly" and justifiable.

watch it. Not only can the programs increase the levels of aggression among the audience, in line with Bandura's experiments; they also foster stereotypes about sex differences in violent behavior. Rarely do we see women portrayed in a Rambo-like way. In movies and soaps about the police it is the male officers who do nearly all of the killing. Television producers are now sensitive to the need to show women in positions of equal status with men, but we have yet to see equality in terms of aggression and violence displayed.

Perhaps the fact that females are shown as the gentler sex has its positive aspects. Girls, who watch less violence on TV than boys in any case, are even less likely to be exposed to aggressive role models that might influence their behavior. Boys, however, receive strong messages about the "manliness" of aggression and are particularly influenced by those programs that show violence to be a justifiable type of behavior. Pure fantasy scenes, or portrayed violence that is subsequently seen to be punished, have little effect. It is the realistic, "praiseworthy" acts of death and destruction that make maximum impact on boys of all ages, and it is this kind of violence that is increasingly being shown in films and on the networks.

While we should be very concerned about these influences, we should also remember that the relationship between television violence and aggression is not quite as simple and direct as some people imagine. Children are exposed to many other sources of influence, not least that of their parents and the home environment. Parents can play a role in counteracting the potentially negative impact of television violence by providing them (and boys in particular) with alternative, nonaggressive models of behavior.

Different styles of aggression?

Girls admittedly are no angels either – a popular notion is that they simply express their aggression in a different and more feminine way. Since girls develop language skills earlier, perhaps they act out their anger through words, not deeds. Since they know that girls should not push and shove, perhaps they are more discreet and more "bitchy" toward their enemies. One study found that a pair of girls playing together reacted to the arrival of an outsider by giving her the cold shoulder and excluding her from participation (boys were more directly aggressive); however, the effect was not long-lasting and soon the children were playing together. It is very difficult to know if the girls' behavior should correctly be called aggressive here, since by aggression we usually mean a conscious intent to hurt or injure. Perhaps girls are more reserved in their dealings with strangers than boys are. We do know that the sex difference is not as simple as a distinction between physical and verbal aggression. Boys in fact are more aggressive in both respects. It is rare, after all, for one child to attack another without at least some angry words preceding the violence. **AC**

69

■ **Violent scenes**. *The young Northern Irish rioter ABOVE is strongly influenced by his social environment. Whether viewers of television violence LEFT can be similarly affected is still a matter of debate.*

THE BOBO-DOLL EXPERIMENT

■ *Young children were shown an adult model attacking an inflated Bobo doll (the toy with a weight at the bottom so that it rocks around on its base). Afterwards, when the children were allowed to play with the same dolls, the boys showed an increased level of aggression toward them as measured by* *the frequency with which they hit the dolls. Girls also tended – but rather less so than the boys – to be more aggressive after watching the aggressive adult. When both boys and girls were rewarded for imitating the aggressive style of the model, the sex differences disappeared.*

▲ **Harsh words**. *Although boys are verbally as well as physically more aggressive than girls, girls rely much more heavily on words than blows when it comes to expressing aggression or retaliating.*

Toys and Play

BOYS are active, rowdy, independent and good at sums. Girls are sweet, well behaved, compliant and good at reading and writing. Boys play with trucks, trains and footballs, and they like games of chase and adventure. Girls play with dolls and soft toys, like to dress up and pretend to keep house. These are the stereotypes all of us are used to, and infants begin to absorb them from the day they are brought home from hospital in their blue and pink blankets.

Yet what is the relationship between these stereotypes and the choices individual children actually make of toys and activities? Their experiences with toys and activities provide them with opportunities to learn and practice a wide variety of skills, not only those considered appropriate to their sex, but their choices seem to reflect their understanding of what it is to be boys and girls.

Whatever their daily environment – their own home, a daycare center, half-day preschool, home daycare – children spend a considerable amount of their day in play involving some type of toy or activity that helps them to grow up. They make their choices from a generous provision of play materials, and researchers have now begun to explore how these materials nourish development.

How we influence our children's choices

One reason for this careful examination of toys and games is that sex differences in this area appear at a remarkably young age – sometimes as early as 18 months, and generally by the age of three. These differences occur much earlier and more consistently than sex differences in social behavior. This is scarcely surprising, as parents con-

70

▲ **Hide and seek** *is a favorite game of girls, as here, and a favorite when boys and girls play together.*

◄ **Dressed up by mother** *for a costume parade. Boys are equally welcome in this event organized by adults, but fewer have agreed to take part. Girls' greater cooperation with such activities allows them to associate more with adults and learn more from them. In one study, girls spent about 60 percent of their time with adults. Boys spent 60 percent of their time away from them.*

Girls and boys have distinct styles of play that involve different toys and games and different levels of involvement with adults. Girls' play is characterized by communication and mutual help, boys' by independent competition.

sciously teach their very young children which forms of play are appropriate to their sex, and do so at a much earlier stage than they begin to guide their social behavior.

As we have seen in earlier chapters, parents and others in the child's social world respond to boys quite differently from the way they respond to girls, both at birth and later. The child's social world includes people who love and care about the new addition to their family – parents, grandparents, brothers and sisters. Through them and the media the social world begins at birth to exert pressure on the child to develop in certain ways, and the evidence indicates that parents and relations tend to perpetuate the common

stereotypes of what they think boys and girls should be like.

Despite the fact that baby boys are on average more vulnerable than baby girls, and are subject to higher rates of infant mortality, the boys are tossed and rough-housed, while the infant girls are held closer, talked to more and treated far more gently. Boys are given masculine toys to play with – blocks, balls, trucks and manipulative mechanical toys – while girls' rooms are stocked with dolls and

▲ **Toys that involve spatial manipulation** *are considered masculine, and they are more often given to baby boys than to baby girls. This may be at least part of the reason why school-age girls are less skilled, on average, at spatial processing than school-age boys – girls who play with boys' toys are better than other girls at spatial skills.*

▲ **Rough-and-tumble** *boys' play can have its origins in very early life. Even as babies, boys are handled more vigorously than girls, and this may condition them to seek greater physical activity later. One theory claims that this rough handling* is the reason why boys avoid adult company more than girls do. Adults, in any event, tend to assume that boys can take care of themselves, and this makes it easier for them to be adventurous and independent. Differences in boys' and girls' hor- mone systems may at least partly explain boys' higher levels of activity, but assertiveness and aggression are also learned socially – many boys' games involve competition for status by showing who is the most daring and strongest.

All children enjoy pretending that they are some-one or something else, but boys' make-believe is filled with fictional super-hero themes, while girls' play focuses on characters in a familiar setting, involved in daily routines.

woolly animals. Researchers have found that masculine toys encourage increased activity – running, scooting or riding – among both boys and girls, while feminine toys encourage quiet, less active movement. Parents themselves encourage even higher levels of activity among boys, by joining in their physical games, while they tend to respond to the girls' games simply with words of praise. It is scarcely surprising then that by the age of two or three, boys are more active and more aggressive than girls.

Adults also respond differently to aggression exhibited by boys and girls. One study found that boys and girls of toddler age hit, pinched and bit to just the same degree, but that adults ignored the girls who hit, and reprimanded the boys. According to some psychological theories, this treatment is likely to encourage, rather than discourage, the boys' aggressive behavior, as subconsciously they welcome this special attention.

How different are boys' and girls' choices?

The preferences of boys and girls for different toys and activities have been documented by researchers since the 1930s. For the most part, activities today do not differ notice-ably from those reported earlier. Boys have consistently shown a preference for bats, balls and trucks, and girls for dolls and toy houses. What has changed, however, is the view taken by researchers of the role toys and activities play in childrens' social and intellectual development.

In the l930s, the choice of toy was thought to depend on a child's development. If the boys chose to play with masc-uline toys, and girls with feminine toys, their development was satisfactory. Children who did not select appropriate toys were regarded as social oddities. A typical example was the "sissy" boy, who preferred to play with girls and dolls, and to spend his time in the preschool dress-up area wearing girls' or women's clothes. Researchers today also believe that a child's choice of toys is important, but for a different reason. They see toys as vital to the child's acqui-sition of social and intellectual skills. From this point of view, both boys and girls who play with dolls and enact family roles are simply practicing the social and verbal skills that will be valuable in later life.

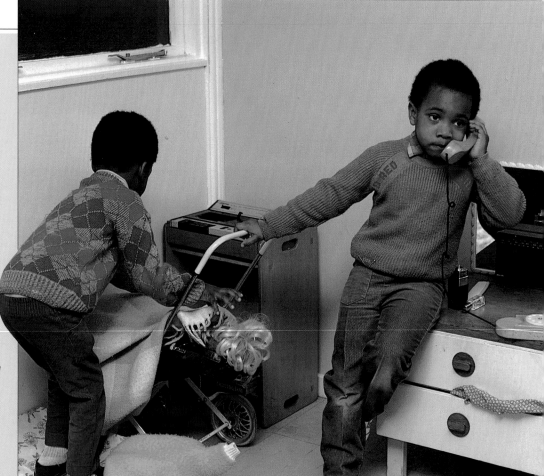

SOCIAL SKILLS

■ *Acting out family situations gives children practice in using the verbal and body-language skills that they observe in adult models. Girls are especially en-couraged in this kind of play and are readily attracted to it. Their make-believe is much more often about daily routines than boys' make-believe, which tends to be filled with super-heroes and highly fictional themes. Many early research-ers believed that a boy's normal sex-role development would be impaired by play-ing at domestic life with dolls. However, such play can be a part of healthy develop-ment in which boys grow up less mystified by females because they develop less rigid views of sex roles and observe and act out the behavior of women, in addition to imitating male role models. All play gives practice at moving from one social role to another and ab-sorbing the rules for playing a role.*

Not only do boys and girls differ in the toys they prefer. Their style of play differs also. In almost every culture, boys are more likely than girls to race and chase each other. This rough-house style of play generally appears joyous and adventuresome to the boys. Parents and teachers, however, used to quiet, less active adult behavior, tend to view this spontaneous, high-energy play with less enthusiasm.

All children enjoy pretending to be someone or something else, but there is one striking difference between boys and girls. Boys' make-believe is filled with fictional, super-hero themes, while girls' play focuses on characters in a family setting, generally involved in daily routines such as breakfast with the family, working at a library or dressing up as a ballet dancer.

In addition to such differences in their choice of toys and games, boys' and girls' activities often differ in whether they are directed primarily by adults or by the children themselves. It is in this area that research has produced some very significant findings.

Choosing where to play

Recent research has attempted to understand the influence of children's choice of activities on their social and intellectual growth. It started by looking at the preschool classroom, as previous research had shown that preschool boys and girls spend their time in very different activities. Boys, for example are likely to work and play farther away from the teacher than girls.

▲ **Parental initiatives** *help to orient boys toward masculine toys and girls toward feminine ones.* TOP *A father makes breakfast fun for a preschool boy.* BOTTOM *From the time they can barely walk, these girls have been given dolls as floppy as themselves. Researchers* *have observed that even very small children will soon put down an opposite-sex toy. Thus girls reinforce parents' decisions to offer dolls and boys reinforce decisions to offer trucks and tractors as playthings.*

◀ **Like father like son.** *Appropriately dressed, a boy plays at sex-appropriate activity with strong male reinforcement.*

73

HOW BOYS' PLAY MAGNIFIES THEIR PREFERENCE FOR MASCULINE TOYS	Masculine toys allow boys to be active and use spatial skills.	Adults encourage boys to use toys that they associate with boys.	Boys develop active and spatially manipulative play patterns that require masculine toys.
HOW GIRLS' PLAY MAGNIFIES THEIR PREFERENCE FOR FEMININE TOYS	Feminine toys allow girls to practice verbal and social skills.	Adults encourage girls to use toys that they associate with girls.	Girls develop verbal and social play patterns that require feminine toys.

GIRLS AND ADULT-INSPIRED ACTIVITIES

▼ **"Miss America Junior"** wears her crown and a winning smile in Atlantic City, New Jersey. Parents are motivated to invest high levels of participation in events that give them hope, through their children, of fulfilling aspirations that are characteristic of their own sex roles. Mothers may be interested in beauty contests for their daughters, fathers in organizing team sports for their sons.

◀ **Sitting next to the teacher** and asking questions, this girl will not only find it easier than her male counterparts to learn the basis of computing, but will also receive subtle tuition in adult behavior – she will acquire social and verbal skills as well as the mathematical ones being taught. However, by sitting farther away, the boys in the class may be developing an independence of thought and action, and practicing how to compete for leadership of a group.

▲ **Like mother, like daughter**. Close contact with the same-sex parent provides both boys and girls with appropriate role models, but girls are more likely to achieve such contact than boys. While helping her daughter learn how to string beads and develop dexterity, this mother also models the skills involved in caring for an infant. Boys learn from other boys, as much as from adults, how to be masculine.

Where children's activities are directed by closely involved adults, boys and girls alike tend to react with compliant "feminine" behavior. Where the adults are relatively uninvolved, "masculine" independent, competitive behavior emerges.

This means that the quality and quantity of the boys' activities inevitably receive less adult attention than the girls'. The researchers thought it was very possible that this difference led to different behavior.

They found that when teachers were intensively involved in organizing children's activities – conveying information, rules and guidance on how to behave – the children reacted by asking for help, complying with the rules, and bidding for the teacher's attention – all typical of "feminine behavior." Where the teachers were less involved, and gave less guidance on rules and appropriate behavior, the children reacted by displaying aggression, independence from adults, and a marked interest in competing against each another and negotiating for leadership – well-documented "masculine behavior."

In all this research, the boys and girls showed similar behavior in similar activities. However, since girls preferred to spend more time around adults, they participated in adult-structured activities more than the boys.

These findings suggest that exposure to activities in which adults are involved, or the lack of such exposure, is a basic underlying process by which sex-typed behavior is developed and maintained.

It was then found from further research that the same was true with schoolchildren aged from 7 to 11. Boys continued to spend the majority of their time (approximately 60 percent) in activities away from adults, while girls spent approximately the same amount of time in activities with the adults.

Again, within the home, similar subtle, but potentially influential, differences have been discovered. Boys spend more time than girls in out-of-home activities, unorganized by adults, while girls spend their time outside the home

▲ **Adult-structured activity for boys**. *Both girls and boys participate in activities organized by adults, but the content of these activities may differ markedly. Girls are more often involved in clubs and groups in which co-operative effort is required – for example, in a choir. Physical activity is less often a focus. Adults usually consider boys to be more physically adept, aggressive and competitive than girls, and they organize more activities for them that encourage these qualities. This, in turn, reinforces the competitive masculine values that boys teach each other when they are not supervised.*

75

mostly in organized activities. The boys, for instance, like to ride their bicycles around the streets, or play with their friends in the back yard. In contrast, the organized activities outside the home preferred by girls include Girl Scout meetings, attending church choir, or going to a movie or sports event with the family. Thus, on average, boys spend more time in activities organized by their friends and less time than girls in activities organized by adults. Their preferences are also unlikely to change very much throughout their lives. In these subtle ways, girls and boys are thus presented with quite different experiences in their social environment and in their day-to-day relations with their parents, other adults and children.

How play creates sex differences

An especially interesting finding of this research is that boys and girls who have spent the majority of their time in adult-structured activities over the first 11 years of their lives do far better on average at both reading and mathematics. Their social behavior is also entirely consistent over this period.

If a child has participated mainly in adult-structured activity, that child generally tries to conform to rules, asks for help and looks for recognition. What was also discovered –

and this was a most important conclusion – was that it is the participation that leads to those social characteristics and not vice versa.

These studies help to explain important differences between boys and girls in academic and social behavior. Boys are treated by their friends and by adults according to the stereotype that they are rough, tough and hardy. Yet the statistics suggests a somewhat different picture. Boys are physically more vulnerable, and are likely to suffer far more acutely than girls from academic problems, behavior disorders and reactions to family distress.

▲ **A will to win** inspires these boys at a Moscow sports center to add psychological warfare to the intellectual challenge of winning at chess. Whether in physical team sports or in board games, boys are more often found pitting themselves against each other than girls are. In one study schoolboys who were friends competed in a situation that prompted girls to help each other (see p81).

Some authorities have argued that the rule-governed games that boys play against each other – while girls play cooperatively and interact with adults – give boys a different moral development, one that enhances their sensitivity to principles of justice and makes them readier to demand fair treatment (see Ch 13).

As boys spend more time than girls do away from adults, they have less opportunity to learn how to adapt to society's expectations, how to cope with crises, how to acquire advanced logical, verbal and organizational skills.

A very likely reason why boys are more at risk is that they do not come into contact with the positive socializing influence of adults to the same extent that girls do. As boys spend more time than girls in activities away from adults both at school and in the home, they have less time to learn what adults can teach children: how to cope with crises; how to acquire advanced verbal, logical or organizational skills; how to adapt to the expectations of society. In this way, boys are less accustomed to the norms of the culture than are girls. When additional stress such as divorce or family distress occurs, the already fragile adult-child relationship between boys and their parents cannot cope, and behavioral problems result.

It is not surprising then that statistics show boys more at risk when the stable family unit crumbles. Nor is it surprising that the average school performance of young boys is far below that of girls. The social skills required to do well in school are primarily those learned from spending time around adults – sitting quietly, asking for help when it is needed, being responsive to adult assistance and following the accepted rules.

Playtime activities organized by children on their own are hardly likely to teach these school-related skills. Yet they are wonderfully well adapted to developing leadership and negotiating skills, and to discovering how to initiate independent projects. These are the skills that many girls fail to learn while growing up, and it has been suggested that this failure may be linked to the high rate of recorded depression, mental illness and lack of achievement among women in our society. These problems are related to lack of assertion, the opposite of the typical male social problems. Since

the development of young children is apparently affected in this way by their preferred choice of activity, it is clearly important to discover the origins of these preferences, and at what age they emerge. There are few behavioral or perceptual differences between girls and boys at birth, but several researchers have pointed out that this does not preclude the possibility that there may be biologically programmed sex differences. Differences in activity level, for example, might emerge in childhood, just as differences in size and strength emerge in adolescence.

Two other theories are currently under consideration. One is that boys prefer to keep to their own activities because they have found their previous experiences with adults generally stressful and even unpleasant. It may be, for

instance, that early rough treatment is an added stress for the somewhat physically vulnerable male. Thus some boys may choose to avoid extended contact with adults in their activities. The second theory is that the reverse is true, and that the majority of boys, who are encouraged by their parents to be independent from an early age, may become so self-reliant that they deliberately seek out activities well away from adults so that they can demonstrate their independent behavior. **CJC**

◀ Boys dominate *the use of adventure equipment while a girl stands by in this lakeside scene from British Columbia. Accustomed to competing with each other for play resources, boys typically push cooperative girls into the background. It is a familiar sight at after-school computer clubs, unless a teacher intervenes, to see boys crowding at all the available screens, pressing for a turn, while the two or three girls who have attended look over boys' shoulders.*

▶ Playing school. *More interested than boys in interacting with the teacher when they are really at school, these Australian girls also enjoy recreating the schoolroom at home, playing at adult-structured activity even when adults are not there.*

HOW BOYS' PLAY MAGNIFIES THEIR PREFERENCE TO BE APART FROM ADULTS	Adults encourage boys to play with less supervision.	Unsupervised boys have to compete with each other for status and leadership.	Boys need to be free to practice competitive skills away from adult control.
HOW GIRLS' PLAY MAGNIFIES THEIR PREFERENCE FOR ADULT-STRUCTURED ACTIVITY	Adults encourage girls to play close to them.	Girls learn social and verbal skills by cooperating with adults.	Girls seek adult interactions in order to practice their social and verbal skills.

Friendship

GIRLS and boys often inhabit different social worlds. It is true that a girl may find herself, for want of any other companions, playing outdoor team games with boys. A boy who has no other playmates may spend many hours indoors with girls cutting out paper dolls. But when they can choose, children mainly have same-sex friends. Outside of the family, they are the main social influence on development.

Sex segregation in nursery school

By two years of age, many children have learned to label themselves as "a girl" or "a boy." There is evidence that infants are *drawn* to the same sex at even earlier ages (see p31). Before the age of six, it is more accurate to say that this bias affects choice of playmate rather than choice of friend. Although preschool children use the word "friend," their ideas about friendship are different from an adult's. They have not yet developed the concept of loyalty and are only beginning to understand those of mutual help and support. Attachments are usually extremely unstable and only last if encouraged by parents. Asking a preschooler which friends from nursery school to invite to a birthday party can be very frustrating. If the child has any concrete suggestions, they may change capriciously from day to day.

Nursery schools are a favorite place for researchers to observe the preschooler's choice of playmates and the nature of their play. The beginnings of sex segregation in play are clearly visible. In a typical study, the younger class (3 to 4 years) in a nursery school was found to play mainly in mixed-sex groups. However, the girls never took part in the fire-fighting fantasy games of boys. The boys joined in family fantasies but would not assume the roles of mother or wife. In the older class (4 to 5) the boys rarely took part in family role play but spent most of their time playing superheroes and police, or constructing wagons and trucks. In a class of English nursery children (aged 3 to 5), only the boys consistently chose same-sex companions. However, in

▲ Being on friendly terms, *whether for adults or two small girls, means attentiveness – including a forward lean. Facial expression is the chief channel for communicating friendship. These children use theirs to show mutual acceptance, interest and understanding.*

► War of the sexes. *Preschool boys take more initiatives than girls in seizing by force the things they want. In some nursery schools they cooperate to reserve toys and facilities for each other, shouting "No girls!"*

HOW FRIENDSHIP CHANGES

■ *Friends have a special, but changing, place in children's lives as they grow. The very expertise of grown-ups limits boys' and girls' power to negotiate the rules and aims of an interaction with them. Exchanges with age-mates are more open to self-expression. The way children share their social world with each other changes as they develop more complex intellectual and interpersonal skills. For the younger ones, friends are girls and boys who share, play together and help one another, but their conceptions of friendship do not include the notion of an enduring relationship. Friendship takes on a new definition when nine-year-olds become aware of individual differences between people. They seek friends who share their interests and have similar personalities. By early adolescence, friends talk about one another's problems and are prepared to help because they understand each other's needs through their similarities of personality.*

Children's friendship choices reflect their sex-role identification. Up to about 10 years of age, this means progressively more sex segregation. After about 14, however, adolescents begin to accentuate their contacts with the opposite sex.

another class most of the boys and all of the girls preferred friends of the same sex. Researchers in Northern Ireland reported a veritable "war of the sexes." Boys at times monopolized resources such as the sand table, and would shout "No girls!" if any came near. Girls were unable to explain to the researchers why they gave in and shrank away. When *they* were in possession of the sand table and tried to exclude boys, the boys insisted on being included, or even took over the table. Boys used the nursery's playhouse, but usually pretended that it was a spaceship or some other nondomestic location.

In a Hawaiian study, same-sex preferences were also apparent. However, here there was a complicating factor. Hawaiian classes contained oriental and white children and both race and sex were found to affect friendship choice. Oriental children played more with orientals and whites more with whites. But for boys, the preference for same-sex friends was stronger than the race distinction.

Another complication is age. Sex segregation has been found to be greater in same-age groups of preschool children than in mixed-age groups. Analysis of this finding suggested that children tend to choose peers whose verbal fluency matches their own. In the preschool years, girls often have more mature linguistic skills than boys. As a result, in same-age groups girls are likely to choose other girls as friends, but in mixed-age groups an older boy might play with a younger girl whose verbal skills match his own.

Boundaries and borderwork at school

Once children start school, friendships develop more easily between children of the same sex than between opposite-sex pairs. In one study, children in 10 classes were asked to name their friends on five occasions throughout the school year. Changes from "friend," to "best friend" and "nonfriend" to "friend" occurred most frequently in same-sex pairs. These friendships were also more stable.

As friendships become more stable, sex segregation increases. It is most marked between the ages of 10 and 14. At school, clusters of friends, whether sitting together in the classroom or lining up to move on to another activity tend to be same-sex. At lunch time, fewer than 5 percent of the freely chosen side-by-side seats will be occupied by boy-girl pairs. High-status boys will influence other boys not to sit at tables where there are "too many girls." Outside on the playground, space is clearly divided, with boys tending to monopolize the large playing fields and courts for team games. Girls use the climbing frames and concrete areas.

▲ **A mixing of the sexes.**
First-year girls and boys sit together during this school lesson, and in playtime, young children, especially preschool nursery children, often play in mixed-sex groups. However, their games already show the beginnings of sex-role behavior: girls do not usually play "fireman," and boys take on only male roles in family games. As the school years continue, girls and boys have more clearly separated play activities.

In observations of schoolchildren in Michigan and California, however, several varieties of *borderwork* have been cataloged, in which girls and boys interact. Contests provide the most visible form of borderwork. Teachers sometimes arrange their class drills so that girls are pitted against boys in spelling and arithmetic. On the playground, children may organize their ball games with boys against girls. Cross-sex chasing is another form – a variant of the same-sex chasing which is a frequent occurence on school playgrounds. There are various names for this sport – "girls chase boys," "the chase" and "chase and kiss." In cross-sex chasing individual identities may disappear and the labels "girl" and "boy" appear instead. Thus Sarah being chased by Ben might shout to her friends: "Help, a boy is chasing me!" "Pollution" seems to arise from the touch of a girl. In girl-girl chasing the giving of "cooties" and "vaccinations against cooties" are important features but this pollution has not been observed in boy-boy chasing. In cross-sex chasing,

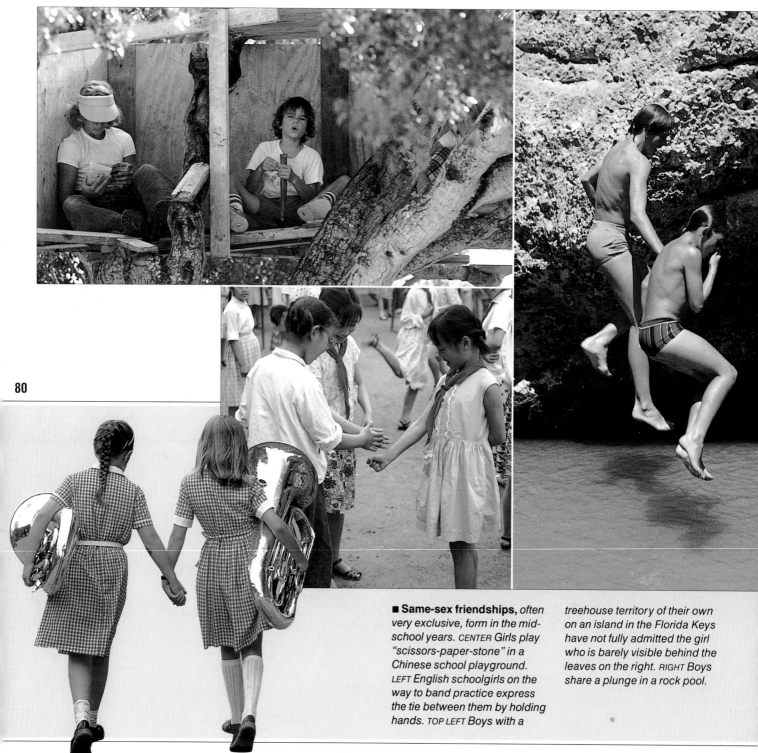

■ **Same-sex friendships,** *often very exclusive, form in the mid-school years. CENTER Girls play "scissors-paper-stone" in a Chinese school playground. LEFT English schoolgirls on the way to band practice express the tie between them by holding hands. TOP LEFT Boys with a* treehouse territory of their own on an island in the Florida Keys have not fully admitted the girl who is barely visible behind the leaves on the right. *RIGHT Boys share a plunge in a rock pool.*

Primary school children work and play in sex-segregated worlds, both in and out of the class-room. In cross-sex chasing, an individual's identity may disappear and the label "girl" or "boy" will appear instead.

boys give cooties to girls and girls give them to boys. Invasions are another form of borderwork. They usually involve boys disrupting the play of girls by grabbing their balls or sticking their feet into the skipping rope. Girls also sometimes invade the playspace of boys. This borderwork allows children to explore the boundaries between them and learn about each other.

The nature of girls' and boys' friendships

Most of children's time is spent in play. They are in school only for part of the day and for little more than half of the year. Outside school, both boys and girls are likely to spend only a quarter of their time in activities such as household chores, homework and religious services. In much of the remainder, girls of 10 and 11 prefer indoor play in small groups of similar age, with dolls or board games. Out of doors also, the activities of girls, such as skipping rope, hopscotch and tag, involve only a few children. Their play is based on cooperation and turn-taking and the resulting friendships are intense and exclusive. Disagreements are expressed indirectly. Secret-telling and secret-keeping are very important, since established friendships might dissolve and new ones form.

In contrast, the social world of 10- to 11-year-old boys is characterized by outdoor play in competitive games. These games require teams and have widely known and agreed sets of rules. To make up team numbers, boys of different ages may be included, so that the groups are large and of mixed ages. Friends might find themselves on different

teams and have to learn to depersonalize their competitiveness and work for the good of the team.

The quality of your friendship relationship is likely to be different if you are a boy or a girl. Comfort-giving between children aged 6 to 12 has been studied by asking them to describe everything they would say to a same-sex friend who was emotionally upset. They were asked to consider what they would say if a friend scored much lower on a test in school; if something on television upset a younger friend; if a friend failed to receive an invitation, or if a friend was ill-treated by a teacher. Both age and sex influenced the number, variety and sensitivity of children's comfort-providing strategies. Older children offered more solutions and more varied ones than younger children, and girls offered more solutions and more varied ones than boys. But this advantage also tended to be available if the respondent was a girl. Regardless of age or sex, children made fewer comfort-giving suggestions when their hypothetical same-sex friend was in a distressing situation with a teacher.

Children say that friends are people who help, share and do other kind things for them. However, a crayon-sharing study found that boys of 5 to 9 years are less likely to share when required to cooperate with a special friend than when they were in the same situation with a neutral classmate. Girls shared with friends and classmates alike.

All the children were asked to name their friends and to rate the same-sex children in their class on a likability scale. Pairs of same-sex friends and of neutral classmates were then observed while they colored geometric figures using a single set of crayons. Only one crayon could be used at a time. They knew that after each figure was colored the child who had done the most would receive 10 cents and the

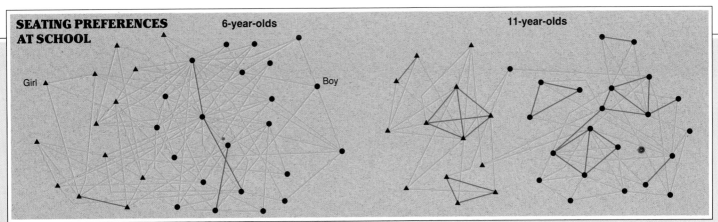

SEATING PREFERENCES AT SCHOOL   6-year-olds   11-year-olds

Girl ▲   Boy ●

■ When children in a class of six-year-olds and those in a class of 11-year-olds were all asked to write the names of the three children they would like to sit near, major differences in the friendship pattern appeared. Here are two diagrams that illustrate the choices made in each class. Triangles represent girls and circles indicate boys. The blue lines show one-way choices: the arrowhead indicates the child chosen. When two children chose each other, this mutual selection is indicated by a red line. The choices of the six-year-olds include numerous cross-sex ones but little mutual choice. Sex segregation is not yet the overwhelming pattern of friendship. The choices of the 11-year-olds produce a different picture: only one girl and one boy made cross-sex choices. There is a noticeable increase in mutual selection, and networks of mutual choices are evidence of the emergence of cliques.

other would receive only 5 cents. Girls shared with friends and other classmates equally. In both types of pairs each girl colored about the same amount of the geometric figures. Boys, especially the 7 and 9 year olds, shared less when paired with a friend and there was a greater difference in the amounts of the figure colored by each child in the friend pairs. Boys also complied less with their friends' requests for the crayon than with the requests of other classmates. Boys' friendships involve competition. This has also been found for male friends at university.

Adolescent friendships

During the first few adolescent years, old patterns prevail. For example, an English study comparing the companionship choices of 11- to 16-year-old white, West Indian and Asian schoolchildren across a year found that the children were more friendly with classmates of their own race and sex but sex was the most important criterion in a friendship. Given the choice, it seems that younger adolescents will

most often associate with members of their own sex and racial group. However, when boundaries are crossed you are more likely to see, for example, West Indian boys with white or Asian boys than with West Indian girls.

For younger children and younger adolescents, friendship patterns inside and outside school are much the same. However, in later adolescence, school and leisure become very different arenas, and the quality of relationships changes. In a study of over 100 groups of teenagers aged 13 to 19 in and out of school, the in-school groupings were relatively large, and they still showed sex segregation. Out-of-school groups were smaller and of mixed sex. The same study found that both boys and girls formed mixed friendship pairs. However, friends in male pairs said they had known each other for longer than did friends in female or mixed pairs. Girls

▲ **Making contact.** *By mid-adolescence for girls, and slightly later for boys, single-sex groups are still the main focus of social life but have become a vehicle for contacts with the opposite sex.*

▶ **A playful encounter** *outside the temple helps a bond to form between two young Japanese as they attempt practice relating to each other without the support, or interference, of friends.*

82

GROUP TO COUPLE

 Girls
Boys

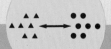

In early adolescence boys and girls form separate single-sex groups.

Growing opposite-sex interactions do not at first cause groupings to change.

In mid-adolescence, mixed-sex groups begin to form and overlap with the old ones.

Sex segregation breaks down as groups merge into a crowd.

In late adolescence, couples become the main form of association and the crowd falls apart.

Teenagers begin to form mixed-sex friendships in small groups outside school. Same-sex friends help boys to build social skills and confidence needed for the dating-couple relationships that become so important later.

had more cross-sex friends than boys and these friends were mostly older boys. The friendships of boys and girls become more intimate in adolescence. This reflects the biological, social and intellectual changes associated with puberty. Teenage girls tend to have more intense, demonstrative, exclusive and nurturant relationships with each other than boys. Boys make same-sex friends more easily than girls and admit new same-sex members to their groups more readily. Adolescent girls report more intimate conversations with friends than do boys but often boys have just as much knowledge about the personal details of their friends' lives. In one study, American adolescents aged 12 to 17 were

asked about their friends, sexual behavior and other activities. The same-sex friends named by girls reported similar degrees of sexual activity, even though they might be different ages. However, the friendship choices of boys could not be explained by reported sexual experience nor by any of the other activities. Girls may show more concern about the faithfulness of their friends and are often more worried about rejection than boys.

In late adolescence and early adulthood, dating becomes important, and there is evidence that the social skills acquired in successful male friendships help boys to form relationships with girls.

In a study, 12 young men and 12 young women, all of them relaxed, active daters, and 12 men and 12 women, all of them anxious, minimal daters, were selected from the replies of almost 4,000 university students to a questionnaire about their social activity. These 48 students were studied intensively. They were asked to provide reports on their social activity, skills and anxiety, to complete a personality test, and also to monitor their ongoing behavior. In addition, ratings were made of their social behavior by peers and by psychologists.

The low-dating women students had satisfactory social relations with other young women. Tests showed that they were as well adjusted as the relaxed, actively dating women. The picture for young men was very different. Male minimal daters had difficulties in their relationships with men as well as with women. Their results on the personality inventory showed them to be less well adjusted than their relaxed, active dating peers. **BL**

▶ **Pairing off.** *Sex segregation is at an end by late adolescence when single-sex groups merge and provide a social framework in which members may practice being couples.*

Skills and Aptitudes

WHO MAKE better lawyers, men or women? Why are so many doctors men? Is there any truth in the jokes about women drivers? Such questions arouse a good deal of passion, and the answers to them are rooted in what we can discover about the different abilities of boys and girls.

There are two basic questions we should ask. First, are there real differences in skills between boys and girls, and consequently between men and women? Second, if there are differences, what causes them? Could it be our genetic inheritance from our parents, or perhaps the things we learn from the people who influence us?

The second question brings us to one of the traditional controversies in psychology: which has the greater effect on abilities – nature (our biology) or nurture (our upbringing)? The answers could have economic and social consequences. Saying that boys and girls are different by nature seems to imply that their differences in performance can be taken for granted. However, if we can agree that these differences result from upbringing and education, then we seem to admit that educational systems and our expectations of the two sexes should be made fairer.

Unfortunately, the answers psychologists can now provide are neither simple nor complete. Thousands of experiments have been performed all over the world in attempts to measure the abilities of boys and girls, but interpreting their results is very difficult. This is partly because human abilities are so complex that it is difficult to work out exactly what is being measured. It is also because these experiments often reach opposite conclusions, even when they are measuring the same thing. Here we shall focus on areas where there seems to be agreement.

How the senses differ

The most logical starting point is probably with our senses. If boys and girls differ in how they see, touch and hear, that would certainly point toward biological differ-

▲ **Two kinds of physical advantage.** *It is the boys, with their large-scale muscular advantage, who are in the lead running down this sandy bank. The girl, whose movements are less fluid, trails at the back. When it comes to using quick, precise movements to manipulate small objects, however, it is girls who excel – from the age of three and a half years.*

Here girls are pretending to make cakes for a tea party, exercising a manipulative skill and illustrating acceptance of a typical role. The extrapyramidal nervous system (controlling large muscles) seems to be better developed in boys, the pyramidal system (controlling fine movements) in girls.

By a combination of nature and nurture, the sexes develop distinctive advantages. Girls have more verbal skill, more acute night vision and better hearing. Boys see and coordinate large-scale movements more accurately.

ences in their skills. Indeed it does look as though there are some differences here. In hearing tests, girls are generally more sensitive than boys. They are more bothered by loud noises, and respond to quieter sounds – a difference that continues throughout life.

Girls are also apparently more sensitive to touch. Even at the age of three months, they are more noticeably calmed than boys by being picked up. But of course this could be due as much to differences in their temperaments as in their sensitivity, so it is not easy to draw definite conclusions about touch.

Boys seem to have an edge in vision, although it is not as great as the difference in hearing. They have the sharper eyesight, with an especially clear advantage if what they are looking at is moving. Yet girls and women have better night vision. We have two separate systems in our eyes, rods for nighttime vision and cones for daytime. Females seem to have the more sensitive rods, while males have the more sensitive cones.

Another fairly simple area where girls and boys might differ is in sports and skills that involve muscular activity. We know that in general men are stronger than women, but

is that all there is to sports and athletic competition? Certainly, boys generally do better at activities that involve big muscular movements. Yet women are consistently better at doing things that involve fine movements. When it comes to psychological tests such as moving a row of small pegs from one place to another on a wooden board, girls as young as three and a half are better than boys of the same age, and this advantage of theirs in quick, precise movements continues throughout the human life-span.

Our muscles, like our eyes, are controlled by two systems. One system in the brain, the "extrapyramidal," controls all our big muscles and big movements, while a separate system, the "pyramidal," controls our fine movements. It is fairly clear that in boys and men it is the extrapyramidal system that is likely to be well developed, while in girls and women it is the pyramidal system.

Who have the quicker reactions, girls or boys? It sounds a simple question, but there is no simple answer. If we ask children to press a button as fast as they can after a light comes on, boys are generally faster than girls. But if we complicate the situation by asking the person to press one button when one colored light comes on, and a different button when a different colored light comes on, girls are faster. There are no simple conclusions to draw from this.

SKILLS AND STEREOTYPES

■ When deciding what skills to encourage in a child, sex matters less than interest and past achievement. Expecting everyone to act according to stereotype – according to our mental picture of the "typical" boy or girl – can lead to wasted talent, for many individuals have talents far in excess of the average for their group.

▶ **Catching like a girl?** *Boys' greater confidence with bats and balls reflects not only a better average ability but the sense of prowess they feel on account of being boys in a world that recognizes boys as better. Social stereotypes greatly exaggerate small average differences between groups, often to the psychological advantage of one group and the psychological disadvantage of another.*

At four, both boys and girls can copy a pattern in two dimensions but are not so equally successful with three-dimensional drawings. There seems to be something about three-dimensional objects that interests boys but not girls.

How thinking differs

Do boys and girls think differently? This is where there is the most disagreement about differences between the sexes and about what these differences mean.

Thinking is a very complicated process, and psychologists are far from certain about what is going on when people have ideas, solve problems, speak, read, calculate, remember and do all the other things that scientists refer to as "cognition." It seems that thinking involves at least two quite different and distinct abilities. One involves putting items into an order one after another. The best example of this process is in learning language, where we string sounds together into words, sentences and speech. Scientists call this "verbal" processing. The other kind of ability involves judging the relationships between objects. This is the kind of thinking involved in mechanical manipulation, such as putting together jigsaw puzzles or blocks, reading a map and finding your way around or fixing a car. This ability is known as "spatial" processing.

Scientists have agreed for a long time that both these processes are different and that what we call intelligence involves both types. All the standard IQ ("intelligence quotient") tests are made up of tasks which measure these abilities. Psychologists know that if they are to arrive at a meaningful picture of a person's intelligence from these tests they must know the separate verbal and spatial scores, because the combined IQ score does not tell them whether a person is equally good on both types of ability or whether that person is very good at one and very poor at the other.

If we look at verbal and spatial abilities separately, we do find that there are real differences between girls and boys. Girls usually do better on tests of verbal ability. They are better readers in school. They speak more fluently than boys. Studies in both the US and England reveal apparent differences in language ability between boys and girls of only 12 and 18 months. By 30 months girls use seven consonants to the boys' five. By the age of four, girls understand what is said better than do boys. Other studies have found that four- and five-year-old girls are more fluent in speaking and use longer sentences than boys. Children speaking such diverse languages as Nepalese and Czechoslovakian show the same pattern. The girls' greater ability to understand language is not due to their more sensitive

A WAY WITH WORDS

■ *Ability in spoken language is slightly greater in girls than in boys. Partly this may be due to innate differences, partly to styles of play. Pretending to read to your teddy bear TOP LEFT and looking after the needs of dolls TOP RIGHT not only allow girls to rehearse their potential role as mothers, they also provide opportunities for the practice of verbal skills. While toys for boys will mainly encourage spatial manipulation skills, girls often prefer playthings with which they can have conversations. Reading and writing ability also tends to develop earlier in girls than in boys. Female superiority in verbal skills is most pronounced from adolescence onwards, but girls in the early years at school BOTTOM maintain a lead of up to 18 months over boys in their level of achievement.*

hearing. On the same tests where four-year-old girls were better at picking out words, four-year-old boys could identify animal sounds and various environmental noises better than the girls. So there does seem to be a real difference in the way boys and girls learn language.

If we look at children with learning problems the differences between the sexes becomes even more marked. Boys with language-learning difficulties, such as dyslexia

and stuttering, outnumber girls by at least five or six to one. Clearly boys are more prone to disruption to their verbal processes. However, under normal circumstances, as boys get older they improve their skills in this area, and by the time they reach the age of puberty, the difference in language ability between the sexes is quite small.

When we look at spatial abilities, a different picture emerges. Here boys tend to do better than girls. This is

DIFFERENT TYPES OF SPATIAL ABILITY

■ To say that boys and men are better at spatial ability than girls and women is only telling part of the story. Three abilities can be distinguished. (1) There seems to be little doubt that moving a three-dimensional object in space is what boys and men do best. (2) But there is a type of spatial ability where males are only slightly better than females. This is called "spatial perception," and it involves orienting yourself or an object in space. This talent is useful for map reading and drawing. (3) A third talent called "spatial visualization," means being able to look at a compli-cated picture and pull out the simple elements that compose it. We use this ability when we have lost something and are trying to find it among other objects or when we do a jigsaw puzzle. Males and females are equally good at this.

■ Spatial skills are commonly accepted to be greater in boys and this is borne out by psycho-logical testing. From the age of eight, boys can more easily per-ceive objects and figures and understand how they relate to each other. They also tend to be better at "mental rotation" – im-agining how an object would look from a different angle. These advantages are reflected in their interest in building complex models.

especially true in "visual-spatial" problems where objects have to be visualized and turned around in space (see below). This process underlies several types of mathematics, and boys, on average, perform considerably better in mathematics than girls (see *Ch11*). This is especially true of geometry and algebra.

We also find that at advanced levels boys do better in most scientific subjects, but of course there is usually a need for mathematical skills in science courses, and if the boys are better at mathematics this would help them to perform better in the sciences. It is noticeable that in sciences such as biology where there is very little mathematics, girls do just about as well as boys.

There is not as much evidence of young boys' spatial skills as there is of young girls' verbal superiority, but what evidence we have points in that direction. If we give a four-year-old boy a three-dimensional object and ask him to make a copy of it, he can usually do it, while a girl of the same age cannot. Girls and boys copy a two-dimensional pattern equally well. There seems to be something about three-dimensional objects that interests boys and not girls.

How these differences affect our lives

There are, then, some basic differences between what even very young boys and girls are interested in, and also between their intellectual skills. What is it that causes these

CREATIVITY IN BOYS AND GIRLS

■ *Research on sex differences in children's creativity mirrors research on adults (see Ch 26). There are no clear overall differences in the levels of creative ability in boys and girls. However, differences have been found in styles of creativity. There are very clear differences in the subject-matter of girls' and boys' drawings at 10 to 11 years. Boys tend to do more mechanical and "scientific" drawings (eg of vehicles, dials and machines) and girls produce more domestic drawings (eg of plates, buttons and clothes). When girls are asked to pretend that they are boys and boys that they are girls these patterns reverse. Children of both sexes are quite capable of acting out the style of the opposite sex simply when asked to do so. Conformity to sex stereotypes does not make it impossible for them to think in an opposite-sex way.* **DJH**

▲ **Equal levels of ability** appear in the creativity test averages for boys and girls, suggesting that there are no sex differences in this area. Studies suggest, however, that children who are versatile in their sex roles are more creative than those who are rigidly sex-typed (see Ch 26).

▼ **Drawing like a boy and drawing like a girl.** Which sex has produced these pictures? Children aged 7 and 9 were given simple drawings of a square and each was asked to turn some of them into pictures that a boy would draw and some into pictures that a girl would draw. In this selection,

Luc (9) thinks that a girl would make a dollhouse and that a boy would make a soccer field. Caroline (7) thinks that a girl would draw a princess and a girl on a bridge. She thinks a boy would make an internal-combustion soft-drinks machine.

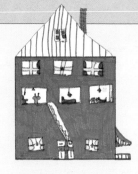

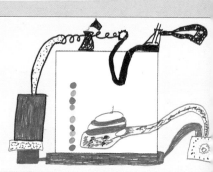

Male and female achievements do not reflect real differences in aptitude. If mathematical skills and verbal skills were all that mattered, there would be many more women engineers, and women would outnumber men in law.

differences? Are boys and girls born with different skills, or do these develop because boys and girls are treated differently from an early age? These are intriguing questions.

It is important to keep a few basic principles firmly in mind, however, if we are to apply any of these ideas to our own children. First, even if a difference in ability is created by a biological factor, this does not mean that it cannot be changed by learning. Indeed, when girls are motivated in scientific and mathematical studies, they do just as well as boys, and scientists are beginning to notice that in recent years the difference between boys' and girls' scores in tests have been getting smaller and smaller. This is probably due to the changing roles of women in our society, which have been giving girls the confidence to go into fields that they would not have considered appropriate before.

Second, the size of the average difference between girls' and boys' abilities has never been very great compared to the difference in ability between individual boys and girls. Even though the average score on a test may be different for groups of boys and girls, it is unlikely that the best boys and girls will be different in their scores.

However, when educationalists calculate the proportion of boys and girls who should go into certain occupations based on the differences in their abilities, they find that for many occupations the number of women is far below what it should be. For example, based on the present differences in spatial abilities between boys and girls, there should be two men for every woman in occupations such as architecture and science where spatial skills are very important. The actual ratio is more like one hundred men to every woman. The same is true for occupations which emphasize

verbal ability. Based purely on natural ability, women should outnumber men in the practice of law, but this is clearly not the case. Therefore, the scarcity of women in these fields is not due to inferior skills, but to social factors which restrict women's training and hiring.

While some real differences in abilities are probably biologically based, they are small and have been magnified far out of proportion by social stereotypes. They should not be used to limit the social, educational or occupational opportunities of either sex. **RE**

▶ **A girl's performance in mathematics and science** *can be as good as a boy's. Males do better, on average, but the best girls may be equal to the best boys, even if they are slightly fewer in number. As social and parental encouragement for girls increases* TOP *they are catching up. This graph shows growing postgraduate degree success for American women not only in the "soft" social sciences but in engineering and other mathematically oriented subjects.*

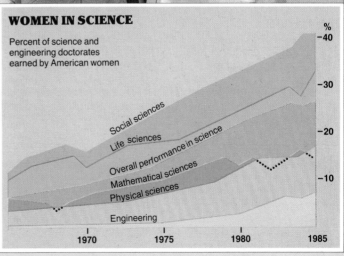

WOMEN IN SCIENCE

Percent of science and engineering doctorates earned by American women

Social sciences
Life sciences
Overall performance in science
Mathematical sciences
Physical sciences
Engineering

%
−40
−30
−20
−10

1970   1975   1980   1985

THE "LATERALIZATION" OF VERBAL AND SPATIAL SKILLS

■ The most tantalizing and also the most frustratingly difficult difference between boys and girls to investigate is the way their brains are organized. A division of function in our brains neatly parallels the measured differences in abilities between the sexes. All human brains are physically divided into a left half and a right half. For most people, the left half is more involved in the kind of verbal activities at which girls excel. And the right half is better at the boys' spatial activities. This is "cerebral lateralization."

We know about this from a number of experiments. Most of them are quite complicated, because the left brain receives information from and sends it back to the right side of the body, and the right brain does the same for the left side. Both halves of the brain communicate very quickly with each other; so it is difficult to distinguish one side's activity from the other's. However, if we present them pictures or sounds quickly we find that the left side is better at working with words and sequences, while the right side is better at putting shapes together in space. If we add to this picture the fact that the left side of the brain controls the right hand and vice versa, we have an explanation of why most people are right-handed. Most of our words are located on the left side of our brain and that is why most people write better with their right hands. Left-handers have more of their language ability in the right brain.

There would seem to be a very simple explanation for sex differences. Why do we not just say that the left side of female brains is more developed, and the right side of the male brain is more developed? Because it does not turn out to be true.

Tests indicate that males have the verbal and spatial processes divided neatly in the way we have seen, but females

have the two types of processes more spread out around both sides of their brains. Women are less "lateralized." What does this mean?

The answer, in a very general way, appears to be that the female brain is better organized for communication between its two halves. On an anatomical level, we can sometimes see a physical difference between the brains of male and female fetuses, with many females having a larger "corpus callosum" – the band of nerve fibers that unites the two halves of the brain. It is possible that the fibers are larger or that there are more of them. That should make it easier for communication: information can go back and forth more easily between the halves.

If we look at the activities girls excel in, we see that these also seem to involve communication. Verbal skills are used to communicate with others and

women on the whole use words more expressively than men. Women are known to be more empathetic than men – they are better at imagining themselves in someone else's situation. They are also better at recognizing faces and understanding what the faces are communicating. A picture therefore emerges showing that women are better communicators than men, that this is based at least partly on differences in the brains, and that these differences probably exist at birth.

LEARNING DIFFICULTIES

If we go a little further and look at studies that relate other factors to brain lateralization, an even larger and more interesting pattern is revealed. We know that left-handed people do more of their verbal thinking with the right side of their brains than right-handed people. More males are left-handed. As we have seen, males are afflicted

with learning difficulties involving words much more often than are females. Indeed, in the extreme case of autistic children, who have little or no language ability, males outnumber females even more significantly. There is some incomplete but fascinating evidence that testosterone has the effect of slowing down the development of the left side of the brain during prenatal development. Testosterone is the most important of the sex hormones that cause a baby in the womb to develop into a boy (see Ch1), and male fetuses have higher levels of it than females. It might just be that a slight excess of testosterone at a crucial stage before birth causes the connections in the brain which underlie verbal ability to shift a bit from the left to the right side and bring about left-handedness. If there is too much testosterone at this stage, the process would go further. Too many ·

COMPARING THE LEFT AND RIGHT BRAINS

■ In their attempts to measure the different abilities of the left and right sides of the brain, scientists have invented special techniques and devices. The two halves of the brain communicate with each other very quickly. Thus it is difficult to isolate the response of one side – free of influence from the other. One way is to present a stimulus to one side for a very short time and ask the subjects to identify what they have just been shown. This is done by means of a "tachistoscope," basically a camera shutter attached to a slide projector so that an image can be flashed on a screen very briefly. What we see with the right eye registers in the left brain, and what we see with the left registers in the right brain. Researchers can thus present a picture to one half of the brain by flashing it

extremely quickly far over in the opposite visual field. When they do this, the results show that we see pictures more accurately when they are flashed to the left visual field while words are more accurately reported when they are flashed to the right visual field. This shows that, for most people, language is handled by the left brain and shapes by the right brain. When researchers using a tachistoscope compare males and females, the males are better at spotting the shapes and the females are better at reporting the words. Another technique is called "dichotic listening." This enables the researchers to measure stimuli that are heard rather than seen. In experiments, a person wears a set of earphones and hears two different equally loud sounds at exactly the same time. When

the sounds are words, most people report only the one they heard in their right ear. The opposite is true for nonverbal sounds. Since sounds from each ear go more quickly and easily to the opposite side of the brain, it seems that once again the left side of the brain is better at receiving words. Children have difficulty with tachistoscope tests and dichotic listening, so a similar technique called "dichaptic stimulation" has been used to test boys and girls. The child is asked to feel two shapes, one with each hand, and after ten seconds is asked to put them down and pick the two shapes out from six shown in a picture. On this test, boys as young as six typically do better identifying the shapes with their left hands while girls of the same age are equally good with their right or left hand.

Boys are more "brain lateralized" than girls are. Their verbal and spatial abilities appear to be more neatly divided between the left and right. However, girls seem to have better communication between the two halves of the brain.

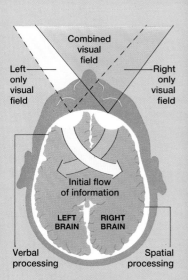

Verbal processing — LEFT BRAIN   RIGHT BRAIN — Spatial processing

Combined visual field
Left only visual field   Right only visual field
Initial flow of information

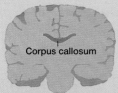

Corpus callosum

Vertical cross-section of the brain

▲ **Left brain, right brain.** *TOP The opposite side of the brain grasps, in terms of its own processing abilities, what each eye sees, then passes the information to the other side through the "corpus callosum" BOTTOM. Words glimpsed with the right eye look like words. Those glimpsed with the left eye are treated more like spatial objects.*

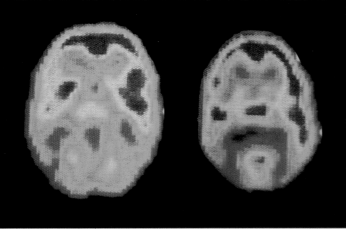

▲ **Left-handedness,** *more common in boys, is thought to result when a prenatal hormone imbalance shifts key verbal processing abilities to the right brain.*

◄ **Brain scans** *of two people trying to decide whether two sequences of musical notes are identical, one listening with the left ear LEFT and the other with the right ear RIGHT. In both, the right brain shows more activity. It performs this kind of task, regardless of which side registers the notes initially.*

connections would be shifted to the right side, and the person would be born with a verbal processing problem such as stuttering, or, more seriously, dyslexia. If there is much too much testosterone at this early stage, the verbal connections would be shifted and disrupted so much that the severe language problems of autism (which include being extremely noncommunicative) would result. This theory, while very speculative, would explain why boys are so much more susceptible to all these conditions than girls.

We can go one level deeper into the biology of this question if we remember that hormones such as testosterone are regulated by our genes. Our knowledge of how genes work is poor, and we know even less of how they control our behavior. However, we do have some very sketchy and controversial evidence that the differences between spatial and verbal abilities originate in these chains of chemicals which tell each cell in the body what to do.

Girls have an XX chromosome pair in each cell, as part of their genetic makeup, while boys have an XY pair instead (see Ch1). The Y chromosome, however, is much smaller than the X and it does not carry as much information about what the body should do. One theory proposes that, because of their Y chromosomes, boys develop more slowly than girls. This allows learning more time to affect them. The theory makes the assumption that spatial ability requires more practice than verbal ability, and therefore boys have more time to develop better spatial skills.

This is only one example of a theory which attempts to explain how our genes work. There are many others, and it will require much work before we can clarify just what connections there are between our genes and our abilities. **RE**

At School

IF BOYS and girls do not differ in overall intelligence, why do more boys than girls repeat courses and leave school at the first opportunity? Why too, in spite of this, do more males go on to take degrees at university? And why do so few women become engineers?

Differences between the sexes in verbal and spatial skills (see *Ch 10*) could account in part for some of these discrepancies, but not for all. One possible explanation could be that they are caused by our schools, including teachers' attitudes and expectations.

In an early experiment on this topic, teachers were given erroneous IQ information that led them to believe some of their students ought to show a significant improvement in their academic performance. Even though the students' names were chosen at random, their performance did improve. Although some psychologists had doubts about this experiment, other studies have supported its findings, and since that time there has been an increasing emphasis on the effect of teacher expectation on performance. Factors

such as IQ score, the reports of previous teachers, the performance of older brothers and sisters, the physical attractiveness of students and even the unusualness of a surname have all been found to alter teachers' expectations.

Obviously the sex of a student may also have an effect – particularly as teachers, as a group, appear to be relatively conservative in their view of appropriate sex-role behavior. Teachers appear to regard boys as more independent and even to encourage their aggression; at least they are more tolerant of male than of female aggression. It is therefore possible that the teachers' views on which subjects suit girls and which suit boys may influence children's performance in the classroom.

Girls excel at reading

Differences in performance between girls and boys have been most consistently demonstrated in most countries in reading and mathematics. Girls read at an earlier age, and maintain a 6–18 month superiority through childhood. Boys show greater ability in mathematics, particularly in adolescence. It has been suggested that teachers expect boys to learn to read more slowly than girls, and that this retards the boys' performance. Research has both supported and questioned this contention. For example, if we compare the reading performance of children whose teachers believe there is a sex difference in reading ability with those who do

▲ **A boy's subject in a boys' school.** *Pupils at Eton College in England carefully discuss the next blow of the hammer. In coeducational schools, boys and girls of this age are now routinely given metalwork and cooking lessons together.*

▶ **Color coding.** *Four children working on an art project are reminded that they are not of the same sex – the rule in this class is that girls wear orange smocks, the boys yellow. Sex segregation at school will also reflect the children's own choices (see Ch 9).*

While there is no difference in the intelligence of boys and girls, more boys than girls go on to be high-achievers. Studies suggest that unconscious attitudes and expectations of teachers strongly influence the final result.

not, we find that only those teachers who believe there is a difference produce pupils who show a difference. However, when teachers are asked to describe their treatment of students, no obvious sex differences are shown. Of course, it is possible that the teachers are not aware of any difference in their behavior and so cannot report it. But if the teachers' behavior in the classroom is examined, it is difficult to identify any way in which they treat the sexes differently.

Teachers seem to be more affected by reading performance than by sex, ironically spending more time with the better students. Indeed, the simple notion that girls read better because they are taught more carefully by mostly female teachers has had to be abandoned, as it has been shown that there is virtually no difference in teaching style between male and female teachers of reading. The pattern of reading achievement for children of both sexes taught by male teachers is the same as that found for female teachers. So, if the teacher does not give more help to girls during reading instruction, why do girls perform better? It has been suggested that girls have a genetically influenced advantage (see *Ch 10*). However, if the difference were caused only by our genes, we should expect it to show up in every culture.

93

▲ **Learning alone and from a teacher**. *Girls find it easier to pay attention at school and to concentrate when they are working on their own. This helps them to excel over boys in reading. According to one theory, however, boys working alone are more likely to experience "autonomous learning" –* *including not just the practice of learned rules, but the development of problem-solving strategies that will contribute – in adolescence – to boys' lead over girls in science and mathematics.*

Both boys and girls think "masculine" subjects are more difficult. Many girls avoid them – but not because of the challenge. They fear that they will appear less feminine and attractive if they out-perform boys in open competition.

It does not. We know that in Germany and Japan there is no difference in reading ability between boys and girls.

Another possibility is that teachers respond more to the behavior of the individual students rather than simply to their sex. This would mean that teachers react to already established sex differences rather than actually creating them. It has been suggested that boys' rowdiness and misbehavior prevents them from paying attention, and that it is as a result of this that they have problems with reading. Indeed, some would say it is the higher activity level of the boys rather than the girls' reading ability that may have a genetic component (see *Ch7*). Furthermore, reading may be seen as primarily a feminine activity in some Western societies, and so boys receive less encouragement at home. Boys certainly are less likely than girls to receive books as gifts and more likely to receive toys that stress exploration, problem-solving skills and creativity (see *Ch8*).

The boys' lag in reading then does not appear to be directly caused by the teachers, so much as by the boys' behavior. Quite simply, they pay less attention than do girls, perhaps because of their greater tendency to misbehave (which seems, to some degree, to be tolerated by teachers), and also because they are discouraged by society's assumption that reading is primarily a feminine pursuit.

Boys excel at science

The girls' lack of success in science and mathematics seems to be far more directly related to their treatment at school. The difference here between the boys and girls, which emerges during adolescence, is found in problem-solving tests and not in simple computation. It has been suggested that one reason for the difference is that boys take more mathematics courses than do girls, and therefore do better in tests. Why do girls take fewer mathematics courses?

Mathematics is seen as primarily a masculine subject, and therefore, as girls reach adolescence, they are less likely to take it. (To show how sex stereotypes work, imagine who would produce these statements; "Oh, I'm terrible with numbers," and "Oh I'm not very good with words.") Interestingly, both boys and girls tend to regard the "masculine" subjects as more difficult. Yet it has been suggested that girls avoid mathematics courses, not because they are difficult, but for social reasons. Girls do not want to be in open competition with boys, nor do they want to outperform them, for fear of being seen as less feminine and attractive. If this is true, one might expect girls in single-sex schools to be more successful at mathematics than girls in mixed-sex schools. This is, indeed, the case.

However, if we examine the performance of boys and girls who have taken the same number of mathematics courses, there are still more high-achieving boys than there are girls. This difference appears to be worldwide (see graph). While it is true that biological explanations have been offered for this, there are alternative explanations. For example, it has been suggested that the difference which emerges in adolescence has its roots in much earlier experience. From their first days in nursery school, males are encouraged to work on their own and to complete tasks, and this "autonomous learning" behavior is essential for the development of problem-solving strategies. Evidence that exceptional mathematicians tend to have worked indepen-

94

BOYS' AND GIRLS' SCIENTIFIC ACHIEVEMENT

Boys

Girls

Italian   English   American   Swedish   Australian   Hungarian   Japanese

▲ **Boys have better science achievement scores** *across the world. Differences in teaching styles and objectives mean that Japanese girls achieve more than Italian boys but* *within each country there is a consistent sex difference. Changing expectations for girls, however, are narrowing the gap in many countries, such as the United States (see p89).*

DIFFERENCES IN MALE AND FEMALE TEACHING

■ *There are surprisingly few differences between male and female teachers in the way that they treat boys and girls. This is true even in the earliest years at school, when male and female teachers both tend to nurture girls involved in feminine tasks and to encourage independence on the part of boys. Overall, however, they seem more influenced by the behavior of a child than by his or her sex. But, there are general differences in teaching style between males and females, which become more noticeable when they are teaching adolescents. Female teachers generally have a more positive attitude toward them. They tend to give more praise and encouragement, and respond more to questions. Students initiate discussions more in the classes taught by women, and receive less criticism. Male teachers tend to concentrate more on the subject in hand, and are more likely to adhere to a strict lecture format. These differences in their style, however, have not been shown to have a very large effect on student performance. This is not surprising, as they represent minor differences. Male and female teachers are much more similar than different.*

dently and not to have had teachers who supplied answers has been cited in support of this theory.

Whether or not this theory is true, there can be little doubt that teachers of mathematics and science expect their male students to do better at these subjects than their female students, and they appear to encourage the difference, albeit unconsciously. They spend more time with the male students, giving them longer to answer questions and working harder to get correct responses from them. They are more likely to call on boys for answers and allow them to initiate classroom discussion. They also engage in more jokes with boys and praise boys more frequently. All of this tends to encourage boys to work harder at these subjects and to promote confidence in their ability. It is, therefore, not surprising to find that high-achieving boys express greater confidence in their abilities in these subjects than do equally high-achieving girls. Such male-oriented teaching is not likely to encourage girls to take many mathematics and science courses, nor is it likely to support girls who do. Thus it seems certain that the difference here between boys and girls is at least exacerbated, if not caused, by schools.

■ **Special attention** *is more frequently given to boys than to girls. TOP A girl receives individual help in learning the computer language Logo. Learning to use its on-screen drawing commands will give her practical experience in solving problems in geometry. BOTTOM An adolescent seeks extra help from his mathematics teacher. Teachers of mathematics and science spend more time with male students, give them longer to answer classroom questions and work harder to get correct answers from them.*

95

How children react to teaching

Besides the specific differences in the treatment of boys and girls in these classes, there appear to be some differences in teachers' behavior overall. Perhaps the most frequently demonstrated is that boys receive more of the teacher's attention. A recent study has shown that unless boys receive at least two-thirds of a teacher's attention, both boys and girls assume that girls are being given more than their fair share.

Generally, criticism of boys is less often directed at the quality of their work and more often at misbehavior or untidiness of presentation. Criticism of girls, however, is generally aimed at the quality of their work, and praise is given for good conduct and neatness. This difference in treatment may cause a more negative reaction to failure in girls than boys. Boys are more likely to see scholastic failure as a result of a lack of effort, and therefore believe that their performance can be improved if they try harder. Girls, however, who are criticized more often for poor work rather than for misbehavior, tend to see failure as the result of a lack of academic ability, and assume that increased effort will not make much difference.

Girls are also less likely than boys to attribute their own success to their own ability. Many studies have demonstrated that this difference exists from their earliest days at school right up to adulthood. After criticism from an adult, the boys' performance of a number of different tasks has been shown to improve, but the girls' performance often gets worse. In one study, 100 teenage boys and girls were given a test that involved matching a digit with a letter. They were given a series of problems and were told they would be graded by an expert. All of them were stopped after doing 15 problems and told they had not done very well. They were then asked why they had not done well. There were three

◄ **Different images for different sexes.** *Boys are more likely than girls to be criticized by teachers for untidiness of presentation. Girls are more likely to be praised for neatness. A typically untidy male image and a typically female image easily become the stereotypes that direct teachers' thinking and also the children's concepts of themselves. Here children display approaches to work that reflect self-image as they create self-portrait figures.*

▲ **Reacting to criticism,** *a girl is less likely than a boy to improve her performance. Girls tend to see failure as demonstrating their lack of ability. Boys are less likely to blame their own inability and more likely to believe that they can succeed by trying harder. Girls tend, as here, to personalize criticism, boys either to disregard it or react against it. When a teacher's view and those of his friends are in conflict, a boy will usually respond more easily to pressure from friends. A girl may find this a more difficult conflict.*

Girls see failure as reflecting on their own ability. They blame themselves when they fail and they are less resilient to criticism than boys, who may see the blame falling on something or someone other than themselves.

---

choices: the expert was unfair, lack of effort, low ability. Boys were more likely than girls to blame the expert, and girls were more likely to blame themselves.

Boys and girls behave quite differently with friends of the same sex. For example, one boy's judgment of another is far more concerned with his level of physical coordination. Boys also appear to be much more influenced by their friends, and are more willing to tolerate adult disapproval than risk rejection by friends, when there is a conflict between the two. Boys are anyway more likely to suffer from such conflicts than are girls. Interestingly, boys who are judged as socially adept by adults are less popular with other boys than are socially adept girls with other girls.

There is less conflict between a girl's view of the world and an adult's, and this ironically may be the reason why girls have a more negative reaction to teacher criticism. Perhaps they personalize the criticism rather than seeing it as part of a teacher's role.

Working together

Boys and girls mix very little at school, but even a very small amount of mixing can have an effect upon their performance. Girls are more likely to play with a single female companion, while boys are more likely to play in a large male group (see *Ch 9*). As the child grows older, however, there may be less sex segregation in the classroom. Girls, in

particular, are less likely to direct their questions solely at one another. Interestingly, in mathematics classes boys who are having difficulties are more successful than girls in getting help from other students, because while girls are equally responsive to male and female requests for help, boys respond more to boys. To improve a girl's performance, therefore, teachers could try to increase the level of cross-sex interaction. Many teachers achieve just the opposite. When they need to break children into groups they often do so in terms of sex. Obviously, it is one of the easier classifications to make for the teacher and also for the student; neither is then likely to forget a student's group. This sort of grouping, however, does not encourage cross-sex interaction and does encourage the development of sex-role stereotypes. One can imagine the outcry if groups were constituted on the basis of race!

The girls' lack of confidence, and their less resilient

▲ **Learning a man's job**. *Few schools encourage girls to prepare for "masculine" jobs, but increasing numbers make the choice for themselves. This 20-year-old American is an apprentice welder.*

WHY DO SO FEW GIRLS BECOME ENGINEERS?

Teachers have higher expectations of boys in science and mathematics and they give them more attention.

Adolescent girls fear that boys will not see them as very feminine if they outperform them in masculine subjects.

Mathematics and science are conventionally seen as more masculine subjects, English and languages as more feminine.

Boys and girls have the same overall intelligence, but small differences in their verbal and spatial skills have been measured.

Teachers tend to encourage boys but not girls to attempt to solve problems independently at a very early age.

School storybooks present men as effective problem-solvers and women as dependent spectators.

response to experiences of failure, are also influenced by the books that they read in schools. Many studies have shown that the majority of the stories in books read by children are primarily about men, and even in the standard texts it is surprising to see just how negatively the female characters are portrayed. The males in these books are generally clever, brave and independent, while the women are incompetent, fearful and dependent. They cannot solve their problems without the help of a male and are constantly worried about their appearance. Exposure to such images is unlikely to foster girls' confidence or independence.

How should boys and girls be taught?

Although girls are treated differently from boys in science and mathematics classes, there is no difference in how male and female teachers treat the sexes (see p94). Hiring more male or female teachers is not likely to affect the differential treatment of the sexes. Instead, it would be necessary to encourage teachers of both sexes to be aware of their behavior and to change it. They could encourage the boys and girls to mix in all subjects. They could make a special attempt to persuade girls to pursue work on their own and solve problems for themselves rather than depend overmuch on set formulas and rules.

School texts could also be changed to include more positive images of girls and women. The toys that parents buy for their children could also be carefully considered. Building toys that encourage autonomous learning and the development of visuo-spatial abilities are appropriate for both sexes.

If this is done it is likely that the girls' present poor performance in mathematics and science could be corrected.

SINGLE-SEX OR COEDUCATIONAL SCHOOLS?

■ For several decades, there has been a trend away from single-sex schooling. It is believed that mixing daily with the opposite sex, especially in the adolescent years, will help children to develop better social skills. In addition, education authorities find it easier to provide a full range of subject choices and facilities within larger schools, and in many countries this has meant joining small local girls' schools with small local boys' schools.

At the same time, research has been accumulating that suggests educational disadvantages, especially for girls, in mixed schools. However, the most important point for parents to consider is a school's policy toward the education of each sex, rather than whether the school is coeducational.

There is a greater tendency to make sex-stereotyped subject choices in coeducational schools. Young adolescents are particularly sensitive to peer pressures that guide boys away from subjects such as modern languages and girls away from science subjects. The pressure not to be one of the few boys to choose French is all the more intense in mixed schools, where choosing French means sitting in a class mainly of girls. For the girls' part, they do not want to seem unfeminine by choosing a traditionally masculine subject like physics. Coeducational schooling makes subjects more available to both sexes, but take-up is sometimes disappointing.

Do the girls who do choose mathematics and science in coeducational schools do less well at them than they would in girls' schools? It has been suggested that they are likely to be motivated, by a desire for femininity, to avoid outperforming the boys. However, proof for this is elusive. Simple comparisons between coeducational and single-sex schools are very hard to make. Single-sex schools are more likely than coeducational ones only to admit children of higher academic ability, to be affiliated to a particular religious denomination or to be private. Each of these factors by itself is associated with higher achievement.

◄ A more strongly masculine environment is hoped for by many parents when choosing a boys' school. Male teachers are expected to be appropriate role models, and young boys are expected to have more scope to develop masculine qualities.

► Freedom from distraction by the opposite sex is a benefit often mentioned by parents who choose a girls' school. There is no conclusive evidence that single-sex schools give girls an academic advantage, but in coeducational schools girls seem to do better in mathematics and science when classes are segregated by sex.

In several studies boys have been found to have lower grades than girls for the same quality of work, and their grades in verbal subjects are much lower than ability would predict, in part reflecting teachers' assessments of conduct.

From what we have seen so far it appears that girls are unfairly disadvantaged in certain classes. Yet boys too may have legitimate grounds for complaint – not about the quality of instruction offered to them, but about the quality of grading.

It seems that boys are generally graded lower than girls for exactly the same quality of work. In 1975 and 1980, in studies involving over a million American high school students, males produced a higher average score than females on objectively scored verbal aptitude tests. They score over three times higher on mathematical aptitude tests. However, the grades they received in the classroom did not reflect their aptitude scores: girls received much higher grades in English and boys received only slightly better grades in mathematics. Other studies have shown that on almost every subject boys are graded lower than they should be from an objective standpoint. It appears that teachers' grades may well reflect factors other than ability – conduct, for example. It may not be surprising, therefore, that boys are less affected by teacher criticism. They may learn only on that teachers' evaluations are far from objective and that academic ability and popularity with adult teachers do not always go hand in hand. **SJM**

Those studies that have compared girls of equal ability at the time of entering their schools typically show little, if any, achievement advantage for girls in single-sex schools.

Evidence that girls do better at boys' subjects when boys are not there, however, does come from the coeducational schools themselves. Experiments creating single-sex classes for mathematics within coeducational schools show favorable responses by girls both in performance and attitude. They see themselves as more likely to perform well and have a stronger sense of the value of their efforts. It is not yet clear whether this effect is lasting. At least one study has shown girls performing less well on return to mixed classes. Segregation for certain subjects within a broad coeducational framework is an idea that is worth pursuing, and one that meets with the approval of many girls.

Girls in coeducational schools are better behaved than boys by most criteria, and are generally perceived so by teachers. In single-sex schools girls' discipline is no better or worse. There is evidence, however, to support the widely held view that boys behave better in coeducational settings. **CR**

99

When Parents Split Up

ABOUT a third of marriages in the Western world end in divorce. As a result, the families of an increasingly significant minority of children are one-parent families. In the United States, 45 percent of children born in the 1970s lived with only one parent at some point in their formative years. By the time they reach the age of 16, some 20 percent of British children will experience divorce in their families.

The upset of the divorce – and the arguments that immediately precede and follow it, can be devastating for all members of a family, but children are especially at risk. Research suggests that the majority of children can successfully overcome the immediate impact of divorce within two years. For others, it brings with it a chain of difficult consequences. In particular, in about 90 percent of cases, divorce means that children are separated from their father. This can have detrimental effects for daughters and especially for sons.

The short-term effects

Divorce has a pattern and rhythm all its own. First there is the disruption and disorganization of the initial separation and the divorce proceedings, followed by an unstable period when the family experiments with ways of adapting to their new situation. Family conflict actually increases after a divorce and this lasts for about a year. It is an especially stressful time for children, as they witness arguments between their mother and father, become entangled in the emotional demands that the parents place on them, and struggle to cope with the loss of a parent and with their own fears of rejection and abandonment.

In the short term, children often exhibit a three-stage "acute distress syndrome": first, agitated upset (which may include blaming themselves for what has happened, concern about the welfare of the absent parent and fear of losing the one that remains); second, apathy or depression; third, loss of interest in the parents, or successful adaptation involving a healthy acceptance of life in new circumstances.

For most children, the experience of a single-parent family comes to an end within five years, during which time the mother is likely to remarry or start a relationship with a man who becomes involved with her children. The child must then come to terms with a new two-parent family. This is more traumatic for some than for others – in Britain

▲ **Day of destiny.** *Every year, millions of children are the victims of parental strife and divorce proceedings; and every day courts have to decide with which parent the child or children will live. In France, where this photograph was taken, most couples who divorce have at least one child; and 42 percent have at least two children.*

Parental acrimony before and after divorce, the separation itself and the subsequent pattern of life can all have adverse effects on any children involved. Boys have more to lose than girls if, as usually happens, the father leaves the home.

almost half of the children registered by the National Society for the Prevention of Cruelty to Children as victims of battering or abuse at home have a step-parent or live with only one parent. In the United States, it is calculated that pre-schoolers living with a step-parent are 40 times more at risk of physical or sexual abuse.

Divorce often involves less prosperity for the parent who has custody of the children. Only about one third of ex-husbands contribute to the support of their families. For financial reasons, the mother is likely to go out to work, if she has not done so already, and usually to a low-paying, part-time job.

When adequate child-care arrangements can be made, maternal employment can be beneficial to both mother and child (see *Ch 7*). However, the very economic necessity that has led to the mother's employment in the first place, or to her suddenly becoming the main supporter of the family, is likely to make high-quality alternative child care difficult, if not impossible, to afford. The child now sustains a double parental loss – the father has left; the mother, through no fault of her own, is absent for most of the day; and there is no suitable mother substitute to take her place while she is out at work.

In addition, following divorce, families often move to less expensive housing in poorer neighborhoods. For the child, this means not only the loss of friends, neighbors and school, but it could also mean an environment with high delinquency rates, a decrease in personal safety and fewer recreational facilities.

Together with economic changes, a father's absence can have indirect effects on children. The mother can no longer depend on the father for assistance with household chores or emotional support. She struggles to distribute her energies in an attempt to perform both parents' roles. For some, this struggle is overwhelming and the result can be an attention-hungry child and a chaotic lifestyle in which

■ A familiar world subverted.
Moving out of the only home they may have known – and quite probably into a less salubrious neighborhood – can be deeply unsettling for young children. Coming to terms with the absence of a parent and the arrival of a step-parent may present even more severe emotional difficulties.

routine chores remain undone and mealtimes and bedtimes become disrupted. Deprived of a partner with whom she can share adult concerns, the mother also loses what may have once been a valuable source of self-esteem and happiness. All these deprivations can put pressure on the child to supply a level of emotional support of which it is not yet capable.

Although most children express a desire to continue seeing their fathers, the initial increase in contact during and after divorce declines over time – although fathers of sons are more likely to maintain contact than fathers of daugh-

ters. This gradual ending of the relationship is particularly unfortunate because continued interaction with fathers has been shown to help children's adjustment and social relations. Some children below the age of five continue to mourn the loss of their father and fantasize about his return for many years.

Effects on sex-role development

A good deal of research has been directed toward establishing what the predictable long-term effects of divorce on the well-being of children might be, and what is responsible for these effects. One of the first areas psychologists investigated was the development of sex-role orientation – a child's underlying perception of himself or herself as male or female. This has usually stabilized by the age of two or three years, when it becomes integrated into the child's own concept of self.

Since the time of Freud, psychoanalysts have stressed the crucial role of the father in the development of appropriate sex-role behavior. Freud in particular focused on the early rivalry between father and son for the attention of the mother – a rivalry that ends with the resolution of the Oedipal complex and the beginning of the boy's identification with the father (see *Ch4*). Social-learning theorists and cognitive developmentalists (see *Ch3*) reject this emphasis on sexuality, but agree that much sex-role learning is based on a child observing the same-sex parent and identifying with him or her.

Thus, there is wide agreement that in the area of sex-role orientation, the absence of a father may have a substantial

▲ **Runaway son**. *The central figures in a case, widely publicized in France, in which a young boy, whose recently divorced mother had been granted care and control of the children, ran away from home to be with his father.*

▶ **A double loss**. *A child whose parents split up may have to face not only the loss of a father but also a home situation in which a mother, beset by financial worries and preoccupied with reviving her own emotional life, finds it increasingly difficult to cope.*

Children who before the age of five lose all contact with their father may mourn his absence and fantasize about his return for many years. If at all practicable, it is especially important that sons should not lose touch with their fathers.

effect on sons. Studies that have focused on this question measure the actual behavior of the child, and include assessments from mothers, teachers or objective judges of the masculinity or femininity of their social behavior. For most of us, social behavior is the most important aspect of our sex roles – it is the observable way in which we interpret how we can and should interact with others as males or females.

Boys who lose their fathers before they are five years old seem to be less assertive and participate less in physical, competitive games in the preadolescent years, but this effect does not appear in younger boys. Either there is a delayed reaction to the father's leaving or, more likely, the effects of his absence are cumulative, making their full presence felt only after years of paternal deprivation. However, the magnitude of this effect on sex-role development is reduced in boys who have older brothers or surrogate father figures. One study reported that, if mothers encouraged them to be assertive, these boys had a more positive masculine sex-role orientation.

This pattern of results runs counter to the predictions of many sociologists, who argue for a "masculine protest" theory of teenage misbehavior. According to this, boys growing up in households headed by women experience a conflict between their feminine sex-role orientation and pressure from society to behave in a very masculine way during adolescence. As a result, they indulge in antisocial behavior as an exaggerated masculine gesture. However, it seems that more feminine rather than supermasculine

COPING AS A SINGLE PARENT

■ *Divorce may be the most realistic solution to a situation that has been destructive for both partners. Children too do better in happy one-parent homes than with two quarreling and unhappy parents. However, if couples separate, it is most likely that one parent (usually the mother) will find themselves coping alone with the children. Here are some principles for coping.*

Bear in mind that conflict between two formerly married partners typically increases during the one-year post-separation period. Make every effort to protect your children from becoming involved in parental disagreements. Do not pry into your children's relationship with your ex-partner by interrogating them when they return from visits. Let the children feel that they can have a loving relationship with the other without causing resentment in you.

No matter what your feelings are toward your ex-partner, your children's adjustment will be greatly assisted if the other parent remains frequently available to them. This may require you to swallow your pride and also to cope with your grief without involving your children in it.

Do everything you can to maintain continuity in your children's lives after the divorce. Those who stay in the

same house and neighborhood, attend the same school, and keep up established friendships make a better adjustment to domestic change.

After divorce, you may go through a period of depression, self-absorption and anxiety, even though there is relief at ending an impossible situation.

This is all part of the normal grieving process, but it can become damaging if it interferes with your relationship with your children. Remember that they, too, need support and encouragement to get through the shock of divorce.

Adult feelings about the divorce are best discussed with

other adults, not with children. It is important to strengthen your network of friends and personal contacts and exchange adult forms of emotional support with them. Do not stay at home on your own. If you do not wish to involve friends or relatives in discussions of your feelings, a professional therapist or self-

▲ However joyful and constructive the relationship between mother and son in a fatherless household may be, the absence of a real or surrogate father is likely to affect the son's sex-role development. In adolescence he may prove to be less assertive and competitive than most of his peers.

help group can provide support. Another reason for maintaining your social network is that friends of the family are an important part of children's social learning experience. By observing and imitating the ways that adults interact, children learn social skills.

During the transitional period following divorce, your ability to discipline your children effectively may flounder. Remember that discipline is not an act of cruelty, but a way of setting limits on behavior that is in children's best interests. You should not feel guilty when you say no. Structure is exactly what children need most at this point in their lives. Remember that increasing responsibilities – areas of accountability such as household duties that children feel they control and can take credit for doing well – make them feel positive about themselves.

Avoid any attempt by your children to coerce or blackmail you into getting their own way. Giving in to their coercion only reinforces it and makes it more likely to continue. Explain the reasons for your rules and stick to them.

However upset your children's behavior may seem during the divorce, remember that most children, like most parents, make a full recovery from its effects within two years.

103

behavior is typical of boys from families headed by women.

For girls, the effects of father loss also make their impact during adolescence. Compared with those from intact families, girls whose fathers are absent because of divorce show more disruption in their relationships with boys and men, including more attention-seeking from males and earlier intercourse. Interestingly, those who lose their father through death show the opposite effect – they are inhibited and rigid toward males and do not date boys very often.

Emotional and social adjustment

How does the absence of a father affect the emotional and social adjustment of children? Early research simply compared children from intact homes with those from broken ones, and assumed that any differences were a direct result of the separation of the children from their fathers. However, a number of findings suggest that it is not divorce or the loss of a father that does the most harm, but the quarreling and disruption that go along with it.

Children whose fathers have died do not show the behavioral problems that are often seen in children from broken homes – clearly suggesting that it is not the absence of the father alone that is responsible for a child's difficulties. In addition, studies confirm that children from intact but quarrelsome homes have more behavioral problems than do children from broken but secure families. Finally, children

Children constantly exposed to situations in which their parents display hatred or contempt for each other are at much greater risk of emotional damage from this than they are from divorce itself or single-parent family life.

whose parents continue to argue and fight after divorce show more problems than do children from conflict-free divorces.

One study that followed families over a number of years before and after the parents divorced revealed that problems

ROUGH PATCHES IN A MARRIAGE

■ *All marriages go through periods of turbulence and conflict, but after children are born, it is important to consider the impact that this emotional turmoil may have on them. Seeing the two people they love most fighting with one another can be a frightening experience, one that can lead to feelings of helplessness and isolation. To ensure that your children are affected as little as possible, bear the following points in mind.*

It used to be thought that arguments were useful for "clearing the air." However, research now suggests that marriages with frequent verbal conflicts are also marriages in which physical fighting is more common. Arguing (as opposed to constructive airing of disagreements) seems to increase rather than decrease the level of interpersonal conflict. "Thrashing things out" may sometimes be less productive than turning attention to other, more positive aspects of the relationship.

Be sure not to involve children in marital quarrels. Using the children as allies ("Mom is mean to Daddy, isn't she?") or as weapons ("You'll never see the kids again if you keep this up") is unfair to the children. Turning them into allies puts them in a no-win situation – they will lose someone's love no matter what they say – and threatening to separate them from the other parent can be terrifying to a young boy or girl who is powerless to control the future.

Discipline of the children has

◀ **It is probably unwise** to try to shield children from every episode of parental dissension; but there is good evidence that children who regularly witness or overhear marital quarrels pursued with real venom can suffer long-term harm. Under such circumstances "staying together for the sake of the children" is almost certainly misguided. Mutual antipathy shown by parents after the divorce can be just as damaging, however.

were apparent in the children's behavior well before separation took place. The evidence suggests that attempts to "stay together for the sake of the children" are misguided – at least when staying together means that arguing and discord continue. In the long term, children are more likely to be damaged by the insecurity and tension caused by unhappy parents than by the acute but transient pain of divorce.

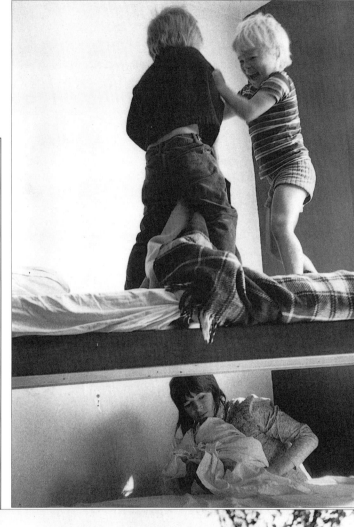

been found to be one of the most common topics of parental quarrels. Do not discuss this in front of your children. Even quite young ones can find ways of exploiting these disagreements. They quickly learn to trade one parent off against the other ("But Daddy said I could"). The result is just the kind of inconsistent discipline that is known to be associated with later adjustment problems.

Each parent should make a special effort to maintain an individual relationship with the children, as this may help to buffer them from the effects of parental conflict. It is vital, however, that this unique relationship is not used as a vehicle for denigrating the other parent. The aim is to assure the children of each parent's continuing love, even when the parents themselves may be at odds.

If you decide to seek help with your family problems, take advice about which therapy to choose. Some experts criticize the widely available technique called "family therapy." In this,

the entire family is considered a communication system and the therapist tries to guide all its members to an understanding of the dynamics behind the conflicts that erupt. However, some research has suggested that this type of treatment can work against the best interests of children, especially when they are young. If they are not ready to be exposed to the private conflicts of their parents – their parents' "hidden agendas" – they are likely to find the process incomprehensible and deeply threatening. Marital therapy – directed solely at husbands and wives – may be more successful, not only in improving marriages but in alleviating behavioral problems in children.

▶ **Sons and daughters will respond** in typically different ways when their parents' marriage is breaking down amid animosity. Daughters tend to withdraw into themselves, reducing interactions with others to a minimum or behaving in a mechanically conformist manner. Sons openly express their anger and fear through constant indiscipline and rowdiness or, more seriously, wanton acts of aggression and destructiveness.

WHEN THE SINGLE-PARENT IS THE FATHER

■ The practical problems faced by single fathers are usually not unlike those faced by single mothers who go out to work; but here are some points particularly worth bearing in mind:

As with single mothers, a single father's relationships with the opposite sex can present special problems for his child. If a relationship is going anywhere, the child should be included in it. A sleepy child who stumbles into the parental bedroom to find that someone has taken Mummy's place will be understandably upset.

at puberty and during adolescence.

Men who have difficulty discussing their own emotions may tend to shy away from talking about such matters with their children, especially their sons. To them, allusions to loss, disappointment and love are equated with weakness, and their reluctance to refer to them may suggest to a child that they are trivial, inappropriate or bad. The single father should recognize that sooner or later the child will need to talk and will deserve a response.

Fathers should make every effort to ensure that the separation and divorce are as amicable as possible and that the child is given access to the mother. Girls especially need an available role model with whom they can maintain a close relationship. The father's task is made easier if the girl can also discuss her personal feelings with a woman – most important

Men who have been emotionally scarred by a divorce may sometimes, without realizing it, communicate a deep distrust of women. A father who brings home a series of dates is effectively telling his son that women are "for fun" and unreliable. A long-term friendship with an adult woman may reassure a son that women can be stable, trustworthy people.

Divorce followed by single parenting can cause anger, resentment and guilt. Even if suppressed, these feelings can subtly color the parent-child relationship. Fathers with daughters and mothers with sons should be especially wary.

Discord has a more powerful impact on the behavior of sons than on daughters, and the two sexes also differ in their typical responses. A wealth of studies examining behavioral disorders in childhood and adolescence have focused on two particular areas of disturbance – under-control – (aggression, conduct disorders and destructive behavior) and overcontrol (anxiety, withdrawal and isolation). Girls typically deal with disharmony in the home in an overcontrolled fashion. They become shy, withdrawn and overly conformist in their attempt to placate the adults in their lives and ease tension. Boys' problems are principally in the area of undercontrol. They overtly act out their anger in their behavior toward parents, teachers and schoolmates, which often results in their being unpopular with their peers and others. The highly visible and disruptive nature of their reactions may also mean that they are more likely than girls to be referred for psychiatric help.

In divorced families, boys usually face the added difficulty that they live with the opposite-sex parent. Although studies suggest that both sexes do better when they are in the custody of same-sex parents, custody policies in which mothers are almost always given the children mean that it is the boys who are likely to face the most difficult situation.

Sons witness more parental battles (because parents are less protective of them), and they receive more inconsistent discipline than do girls. Women who experience divorce as a rejection by a husband upon whom they felt dependent often become erratic, depressed, self-involved and ineffectively authoritarian during the following year. They are more likely to get into an escalating pattern of mutual coercion with their sons than with their daughters.

Boys also receive less positive support and nurturing from parents, peers and teachers during and after a divorce than girls do. It is as if we expect them to cope better than girls, and so are less attentive to their distress. This is particularly unfortunate in the light of the evidence that boys are more susceptible to a variety of biological and psychological stress-causing factors than are girls.

As children reach adolescence, behavior that until now has simply been troublesome may begin to take the form of delinquency. Teenagers from broken homes are more likely to appear in court and be judged delinquent. However, care must be taken when drawing conclusions from this, since the decisions to refer children to court may be influenced by the very fact that they come from broken homes. A single mother is perceived by many to be an ineffective caretaker of her children. Social workers, police and judges are more likely to feel that a child should be removed from such a mother in his or her own best interest. Surprisingly, more girls than boys from single-parent homes are targets of judicial intervention.

By asking teenagers to say whether they have committed a variety of different offenses, it is possible to examine the association between broken homes and delinquency more directly. Such studies find that there is a slight relationship

107

◄ **Girls as young** *as one year old often behave in a flirtatious way toward their father. In a two-parent family, a daughter soon understands that she has no exclusive female claim on her father, but when no mother is present, fathers should be wary of encouraging this flirtation, no matter how endearing it may be. For their part, fathers raising daughters often become overprotective and can inadvertently communicate a mistrust of the outside world – and especially of men. While a mistrust of unknown men may be appropriate, a general fear of the male sex will not stand a girl in good stead later on.*

◄ **Boys are more susceptible** *than girls to a variety of biological and psychological stress-causing factors. Yet in the aftermath of divorce it is the distress of daughters that is more often recognized and attended to by parents, teachers and peers; boys are simply expected to cope. In young boys affected by divorce, troublesome behavior associated with a lack of paternal discipline or the stress of adjusting to a stepfather may, in adolescence, become delinquent.*

between having divorced parents and admitting to a large number of delinquent acts, although the types of acts admitted are usually "status" offenses – running away, smoking marijuana, playing truant and so on – rather than more serious crimes such as burglary or car theft.

Contrary to popular belief, the family structure that is most likely to lead to delinquent behavior in boys is one in which the mother remarries and the adolescent son has to adjust to the presence of a new stepfather in the home. As for the effect of the broken home, there seems to be no difference in how it affects each sex in terms of adolescent misbehavior. Boys are always more likely to get involved in crime than are girls – and this may be due more to society's discrimination between the sexes than to the serious effects of divorce on children, which are just as powerful for girls as they are for boys.

Why children suffer

A number of theories have been offered to explain why divorce produces these negative effects on children's development. One of the most well known is the "maternal deprivation hypothesis." According to the British psychologist John Bowlby, children experience a critical period, extending from birth through the first years of life, during which they form an intimate and lasting attachment to their mothers. From a social viewpoint, this early bond fosters trust and love in the child and forms the basis for all his or her later relationships. Any disruption of this bonding process, Bowlby argues, such as the mother going out to work, may result in the child developing a mistrust of others, a sense of isolation, and an "instrumental" view that human relationships are to be taken advantage of but not invested in.

However, these ideas do not tally with the facts of child-

hood separation. Bowlby believes that the nature of the mother-child bond has a different quality to the relationships that a child develops with other adults, but we know that infants can and do form bonds of equal intensity and quality with fathers, brothers and sisters, and adult caretakers. His argument that separation from the mother before the age of five is especially damaging is not supported by other research, which indicates instead that daily involvement, which is nevertheless not day-long involvement, is enough for the development of an emotionally satisfying bond between mother and child (see Ch 7). Bowlby's theory has also been criticized for failing to predict the sex differences in children's responses to the situations surrounding and created by divorce.

Others have suggested that disruption of children's parental modeling is at the heart of any damage that may

▶ **Widening the family circle.**
A single mother and her daughter browse through the family photograph collection – a regular event in this household, over the years, and a useful means, as this still-youthful mother knows, of instilling in her daughter's mind a sense of belonging to a "real" family.

In one-parent families, the extended family – grandparents, aunts and uncles,
cousins – and a network of family and personal friends can provide a background of extra security for the child. When they are dependent on only one parent, children are often – and not unrealistically – frightened about what might happen if the parent is unable to care for them. They need to know that they are loved or held in special high regard by other adults as well.

Parental inconsistency in applying standards to their children's behavior – often one of the signs of a marriage in jeopardy, and a common feature of post-divorce child care – is strongly associated with antisocial habits in sons.

result from divorce. Children acquire different styles of behavior, skills and abilities through exposure to others – especially adults. Behavioral problems might occur because a child loses an appropriate role model or because substituted adult models display aggressive or otherwise antisocial habits.

Because children show a preference for imitating the same-sex parent, the loss of the father would be expected to have a more marked effect on sons. Indeed, boys' adjustment is made easier when they are raised by their fathers, and fatherless sons who spend time with other adult males seem to be less affected by paternal loss. The fact that quarrelsome marriages are even more likely to lead to childhood problems is also explained by this theory. Aggression is readily imitated by children, especially by boys. If fathers respond to marital disagreements by anger and mothers by withdrawal, we would expect to find undercontrolled disorders in sons and overcontrolled disorders in daughters – which is exactly what we do find.

A third theory is that erratic or inappropriate discipline is the source of children's behavioral problems. Parents who are preoccupied with their own disagreements are likely to be inconsistent in their response to their children's misbehavior. In addition, disagreements over discipline are often the cause of arguments between parents, and this can be especially damaging to a child.

One study that followed families over a number of years found that the more parents disagreed about disciplining children, the more likely the couple was to separate and, later, for their sons to develop undercontrolled and their daughters to develop overcontrolled behavior. Psychologists frequently warn families that inconsistency in applying and enforcing standards of behavior often results in a pattern of undercontrolled aggressive behavior – precisely that seen in sons badly unsettled by the consequences of divorce.

Discipline by the father seems to be particularly important in controlling sons, and the loss of a father can have a noticeable effect on their behavior. When the father is absent and the mother's control is weakened by her own adjustment difficulties, the beginnings of manipulative and coercive behavior on the part of the children can be seen – especially in sons.

Divorce is a difficult time for everyone involved, but for children, the emotional distress is compounded by their powerlessness to affect the final outcome. Expecting boys to be tough, parents tend to expose them to more discord and uncertainty than they can cope with, forgetting that they need all the support that their sisters do. A girl's withdrawn silence may evoke more sympathy than her brother's fighting and may cause him to be overlooked in all the drama, but it is important to remember that, in the end, the messages they are both sending us are the same. **AC**

◄ The father's presence.
Many psychologists support the view that the formation and nourishment of a bond of attachment between child and mother is indispensable to the emotional well-being of every child, girl and boy alike. Others do not go quite as far as this, maintaining that what is crucial is the presence of a constant caregiver – who could be another woman or the father himself. Whatever the truth of the matter, it is known that the overwhelming majority of children have a preference for modeling their behavior on the same-sex parent. And in cases where parents split up and a son loses his father (which is what most frequently happens), his repertoire of masculine behavior may be moderated – or impoverished (depending on your point of view), or there is a likelihood of antisocial behavior.

Moral Development

BARELY a century ago, it was taken for granted that women have a "natural" moral inferiority to men. Women were thought capable of worthy sentiments but it was men who had the intellectual skill to apply complex principles of justice. Sigmund Freud, the first great investigator of moral psychology, did not agree that *nature* makes women inferior, but he did think that their early childhood experiences do, and that this is inevitable (see *Ch 4*). Today there is less of a fashion for speaking of moral inferiority and superiority. Experts feel much less certain that they are qualified to say who knows better when people have different moral outlooks. However, they continue to ask whether men and women at least *have* different outlooks, and whether this reflects the way boys and girls are raised.

Caring about people and caring about rules

It is certain that moral outlook is part of the stereotype of male-female differences. In questionnaires, people overwhelmingly endorse the view that men are more objective (implying that men are more likely to judge rights and wrongs abstractly), while women are more empathetic – more aware of other people's feelings – and more caring (implying that they are more likely to try spontaneously to do good). Women have the image of caring about people. Men have the image of being concerned about rules.

Some psychologists – for example, the American researcher Carol Gilligan – believe that this stereotype reflects a very general difference that distinguishes females from males throughout life, beginning in infancy. Girls and women tend to attach or "connect" themselves to others, whereas boys and men tend to be individualistic and "separate" from others. The feminine orientation is supposed to give women a greater interest in relationships, while the male orientation is supposed to give men more interest in individual achievement. Gilligan believes that males are concerned about justice and rights, whereas female are concerned about care and responsiveness. From a boy's or a man's perspective of separateness, socialized

Are boys taught to be more rule-minded, girls to be more caring? Research suggests both sexes are caring and empathetic in situations that call for this, although females are more often placed in situations calling for a caring attitude.

living requires an intricate moral system of rule-governed rights – in order to resolve individual, competing claims to fair treatment. Such a morality is needed to create links between people who are assumed to be fundamentally in conflict. In contrast, the girl's or the woman's orientation toward connectedness requires only a sensitivity to the needs of others and a benevolent attitude, both of which are dominant in the feminine morality of care.

To explain the origin of the difference, Gilligan adopts the point of view of Nancy Chodorow in her feminist revision of Freudian theory (see *Ch 4*). According to this argument, distinctive male and female orientations are formed early, and irreversibly, in the mother-child relationship. Because women are almost universally responsible for early child care, boys establish their noncaring identities through contrasting themselves with their mothers, whereas girls, identifying with their mothers, "emerge with a stronger basis for experiencing another's needs and feelings as one's own."

A careful review of the evidence, however, reveals that the common stereotype greatly exaggerates the differences between boys and girls and men and women. Both sexes are caring and empathetic in situations that call for this, although females are more often *placed* in caring situations. Both apply principles of justice when appropriate, and developmental studies find no significant variation between boys and girls as their judgment of right and wrong matures.

Empathy and caring

Comparisons of children in a large number of cultures have found that girls are more likely to take an interest in someone else's needs – to be "nurturant." Until the age of

about five or six, girls are not more nurturant than boys, but they are expected to play with and take responsibility for younger children, and they show more willingness to do this. By middle childhood, sex differences in nurturance appear as girls show themselves more responsive to the needs of others.

This difference is most pronounced in cultures that treat boys and girls differently, where girls, more often than boys, are asked to do household tasks, to take care of infants, or to do work that keeps them close to home and in the company of women. Because the general pattern in cities in North America and Europe is to require very little household work of either boys or girls, the sex differences in European and American children are less pronounced than in those of largely rural, underdeveloped countries, where girls do help a great deal with child care and housework. Anthropologists attribute girls' greater nurturance simply to the fact that they spend much more time in the company of babies and young children.

Boys and girls do not differ much in the extent to which they can *recognize* other people's feelings. Girls are somewhat more likely than boys to show an emotional response, but the difference is small and is more likely to occur when the feelings involved are happiness or pride than when more negative emotions such as sadness are involved. It

111

◄ **Caring about people**. *Both boys* LEFT *and girls such as this one* FAR LEFT *in Namibia, shyly shielding her brother's face from intrusion by the camera, learn to take an interest in the needs of others, especially their younger kin. By social custom in most countries, girls more than boys are expected to take a caring role. As a consequence, sex differences in the readiness to do so are well developed by mid-childhood, except in industrialized urban settings where little help with child care is expected from either girls or boys.*

► **The decision whether to confess**. *At different levels of development, children take into account different kinds of reason for doing what they consider right. In the earliest stages fear of punishment and the need for approval dominate their thinking. By late adolescence, some may be moved by a profound commitment to moral principles. No differences between girls and boys in moral reasoning have been detected.*

appears, then, that there is not a strong tendency for girls to be more empathetic than boys.

What is interesting, however, is that the personality characteristics of boys who are high in empathy are quite different from the characteristics of empathetic girls. Empathy in boys is associated primarily with intellectual ability, whereas empathetic girls are generally remarkable for their self-confidence and sociability.

Some studies of generosity, helpfulness and comforting report sex differences, and some do not. Those that do report a difference have found females to be more generous or helpful, but the differences are not large. Also, in some other forms of selflessness, such as the willingness of a by-stander to intervene in a situation where a stranger needs help, males show a slight tendency to be more willing. It seems therefore that the differences between boys and girls in the areas of empathy and caring are subtle and complex enough to cast doubt on the familiar stereotypes.

Rights and wrongs at play

In the 1920s the Swiss psychologist Jean Piaget studied children's marble games in Geneva, and he identified four stages in which play reflects a respect for social rules. Piaget outlined these four stages and explored their implications for children's moral development. He also noted some differences between boys and girls.

In toddlerhood and beyond, children will spontaneously make up their own playful rituals. For example, Piaget watched his daughter playing a self-invented game in which she repeatedly rolled marbles into the button pockets of an

▲ **A disordered "state of nature"** *reigns in this relationship between toddlers. Among the first rules that we attempt to teach young children are rules for sharing. They are taken to heart only gradually, and spontaneous displays of generosity and kindness may be brief and infrequent at first. The art of* friendship develops as children become more skilled at understanding and giving the loyalty and consideration that is normally thought due to a friend. Depending on the example of parents and other models, concern and consideration may extend beyond the ties of friendship.

If experience of game rules has an influence on sex differences in moral development, it is very likely to be a declining influence. Increasingly, girls are taking an interest in team sports and games with complex rules like those of chess.

overstuffed chair. This game had no social rules that could be shared with anyone: it was an individual rather than a collective game. It did, however, have a basic regularity in its repeated ritual of rolling the marbles into the same place and then retrieving them. Such regularity is a first step in the child's advance toward games with real social rules.

By the late preschool years, children understand that game rules are not simply personal rituals that one enjoys repeating. Rules are seen as obligatory – so much so, in fact, that children believe that rules must be taken literally and must never be changed. It is as if they were "handed down from above." This stage represents a positive step forward developmentally for the child, because the child is now aware of an obligation to follow rules. However, the child's unbending attitude toward them is unrealistic and actually leads to more, rather than fewer disputes over rule violations.

During their first years in school, children come to understand rules as agreements between people, who can also agree to change them if that suits all concerned. This is more of an "inside" view of social rules, leading to a more cooperative and consistent attitude toward them. It also engenders a sense of full, equal participation in the control of the game and an enduring respect for social and moral rules. Eventually, by adolescence, respect for rules may trigger a fascination in the very process of rule creation. At this fourth developmental stage, adolescents derive great

pleasure from inventing new systems on their own. In some cases, this can lead to an interest in exploring political ideologies and an attempt to create hypothetical utopian social systems.

There is evidence, beginning with Piaget's own observations, that some girls take less interest than boys in competitive, rule-governed games such as team sports. Instead, many girls seem drawn more to activities such as hopscotch or guessing games, that revolve around small interpersonal encounters (see *Ch 9*). To the extent that this is true, it means that boys have more opportunities to explore formal rules systems, whereas girls have more opportunities to explore the interpersonal aspects of moral sensitivity. Such differences in their experience could contribute to sex differences in moral attitude. Girls, however, are taking an increasing interest today in competitive team sports, from rugby to baseball, and if experience of game rules *is* an influence for sex-differences in moral development, it is likely to be a declining one.

Rights and wrongs in real life

Research shows that, in thinking about dilemmas in their own lives, most people follow both rules and feelings. When asked "Have you ever been in a situation of moral conflict where you had to make a decision but weren't sure what was the right thing to do?" a few people – and it is important to note that this is only a minority – tend to focus much more on one orientation than the other. When this happens, it is the males who focus primarily on concepts of justice, whereas it is the females who focus primarily on a

◄ **Laying down the law.** *TOP very small children first learning to follow rules take a rigid view of them, and much playtime is spent in squabbling about what is fair. BOTTOM A friendly confrontation over school playground rules.*

► **Games with complex rules,** *such as team sports and chess, are traditionally for boys, a stereotype that is broken here. Their games supposedly give boys a "justice orientation" while girls develop a "caring orientation" in games that practice social skills. However, psychological testing has shown no differences in male and female ways of thinking about questions of fairness.*

morality of care. It seems that this difference can be explained by the kinds of dilemmas that men and women choose to talk about. Some moral conflicts, such as a decision to end an unwanted pregnancy through abortion, seem to be linked with a care orientation. Other dilemmas, such as when it is right to go against the rules in order to help a friend or loved one, elicit a justice orientation. There is a slight tendency for some women to remember more dilemmas of caring and for men to remember more dilemmas of justice.

Comparisons have also been made of how girls and boys progress through distinct stages of moral development. The established tests of this derive from the work of Lawrence Kohlberg, who distinguished six stages of increasing maturity in moral judgment. Each stage represents a difference, not necessarily in the way that we would behave, but in the kinds of reasons we would give for saying that we ought to do something. Although many people do not reach the highest stages, Kohlberg believed that all people, everywhere, go through stages in the same order. Earlier forms of moral reasoning continue to be important during later development – even in full maturity we base some of our thinking on stage 1 reasonings.

The first two stages are "preconventional" – our reasons for doing the right thing do not yet include a personal commitment to upholding social conventions. Instead we act out of fear of punishment and for the rewards that those in authority (such as parents) can give us. In *stage 1* (beginning at about 3 to 6 years of age for most children) we are concerned simply to avoid punishment. At *stage 2* (beginning at 5 to 9 years) we learn that when we do the right thing this helps us to serve our own interests because of the rewards we are offered.

The next two stages are "conventional." The focus shifts from individuals with authority to the authority of a group,

▲ **Debating the future of society**. *In early to mid-adolescence young people develop a concern for the institution of society and want to help prevent a breakdown of the system as a whole. In the second half of adolescence, many go a stage beyond this. They become concerned to reason out what the system as a whole should be like. Here freshman American college students argue the issues.*

WHO CHEATS, AND WHY?

■ *Developmental psychologists have found little relationship between cheating at school and moral development, at least in terms of Kohlberg's moral stages (see main text). Their research also suggests that there is no sex difference in honesty or cheating: both boys and girls are likely to cheat. In fact, they appear to be very likely to cheat.*

In a survey, 134 American university students, 60 men and 74 women, were asked about their own behavior when they were at school, and about their reasons for and attitudes toward cheating. A very large number of them (96 percent) admitted to cheating at school. There was, however, little difference between boys (95 percent) and girls (97 percent). Students of both sexes are also likely to cheat on the same subjects – 88 percent of boys and 92 percent of girls said that they were more likely to cheat in science subjects than in arts.

This may be a reflection of the perceived degree of difficulty of science subjects, as fear of failure is a major reason given for cheating – 80 percent of boys and 89 percent of girls speak of cheating because of fear of failure. Noticeably fewer boys (39 percent) than girls (58 percent) admit to cheating because they were too lazy to study for examinations. **SJM**

WHAT DO GIRLS AND BOYS THINK OF CHEATING?

■ *There are no large or obvious sex differences in cheating at school. But do boys and girls think that there are significant sex differences? They appear to. When boys were asked to think of their five best male friends and their five best female friends and to say which group cheated more in high school, 43 percent chose male friends, only 10 percent chose female friends and 47 percent said that there was no difference. A similar pattern of results is found for girls – 45 percent chose male friends, 13 percent chose female friends.*

Although there is no sex difference in admissions of cheating, boys and girls still tend to believe that boys are more likely to cheat. It can only be assumed that this is the result of the sex stereotype (inaccurate in this case) that girls are better behaved as students. Although the vast majority of students cheat in high school, they at least appear to think that it is wrong to do so. Only 20 percent of girls and 27 percent of boys believed that cheating is reasonable. In this case, attitudes appear to have a small effect on behavior. **SJM**

Several experiments have followed the same people's moral development scores over many years. Girls' and women's judgment has been found to mature through exactly the same stages as a male's, and the scores are comparable.

such as the family, a peer group, or society at large. At *stage 3* (beginning at 7 to 12 years) we feel the need to be a good person in our own eyes and in those of others. We care for other members of our group and desire to maintain rules and authority which bring about predictable behavior. We distinguish good from bad intentions as well as right from wrong actions. At *stage 4* (beginning at 10 to 15 years) we develop a concern for the institution of society as a whole. We want to prevent a breakdown in the system, and when considering whether something is right or wrong we ask "What if everyone did it?"

The final stages are "postconventional," going beyond received conventions. At *stage 5* (beginning at as early as 12 years for some) we feel a contractual commitment, freely entered upon, to family, friends, trust and work obligations. We become concerned that laws and duties should be based on rational calculation of the maximum benefit that all concerned might derive from the existence of rules. In one study, 10 percent of American 16-year-olds had reached this stage.

In *stage 6*, an exceptional stage of moral development, judgments of right and wrong are influenced by a sense of personal commitment to universal moral principles, and by a distinction between principles and mere rules: although a person who thinks like this recognizes that laws or social agreements are usually valid because they rest on

such principles, they feel they must follow moral principles even if they are in conflict with the law.

Researchers have conducted a great number of studies relating to Kohlberg's theory, and the evidence does seem to support his claim that moral judgment matures in a predictable way as we develop. Kohlberg's sequence of stages seems to stand up well in cross-cultural studies. However, an early objection was that the sequence might not reflect the development of girls as effectively as it reflects that of boys. The original sample that Kohlberg used to test his definitions was made up entirely of boys. Carol Gilligan and others have argued that, as a result, his theory fails to take into account the rather different approach to morality taken by women. They believe that it places girls at a disadvantage when comparing them with boys because Kohlberg's interviews pose hypothetical conflicts of justice, in which the rights of different parties have to be weighed. Since women may see morality as a problem in care rather than justice, they may be ill prepared to reason about the focal issues under investigation, and are likely to score lower than men.

However, careful reviews of the evidence report that if girls and boys or men and women of equivalent educational and occupational backgrounds are compared, there are no sex differences in their scores on Kohlberg's six stages. What is more, in several experiments in which the same people have been studied over many years, it has been found that girls' and women's moral judgment matures through exactly the same developmental sequence, and in the same order, as that of males. **A C I WD**

PRECONVENTIONAL MORALITY

1 "Will I be punished?"
beginning 3 to 6 years

2 "Will I be rewarded?"
beginning 5 to 9 years

CONVENTIONAL MORALITY

3 "What will people think of me?"
beginning 7 to 12 years

4 "What if everyone did that?"
beginning 10 to 15 years

POSTCONVENTIONAL MORALITY

5 "Should I feel obliged to do this?"
beginning as early as 12 years

6 "Is it right according to universal principles?"
exceptional

115

▲ **Kohlberg's six stages**. Each stage represents an increasing level of maturity and sophistication in moral judgment. The early forms of reasoning continue to be used even after later ones develop.

▶ **At the age of 13**, a Jewish boy becomes personally responsible for following the religious law. He becomes "bar mitzvah," a "son of the commandments." This entitles him to play a man's full part in the ritual of the synagogue, and a central part of the ceremony celebrating this passage into manhood is his exercise of his synagogue rights by reading

from the Torah. A girl becomes too a fully responsible "bas mitzvah," a "daughter of the commandments" at the age of 12, but this is not usually marked by as much ceremony. The ages of 12 and 13 fall within the range in which researchers most commonly find children reaching Kohlberg's fourth stage of moral development, when our conventionality goes beyond mere conformity to other's expectations of us to reach a personal concern for upholding rules.

Getting Into Trouble

ASK THE PARENTS of any adolescent girl, and they will tell you that daughters cause more sleepless nights and worry than boys. Yet the objective evidence tells us that girls are far less likely than their brothers to get involved in trouble outside the home.

In almost all industrial countries, more than a third of adolescent boys who live in towns and cities get into some kind of trouble with the police, while the comparable figure for girls is only about 10 percent.

In many cases, "trouble with the police" amounts to no more than being stopped and warned, or having illicit alcohol taken away. But in one American study, 40 percent of a sample of boys born in the same year in Philadelphia were formally arrested before the age of 18.

The kinds of trouble that girls and boys get into also differ. A significant minority of the boys who appear in juvenile courts are charged with serious crimes such as stealing cars, breaking and entering or acts of violence against people. Only a much smaller proportion of the girls appearing in court are charged with such serious offenses. The overall number of girls getting into trouble, however, is

rising in many communities, including trouble for genuine criminal offenses. What accounts for the sex differences, and for the fact that they are becoming smaller? What can parents do to keep girls, and boys, out of trouble?

Girls and the "status offense"

When adolescents get into trouble, the trouble is different for boys and for girls. Young people who appear in court can be brought there for two kinds of reasons – either because they have been accused of a crime or because they are thought to be in need of care and protection. Acts such as truancy, running away and incorrigibility (none of them grounds for bringing an adult to court) are enough to warrant a court appearance in the case of a juvenile. In the United States, these "status offenses," as they are called, account for 70 percent of all court appearances by girls, as compared to 31 percent of those by boys.

A study in New York City indicated that girls made up 100 percent of cases involving promiscuity, cohabiting, spending the night with a member of the opposite sex and association with undesirable friends. As one American judge put

Boys get into more trouble than girls, and more serious kinds of trouble. However, girls are now increasingly involved in all types of delinquency. A reason for this may be a shift toward greater participation in group friendships.

it: "The offense of most of the young women going before the court is nonconformity to a social model of accepted behavior for young girls. We talk about promiscuity in girls, but I have yet to see a boy brought to court because he is promiscuous or simply because he fornicates."

Although girls, as status offenders, have not committed any criminal offense, we treat them even more harshly than boys. In one study, 53 percent of the female status offenders (compared with 7 percent of the male status offenders) were detained in an institution while awaiting trial, instead of being allowed to go home. While in detention, girls are checked as a matter of routine for virginity, sexual disease and pregnancy. After the court appearance, girls are again

less likely than boys to be sent home – although girls comprise only one-sixth of the court caseload, they compose half of those recommended for placement in an institution. It is clear then that girls are more likely to appear before a court because of their "immoral" behavior, but are they really more likely than boys to commit status offenses? And are boys more likely to commit "real" criminal offenses? One way to answer the question is to ask adolescents themselves. If we rely on official reports alone, we may be measuring the discriminatory practices of the police and courts rather than any real differences in behavior between males and females.

In a survey, high school students in Seattle, Washington, were asked to fill out a questionnaire anonymously, indicating whether or not they had ever committed any of a variety of offenses (see box). The sexes were roughly equal

◄ **Stopped by the police.** *Our image of a boy in trouble tends to be of one from a poor background, and subject to low parental control and support, who is accused of a property offense – theft or damage. This stereotype is confirmed by criminal statistics around the world, but children of every class and both sexes are interested in exploring the boundaries of acceptable behavior, especially during adolescence.*

▲ **A girl "in trouble"** *conventionally means a pregnant one. The majority of girls who come into contact with authority have not committed crimes but are considered to be in need of care and protection, like this girl in a home for unmarried mothers. The father of her baby is unlikely to receive any attention at all.*

CONTROLLING CHILDREN'S BEHAVIOR

Studies show that the "authoritative" style of parenting (one that is high in both caring and control) is the most effective in managing children's behavior. The "authoritarian" approach (low caring and high control) makes children withdrawn, while the "permissive" one (high caring and low control) results in poor self-control. The basics of effective control are that parents have to state rules clearly, monitor compliance and punish violation. For punishment, hitting is much less effective than withdrawal of privileges or parental approval, combined with an explanation of why this is being done.

Displeasure at poor behavior should always be balanced by plentiful approval of pleasing behavior. Punishment should be consistent. If parents punish only when they are in a bad mood, the child learns that his or her own behavior has no reliable consequences, and also that lashing out at others is an acceptable way to manage discontent. Irritable and ineffective parents tend to have aggressive children who can bully them into getting what they want. Indifferent parents are more likely than others to produce children who steal, because they know how easily they can get away with it.

117

in the percentage admitting to truancy, running away, defying parents, shoplifting, petty theft, drinking alcohol and using marijuana, barbiturates, speed, hallucinogens and heroin. In fact, girls and boys were most alike in precisely those status offenses that result in girls but not boys appearing before a court.

The fact that girls get into trouble for these offenses seems to represent a difference in adult reactions to the behavior of boys and girls, not a difference between boys and girls. As the offenses become more serious, however, more genuine differences between girls and boys appear. Many more boys than girls admit to stealing cars, armed robbery, breaking and entering and carrying weapons. All this leaves experts with an important question: why are girls (and women too) so much less likely than their male counter-

parts to get into trouble with the law for serious offenses? It is a question to which a bewildering number of answers has been offered. None of them is conclusive.

Boys and "serious crimes"

In all cultures, males exceed females in criminal behavior, and this universality has been enough for some experts to conclude that the difference must be inbuilt – a naturally masculine characteristic. This certainly is the traditional view. At the turn of the century, the Italian father of criminology, Cesare Lombrose, pioneered the idea that criminal women were abnormal, because they lacked the "female qualities" of maternal drive, passivity and low intelligence. These qualities, he thought, normally moderated the effects of women's "natural moral deficiency," jealousy and childishness, which together would lead to criminal activity.

Sigmund Freud echoed this view, but had an explanation based on early childhood experiences. He saw female delinquency as a failure to achieve the "normal" feminine state of passivity. He argued that the young girl usually learns to transfer her original love for her mother to her father, and in doing so she identifies with and imitates her mother's

▲ **In custody.** TOP *Two young detainees in the youth remand center at Strangeways prison in Britain, where young people are more likely to receive custodial sentences than in most other countries. Researchers suggest that rather than deterring crime, imprisonment both reinforces criminal tendencies and allows prisoners to acquire new criminal skills.* BOTTOM *Suspected child pickpockets in Paris. French minors cannot be held in detention after nightfall. These boys and girls will be free in a few hours to return to the tourist haunts where they were arrested.*

Boys and girls are most alike in precisely those offenses that often bring girls but not boys before the courts. As offenses become more serious – involving violence and breaking and entering – genuine differences between the sexes appear.

passive role (see *Ch4*). The "tomboy" quality of girls' delinquency, he believed, could only be explained by a developmental failure which left the girl identifying with her father instead of her mother.

As recently as the 1970s similar ideas were being reinvented by American criminologists. A whole line of research was undertaken with a view to demonstrating that the sex-role identification of female delinquents was more masculine than that of nondelinquents. However, studies that asked adolescents to rate themselves on masculinity and femininity showed no relation between delinquency and a more masculine self-image among girls. In fact, one

study, which asked delinquent and nondelinquent girls "what kind of person they would like to be," indicated that delinquents, contrary to Freud's ideas, do not aspire to be any less feminine than their conventional sisters.

It has been suggested that "supermale" men with an abnormal XYY chromosome makeup might be especially prone to criminal behavior. However, the extra Y chromosome is too rare among men to be significant. In a major survey it was discovered in only 16 out of 4,000 men. Then too, if the answer lay in the Y chromosome, we should expect the abnormal XXY makeup to appear among women with criminal records.

A study was designed specifically to investigate this possibility. It found no female prisoners with a Y chromosome. The most likely explanations seem to lie rather in up-

WHAT ADOLESCENTS ADMIT TO

■ When a survey of American high school students asked them to report anonymously on their own delinquent behavior, few differences emerged between boys' and girls' involvement in minor offenses and misbehavior. Boys, however, were more likely to admit to serious crimes. Here are the questions they answered and the percentages of girls and boys answering yes.

HAVE YOU EVER...	% BOYS	% GIRLS
Broken into a house, store, school or other building and taken money, stereo equipment, guns or something else you wanted?	14.9	4.6
Taken things worth between $10 and $50 from a store without paying for them?	13.9	14.7
Threatened to beat someone up if they didn't give you money or something else you wanted?	15.3	7.0
Carried a razor, switchblade or gun with the intention of using it in a fight?	15.1	6.4
Beat someone up so badly they probably needed a doctor?	12.8	6.0
Taken a car belonging to someone you didn't know for a ride without having the owner's permission to drive it?	8.5	1.3
Tried to pass a check by signing someone else's name?	3.5	1.2
Intentionally set a building on fire?	2.4	0.8
Grabbed a purse from someone and run with it?	1.2	0.5
Taken little things (worth less than $2) from a store without paying for them?	57.6	40.5
Broken the windows of an empty house or other unoccupied building?	53.3	13.8

	% BOYS	% GIRLS
Bought something you knew had been stolen?	33.2	9.9
Picked a fight with someone you didn't know just for the hell of it?	15.3	7.8
Helped break up chairs, tables, desks or other furniture in a school, church or other public building?	8.5	1.2
Jumped or helped jump somebody and then beat them up?	12.2	10.3
Slashed the seat in a bus, a movie house or some other place?	9.9	3.5
Punctured or slashed the tires of a car?	7.4	0.9
Drunk whiskey, gin, vodka or other "hard" liquor?	70.3	71.3
Smoked marijuana?	73.1	73.1
Sold illegal drugs such as heroin, marijuana, LSD or cocaine?	36.4	8.4
Taken barbiturates (downers) or methedrine (speed or other uppers) without a prescription?	15.2	15.9
Used cocaine?	20.2	13.9
Taken angel dust (phencyclidine), LSD or mescaline?	13.3	10.9
Used heroin?	0.7	0.9
Stayed away from school when your parents thought you were there?	60.1	57.4
Gone out at night when your parents told you that you couldn't go?	45.4	27.3
Been suspended or expelled from school?	51.3	33.2
Run away from home and stayed overnight?	15.1	17.9
Hit one of your parents?	8.9	10.3

119

bringing, in our concern that girls should develop as more cooperative and caring people than men, and that boys should develop independence and assertiveness. It is easier for attempts to develop a typical male personality to misfire as rebelliousness and aggression than for a girl's upbringing to lead in this direction.

Delinquency and liberation

In the l960s there was a significant increase in crime among females. Coming as it did at the same time as the women's liberation movement, this prompted new theories about sex differences in delinquency.

Could it be that, as women became freer to develop their potential and to realize new goals in life, their criminal behavior would also come to resemble that of men? Would women's newfound freedom bring with it the freedom to fight and steal? What was it about the changes that were taking place in women's roles that was producing an increase in female crime? Expert opinion was divided over the answers to these questions.

Some interpreted the liberation movement as a movement of women demanding the right to be like men. They expected that as women cast off the old traits of passivity and dependence, some would display their rejection of the old values by joining street gangs and fighting like boys.

This view, however, turned out to be fundamentally wrong. The ratio of boys to girls in street gangs stayed where it had always been – at around ten to one. The major increases in female criminal activity were in theft and drug offenses rather than in the traditionally masculine crimes of violence. One study even found that girls who endorsed

traditional sex-role views (eg "women belong in the home") were actually more likely to be delinquent than more liberated young women.

Other experts argued that the new sense of liberation caused an increase in female crime by encouraging women to be responsible for their own material support and thus to be exposed to the same strains and stresses that had traditionally driven men to crime. For example, some have suggested that male delinquency is largely caused by the

■ **Free-roaming boys and sheltered girls** *make most of the difference to traditional statistics for boys' and girls' delinquency. Spending more of their social lives indoors, girls have had less opportunity to come into conflict with authority. Male delinquency is often a group activity, petty offenses being committed to gain social standing, rather than for purely financial motives.*

One study found that girls who endorse tradition – "women belong in the home" – are more likely to be delinquent than more liberated ones. Other studies find a higher rate of delinquency among girls whose opportunities are blocked.

strain society imposes on working-class boys, by encouraging them to seek economic and material success while at the same time denying them any real possibilities of realizing it. When the boys see expensive cars, stereos and designer clothes on television and in wealthy neighborhoods their anger leads them to find criminal ways of obtaining these rewards of material success. By encouraging girls to aim for economic self-sufficiency and even wealth, some say, we are giving the same double message as we give to working-class boys, and the result will be an increase in female crime.

This argument does seem to have some evidence on its side. It does, for instance, predict an increase specifically in property offenses, which is where the major changes did indeed take place. Some studies also show that girls who give positive responses on a questionnaire which measures their perception of blocked opportunity also admit to higher rates of delinquent behavior. In fact the relation between delinquency and blocked opportunity is even higher for girls than it is for boys.

However, two other important findings seem to go against this argument. First, studies that have tried to identify links between women's crime rates and rising levels of industrialization and economic development have largely been unsuccessful. Second – and this is especially important – the majority of female delinquents are from the kind of backgrounds which are least likely to have been affected by the career aspirations of the women's liberation movement –

the poor, the undereducated and the nonwhite. In fact, there has been a marked increase in juvenile criminal activity especially among families living at the poverty level. These families are mostly headed by single-parent women who rely on government assistance for survival, and who have few aspirations to find jobs of the kind that might be blocked by sex discrimination.

Some experts believe that the rise in female crime might be due to changes in the traditional ways that we bring up our daughters. Girls, more than boys, have generally been subjected to stricter supervision and tighter controls within the family. The premium placed on being "good" has always been stronger for girls than for boys. While a boy's way up the social ladder might be through education and career, a girl "married up." To ensure that she would make a good marriage, parents traditionally kept the girl close to home. There she was safe from the sexual temptations of the streets – any girl with a "reputation" lost her value on the marriage market. In the safety of the home, she was taught to cook, sew and care for children – to become a well-behaved model for the daughters that she in turn would raise one day.

Today, parental controls have certainly begun to loosen, but their legacy remains. An American study of 1,752 teenagers chosen at random suggests that girls, compared to boys, spend more time with their families, see the family as more influential in their lives and attach more importance to their family's aspirations for them.

Boys and girls who come from homes where the parents closely supervise their whereabouts, who feel that their parents understand them, who feel wanted by their parents

▲ **A lack of parental supervision** that endangers the safety of small boys may later contribute to their greater delinquency by comparison with girls. Parenting styles that emphasize parental control *without care and those that emphasize care without control are both associated with higher rates of delinquency.*

▲ **Being a part of the group** means joining in with its resistance of adult authority. By combining care, control and sound explanations for your rules throughout a child's development, you face a better *chance that your adolescent will choose groups whose values do not conflict strongly with your own.*

and are confident that their parents would stick by them in times of trouble, are certainly less often in trouble with the police than those from colder families. Yet, it is interesting to note that, even in supportive and closely supervising families the boys are still more delinquent.

Delinquency in groups

Another influence for change is a shift in the pattern of girls' friendships. Girls are more likely to be one of the gang than was once possible, and it is when they are in a gang

that adolescents are most likely to get into trouble. Most delinquency aims at winning group approval. Questionnaire studies as well as police reports agree that adolescents are more likely to break the law in groups than alone. The payoff for much of this risk-taking is the acclaim of the audience – it is not the same without friends around to appreciate your daring. Once teenagers are out with friends on the streets or in the clubs, parents have to hope that the values they tried to instill in the earlier years will influence their choice of companions and help them to moderate their

---

AMERICAN STREET GANGS

■ It is estimated that there are as many as 52,000 youth gang members in the United States, including about 5,000 girls. The vast majority come from inner city areas, from the poorest and most recent immigrants.

Los Angeles and Chicago both have a high concentration of Chicano (Mexican American) gangs, while New York City gangs are principally Puerto Rican, Jamaican and Haitian. Each gang has a distinctive name, claims control over a "turf" (territory), wears "colors" (gang emblems) on members' jackets, has a leader and also special officers (such as a Sergeant-at-Arms and a Godfather). The members join in illegal activities that occupy the gang.

The youth gangs of the 1950s, like those in West Side Story, were mostly involved in small-time crime and most of their aggression was directed toward other gangs at "rumbles," where prearranged agreements limited the use of lethal weapons. Today, in contrast, gang deaths in Los Angeles are running at over 200 per year and typically involve a bullet fired from an unmarked car driven by a rival gang member.

The gangs' principal source of income is from street drug selling, robbery or acting as strong-arm men to protect

dealers from takeovers. Large sums of money are involved and gang killings are less to do with "heart" these days than with profits.

Many street gangs have branches in state prisons where individual gangs form alliances, often along racial lines ("The Arian Brotherhood," "The Mexican Mafia"). They control the flow of drugs into the prison, and gang leaders, even when incarcerated, organize street activity and order "hits" to be made from behind prison bars.

Young women make up about 10 percent of youth gang members. They are usually affiliated to a male gang, and take a feminized version of the male gang's name. They have their

own leader or Godmother, perform their own initiation rites and discipline their own members. Often they choose a boyfriend from their brother gang, since it is forbidden to become romantically involved with boys from rival groups. Entry into the gang usually depends upon the girl's willingness to "get down" (fight), and gang wars between girl affiliates are not uncommon, but fists and knives rather than than guns are most often used.

The girls organize shoplifting rings, "panhandle" (ask passers-by in the street for money) and hide their boys' weapons and drugs when the police appear, since they cannot be searched by male

officers. While the boys' ties with the gang are most often weakened by long prison terms or severe injuries, girls often leave the gang after they have their first child.

▼ **The extreme of juvenile delinquency** is found in highly organized street gangs in large American cities. Gang conflict goes beyond mere neighborhood rivalry, as profitable trade in drugs, robbery and strong-arm protection racketeering depends on the control of local territories. Killings are a common feature of this conflict.

Adolescents are more likely to break the law in groups than alone. Their reward is audience acclaim for daring. As girls come to spend more time out in the company of friends, they become more prominent in delinquency statistics.

adolescent determination to test the limits of conventional behavior. Traditionally, adolescent girls spend their time away from the excitement of the streets. Their friendship groups tend to be smaller and more intimate than those of boys, and a lot of their time is taken up with talking rather than doing. Gathered in each other's bedrooms, girls try out makeup or talk about rock stars while their male counterparts are ranging more widely away from home.

The boys have much more opportunity for mischief, and they are more accessible to the arm of the law, which most typically touches them for such minor offenses as loitering and underage drinking.

It is only recently that social scientists have begun to study changes in girls' peer groups and to examine the impact of delinquent friends on girls' antisocial behavior. They note that girls who spend a lot of their leisure time in mixed-sex groups are the ones most likely to become involved in delinquent behavior – certainly more likely than girls who go around with a single boyfriend or girlfriend. Although it is usually the boys in the group who start trouble, the majority of girls who become involved in delinquency say they do it to win the approval of their girlfriends rather than the boys.

Perhaps this is where liberation has had one of its most important and subtle effects – in the relationship between young women. Rather than being competitors for the romantic attention of boys, girls may be discovering a new camaraderie with each other, away from the confines of their parents' homes. **AC**

▲ **Female camaraderie**, as two girls share a sense of fun with each other and the boys they are with. Girls who spend more of their social life in mixed-sex groups tend to figure more prominently in delinquency statistics than those who mix mainly with other girls, but a majority of girls who become involved in delinquency that boys initiate say that they join in to impress the other girls rather than the boys in their group.

Puberty

PUBERTY, marking the end of childhood and the beginning of adolescence, is a period of rapid and sometimes bewildering changes. As the adolescent watches these changes occur, he or she may be alternatively fascinated and terrified, pleased and disappointed, self-confident and self-conscious.

Puberty is both a public and a private event. The adolescent feels it to be a deeply personal one, but sometimes it is a painfully evident one to parents and friends, who make it not only a biological experience, but a social one as well. Puberty marks the introduction to adulthood, as the girl becomes a woman and the boy a man.

What happens biologically?

The biological aspects of puberty include growth-rate changes, sexual maturation and hormone changes. Physical transformation from a child's body to that of a reproductively mature adult begins with changes in the hormone system that precede the visible signs of puberty. Until middle childhood, the system that was so active during prenatal development (see *Ch1*) shows low activity, and hormonal output is very low. Then, two independent processes occur. *Adenarche*, or increases in adrenal output, occurs first around age 7. *Gonadarche*, the activation of a system of hormone exchanges between the hypothalamus and the pituitary (both in the brain) and the gonads (testes in boys, ovaries in girls) occurs around age 8 or 9. There is an increase in hormones that stimulate the gonads. It is believed that puberty is triggered by the lifting of a suppression of the release of the sex hormones. Both growth and sexual maturation during puberty are in part under the control of sex hormones. Androgens (male sex hormones) will promote muscle development, beard growth, chest hair and larynx enlargement. In girls, estrogen will be responsible for breast development, thigh widening, fat deposits, salt and water metabolism and an increased

▲ **The tall and the short.** *Differences in growth spurts make it difficult to guess children's ages around the time of puberty. From appearance alone, it is impossible to tell whether a group is of widely mixed years* *or includes late and early developers all of the same age. Not until late adolescence will it be clear who is going to be a tall or a short adult.*

▲ **A time of transition.** *Having barely established her identity as a girl, an early adolescent turns her thoughts to the passage to womanhood.*

▶ **Body image** *is often distorted in girls who develop early. They may see themselves as overweight by comparison with as yet undeveloped classmates who seem to reflect society's ideal of slimness. This may lead to unnecessary dieting. In combination with other pressures of adolescence, it can reach the self-starvation extremes of anorexia nervosa.*

Puberty brings the biological changes that make a girl physically a woman and a boy physically a man. It is also a time of emotional and social adjustments, in which adolescents experience an intensification of sex-role learning.

sense of smell. Progesterone will prepare the body for pregnancy through enlargement of the breasts and alteration of the uterus.

The first event of puberty following hormonal increases is a growth spurt. Only at one time in life is growth more rapid: during the fetal period and the first two years – growth rates slow down during childhood. The acceleration that occurs during puberty is psychologically more significant than earlier growth since the adolescent, unlike the fetus or infant, scrutinizes the body changes carefully, intensively and self-consciously.

During the peak year of the adolescent growth spurt, which usually arrives two years earlier for girls than boys, children shoot up between 6 and 12 centimeters (2-5in). The girls' spurt usually comes around at age 12, the boys' around at age 14. It comes earlier in years for girls, and also earlier in their sexual maturation sequence. In both sexes, it affects all body parts, not just height, and different parts develop at different rates and times. The head, hands and feet reach adult proportions earliest. Next, leg length

increases, followed by body breadth and shoulder width – a boy's pant-legs stop getting short a year before he stops growing out of his shirts. The muscles also grow in size and strength during puberty, especially in boys.

The boy's sequence in sexual maturation is as follows. First, some time between 9½ and 13½ years of age, the testes enlarge. About a year later the penis begins to grow. And a year after that, the boy typically experiences his first ejaculation. Hair begins to increase on all parts of the body at the same time as the testes and penis are becoming mature. Pubic hair appears first, followed by body and facial hair a few years later. Facial hair starts at the corners of the upper lip and ends of the sides of the face and border of the chin. Hair development continues throughout the entire pubertal period. The breaking of the voice, a phenomenon that causes many an adolescent boy to blush, is that last obvious sign of puberty. It results from the enlargement of the larynx, causing the voice to deepen. Thus, voice changes do not herald the beginning of puberty, as some people believe, but occur late in the sequence.

For girls, the first sign of sexual maturity is breast-

GROWTH AND MATURATION

■ **The growth spurt** *starts as early as 9½ in girls. The average girl starts her spurt at 10½ and finishes at 14. Boys may begin as early as 10½ – on average at 12½, finishing at 16. Slower growth continues until about 18.*

Aged 10 years   Aged 14 years   Aged 18 years

Hair growth

Age		8	9	10	11	12	13	14	15	16	17	18
Growth	Boy				Early			Growth spurt			Late	
	Girl											
First menstruation												
Breast			Early development			Average development				Late development		
Pubic hair	Boy											
	Girl											
Penis												
Testis												

■ **Sexual maturation.** *In early puberty, a girl's face becomes fuller, her pelvis begins to grow and fat deposits appear on the hips. Her breasts may bud as early as 8, on average at 10½. First pubic hair, long strands along the labia, usually appear around 11. Glands begin to produce oily secretions for the scent traps created by developing underarm and pubic hair. After the growth and body-fat spurt has begun, first menstruation (menarche) occurs. Typically, a boy's sexual maturation begins with growth and enlargement of the testes and scrotum, as early as 9½, but on average at 11½. Pubic hair usually appears at the base of the penis around 12. There may be a slight breast budding, but this disappears in 1 to 1½ years. By 15 the voice has usually deepened and hair appears under the armpits and on the face. The boy will probably by now be having ejaculations. Both boys and girls are fully mature at 18.*

125

budding. This occurs between 10 and 14 years of age. The breasts become elevated and the nipples enlarge. The second sign is usually the appearance of pubic hair. Then, the internal sex organs (uterus and vagina) and external sex organs (clitoris and labia) mature. Only after these signs of maturation occur does first menstruation (menarche) begin. Following menarche, body hair appears, hips broaden and fat deposits increase. A truly mature cycle of ovulation (pro-duction of eggs that can be fertilized to produce new human life) followed by monthly menstruation may not be estab-lished, however, until several years after menarche.

The timing of puberty

It is vital to remember that these biological changes can occur very rapidly or very slowly. For girls, the time between breast-budding and full breast growth can take anywhere from 1½ to 6 years. From beginning to end, puberty for boys lasts anywhere from 2 to 5 years. It may begin in ele-mentary school or in high school. We can take three normal, healthy 14-year-olds, and, in height, sex organs and other characteristics, one of them might look like an 11-year-old preadolescent, one like a 14-year-old midadoles-cent and one like a 17-year-old late adolescent. Yet all three will be normal. They might have different social experien-ces, however, depending on their physical maturity.

In Europe and the United States the age of menarche has declined four months per decade since 1850. In 1833 an adolescent girl did not menstruate until she was, on average, 17 years of age; today, European and American girls first menstruate at 12 or 13 years of age. Better nutrition and general health help to explain this change. It seems that the growth spurt and menarche are partially dependent on weight. Weight is also important for the maintenance of menstruation. Girls who have a condition in which they stop eating (called anorexia nervosa) cease menstruating as soon as their weight drops 10 to 15 percent below a critical weight. Some women athletes, whose proportion of body fat is low, also stop menstruating. Both groups begin menstru-

HOW DO WE GREET PUBERTY?

■ *First menstruation (men-arche) may pass with celebra-tion, disdain or no comment, depending on the culture. Industrialized societies usu-ally have no formalized rites of passage for children at puberty, but some families do celebrate the event. As one American girl described her first period: "When I discovered it my mother told me to come with her, and we went into the living room to tell my father. She just looked at me and then at him and said, 'Well, your little girl is a young lady now!' My dad gave me a hug and congratulated me and I felt grown up and proud that I was a lady at last." Unfortunately, the event is not always acknow-ledged with pride. Another girl recalls her experience: "I had no information whatsoever, no hint that anything was going to happen to me...I thought I was on the point of death from internal hemorrhage...What did my highly educated mother do? She gave me a furious lecture about what a bad, evil, immoral thing I was to start menstruating at the age of eleven! So young and so vile! Even after 30 years, I can feel the shock of hearing her con-demn me for 'doing' something I had no idea occurred." In spite of a lack of a formal rite, adolescents do learn about their society's beliefs. Much of the information about menarche for girls and first ejaculation for boys is contradictory and nega-tive. On the one hand, men-arche and ejaculation are thought to be traumatic and up-setting events, while on the other they are symbols of sexual maturity, of becoming a woman or a man. Even though it signifies maturity and adult-hood, girls are told to hide the fact that they are menstruating by "acting normal" and "not let-ting anyone know," and boys are given similar messages about ejaculation.*

▶ **Sharing their experiences**. *By six months after first men-struation about 80 percent of girls may have begun to dis-cuss the experience with girl-friends. Before the event, most expect to tell more girlfriends immediately than they actually do, and 75 percent tell only their mothers.*

Even though it signifies maturity, mothers tell girls to hide the fact that they are menstruating – by "acting normal" and "not letting anyone know." Boys receive the same message from more diffuse sources when they begin to ejaculate.

ating again as soon as body weight and body fat rise. Thus, the earlier puberty that we have seen over the last century is probably due to the fact that children are growing and gaining weight more quickly than ever before. However, prosperous industrial countries are probably close to reaching the lowest age possible for puberty in normal children.

How children react

Experts used to characterize early adolescence as a universally stormy period. This picture has not been substantiated, but, for some children, increases in negative emotions do seem to occur between late childhood and early to middle adolescence. The activation of the hormone system seems to increase excitability, arousal and emotionality. Sexual arousal also seems to be associated with hormonal increases for both boys and girls. These changes in turn may influence behavior. Increased excitability and arousability may result in more rapid and/or more intense mood fluctuations. They may render a girl more sensitive to negative reactions of peers and parents with the result that she has emotional interchanges with them. Hormone changes are associated with aggressive feelings in boys and both

aggressive and depressive feelings in girls. These may be greatest when the hormone system is being turned on; in a study of 100 early-adolescent girls, negative feelings increased as the hormone system was undergoing its greatest change. They leveled off or dropped after hormone changes had reached their limit.

In general, menarche heralds increases in social maturity for girls, increased peer prestige, self-esteem, heightened self-awareness of one's body and heightened consciousness of self. Somewhat ambivalent emotional reactions to menarche are reported. Typically, girls describe both positive and negative feelings – they are excited and pleased, scared and upset.

Girls who are early and girls who are unprepared for menarche report more negative experiences at menarche than on-time or prepared girls. In addition, not being prepared seems to have long-term effects – adults and late adolescents who remember being unprepared report more severe menstrual symptoms, more negative attitudes about menstruation and more self-consciousness. Being unprepared typically means lack of information from the mother, because she is still the primary source of information about menarche for the majority of girls.

Girls almost never discuss menarche with boys but do have extensive exchanges with girlfriends. Even with girl-

▲ **Adolescent moods** *are influenced by hormone changes. Boys become more aggressive. Girls may react with aggression and by becoming easily depressed. Characteristic adolescent lethargy may result in part from hormone changes and from tiredness due to the growth spurt. However, these direct hormonal effects are small compared to social factors, such as the pressures of adjusting to new roles.*

▲ **Talking man to man.** *Boys do not readily discuss their pubertal experiences with parents or friends. They do not usually tell anyone when they begin ejaculating, as this may involve masturbation, an activity which most boys engage in secretly but deride publicly when joking with friends. This helps them to ease tension about the topic by bringing it into conversation, while at the same time avoiding situations that might lead to homosexual experiments. Sex-education talks with a father are characteristically one-sided and abstract. The father does most of the talking and there is little self-disclosure.*

friends, reluctance to discuss menstruation occurs immediately after menarche: premenarcheal girls expect to tell more girl friends than they actually do, and according to one study only one-quarter tell anyone other than their mothers when they first menstruate. They are reluctant to discuss the event for about six months; by that time approximately 80 percent of girls talk to their girlfriends. Thus, little information seems to be exchanged immediately, although later on, friends share stories about symptoms and negative attitudes. Girls also may select friends who reached menarche at about the same time as them.

In late elementary school girls, the beginning of breast development is associated with positive body images, good peer relationships and better adjustment. At the same time, pubic hair growth is not. Different pubertal events have different meanings to adolescents.

Very little is known about the psychological meaning of pubertal changes to boys. It is believed that the occurrence of ejaculation, or spermarche, is as significant for boys as menarche is for girls, although there is little research. In one small study, boys who had had an ejaculation were extremely reluctant to discuss the experience with parents or peers.

None had talked to peers about their own experiences, although all joked about it. This secrecy may be in part due to spermarche's link to masturbation, a relation that does not exist for menarche.

Early-maturing boys seem to have social and emotional advantages over late maturers. Some of these persist into adulthood. In contrast, early maturation does not seem to be an advantage for girls. Maturational timing in girls influences physical development, preparation for and feelings about menarche, body image and self-image, deviant behavior and relationships with parents and peers. For example, early-maturing girls seem to have a poorer body

▲ **Falling in love**. By mid- to late adolescence many are experiencing the joys and sorrows of first love. Social expectations favor intense involvements in which partners form highly idealized images of each other. When the first excitement wears off, and the lovers take a more realistic view, a break-up almost always follows, with considerable emotional pain, but with a deepening of experience.

▲ **Intensification of sex roles**. As children move into puberty, boys become more and girls become less assertive. Boys begin to occupy more public space, while girls become more practiced at making their bodies small. In family interactions, mothers have been observed to expect more compliance with their wishes from daughters who have had their first menstruation. However, families expect boys to become more independent.

Early-maturing boys seem to have emotional and social advantages over late-maturing boys. With girls, the pattern is reversed – early maturers have a poorer self-image, regard themselves as overweight and have more conflict with parents.

image than on-time or late girls. In American studies, this poorer image persists through elementary school and junior and senior high school. Body build is evaluated by peers and prestige depends on being slim. Early maturers do not conform to the cultural values that favor thinness and prepubertal figures. Excessive dieting is a common response.

Early maturers may engage in adult behavior such as smoking, drinking and sexual intercourse at a younger age. However, by late adolescence, these differences between early and late maturers disappear. We know very little about the effects of maturational timing on parent-child relationships, but research suggests that early-maturing girls are more likely to experience conflict.

The intensification of sex roles

Pressures to act in sex-stereotyped ways increase as the mature body emerges. Some psychologists see these pressures especially in the family, where boys and girls are expected to establish their growing adult identities in different ways.

Parent-child interactions at early adolescence suggest that it is easier for boys than for girls to establish their independence. In observational studies of families, as puberty progresses girls are interrupted more, ignored more and are less assertive, while boys assert themselves more. Without showing it openly, mothers seem to exert more power over their daughters after menarche than before. Pressure to identify with the mother increases and so does compliance with her wishes.

At the same time, boys may be experiencing increasing problems in establishing intimacy. This aspect of adolescence is not well studied, but the fact that it is culturally unacceptable to talk about male pubertal changes, and the feelings they engender, may be a pivotal experience. In contrast, almost all girls today talk over pubertal changes with their mothers and their close girlfriends. **JBG**

▶ **Setting out**. *With the transition to sexual maturity complete, and perhaps with one or two adolescent romances safely behind her, a young woman gets ready to enjoy an evening. Her adult life lies before her.*

129

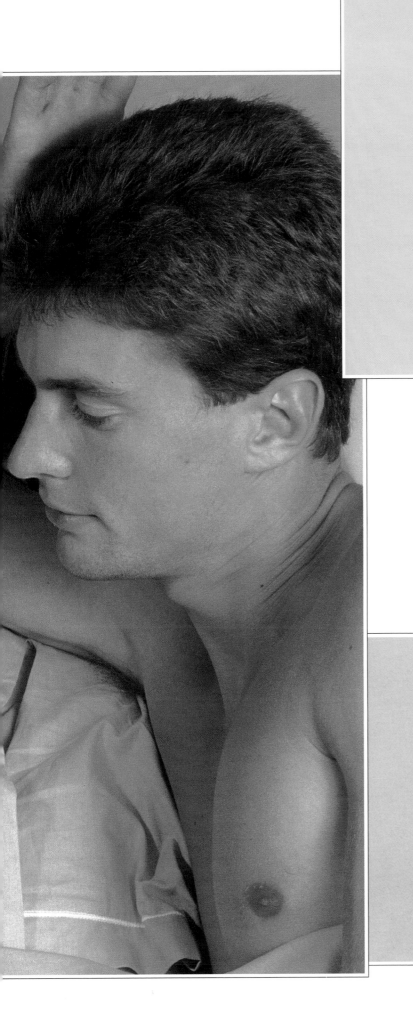

2

ADULTHOOD
MEN AND WOMEN

THE OPPOSITE SEX PART TWO

Evolution

Throughout the world, men and women differ from each other in the roles they play and in their patterns of behavior. Much of each society's culture – its institutions, language and beliefs – reflects these differences. How far are they "natural" – the product of millions of years of evolution? Many scientists have argued that the differences that are common to all societies are part of the success of the human species at adapting to its environment and are therefore best not tampered with. Others argue that there is no biological basis, apart from reproductive organs, for the roles and styles of behavior adopted by men and women – the male and female worlds are defined by social custom. The truth doubtless lies somewhere between these extremes. Just *where* it is impossible to say.

Rival myths about our past

A familiar evolutionary picture originally championed by Charles Darwin, the father of evolutionary theory himself, features our male ancestor as a heroic character, who spent his life hunting, and fighting in defense of his family, activities that were to become the driving force of human evolution. The male, according to this scenario, was solely responsible for the enlargement of the human brain, for our upright stance, and for the development of our technology, language and culture. Females, in contrast, because of their reproductive function, stayed close to a home base, rearing the young, were economically dependent on males and had no impact on the development of human characteristics.

Feminist scholars have appropriately dubbed this the "coat-tails" theory of human evolution. Some, perceptively, have also pointed out that it is not unlike other myths that males have fostered in all cultures, which have a common narrative structure and often take the form of a "hero story," with man in the role of hunter and protector.

► **Man the hunter and woman the gatherer** *are characteristic of almost all preagricultural human societies. The same division of labor may have been characteristic of the species from which we have evolved. Probably neither sex has been more important than the other to the survival of our species. When meat is plentiful, it is men, such as this Greenland Eskimo capturing a seal, who supply most of the food for a hunter-gatherer community. Eskimos eat almost nothing but meat and fish. When hunting is sparse, as in the Amazonian forests* INSET, *women, such as this Yanomamo Indian carrying peach-palm fruit, play a more important part in feeding the population. Among southern African Bushmen, women gather 70 to 75 percent of all food consumed.*

Hunting, gathering and sharing the food obtained are survival strategies that evolved naturally for humans. How significant for present-day life are the sex differences that characteristically appear in this most traditional of lifestyles?

Unsurprisingly, there has been a conscious effort to devise rival scenarios that emphasize the role of the female in human evolution. These theories assume that during the earliest phases of our development as a species – some 2 to 3 million years ago – our ancestors depended predominantly on plant food. Here "woman the gatherer" occupies center stage, through her ability to obtain plant food. She invents tools, and carrying devices for both infants and food, which allow her to travel long distances and be economically independent. The more extreme of these theories, which all but ignore the evolutionary contribution of males, have been called "apron strings" scenarios.

Is this controversy all just storytelling – with the prize going to the teller of the most plausible and pleasing story? At one time, when there was little evidence of any sort to help us evaluate alternative scenarios, the answer was surely yes. In fact, for much of the 20th century the "man the hunter" story depended almost entirely on Raymond Dart's discovery at Taung, South Africa, in 1924, of what was then the earliest hominid (human-like) skull, and on his later descriptions of the bone-smashing and killing activities by these earliest of hominids – the australopithecines. His picture of a club-wielding, predatory man-ape fired many imaginations. The current situation is much changed. There is substantial new archeological evidence against which we can test alternative evolutionary scenarios. We also have a much richer understanding of the social organization of our closest living relatives, the African apes.

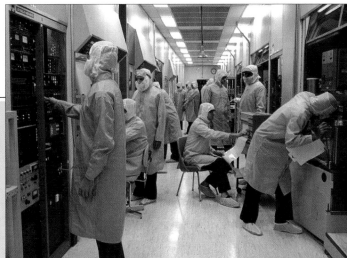

▲ **Hunting for new solutions** *to technological problems, would you need the genes of someone born to find and kill game or those of someone born to find and bring home edible plants? Some writers speculate that the task of bringing down moving game has given the human male more need than the female to develop visuo-spatial abilities and so mathematical aptitude. However, social pressures, rather than biology, may deter women from participating more fully than they do in work of the kind being done here – developing new computer systems.*

133

Social organization in animals depends on how they get their food. In later hominid society, men hunted and women gathered, but our earlier ancestors ate nuts, seeds and roots and probably spent a good deal of time in trees.

We know from studies of other animal species that their social organization depends very largely on how they get their food, and this is certainly the key issue in studying the evolutionary origin of human sex roles. Until relatively recently, all humans depended on hunting and gathering for survival. Even today, in groups such as the southern African Bushmen, the characteristic features of social organization are a home base, food-sharing and a division by sex of the work of feeding the band (with men hunting and females gathering). In these societies, although the plants gathered by women make up the predominant portion of the total food-supply, it is nonetheless clear that hunting is important to the basic division of labor. In hunter-gatherer groups that followed herds (such as the North American Plains Indian) or lived near water (such as coastal Eskimos, or salmon-eating North American Indians of the Pacific Coast) the hunting and fishing activities of men provided almost all of the food. It is of interest to identify when meat became an important element in hominid diet.

The earliest known hominid

The earliest human-like traces now begin with an australopithecine skeleton widely known as "Lucy," discovered in 1974 in Ethiopia. Classified as *Australopithecus afarensis*,

Lucy died at about the age of 23 around 3.5 million years ago. She was small-brained and stood on two legs. Judging from the limb bones, she spent a good deal of time climbing in trees.

Unlike modern apes, her species was not a forest one. Like other australopithecine species, it lived in more open country with clusters of trees, such as are still found today in East Africa near rivers and lakes. Of small body size – 35-65kg (75-145lb) – these creatures very likely relied on trees for protection from predators, such as leopards, saw-toothed tigers and other large carnivores. Their jaws and the shape of their teeth suggest that they chewed hard, gritty foods – hard-shelled nuts, seeds, tubers and roots. Several skeletons have been found together, and at one famous site a series of fossilized footprints suggest that they lived in groups. There were, however, no signs of stone tools.

This minimal reconstruction of Lucy's lifestyle can be further enriched by looking at our closest surviving relatives, the gorilla and especially the chimpanzee. While these live in very different environments from those inhabited by the australopithecines, it is likely that ancestors of the gorillas, chimpanzees and the australopithecines diverged from a single species some 5 million years ago. We can guess from

134

■ **A trail of footprints** *and a dented piece of skull are typical of fragments from which anthropologists such as Mary Leakey* RIGHT *attempt to reconstruct early hominid life. The footprints make it plain that australopithecines were comfortable walking upright. Fitting a set of leopard's fangs to the broken skull suggests the hazards of life 3 million years ago. A polygynous mating system can be conjectured, by analogy with modern social mammals, from the fact that males were twice as heavy as females.*

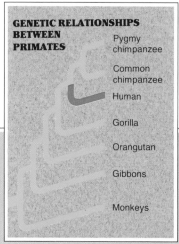

GENETIC RELATIONSHIPS BETWEEN PRIMATES

Pygmy chimpanzee

Common chimpanzee

Human

Gorilla

Orangutan

Gibbons

Monkeys

■ *Genetic relationships between humans, chimpanzees and other primates. Scientists do not agree about the exact distances between species, but humans and chimpanzees probably shared a common ancestor which arose after the branching-off of the gorilla, and we may be a nearer relative of the other primates than the chimpanzees.*

the behavior of the modern apes that this common ancestor as well as Lucy and her fellow australopithecines lived in relatively closed social groups, defended primarily by males. Females left the group to mate, and the males were polygynous (mated with more than one female).

This reconstruction is consistent with anatomical evidence. First, Lucy's brain is essentially ape-like in both size and the surface features discernible from the inside of her skull. We can expect her behavior to have been very ape-like as well. Second, male australopithecines were almost twice as large as females. Among most mammals generally, a marked difference in size and shape between males and females (sexual dimorphism) is associated with a polygynous mating system – presumably the outcome of combats selecting the largest males as sires. It is also possible that battles between australopithecines resulted in the

THE AGGRESSIVE MALE

■ It is easy to believe that Western society especially, with its emphasis on masculinity and a macho image, and not human nature, is responsible for aggressiveness in the human male.

We know about many societies that are not nearly as overtly violent and warfaring, where male aggression is discouraged from childhood. However, even in these relatively peaceful communities, males readily learn that they are more prone to violent urges than females, as is evident, for example, from watching boys at play.

This difference between male and female is by no means universal among primates. In some monkeys and apes (gibbons, for example), especially where there is little or no difference between the sexes in the size of their teeth or bodies, females are at least as

aggressive as males, or, as with squirrel monkeys, may even dominate them. At one time, human male aggression was believed to be unique. But Jane Goodall's years of study of chimpanzees in the wild has proved this to be incorrect.

Adult males, on average, attack another chimpanzee twice as frequently as do adult females. Meetings between chimpanzee communities frequently lead to male fights. A considerable part of a male's life consists of regularly patrolling his community's

borders, which sometimes leads to confrontation, fighting, death and the acquisition of the loser's territory. Goodall has suggested that this coordinated adult male activity, if present in early hominids, could have been an early form of human warfare.

135

OUR CLOSEST RELATIVES

■ On anatomical grounds, the African apes and humans have been regarded for more than a century as close cousins. Charles Darwin used this to justify comparative studies of behavior, such as the facial expression of emotion. Many Victorians were morally outraged at Darwin's claim that humans and apes were descended from a common ape-like ancestor in the not-too-distant past. However, modern evidence has strengthened Darwin's case. Using a variety of techniques, molecular biochemists have found that humans and African

apes share about 98 percent of the chemical structure of their genes. Even more remarkable is the finding that humans and the two species of chimpanzee (the common and the pygmy chimpanzees) have more in common genetically than either has with the gorilla, in spite of the closer resemblance between the gorilla and the chimpanzee. Some authorities have begun speaking of "the three chimpanzees." This finding provides a stronger rationale for comparative behavioral studies than even Darwin had proposed. ABOVE A female

chimpanzee uses a stick to gather termites, in much the same way that early hominid

females might have done while males cooperated in hunting small animals.

survival of the larger males, and that this is at least part of the reason why men today are aggressive.

On the basis of sexual dimorphism, the gorilla suggests the most likely model of an australopithecine mating system. The gorilla male weighs 140-180kg (310-400lb), the female is only about 90kg (200lb). They live in small, mixed-sex groups under the constant control of a dominant male – called the "silverback," because he grows a crest of white hair on his neck and shoulders upon assuming dominance of the group. He mates polygynously with all females in the group and, when fertile, they mate monogamously, only with him. A less likely model is the promiscuous mating system of the chimpanzee. The male weighs 40-90kg (90-200lb). The female weighs 30-80kg (65-175lb). Each male in a troop potentially mates with each female.

There is no evidence to suggest among australopithecines a division of labor by sex in feeding the population. If they were very gorilla-like, there certainly was none. Male and female gorillas feed on the same herbs, shrubs and vines without dividing the work of picking them, and without sharing. If there *were* differences in getting food, they would probably have been chimpanzee-like. When the opportunity arises, male chimpanzees cooperate in stalking and killing small mammals, such as young gazelles and monkeys, while female chimpanzees specialize in "termiting" – fashioning grass stems for extracting termites from their mounds. Food-sharing among chimpanzees, however, is rare, and the basic feeding strategy is a self-serving "feed-as-you-go" one. Australopithecines may have been similarly opportunistic – supplementing the basically vegetarian diet we know of from their teeth by eating meat or insects as they became available – abandoned carnivore kills may well have presented such opportunities.

When did we become meat-eaters?

Later descendants of Lucy, some 2 million years ago, almost certainly depended on meat from medium to large mammals for a significant portion of their diet, and in so doing may have ushered in the first division by sex of food provision. We know this from relatively rich archeological evidence at Olduvai Gorge, East Africa. This site contains a layer of deposits that was formed about 1.75 million years ago when it was covered by volcanic ash. By this time several species of hominids shared eastern and southern Africa, but very likely only one, known as *Homo habilis*, was the direct ancestor of all later humankind. Compared to *Australopithecus*, the teeth of *Homo* are generally smaller, and the molars not as specialized for tough grinding and crushing. They are suited to a much more varied diet. *Homo* also had a significantly larger brain than Lucy, considerably bigger than the brain of an ape of similar body weight. Some scientists, from close inspection of the impressions left by the cerebral cortex on the inside of fossilized skulls, suspect that these 2-million-year old hominids may well have had the power of speech. They also made crude stone tools.

◀ **Eskimos skin a bear**, *preparing to take meat and hide back to their home base. Early hominids probably scavenged and hunted for meat, but we do not know how or even whether they distributed it within their communities. It has been suggested that females evolved to depend on men for meat, but many subsistence agricultural societies are almost completely vegetarian.*

■ **Division of labor** *according to sex in subsistence-based cultures.* RIGHT *Men do most of the hunting, fishing and trapping of animals, as well as related jobs, such as preparing fishing nets and making hunting tools. Women cook and sew,* and CENTER *gather wild plants. In subsistence-agricultural societies, men usually fell trees and clear land and often prepare the soil and plant the crops but* LEFT *more women than men tend and harvest them. Women also grind the grain. Men tend to do work in which the heavy musculature of their arms and shoulders is an advantage.*

TENDING AND HARVESTING CROPS

Proportion of societies studied

Men usually

Men always

Either sex

Women usually

Women always

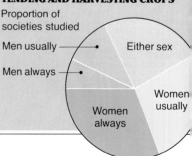

HOW EARLY HOMINIDS MADE A LIVING

■ *There are differing theories on how our ancestors dealt with the meat they scavenged. One suggests that man became a biped specifically to enable the males to carry the meat back to a home base for sharing with the females. According to this theory, the provisioning of females by males then promoted a monogamous mating system and permitted females to increase their reproductive output. Available evidence does not help much in assessing this story. It is not known whether scavenging was an* exclusively male activity, nor whether meat was transported, let alone brought to a home base for sharing. While the latter is a possibility, it is equally likely that carcasses were taken to points where tools were "cached" for processing. It is even possible that early hominids carried their stone tool kits to the carcass, dismembered it and consumed it on the spot. West African chimpanzees have been observed to carry wood or stone hammers to trees where they use them to open nuts.

Our "australopithecine" ancestors were ape-like in both body and behavior. Males were twice the size of females and usually had more than one mate. We can only speculate about a possible division of labor by sex in these species.

Homo erectus, another toolmaker, succeeded *Homo habilis* about 1.5 million years ago.

Large brains require special diets, as neural cells consume energy at five times the rate of other cells, and use up this energy constantly even when we are asleep. And so we come back again to the question of hominid diet. There is evidence that by now hominids were certainly eating meat. First, the layer at Olduvai contains not only the bones of *Homo habilis* but also some 60,000 animal-bone frag-

ments over a 300-square-meter area of former lake front. Many of the identifiable bones are those of large animals, such as wildebeest, weighing 115-340kg (250-750lb), which accumulated over a period of one to two years. These bones are marked by cuts, exactly as you would expect if hominids were removing flesh from limbs, while the way the bones have been broken indicates that the hominids were also after the nutritious bone marrow. The concentrated protein and fat yield from these sources (unlike that from plant foods alone) would have made it possible to meet the fuel demands of a larger brain. Analysis of some of the tools found at the site suggests that they were indeed specially manufactured and used for butchering purposes.

Lifestyle 2 million years BC

There is still substantial debate about how *Homo habilis* and *Homo erectus* might have acquired meat, and what it implies about social organization. Did these creatures kill the animals, butcher them and then carry the meat-rich parts to a safe, central place and share them there with other members of the group? Or did they scavenge the remainder of abandoned carnivore kills on a more opportunistic basis, consuming everything on the spot? These are just two of several possible scenarios that could account for the accumulation of bones and tools.

From both the number and types of skeletal parts present at the site, as well as the presence of carnivore tooth marks on the bones, we can assume that they generally scavenged rather than hunted their meat. However, as the depth of the toolcut marks suggests that plenty of meat was left on the bones, these hominids may well have confronted and chased off the carnivores while still in the early stages of consumption. Wild chimpanzees are quite capable of routing leopards and other carnivores by shouting, wielding

137

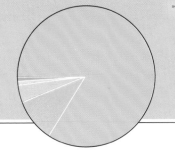
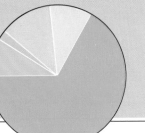

GATHERING PLANT FOOD   **HUNTING, TRAPPING AND FISHING**

◄ **Producing food and caring for young** *are jobs that women combine in most human cultures.* ABOVE LEFT *An agricultural community in Maputo, Mozambique.* BOTTOM LEFT *Yanomamo women of Brazil set out on a fishing expedition. Women may have evolved a different style of communication from men in order to be more sensitive to children's needs (see Ch 27).*

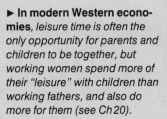

► **In modern Western economies,** *leisure time is often the only opportunity for parents and children to be together, but working women spend more of their "leisure" with children than working fathers, and also do more for them (see Ch 20).*

large sticks and throwing stones. These early hominids were no doubt equally capable of doing so.

As this kind of "confrontational scavenging" must have involved elements of physical prowess and high risk, it may well have been a largely male activity, especially as, from a reproduction standpoint, males are more expendable than females (the number of females, rather than the number of males, in a group sets the limit on how many offspring it can have). Large quantities of meat could then have been carried to a central place, to which several subgroups would return for feasting and celebrations. If females were at the same time gathering plant food (and probably fish, grubs and other small animals), this scenario then amounts to a division of food production by sex, not unlike that among modern hunter-gatherers.

It has been argued that this pattern of food-sharing would create an evolutionary pressure away from a gorilla-like mating system. A dominant male scavenging for meat would not be able to supervise females, and subordinate males that mated with, and shared food with, the unsupervised females would have more reproductive success than those that did not. Females adapted to seek a stable relationship with a protective and providing male might have had more

surviving offspring, and so would males adapted to exclude other males of the group from access to "their" females.

It is important to realize that this is just one of several possible scenarios for the origin of sex roles that is consistent with present evidence. It is crucially dependent upon the existence of a home base that would have facilitated division of labor and food-sharing. Current evidence is equally consistent with models that do not include either a home base or food-sharing. Thus, while human sex roles are likely to have originated in the manner suggested, exactly when this occurred cannot be said with any certainty.

There are important differences between this scenario and the "coat-tails" and "apron strings" versions. In this theory, the activities of neither sex are devalued and neither sex is dependent on the other for the evolution of human characteristics, such as development of an upright stance, a large brain and language. Studies of the foraging activities of monkeys and apes, especially of how both sexes locate plants and insects and then extract the food with tools, indicate that both sexes of early hominids would have been subject to similar selection pressures.

It is clear, too, that as brains enlarged, necessitating a prolonged infancy period and hence greater immaturity of the young at birth, there was a greater need for a male contribution to infant care. This was probably a main feature of the gradual transition from *Homo erectus* to our own species, *Homo sapiens*, which began about 500,000 years ago. Changes in the female pelvis, which may have been linked to a reduction in the human gestation period from 11 to 9 months, are one of the features that marked the emer-

EVOLUTION DOES NOT EQUAL GOOD

■ *Is what evolution has produced (what is "natural") necessarily good? Not always. We readily learn to crave sugar, probably because of our fruit-eating ancestry. In our new environment offering an abundance of processed sugar, we are now suffering from unhealthy side-effects. By the same token, it is possible to consider that we might benefit from managing and modifying inherited patterns of social behavior, such as innate aggressive tendencies – or perhaps even a natural tendency, if there is one, for men and women to have sharply defined roles.*

138

▼ **The sexes have become more alike** *over 3 million years of evolution. "Australopithecus afarensis" males of 3 million years ago weighed about 65kg (145lb) and were about 1.5m (5ft) tall. This was twice the weight of the females, who were only about 1.2m (4ft) tall. "Homo erectus" (about 1.5 million years ago) was taller, though still shorter than modern humans – "Homo sapiens sapiens." In both of these later species, the difference in size between males and females is much less.*

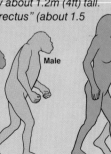

Female   Male

Australopithecus afarensis

Homo erectus

Homo sapiens sapiens

▲ **Male-female body-type differences** *(sexual dimorphism) are only slightly apparent in this view of modern humans. A female Japanese film star poses for photographers at the Cannes film festival while slender youths watch with interest.*

"Homo habilis," a meat-eater, may have been the direct ancestor of all humankind. Scavenging or hunting for meat was probably a male activity, but we cannot be sure how, or even if, the meat was divided among group members.

gencé of modern humans, *Homo sapiens sapiens*, between 50,000 and 100,000 years ago. The shorter gestation period would have meant even greater immaturity at birth, and greater dependence on both mothers and fathers.

Evolution versus culture

A notably common reaction to all these scenarios, especially among social scientists, has been to discount altogether the importance of evolution in the development of

sex roles. Most will agree that there is some form of division of labor by sex in all known societies. However, they claim that the origins of all these differences lie in certain common elements of human culture – where we live, what we eat, the way we rear our children. Culture itself is seen as a learned, shared system of behavior, beliefs and values, spread throughout the world through language and trade.

There are serious problems, however, in dividing the human animal in this way, into culture and nature. Chief among these is that while culture may grow and evolve at a rate independent of that for biological evolution, its growth and form are not independent of biological processes. Culture is very much a product of the human brain, whose learning processes, like our senses, are shaped and constrained by evolutionary pressures. A full understanding of ourselves therefore cannot exclude our evolutionary history.

It is also important to note that evolutionary theory need not, as we have seen, imply that there is an inherent inequality between the sexes, only that there is a difference in their roles.

It is only comparatively recently, some 10,000 years ago, with the beginnings of agriculture, that the economic role of women, and hence their political power, became diminished. With the advent of efficient, large-scale food production and storage, women stayed closer to home than in preagricultural days, while men gained greater opportunity for the acquisition of goods and political power. It is socio-economic history, not evolutionary history, that has introduced inequality in sex roles. There is nothing in our "nature" to justify it or to block change. **HDS**

▲ **Male and female body-types**. *Men have evolved a triangular torso, with broad shoulders and narrow hips, women an "hourglass" shape. With hips broader than waist, a woman is adapted to carry and give birth to a baby. Powerful musculature in men may well have arisen from a hunter's need for a strong throwing arm. Infants with a father able to protect the mother, especially during her vulnerable last months of pregnancy, would survive more easily. Female musculature is disguised by the extra layer of body fat under a woman's skin. If she loses this (for example, through excessive dieting or athletic training) she will become temporarily infertile. A man's "Adam's apple" arises from the larger male larynx, which also produces the deeper male voice. Body hair is more prominent in males.*

▲ **Social evolution** *and new technology have made strength less important in the division of labor by sex. Women are still concerned with child-rearing and men usually occupy the most prestigious jobs, but the borders between men's and women's roles have blurred.*

139

REPRODUCTION: MALE AND FEMALE STRATEGIES

■ *Producing and bringing up a child is hard work. It takes time, nutritional resources, money, and a great deal of effort. Generally we consider the effort worthwhile, because it gives us satisfaction, but it is also worthwhile in another sense. By investing resources in children, parents are able to ensure that copies of the genes they carry are transmitted to the next generation.*

"Parents" means a father and a mother. We have evolved from creatures that reproduced sexually. This ensured that their populations were buttressed against changing environments by genetic diversity. Instead of each member of a group being an identical clone of a single mother-ancestor, each individual was a uniquely different combination of inherited traits. When a new disease or a change of climate struck at a weak point in their makeup, our ancestors were not equally susceptible. Some survived and reproduced, because by luck they were adapted to the new circumstances.

Because human infants are relatively immature and helpless compared with those of other primates, they require a tremendous investment of time and energy in their early years. This may be the reason why, in our species, the usual pattern is for both parents to play a substantial part in caring for the children. Yet, however much men may share the responsibility, there are some biological facts which have made, and will always make, the parents' contribution to reproduction inevitably unequal.

WOMEN BEAR THE BURDEN

In mammalian species the female carries the burden of pregnancy and childbirth. Beyond these risks she must then nourish the offspring with her milk. In some societies, such as the Bushmen of the Kalahari, the children are

quite literally a burden, since the women have to carry them as they forage for plant foods, the most important part of their diet. This means that they cannot afford to have babies at frequent intervals, and the average interval between births is kept to about four years. This is accomplished partly by abortion and partly by the fact that an undernourished woman becomes infertile while breast-feeding, a stage that Bushmen mothers prolong.

MEN CAN FATHER MORE

Women's ability to reproduce is limited, by age (because the chances of becoming pregnant are low before the early teens and after the late forties) and by physiology (because ovulation occurs only once a month, and it takes at least nine months to produce a baby). The maximum number of births ever recorded for one woman is 69 (by an 18th-century Russian who had several sets of triplets and quadruplets). Men, however, are not so limited, and a powerful man who can monopolize many

women may be much more prolific. One Moroccan king is reputed to have fathered 1,056 children – though estimates vary.

MATING ADAPTATIONS

Human males might have evolved to impregnate many females indiscriminately. The ones who have most successfully transmitted copies of their genes to future generations, however, are those who have had a tendency to invest care and resources in one or more carefully selected wives and their children. This means that children have improved

chances of survival, and having a wife or wives reduces the risk that a man's sperm will have to compete with those of other men in a woman's reproductive tract. Men are known, in addition, sometimes to seek sexual novelty outside of marriage, and this may be a supplementary adaptation for reproduction. However, it will not result in surviving offspring nearly so often. In most societies, a woman reduced to prostitution cannot care as successfully for children and the sperm competing to join with her eggs are from many men. In affairs with married women, a man's sperm

▲ **Attraction to young women** *gives men a better chance of passing copies of their genes to future generations – young women have more reproductive potential. A relationship with an older partner is more common for women, especially when the man controls resources that she and her children need. Women are less impulsive than men in forming a relationship.*

▶ **Love of children**, *especially those we recognize as our own, is just as important an adaptation for reproductive success as our sex drive. A Bushman mother in southern Africa* TOP *and a Yanomamo father in Brazil* BOTTOM *display their commitment to their young. About 90 percent of children are genuinely offspring of the men who claim them.*

> *Do men and women have incompatible stakes in sex and reproduction? Infidelity may offer a woman or a man marginal opportunities for reproductive advantage, but the main evolutionary pressure is for stable procreative relationships.*

must compete with her husband's, which usually have an advantage – he normally sleeps with her more often and sperm survive for up to eight days.

Female extramarital sex, on the world scale, is almost as common as male extramarital sex (see p161). Husbands are often enough cuckolded that high sperm counts, as well as frequent sex, are a competitive adaptation for even a strictly monogamous male. Human sperm counts are almost three times those of the gorilla, a species in which a fertile female is effectively monopolized by one male. (Chimpanzees, which have a very promiscuous mating system, have nine times the sperm count of a gorilla.) The scrotum, a physiological trait that humans and chimpanzees share, aids storage of sperm, and thus high counts, by keeping the testes cooler than the internal body temperature. The human penis, at an average length of 13cm (5.3in), and the chimpanzee penis, at 8cm (3.2in), are both much longer than the gorilla's, at 4cm (1.6in). This enables human and chimpanzee sperm to be placed as close as possible to the eggs that they exist to fertilize.

Why should women, who need stable families in which to raise their children, have inherited any propensity to mate with more than one man? Several possibilities suggest themselves.

In about 10 percent of marriages, the husband has low fertility or is infertile. Over hundreds of generations, it is plausible to suppose that this situation would create an evolutionary disadvantage for women who were emotionally incapable of mating with anyone but their primary mate.

Increased genetic diversity in her children might also be a reproductive advantage to a woman. Just as whole populations are buttressed by genetic

diversity against extinction, so a woman will have more chances that copies of her genes will survive for generations to come, when, in her children, they are paired with sets from diverse males. Another advantage of multiple mating is that the woman may be drawn to a secondary mate whose genes are superior to her husband's and

offer better survival and reproductive prospects in offspring.

It has been speculated that women's pendulous breasts and the fact that they are always sexually receptive are adaptations to give the human female more control over her reproduction. In other species, pendulous breasts only appear when the female is nursing, and

they are a sign of infertility. Other primate females send specific sexual signals – eg a colorful swelling of skin in the anogenital area – during the fertile stage of their ovulation cycle. Thus it is harder for a human male than for a gorilla to know what is the precise moment when he should be guarding his mate most closely.

MATING CHOICES

In most societies, a woman who has extramarital sex risks the often violent jealousy of her husband and also serious social sanctions against female adultery. Often even women who have been raped are blamed for it. To guard against the possibility of female extramarital sex, some societies practice purdah - the veiling of women – not only literally, but by restricting their mobility in society.

On the whole, the risks and rewards of extramarital mating work out to be less favorable for women than for men. Because of this, and because females bear most of the burdens of reproduction, they have more to lose from making an unsuitable choice of mate. We would therefore expect them to be more choosy than males. Computer-dating studies have shown that women are much more inclined than men to evaluate their prospective partner carefully on a whole range of attributes (such as intelligence, status, religious views and background). The only attribute which did not seem to count was physical attractiveness. Similar considerations apply in arranged marriages, where the economic and social status of the prospective husband is the major concern in marrying off a daughter.

Men value attractiveness, youth and a good figure in the initial stages of finding a partner – characteristics that seem to predict reproductive potential. **PW**

141

Sexuality

YOUR sexual response to someone is not an automatic reaction. Unlike many animals, humans do not have a wholly inborn sexual reaction to specific sights or smells. Sexuality is largely learned. It is not only the result of your biology, but also of culture and your own personal history. Whether or not a certain sight, smell or activity is sexually arousing depends on three factors. First, it must fit the socially defined image of the sex you are attracted to. For example, a man is more likely to appear sexy to a woman if he acts and looks like her ideal of a man. Second, your own personal experiences add to your list of "What is arousing?" If you have had an exciting, satisfying sexual encounter on the beach, you are more likely to list beaches as exciting. Finally, circumstances influence how you feel. Nothing looks very attractive when you are in poor health, or tired or preoccupied with problems. To all of these variables, should we add, as well, that your sexual response depends on whether you are a man or a woman? Can you, by better understanding the differences and similarities between men and women, make sex more rewarding?

The neighboring sex: how we are the same

Imagine a naked man and naked woman. What parts of their bodies are you focusing on? Are you intrigued by their similarities: their eyes, ears, arms and legs? Or are you fascinated by the differences between them? Most of us appreciate the obvious sexual differences, but men and women are actually more alike than different. Biologically, we are more neighbors than opposites.

There are two reasons for the similarities. First, male and female sexual organs develop from the same type of body tissue. During prenatal development, the same tissue will become either the head of a penis or the head of a clitoris. It depends on whether there are high levels of male sex hormones (androgens) during prenatal development (see *Ch1*). For this reason, the penis and the clitoris share the same abundant number of nerve endings, and consequently both are very sensitive to touch. Other parts of the men's and women's reproductive systems also develop from the same types of body tissue: the scrotum and the outer lips of the vulva; the testes and the ovaries.

▲ **Sensuality in a sensual setting** *for holiday-makers in Spain. Our sexual response depends partly on our mood, including the effect that the setting and its associations has on our emotions.*

▶ **More alike than they are different**, *a man and a woman begin a sexual experience that is essentially the same for both. Through similar stages of excitement they rise to a climax that has no distinctively male or female claim on it.*

SEXUALITY

Much more than biology controls our response to sexually exciting situations and people. Sexual attitudes and behavior are heavily influenced by social norms, and they exaggerate the differences between a man's and a woman's sensuality.

The second reason why men and women are biologically similar is that there are parallel processes in male and female sexual functioning. The testes and the ovaries do the same work: both produce sex hormones as well as mature cells (sperm or ova) for reproduction. Both the head of the clitoris and the head of the penis are the central sensitive sites of sexual arousal; they both become erect when stimulated. Similarly, lubrication glands in both men and women become active during sexual arousal.

The two most important physiological responses that accompany sexual stimulation are the same for men and women. The first is *vasocongestion*, or the flow of blood to the penis or clitoris and surrounding tissue. This blood flow is the cause of erection in both males and females. The second is *myotonia*, or the increasing tension in muscles, primarily in the pelvic region. It is the rapid contraction of these muscles that creates an orgasm. These two events –

erection and orgasm – are similar for men and women because the organs involved in these processes are similar.

Research has found that the sexual response cycle is very similar for men and women, and many old myths have been dispelled. Women, for example, need no longer be misled by their boyfriends who assure them that if a man is sexually aroused and does not experience the release of orgasm, he will be in pain. Discomfort is a better description than pain, and women have the same experience as men: sexual arousal without the release of orgasm feels uncomfortable. With the rapid muscle contractions of orgasm, the blood flows rapidly from the pelvic area, causing a warm sensation. If there is no orgasm, both men and women will be uncomfortable while the blood slowly recedes.

The experience of orgasm appears to be very similar for both women and men. Consider these descriptions:

"My orgasms feel like pulsating bursts of energy starting in my pelvic area and then engulfing my whole body."

"An orgasm feels like a dive, magnified many times over."

"Throbbing is the best word. The throbbing starts as a faint vibration, then builds up in wave after wave where time seems to stand still."

"There is a warm rush from my toes to my head, a strong pulsing rhythm."

143

▲ **Mature love**. *Sexual activity is greater in the early stages of a marriage or other sexual relationship, but declining frequency is not a result of physical changes that come with aging. The novelty of sex may wear off, and other demands, such as young children and stressful careers may rechannel our energies. Couples are sexually active throughout the age-range, and may become more active at a later, more relaxed time of life.*

Men too are capable of multiple orgasms. Orgasm is the rapid contraction of pelvic muscles. It is not necessarily accompanied by an ejaculation. Men can learn to delay ejaculation during a series of increasingly intense sexual climaxes.

The first and last were by women, the other two by men.

Indeed it is only by appreciating how alike we are, in the way our bodies work, that we can begin to understand what the other person feels during sexual activity. "I know how good this feels to me when you do this, and so now I understand how good this feels to you when I do the same."

The opposite sex: how we are different

Similarities, however, are not the whole story. Men and women also differ in the ways their bodies work.

Although orgasm is the same for men and women, only men ejaculate. This is the release of semen and usually it occurs when a man has an orgasm. But a man can ejaculate without having an orgasm – for example, during a medical examination in response to a doctor massaging the prostate gland, or have an orgasm without ejaculating because previous ejaculations have used up his supply of semen.

Contrary to some reports, women do not ejaculate. In recent years a lot of publicity has been given to scientists who claim that there is a sensitive area within the vagina that is similar to men's prostate glands. Stimulation of this "Grafenburg spot" (G-spot) may cause an urge to urinate, and further stimulation may then cause the woman to have an orgasm and release fluids. Hence, the "female ejaculation." The evidence for this is weak. First, only a small percentage of women report an ejaculation-like experience. Second, there is disagreement about the type of fluid released by these few women. Some laboratories claim that the fluid resembles seminal fluid without sperm, while others claim that it more closely resembles urine. The most that such research can claim is that a few women may release a fluid during orgasm, but this is not common.

Men experience a "refractory period" – a period of time after ejaculation when they cannot be sexually aroused. This is usually brief, lasting 2 to 30 minutes. It tends to increase with age, and in some men it can even be as long as 24 hours. With most men it varies, depending on their prior experiences and expectations, their health and fatigue, and their relationship with their partners. Women do not have a refractory period; with effective stimulation, they can therefore enjoy a rapid sequence of orgasms. However, some women find further stimulation painfully intense, because of the heightened sensitivity of the clitoris.

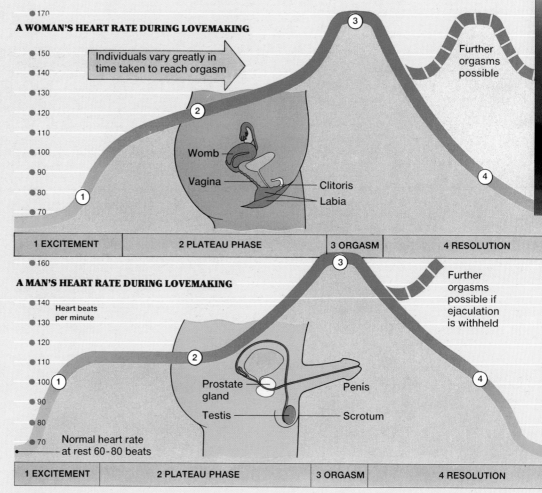

THE SEXUAL RESPONSE

1 *Blood flows into the pelvic region. Penis and clitoris become erect. The vagina lubricates and expands, as the womb enlarges. The testes enlarge and elevate, and the labia swell and become erect. Nipple erection occurs in women and some men. The breasts enlarge.*

2 *Muscle tension increases. The erect clitoris retracts beneath a hood. The penis becomes more fully erect. Its head increases in size and may deepen in color. The labia become fully erect and deepen in color. Testes continue to increase in size, and lubrication fluid is released through the penis.*

3 *Rapid involuntary spasms of the pelvic region, including contractions of the womb. The prostate gland contracts, releasing fluids that mix with sperm. Ejaculation occurs as rapid muscle contractions force semen out of the penis.*

4 *The body returns to normal.*

A WOMAN'S HEART RATE DURING LOVEMAKING

170 · 150 · 140 · 130 · 120 · 110 · 100 · 90 · 80 · 70

Individuals vary greatly in time taken to reach orgasm

Womb · Vagina · Clitoris · Labia

Further orgasms possible

| 1 EXCITEMENT | 2 PLATEAU PHASE | 3 ORGASM | 4 RESOLUTION |

A MAN'S HEART RATE DURING LOVEMAKING

160 · 140 · 130 · 120 · 110 · 100 · 90 · 80 · 70

Heart beats per minute

Normal heart rate at rest 60-80 beats

Prostate gland · Testis · Penis · Scrotum

Further orgasms possible if ejaculation is withheld

| 1 EXCITEMENT | 2 PLATEAU PHASE | 3 ORGASM | 4 RESOLUTION |

Due to the absence of the refractory period that a man experiences after ejaculation, women have the capacity to have multiple orgasms – two to six within a sexual encounter. Not all women experience them. It depends on their individual preferences and effective stimulation.

Men do not usually have multiple orgasms, but they are capable of them – because orgasm and ejaculate are separate processes. Orgasm is the very rapid contraction of muscles, and ejaculation is the release of semen. Learning and expectations are central to the expression of sexual desire, and generally they associate orgasm with ejaculation, but sex researchers have found that men of various ages have learned to focus on maintaining excitement, rather than focusing on quickly achieving a final orgasm-ejacula-

▲ **Building excitement**. *On average, women reach an orgasm after eight minutes of sexual intercourse. Since the penis is usually more directly stimulated than the clitoris, men may reach orgasm more quickly. However, orgasms are more intense if they are delayed, and through control and practice, a man can learn to build up by progressively stronger non-ejaculatory orgasms to a final, intensely felt one.*

CLITORAL OR VAGINAL ORGASM?

■ *The clitoral orgasm/vaginal orgasm controversy began with Freud. He viewed the clitoris as an inadequate substitute for a penis, and decreed that women who relied on stimulation of the clitoris for sexual pleasure were immature. A mature woman, he said, relied on stimulation of the vagina by her male partner's penis as the primary means of sexual pleasure.*

The view that there were two different types of orgasms – clitoral or vaginal – was supported by actual clinical reports that only some women have orgasms during intercourse. It was further supported by women's own reports that orgasms stimulated by manual or oral contact felt different from those during intercourse.

Research shows, however, that the clitoris is the center of sexual arousal and nerve activity, regardless of the method of stimulation. When a woman has an orgasm during intercourse, it is because the thrusting of the penis pulls the inner lips of the vulva, rubbing the clitoris. It is even the center of sexual arousal for those few women who can achieve orgasm from breast stimulation alone.

Why then do orgasms during intercourse feel different from those during other types of stimulation? It is because orgasm is the very rapid contraction of the pelvic floor muscles. During intercourse these muscles are contracting around a penis, and cannot contract as much as they can when nothing is within the vagina.

tion. When they feel that ejaculation is near, they stop thrusting and let the rapid muscle contractions of orgasm happen. After a brief pause (15-20 seconds), they resume thrusting. They repeat this as many times as they desire (reportedly up to 25!) and then ejaculate with the last orgasm.

Another difference between men and women is that men have orgasms more consistently than women. Men have orgasms almost every time they have sexual intercourse, while women average only 50 to 75 percent. These statistics may seem surprising, in view of the evidence we have on male-female similarities, but they draw our attention to the fact that our most important sex organ is the brain. It is the brain that absorbs the following lessons of our culture, and these are so consistent that they seem, mistakenly, to be dictated by nature:

Men are sexual; women are sex objects.
Men need sexual release to be healthy; sex is something women do to please men.
Men's urges initiate a sexual encounter; women's role is to say "yes" or "no."
A man's orgasm signals the end of sexual intercourse; since the woman is only there for the man's pleasure, her orgasms are less relevant.

These messages are taught in novels, movies, songs, folk wisdom and jokes. It is not surprising then that women have orgasms less consistently than men. Men and women enter the bedroom with different expectations.

Along with this, there is the common experience that, compared to men, women are slow to reach orgasm. There is a time difference, however, only during intercourse. When masturbating, women control the stimulation, and they reach orgasm just as rapidly as men. During intercourse, however, women are likely to need more stimulation than men, because the stimulation of the clitoris is indirect rather than direct.

Do men desire more novelty?

Men are said to find the prospect of a new partner more exciting than women do. If this is true, biology *might* be the reason. It is sometimes argued that men are naturally adapted to opportunistic reproduction of their genes by mating with as many different women as they can, while women are adapted to establishing stable relationships that will provide a sound base for child care. However, males also gain reproductive advantages from stable families for their children. In addition, men like to know that they are the fathers of the children they support and help to care for. For both of these reasons, male-dominated societies have ample motives for teaching women that it is unwomanly to be excited by the prospect of a new partner (see p140).

An exclusively male instinct for sexual opportunity has been suggested as an explanation of why men love to look at erotic pictures, while women hate them. However, both women and men enjoy, and become sexually excited by, pictures and stories of sexual activity. Another mistaken belief is that men enjoy pictures or descriptions of genitally focused sexual activity, but women enjoy them only if some romance is involved. Research shows that both men and women are aroused by descriptions and pictures of genital caresses – with or without romance. Also, both women and

▶ **Aiming at a male eye,** a Hong Kong nightclub advertises the sights within. Men are more easily aroused by displays of female availability, women by erotic pictures that include participants with whom they can identify. Research shows that romance does not have to be an element in pictures that stimulate female arousal, but it must be possible to imagine the woman in the scene being valued as a person.

Men's and women's fantasies are not equally well addressed by available erotic material. Perhaps the signs on the pornography shops of the future will read "For Men Only" and "For Women Only" instead of "For Adults Only."

men are more aroused by pictures or descriptions of women being touched than by pictures or descriptions of naked men. This is because both men and women learn that women are the sex objects in our culture. When viewing pornography, men are aroused by images of women because the women represent their objects of desire. Women are aroused because they see themselves as the woman in the picture.

Why is it then that almost all pornography is bought by

men? Because it is designed by men for men. The majority of the material appeals solely to men's fantasies, concentrating on the story of "Man conquers woman," using different settings and a variety of storylines. The women are conquered by the man's amazing organ or by his amazing skill. Women do not find this exciting. To be aroused, they have to be able to project themselves into the scene ("That's my thigh he's rubbing.")

In most pornography, women are portrayed as victims. They are dominated, degraded and abused. For most women, that is not arousing. What they like is erotica – stories that show people caring, loving, caressing, with an equal sharing in the touch and pleasure.

Men's and women's different emotional responses to erotic materials really indicate a difference in their primary fantasies. These fantasies are not equally addressed by current pornography. As long as men and women have different sexual scripts, they will have different fantasies and will, consequently, find different stories or images sexually arousing. Perhaps the signs on pornography shops of the future will read: "For Men Only" and "For Women Only" instead of "For Adults Only."

The pursuer and the gatekeeper

Many of the differences between the sexuality of men and women are not the result of biological differences, but of the the sex roles imposed on them.

Successful achievement at work means getting a lot while giving a little; so it is not surprising that the man brings the same philosophy to his personal relationships. To be successful in a sexual encounter, a man must achieve an erec-

▲ **The female form** *can be admired for its sheer beauty, and this is distinct from feeling a sexual response. To be attractive to your partner, it is more important to cultivate a positive self-image and the behavior that goes with it than it is to be handsome or beautiful.*

▶ **Aiming at a female eye,** *a male striptease artist practices his craft. Men will pay money to sit silently in a dark room watching a woman remove her clothing, but only the audience-participation style of male striptease has proved a commercial success.*

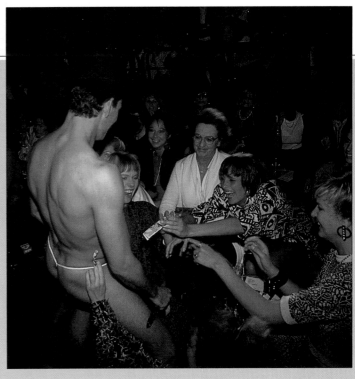

147

tion and orgasm. Others scathingly condemn a man when he does not perform "like a man" sexually. We call him impotent, which means powerless. As it is the man's role to be the aggressive initiator, he selects the woman, asks for the date, decides the time and place and makes the first moves toward physical contact. A man is taught to be the pursuer in everything from first eye contact to first orgasm. He aggressively pursues his goal in spite of the woman's objections. He has learned to "not take no for an answer."

While the primary message to men is to achieve, the primary message to women is: "You're nobody till some-

body loves you." Even in these liberated days, in several ways our culture encourages women to establish their identity by establishing a relationship with a man: the majority of women still change their last names when they marry, and most forms that we fill out still request that you designate "Mr," "Miss" or "Mrs." It seems important to know if a woman is married or single – even if she is just registering her bicycle.

A woman is most likely to "get a man" if she fits his expectations. She must be sensitive to the needs of others, yielding, soft-spoken and affectionate. Yet she must play a double role. She must be soft and yielding enough to attract the man's attention, but then she must keep him at a distance and fulfill a gatekeeper role. Having aroused a sexual desire, she must say, "No."

She must remain mindful that what she wants from the man is commitment. This exchange of sexuality for commitment has been, and remains, part of our sex roles. So, as he pursues her, she keeps the gate closed. Slowly they dance, trading small commitments ("Want to go out again next Saturday?") for small sexual favors (kissing, then deep kissing, then fondling). If the partners continue to dance, this pattern will culminate in an emotional and sexual climax.

A quick way to appreciate the effect of sex roles on personal relationships is to consider the two phrases, "she got a man," and "he got a woman." They may sound the same, but we all know they mean different things, and these different meanings reflect the sex roles. The first indicates commitment, the second sexual scoring.

■ **Playing a double role.** *RIGHT A woman must be yielding enough and make herself attractive enough to win a man's sexual attention. TOP But she is expected to be the less eager of the two – mindful that what she wants from the man is commitment. The division of roles into male pursuit and female resistance are often difficult to shed when the couple become sexual partners. This can be an obstacle to mutual satisfaction.*

"She got a man," and "He got a woman." These phrases have the same grammar but different meanings. The first is about winning a commitment and the second is about sexual scoring. They reflect a fundamental sex-role division.

Just as, physiologically, women and men are more alike than different, this is probably also true psychologically. Both women and men want exciting, passionate sex as well as the stability of a long-term relationship grounded in love and respect. Yet, ironically, the woman who displays passivity to attract a man may then find that this passivity makes it difficult for her to teach him what excites her sexually. A man may attract a woman because he is a powerful, aggressive initiator; but this very quality makes it difficult for him to enjoy sex when she takes the initiative in love-making. Thus the very sex roles that make us attractive to one another are also the same sex roles that make it difficult for us to be successful sexual partners.

Enhancing sexual pleasure

What can we learn from the experts to increase sexual pleasure? A starting point is to recognize that good communication makes for better sex. It is by talking to each other that two people develop intimacy. As we share ideas and humor, we feel emotionally close. Our desire to touch each other increases. Some problems come, however, when we start making love. Far too often we focus on our own performance. "Am I taking too long?" "Am I lubricating enough?" "Will I get an erection?" "Will I be able to have an orgasm?" The very goals of pleasure and orgasm are thwarted by this critical self-monitoring. Rather than enjoying our sensations, we sabotage our own pleasure. To over-

come this pattern of self-monitoring, sex therapists recommend *sensate focus* exercises.

Our hands have more nerve endings than our genitals, and the sensations we receive when we touch our partner can be a powerful source of pleasure and sexual arousal. Sensate focusing means taking our attention away from mental self-monitoring and shifting it to the physical sensations from our own hands and from those parts of our body that are being touched.

The first step is to take turns touching each other, but at this stage avoid touching each other's genitals or breasts.

▲ **Unwanted attention.** *Culture and individual personality all affect how aggressively a man will pursue his sexual demands and how much respect he will pay to a woman's signals that she wants to be left alone. Most cultures expect women to avoid placing themselves in situations where they may become objects of unwanted attention – for instance, not going out at night without a male protector. These patterns give women less social freedom than men.*

HOMOSEXUALITY

■ *Throughout history a small percentage (estimates range from 4 to 14 percent) of people have been attracted to people of the same sex. Exact statistics are difficult to obtain because in most cultures homosexuality has been viewed as an unacceptable form of sexual expression. Open acceptance of homosexuality as an alternative lifestyle is still uncommon except in large cities, partly because it is so hard for heterosexuals to understand the homosexual point of view. Ask a few heterosexual men why they are attracted to women. They'll probably mumble something about "...because it's natural" or "...because I'm a man." Heterosexual women's answers sound similar. Most people cannot explain why they feel attracted to the people who excite them. The same is true for homosexual men and women. They do not know why they feel attracted to people of the same sex – they just are. There is not even agreement on what causes homosexuality. The theory most favored by homosexual activists is a biological one: their sexual orientation has been set since birth, as a result of genetic determination or prenatal development, rather than consciously selected. A higher than average tendency toward homosexuality has been found among women who were accidentally exposed to excess levels of hormones while still in the womb. However, not all homosexuality can be explained in this way and about 50 percent of the women*

exposed to masculinizing hormones are exclusively heterosexual (see Ch1). Psychological theories have attempted to link homosexuality to various parent-child patterns: a domineering mother and an absent or passive father; an indifferent mother and emotionally expressive father; parents who were emotionally unresponsive; and parents who were emotionally too responsive. Others suggest that homosexuality is learned, by early pleasurable homosexual experiences or by early frightening heterosexual experiences. None of these theories, however, are supported by systematic analyses of homosexual men's and women's childhood experiences. Many people change their sexual expression over their lifetime. Is homosexuality then a biological predestination or a conscious choice? How large a role do parents play? We do not know. Nor do we know what causes heterosexuality. What we do know is that homosexual women are more likely than homosexual men to establish a long-term committed relationship. Homosexual men are much more likely than homosexual women or heterosexual men and women to have brief sexual encounters. These patterns fit the same sex-role stereotypes as those of heterosexuals. Women seek commitment and men seek to avoid commitment. There is much speculation that the threat of AIDS will change these patterns; but so far there is no clear evidence of such a trend.

While touching, focus on the textures, contours, shapes of your partner's body. There is no specific goal to the touching – this is not touch-as-massage or touch-as-sexual-arousal. You focus on the pleasurable sensations in your hands – the different feeling of body hair and skin on your partner's back, neck and abdomen, while your partner focuses on the pleasure of this stimulation. Then it is your turn to be touched.

Do this for several evenings before moving on to step two. And, most important, while in this way you are learning more about the pleasures of your own and of each other's bodies, intercourse is not allowed.

The second step is again to take turns touching each other, but this time include each other's genitals and breasts. However, they should not be the starting point. Begin by taking turns at general touching, as in the first step, perhaps with the woman sitting between the man's legs with her back to his chest, so that he can easily touch many parts of her body. When it is his turn, he can lie down while the woman faces him, sitting cross-legged between his legs with his legs draped over her knees. As before, when you are touching, focus on the pleasurable sensations from your hands, and the fun of exploring the shapes and textures of your partner's body, with no demands for sexual arousal. When you are being touched, focus on the pleasure of being touched. You can silently communicate your preferences by

APHRODISIACS – DO THEY WORK?

■ Is there a sure-fire, guaranteed ambrosia that will increase your sexual desire and powers, and bring new heights of passion and ecstasy? The pursuit of this dream sends thousands of people out to purchase an amazing range of potions, powders and perfumes sold as aphrodisiacs.

There are exotic products: ground reindeer antlers, ginseng root, rhinoceros horn, animal testes, turtle eggs and Spanish fly (cantharides) – prepared from dried green blister beetles. More common items include alcohol, perfumes with musk, oysters, room deodorizers, liquid incense and chocolate. There are prescription drugs: PCPA, L-Dopa, bromocriptine mesylate, papaverine hydrochloride and naloxone – and street drugs: marijuana, MDMA ("Ecstasy"), LSD, barbiturates, cocaine, Quaaludes, amphetamines and amylnitrite ("poppers").

Do they work? Despite the money spent, none of these will increase your sexual desire or power – unless you believe they will. Most of them are harmless. Ginseng root, for example, provides some vitamins, but it does not increase sexual desire, except for the increase that may be caused by relaxation. Most of the prescription drugs have no effect on people who are healthy. The reported effect of increasing sexual desire is probably a side-effect created in patients who are feeling some relief from their painful symptoms. The perfumes with animal pheromones are interesting in that they seem to heighten attraction, but they do not trigger irresistible desire in humans.

Some preparations are dangerous. Spanish fly irritates and inflames sensitive mucous membranes. The "joke" in the fraternity house is to slip some Spanish fly into a girl's drink, and she will become your willing partner, eager for your strong penis to scratch the itch within her vagina. Actually, the "itch" is a painful irritation in both men and women. Deaths have been reported, due to kidney failure or convulsions, after large doses of Spanish fly. Street and prescription drugs can upset the delicate balance of hormones in our bodies, and can create dangerous side effects. Long-term use of alcohol, cocaine, barbiturates and narcotics can completely suppress sexual desire. High doses of amphetamines can weaken blood-vessels and decrease the flow of signals to and from the brain. Some of the items sold as aphrodisiacs appear to enhance sexuality because they reduce inhibitions, but this reduction in inhibition is accompanied by a reduction in erection and lubrication in both men and women. In Shakespeare's words, alcohol "provokes the desire, but it takes away the performance." The same is true of the hallucinogens (LSD and marijuana). Also, these drugs actually reduce sensations from the skin rather than intensifying them.

150

You may read that the average couple has sexual intercourse 2.8 times a week, but do beware of equating frequency with fun – this is the way to turn sex from enjoyment into work. Every couple has its own happiest level of performance.

placing a hand on your partner's to guide movement and intensity of touch. But this hand-guiding is a suggestion, not a demand; the touch is to be guided by the toucher's interests, not by the receiver's preferences. This step is very important, and deserves several sessions.

The third step is to progress to touching each other at the same time. As you touch each other, concentrate on the pleasures received by touching, as well as those received from being touched. Do not worry about "Am I doing OK?" The goal is "getting lost in the touch" – both the giving and receiving. Focus on the sensations for several evenings before moving on. Intercourse is still for later.

The fourth step is to continue the methods of step three, but with the woman straddling the man while he lies on his back. This position allows the man to relax, and allows the woman to play with his penis, to rub it on her breasts, vulva, and even to insert the head of the penis into the vagina. You are advised to practice this focus on mutual touch for a few evenings before proceeding to full sexual intercourse.

Sex as work

There is a tendency to make our fun into work: to swim the most lengths, to ski on the highest mountain or to win the tennis match. Activities that were originally undertaken for pleasure become subject to the same standards of performance that we use to judge our work. Sometimes, with disastrous results, we even bring this competitive attitude into the bedroom. For example, you may read in a magazine that after five years of marriage, the average couple has

sexual intercourse 2.8 times per week. Do you begin to wonder if you are above or below the average? One danger of sex research is that the findings often become the new standards of performance. But do not confuse frequency with fun. Look carefully at the research. Does it count as sexual intercourse if the man orgasms but the woman does not? And what if neither has an orgasm, but they both had fun? All too often we talk about sexuality in the way we talk about workers in a factory. Lovers are adequate, the stimulation is effective, and the orgasms are tallied as part of the week's products. In this language, sex is a task, rather than a pleasurable pastime. Orgasms become the goal, rather than a joyful, slow rise of excitement. Both women and men have orgasms more rapidly during masturbation than during sexual intercourse. Yet most women and men prefer sexual intercourse, and they prefer intercourse with someone they love. It is clear that the number of orgasms is not the primary measure of sexual pleasure. The process of arousal and the pleasure of touching and being touched are more important than the product of orgasm. **EC**

▲ **The unhurried approach** *to love-making is the most rewarding approach.*

151

▶ **Stages in sensate focusing.** *To take the mind away from worries about performance, sex therapists recommend practice at shifting attention to physical sensation instead, concentrating on the hands, since these are our most sensitive organs of touch. Each stage should be practiced for several evenings.*

◀ **The only true aphrodisiac** *is the mind. The most powerful sexual enhancer is belief – our belief in the power of a drug, the power of moonlight, or the power of love.*

4 With the woman straddling the man, who lies relaxed on his back, allow each other to enjoy unhurried mutual genital touching.

3 Touch each other at the same time. Lose yourself in the pleasure of giving and receiving touch.

2 Without demanding sexual arousal, focus on the pleasure of being touched, including touching of the genitals.

1 Take turns feeling the pleasurable sensations that the textures, contours and shapes of the other's body can create in your hands.

Attitudes to Love

IS LOVE different for men and women? It is commonly believed that women are the romantic sex, and that men want to "love them and leave them." But is this really so? Studies have compared how much men and women love and like their partners, how romantic they are and how likely they are to take the initiative in ending a relationship. The results of these studies do not support common stereotypes.

Sex differences in love and liking

Student couples were asked to complete a questionnaire designed to measure how much they loved each other. They answered yes or no to such statements as "It would be hard for me to get along without X" (indicating emotional attachment), "I would do anything for X" (indicating caring and commitment), "I feel I can confide in X about virtually anything" (indicating intimacy). They were also asked to complete a questionnaire designed to show how much they liked each other – with statements such as "I think X is one of those people that quickly win respect." Some very interesting differences between the sexes became apparent. Men and women love their partners equally well, but there is often a difference in how much they like them, because women make a clearer distinction than men between love and liking. Men who rate their partners high on love tend to rate them high on liking too. Women more often rate a partner high on love, but not as high on liking, or high on liking but not as high on love. Indeed, many men find it positively

difficult to accept a woman as a friend without having her as a lover, while women are very ready to have close male friends with whom they are not sexually intimate. It also seems that men are more likely to link love with sex, so that it is hard for men to be emotionally close to a woman and not have sex, while women can appreciate emotional closeness that has nothing to do with sex.

This difference between the sexes in love and liking not only creates different expectations in their relationships with the other sex, it also causes problems in their relationships with same-sex friends. Since men associate strong liking with love, and love in turn with sex, it is hard for them to feel emotionally close to other men without considering this to be homosexual. Women, however, can feel close to another woman without sensing a sexual involvement.

How does love develop?

We can think of relationships in terms of "social exchange." In a social exchange, you do a favor for a friend, and your friend does a favor in return. This sounds like economic exchange, but it differs from it in several important respects. Economic exchange usually involves only tangible, or at least well-defined, commodities such as goods and definite services, while social exchange can also include highly intangible social gestures and expressions of feeling. Also, in economic matters the conditions of exchange are spelled out in advance. You know exactly what you must do in return, and when – such as pay so much

◀ **An exchange of affection** such as this could easily be interpreted in typically different ways by the man and woman involved. He might view it as a token of love entailing physical desire, and so automatically see it as part of the prelude to sexual intercourse. She might regard it as a token of love in the sense simply of emotional closeness, with no thought of sex. If their expectations do – and continue to – reflect this difference, their relationship will inevitably run into difficulties.

For most women, liking, loving and having sex are separate ideas that need not entail one another. But for many men, even the idea of forming a close friendship with a woman is inseparable from the idea of becoming her lover.

money on delivery. In contrast, social exchanges involve "unspecified obligations." When you invite someone to dinner, you expect them to invite you back in return, at some time. But you do not say, "I'll have you over for roast beef on Saturday, if you will invite me for salmon on Sunday." Specifying the obligations changes the relationship from a social one to a commercial one – just as paying a prostitute a specified amount of money defines the transaction as one based on economics instead of mutual interest and concern.

In love affairs, what are exchanged are feelings of love. Even the selfless love of a mother is based on the desire for something in return – the love of the child. We may not like to think of love affairs (or even friendships) as being based on exchange. But the way we judge whether or not someone still loves (or likes) us is by asking ourselves the question, "What has he done for me lately?"

The key to these unspecified obligations is trust. You trust that your friend will eventually do a favor in return, so you need not worry about when. You trust that your lover will demonstrate love in return in some way, so you need not specify how. But when relationships first begin, you do not know whether you can trust the other person. When you offer a favor to a potential new friend, the offer might be rejected. Or the favor might be accepted, but the other person

might not reciprocate. Similarly, when you offer love to another person, you risk rejection or lack of love in return.

So love affairs, like friendships, typically start out slowly. You offer a few rewards, and if they are accepted and reciprocated, then you feel some trust and are willing to offer more. As long as the other person keeps reciprocating, the relationship continues to develop. This has two important implications.

First, the process of developing trust (and the intimacy allowed by trust) typically takes time. As a result, people

■ **What keeps love alive**? *Although romantic "love" (infatuation) and altruistic "love" (self-sacrificing benevolence) are, for a while at least, self-sustaining, the key to enduring love relationships is reciprocity: a constant exchange of emotional and economic "gifts" and "favors" to the satisfaction of both partners. Fundamental to mutual love in most circumstances are small signs of affection, trust and regard, exchanged with spontaneous warmth, as LEFT. If the scene ABOVE epitomizes this couple's relationship, love is unlikely to bloom.*

build up investments of time, effort and emotion in their love affairs. Giving up those investments makes ending a relationship difficult, even if it is no longer as rewarding as they would wish. We see evidence of this in the reactions of people who have recently been divorced. In interviews, divorcees typically have very ambivalent feelings. They are glad the marriage is over, but they miss their former partner too – they want the former intimacy, but still cannot bear living together (see Ch 19).

Second, love affairs cannot progress if they become too one-sided. The relationship may continue for a while, as the one that is more committed makes extra efforts to get equal commitment from the other partner. But the effort comes at a cost. Eventually, the former will begin to feel exploited, or the latter will tire of the pressure to become more committed – and one or the other will try to end the relationship.

When break-ups occur

As love affairs are private matters, then you would expect them to end whenever the two persons decide that they should go their separate ways. But in a study of university students, it became clear that there were certain specific times of year when couples were especially likely break up – September/October, December/January and May/June. These times correspond with the beginning and end of classes, when changes occur that are quite external to the relationship. External events appear to affect breakups in two ways.

First, they raise issues about the relationship. During the break-up months, students need to make decisions about their class schedules, their jobs and their living arrangements. These decisions, in turn, have implications for their dating relationship and vice versa. "Should we coordinate our class schedules?" "Should I take a summer job in another town, or should we try to stay together?" These are times when it is necessary to decide whether or not the relationship is worth extra effort to keep it going.

Second, external events make it easier to call off a relationship. They provide convenient excuses. It is easier to say, "While we're apart over the vacation, we ought to date others," than it is to say, "I've grown tired of you, and don't want to see you again." In addition, the external changes make it easier to meet potential alternative partners, and this reduces the risk of not finding a new partner should the old relationship end.

While the particular break-up months found for these students might not apply to those who are not at university, the same principles are likely to apply. A change of jobs or living arrangements could affect the timing of a break-up, whatever the month.

The need for external factors to ease break-ups is underscored by the finding that rarely were they completely mutual. In one survey, it was only in 7 percent of break-up cases that both former partners reported that they were equally interested in ending the relationship. The ambivalence involved in ending a relationship is compounded by feelings of guilt and embarrassment arising from the knowledge that the other does not want it to happen.

Sex differences in breaking up

The stereotype is that it is the man who cold-heartedly "loves" a woman then leaves her. Perhaps this applies to sex (not love) in a one-night stand, but it is not the case in loving relationships. It is, of course, often difficult to identify which partner is breaking away. Both men and women tend to say, "I wanted it to end," or "It was mutual," instead of

▶ **Student romances,** *intensely felt as they usually are by both partners, seldom outlast student days – and often founder during vacations when, it seems, temporary separation gives time for reflection and does not necessarily make the heart grow fonder. In relationships in which both partners perceive each other as about equal in status and desirability, it is the more practically-minded girl who is likelier to call it off. The extent to which the spread of AIDS will inhibit student experiments in premarital sex, in the long run, is still a matter of conjecture.*

Men may be proverbial lovers and leavers of women, but research shows that women are more tough-minded than men in assessing their love relationships, more likely to initiate a break-up, and more resilient after the parting.

saying that their partner no longer wanted them. This serves to protect self-esteem. Nonetheless, research has shown that women are somewhat more likely than men to say, "I wanted it to end." In addition, they report more relationship problems than men. Women do seem to be the more sensitive to what is happening in relationships, and they have more influence in determining their outcome.

It has also been shown that rejected men have more difficulty coping emotionally with the break-up than women in the same situation. Men become more depressed and lonely, and they also have a harder time remaining friends with their former partner after the break-up. Their upbringing teaches them to avoid expressing their emotions, but they are more vulnerable than their tough facade leads us to expect. In contrast, a girl's upbringing encourages women to concern themselves with personal relationships, and so they learn to manage their emotions better than men.

LOVE AND PREMARITAL SEX

■ Research studies with American students revealed three different attitudes to premarital sex. Some people felt that premarital sex was wrong, and avoided it even if they were in love. For instance, one man admitted that he wanted to have sex, but his partner did not, and out of love for her he did not try to insist. These people were called the Sexual Traditionalists. In contrast, the Sexual Moderates felt that premarital sex was acceptable provided that you were in love. For them, intercourse marked a stage of increased commitment

in their relationship. Finally, the Sexual Liberals felt that sex with someone you love was great, but that sex was also acceptable with someone with whom you are not in love. To them, sex

was a means of developing emotional closeness. Because of these differing orientations there were therefore couples who were having sex because they were in love, couples

having sex even though they were not in love, couples avoiding sex because they were not in love, and couples avoiding sex even though they were in love.

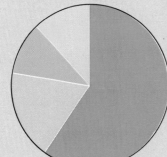

▼ **Male premarital sex** – how widespread it is in over 100 different cultures surveyed.

- Very common
- Fairly common
- Fairly uncommon
- Uncommon

▶ **Female premarital sex** – how widespread it is in over 100 cultures surveyed around the world.

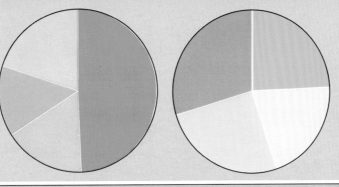

◀ **Social attitudes toward female participation in premarital sex** – as reflected in a survey of nearly 150 cultures around the world.

- Approval
- Tolerance
- Moderate disapproval
- Strong disapproval

WHICH SEX IS MORE ROMANTIC?

■ *Since women read romantic novels more than men, people think that women are more romantic than men. Actually, this probably reflects the differences between men and women in their attitudes toward sex. As we have seen, women associate love with emotional closeness while men tie it more closely to sex. In sexual activity, women want to cuddle, while men want to proceed to what they consider the "main event." But when it comes to positive endorsement of romantic ideals, are women really more* romantic? In one study in the United States, male and female students were asked if they disagreed or agreed with statements such as, "To be truly in love is to be in love forever," and "As long as they at least love each other, two people should have no trouble getting along together in marriage." Significantly, men were more likely to agree with these romantic ideas than women. But, of course, having romantic ideals does not necessarily translate into romantic behavior.

▲ **A woman's greater practical-mindedness** *in approaching marriage is probably connected with her biological role. Most women who foresee themselves bearing children and assuming primary responsibility for their nurture in circumstances of dependence on a partner are likely to take a longer-term view of their partner's potential for contributing to family well-being.*

WHERE DO ROMANTIC NOTIONS COME FROM?

■ We tend to surround our customs with myth and ritual, in order to give them meaning. To "explain" love and to teach it to children, we have borrowed romantic notions from the art of courtly love which developed in the 12th century. Many of the men in attendance then at the royal courts in Europe had little else to do but write poetry and love songs to win the favor of young women. This courtship had little to do with winning sexual favors, and even less to do with marriage. Indeed, at the time, it was believed that marriage killed romance. Since marriage was based on duties and obligations, how could passion survive in such an institution? Some of the ideas about romantic love were incorporated into fairy tales which have been passed down through the generations. When we began selecting our own marriage partners based on "love," we used these fairy tales to explain how love works.

▲ **"Got my man!"** *Wedding days traditionally belong to the bride. While both partners gain a mate, companion and caregiver, the bride who also gains the security of an economic base has a double reason for celebration. Although times are changing, most men still expect to be the family's chief income-earner and provider; most women still expect to be in charge of raising the children and, if earners at all, to be secondary earners.*

Women are more practically-minded than men when choosing a marriage partner. This may be one of the reasons why partners who "marry for love" today tend to be as much like each other as they were when marriages were arranged.

Is love blind?

For centuries, marriages were arranged by parents. They were important in determining political alliances and the inheritance of property. These matters were considered far too important to be decided by the emotional whims of adolescents. But with the industrial revolution in the 19th century, economic survival was less tied to inheritance. Young people increasingly escaped from parental control and made their own choice of marital partner.

Social critics in Europe first heard about the trend to base marriage on love as an American oddity. They called it a "pathological experiment," arguing that love would blind people to practical considerations, with disastrous results. But are young people really blind when they select dating and marriage partners?

Traditionally, parents encouraged young people to marry those with similar social characteristics – those of similar age, education, class, ethnic background and religion. Many studies have found that partners still tend to share characteristics, exactly as they used to do.

Among student couples, research shows that partners tend to be alike in age, educational goals, intelligence, and physical attractiveness (as judged from photographs by a panel of students). They also tend to be alike in height, religion and their attitudes to sex roles, to romantic ideals and to having children. Research also shows that breaking up is especially associated with being mismatched on age, educational plans, intelligence and physical attractiveness. Young people do not seem to be totally blind to practical considerations, even when they select their own partners.

Love is not enough

Couples who were more intimate at the beginning of a two-year study tended to stay together for the whole period. They reported greater feelings of closeness and a higher likelihood of eventually marrying. They were readier to disclose their feelings, and had recorded higher Love Scale scores. They had dated longer, on average, and were more likely to have been dating their partner exclusively. The development of intimacy was clearly an essential element in the survival of these relationships.

At the same time, intimacy did not guarantee staying together. While most of those who stayed together had previously said that they were "in love," about half of the couples who eventually broke up had originally been "in love."

In addition, there were two measures of intimacy which did not predict staying together. Couples who reported having had sexual intercourse were more intimate on other measures, but were no more likely to stay together than couples who had not had intercourse. Similarly, couples who were living together were more intimate, yet no more likely to stay together. Having sex or not does not predict staying together or breaking up.

Couples who were living together reported that they were under pressure from parents either to get married or break up. In addition, they faced problems of getting along with each other that could be ignored while dating, but which made life difficult when they were living together. These stresses seemed to counterbalance the positive effects of the increased intimacy of living together, and lessened their chances of staying together.

Among those who marry, of course, still other factors influence whether the relationship will last, since marriage involves a public and legal commitment, as well as a private commitment between the couple. **CTH**

157

■ **Like pairs off with like**. *The striking thing about most young couples is their similarity. Partners who stick together are, very much more often than not, alike in respect of age, intelligence, social background, educational goals and level of physical attractiveness.*

Marriage

IT HAS BEEN said that in every marriage there are actually two marriages – his and hers. Is this correct? And, if so, in what way *is* marriage different for men and women?

Sociologists argue that every group needs two leaders. The first deals with external demands and tries to keep the group on course. The second deals with internal matters, such as resolving conflicts and meeting emotional needs. Studies of marriage have found a very similar division of roles. Husbands traditionally deal with the outside world (employment and politics), while women take primary responsibility for domestic matters.

Women's involvement in employment and politics has been increasing, but even when women work outside the home they are still in charge of domestic tasks. Surveys show that working wives do somewhat less housework than nonworking wives, but their husbands do no more than the

husbands of stay-at-homes – instead, less housework gets done overall. As more women have taken on, or begun to share, what was traditionally the husband's role, they still have not been able to give up the burdens of the wife's role. In this sense, then, marriage is certainly different for men and women. It makes unequal demands on them.

Who has more power in marriage?

Historically, in the Western world, men have had more power than their wives in marriage. Why? One reason is that, traditionally, men are supposed to take the initiative and make the major decisions in marriage. Another factor is

DO WE SEE MARRIAGE DIFFERENTLY?

■ When couples are asked questions about their marriage, their answers often differ. For example, partners often disagree on who has more power or how often they have sex. If this disagreement were due to men's and women's different roles in marriage, then the answers ought to differ according to sex. However, when you average all of the men's answers and compare them to the average of all the women's, men as a group do not differ from women as a group. Disagreement seems to reflect the fact that two people will view their relationship differently, no matter what their sex. This conclusion is further supported by an extensive study of dating relationships. On every question

that was asked, at least some couples disagreed. Agreement was highest on factual questions, such as how long ago they met, and lowest on subjective matters, such as who was more involved in the relationship. As with the married couples, the men's answers did not differ consistently from those of the women.

In addition, the amount of disagreement was no greater for couples with traditional attitudes about men's and women's roles in marriage than for couples with more egalitarian views. Instead, the disagreement was higher for the couples who communicated less. Moreover, the couples with greater disagreement were more likely to break up.

▶ **Leading his family** across the stream, a father extends a helping hand. Every group has two leaders. One deals with external demands and keeps the group on course. The second deals with internal conflicts and emotional needs. In the common image of marriage, its leader in external matters is the husband. Its internal leader is the wife. However, the reality of power sharing in marriage is often much more complex and difficult to observe.

▲ **Equality of endeavor within a marriage** is given ceremonial expression by a newly wed couple in East Germany. Realizing their ideal will depend heavily on both husband and wife understanding and agreeing to the expectations of the other – on their sharing a common standard of what counts as useful endeavor toward worthwhile marriage goals.

How different is marriage for a husband and a wife? Sex differences appear in the division of power, in the way partners communicate, in their sensitivity to the problems of the relationship and in the burdens that partners carry.

that men, on average, are somewhat stronger physically than women, and therefore more capable of enforcing their will by brute force. But equally important is that men's education, employment and other involvements outside the home have given them greater income, social status and expertise. Significantly, research has found not only that husbands make more decisions than wives, but also that husbands with more income and social status have more power than husbands with less income and social status. However, this varies between cultures – in some societies husbands' actual resources are less important than beliefs about who ought to exercise power.

Power, however, is relative. My power over someone else depends upon our relative dependence upon each other. If we each have something the other wants, and are equally dependent on each other, then neither has the power advantage. But if one person is more dependent, that gives the other person more power.

Dependence can include emotional involvement, not just material rewards. If one of you is more emotionally involved in your relationship than the other, that one is also more dependent and therefore tends to have less power. Also those who rate their partners as being more attractive are more likely to be more dependent and to report that their partners have more power.

Generally, men are observed to employ direct forms of power, such as physical coercion or appeals to authority, expertise or knowledge. Women, on the other hand, use indirect forms, such as helplessness or appeals to affect-

▲ **Giving away his daughter.** *An Australian sets out to perform a rite that symbolizes the transfer of a possession from one man to another. In modern marriage, however, this concept has lost much of its* *meaning as the image of a rewarding, even romantic, life's relationship between equal partners has come to dominate the expectations with which marriages begin. In general in Western countries, husbands'* *expectations are more romantic than wives', and men are more easily disappointed by the humdrum practicalities of married life.*

159

When a wife exercises more power than her husband both partners are less likely to report that the relationship is satisfying. The woman's dominance violates the new ideal of equality as much as it does the traditional pattern.

ion. When asked how they get their partners to do what they want, men are more likely to report that they use the direct styles of asking, telling and talking, while women are more likely to use the indirect styles of pouting, being nice and hinting (see *Ch24*). For example, a wife may leave travel brochures around the house until the husband finally notices them and suggests, "Why don't we take a vacation?" She then replies, "What a great idea; I'm glad you thought of that."

Husbands and wives often have different perceptions of who has more power in their relationship. Why is disagreement so common?

One reason is that when they think about who makes decisions, they do not have the same decisions in mind. In one interview, the wife felt she had more power because she made the "important" decisions such as how to decorate their new apartment. From her husband's perspective,

however, that was a minor decision which he had happily delegated to her.

In addition, people are more aware of what they have done than of what their partner has done. When husbands and wives are asked who does what share of the housework, husbands always underestimate what their wives have done and vice versa: you remember the two hours you spent cleaning something, while your partner might not even notice that the cleaning was done. Similarly, when dating couples were asked who had more say about sex, the men claimed they did (because they were the ones who usually initiated it) while the women claimed they did (because they were the ones who decided whether or not to veto it).

Finally, untangling who exercises power is difficult when delegation of power is involved. There is an old joke in which the husband says, "I make all the major decisions in

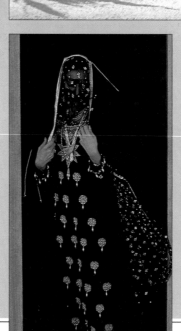

■ **Marriage systems**. TOP A Kenyan husband directs his wives' work in the fields. BOTTOM LEFT Of 849 cultures surveyed, 708 practice polygyny (one husband, more than one wife). Only 137 are mainly monogamous (one husband, one wife) and only 4 polyandrous (one wife, more than one husband). But polyandry is usually controlled by men – for example, by a senior and a junior hunting partner among the Aweikoma Indians in southern Brazil. A less total wife sharing occurs in about 30 percent of cultures – for example, among closely related Eskimos. Ceremonial wife lending includes the consummation ritual performed by men of the groom's family in many societies in New Guinea.

▲ **Deference customs** proclaim inequality in marriage. Worldwide, wives defer publicly to husbands, as when a Greek woman walks behind her mounted husband. It is difficult to know how much power such men wield in private, however.

◄ **Purdah** – secluding women from the view of all men but the husband – is seen here in the United Arab Emirates. This practice represents the control of women by men, but some women who practice it believe it makes marital relationships more exclusive and valuable.

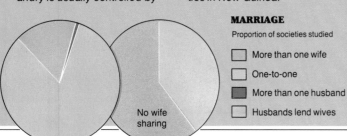

MARRIAGE
Proportion of societies studied

☐ More than one wife
☐ One-to-one
■ More than one husband
☐ Husbands lend wives

No wife sharing

my family, and my wife makes all the minor ones – including which decisions are major and which are minor." If a man says to his wife or girlfriend, "Let's go to a movie – you pick which one," and she selects the movie, is he exercising power or is she? It could be that the important issue is whether or not to go to a movie, in which case he delegated the minor part of the decision to her. On the other hand, he may have known that she preferred to go to a movie over

anything else, and would not go unless she picked the movie; in that case his "delegation" was merely an acknowledgment that she was calling the tune.

It is not surprising then that husbands and wives disagree on who has more power. And does it really matter who has the greater say? If they both think that the man should have more say, and feel that he does, or both think that they should have equal say and feel that they do, they generally

WHO IS IN CHARGE AROUND THE WORLD?

■ *Which marriage partner dominates and which submits in different communities? Who makes the family decisions? Who gets his or her way in case of conflict? What are the general patterns of equality or inequality? The problem with answering these questions is that power relations are hard to observe. People in a community may say that husbands "rule," but what really happens when husbands and wives are alone? Although men almost always dominate the political arena, women appear to have a great deal of domestic power and informal influence. Furthermore, power relationships between husband and wife probably vary a great deal within any society, responding to the personalities in each family. What anthropologists have been able to document are deference customs. These are the standardized and public*

gestures that express inequality on the symbolic level. They are ritual expressions or cultural expectations of an unequal relationship. Common examples are bowing, kneeling, walking

behind, respectful speech, giving the honored person the best seat or best food, always keeping oneself lower or standing to greet the person. Extreme deference customs

characterize the autocratic civilizations of old Japan, China, Hindu India, Egypt, the Middle East, Latin America and Africa. There is a strong association between deferential behavior within the family and autocratic states. Within these societies, deference is shown by lower classes to upper classes, women to men and younger men to older men. Wife-to-husband deference patterns (not always extreme) are widespread in other societies, too. All of the deference customs listed above, from sitting on the floor while the husband takes the chair, to always giving him the choice pieces of food, are seen. In contrast, there are few examples of husband-to-wife deference. Most are European, remnants of the medieval chivalric code. Stylized "good manners" toward women are not common in most of the world's cultures. **CE**

161

▶ **Governing the finances** *of a household is an important indication of overall power. The friends and relatives of these newly wed Indians in Britain have pinned money to the groom to acknowledge his control of how their gifts will be spent. A survey in 1987 revealed that American husbands are more tolerant than ever before of their wives' working, but they feel just as discontented as they did 20 years ago if their wives earn more than them.*

▼ **Faithfulness in marriage** *is valued highly around the world – especially the faithfulness of women. But women have extramarital sex in more than 73 percent of societies. In the 1950s about 25 percent of US wives had slept with at least one other*

man after marrying. Less scientific surveys (in which women respond to questionnaires in magazines) record figures of more than 50 percent for the 1980s. In a 1987 survey 12 percent of married people in France rated themselves as

currently unfaithful, with husbands outnumbering wives 2-1. Husbands in only 74 of 135 societies studied are highly confident that their children are their own, and blood-sample tests in both the United States and among Amazonian Indians reveal that about 10 percent of children are not related to the fathers who claim them.

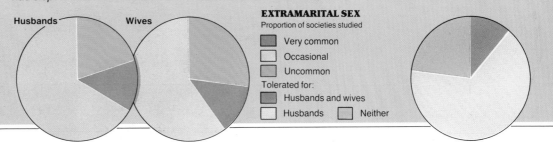

Husbands   Wives

EXTRAMARITAL SEX
Proportion of societies studied

- Very common
- Occasional
- Uncommon

Tolerated for:
- Husbands and wives
- Husbands   Neither

report being satisfied with the marriage. However, there is a significant difference if they report that the wife has more say. In this case, both partners are less likely to feel satisfied with the relationship. The woman's dominance violates both the traditional pattern and egalitarian ideals.

Do we communicate differently?

Just as there are differences between husbands and wives in the exercise of power and influence within marriage, men and women differ also in their styles of communication. Men are more likely to make direct statements, while women are more likely to ask questions. Even when they do make a statement, women are more apt to end with a question: "It's too cold to go out today, isn't it?" Women tend to phrase requests more politely: "Would you please shut the door?" Men use more direct commands: "Shut the door!" In marriages, wives initiate conversations more than their husbands, but the responses of their husbands usually determine how long the conversations last and in which directions the topics lead.

As for the content of their conversations, it is a compromise. Women generally reveal more personal information to their women friends than their husbands do to their men

Wives initiate more conversations than husbands, but the responses of husbands usually determine how long the conversations last. A wife is more likely to ask a question, a husband more likely to make a direct statement.

friends. Indeed, women's friendships tend to be based on sharing feelings while men's friendships are based on doing things together, such as engaging in or watching sports. In marriage, however, the greater openness of the woman encourages the man to open up, while the reticence of the man discourages the woman from opening up as much as she would to her own female friends. There are therefore fewer differences between the sexes in the content of their conversations within marriage than there are in what they are ready to discuss with friends of the same sex.

Nonetheless, some differences have been identified. Wives disclose more feelings, while husbands disclose more facts. Marriage partners also differ in the reasons they give for *not* revealing things to each other. Wives report that they do not want to burden or worry their husbands, or that their husbands would be unresponsive to their problems. Husbands report that they try to separate home from work, and that their wives do not know enough about their work to understand their problems.

Research also reveals that women tend to be better than

▲ **Relaxed intimacy** *with a partner is an ideal of Western culture, and public affection and togetherness are taken as a sign of the soundness of a marriage. However, traditional cultures measure the success of a marriage mainly in terms of economic achievement and reproductive success. Displays of equality in the relationship between husband and wife may be discouraged.*

▶ **Good communication** *is essential to a happy and enduring relationship. Talking problems over and agreeing on the responsibilities of each partner are both important, but so is the ability to laugh and have fun together. This promotes intimacy and commitment. Being relaxed with each other and laughing together imply the trust that people need in order to draw close enough to provide each other with lasting emotional support.*

men in sending nonverbal messages, and more accurate than men in decoding them. Women engage in more eye contact, and differ in their body movements (see *Ch 27*).

Since husbands and wives have different styles of verbal and nonverbal communication, it is not surprising that they often have difficulty communicating with each other. Many couples learn to adapt to these differences, but other couples talk past each other, eventually developing patterns of interaction that are increasingly negative. When "distressed" marriages are compared with "satisfactory" marriages, we find that distressed couples express less

positive emotion and more negative emotion than satisfied couples. The differences are especially pronounced for nonverbal expressions of feelings, such as glares or frowns. In addition, the response to a negative expression is more likely to be a similar expression, while this is not necessarily true of a positive expression. If he frowns, she frowns; if she glares, he glares; but if one smiles, the other may not smile back, but may frown or look away instead.

When couples are unhappy, they are more likely to assume that the partner has discreditable motives for doing something instead of creditable ones. A gesture such as a bouquet of flowers is taken as a sign of feeling guilty for unfaithful behavior rather than as a token of affection. A laugh is interpreted as derision instead of enjoyment of each other's company. As a result, there is a spiral of increasing bad feeling, miscommunication and distrust.

Do men "love 'em and leave 'em"?

When relationships do deteriorate, who is more likely to be aware of it and act upon it? Women report more problems in dating relationships and are somewhat more likely to break them up (see *Ch 18*). Several studies have found this to be true for marriage as well. Often a man is

---

HOW CLOSE ARE MARRIAGE PARTNERS?

■ *In modern Western society, marriage ideally includes intimacy and sharing. Husband and wife live in the same home, eat meals together, share a public social life and jointly own possessions.*

However, this degree of togetherness is not typical of other cultures. In fact, aloofness between men and women in certain societies may be vital in maintaining the aggressive personalities needed for warfare. Husband and wife may even sleep in separate dwellings.

For instance, within traditional sub-Saharan Africa, the common arrangement is for each wife to have a hut in the family compound; her husband either has his own hut, or rotates between his wives. In

New Guinea, husbands often sleep in the men's house, a building strictly off-limits to women.

Modern Western society appears rather extreme not only in togetherness but also in the amount of intimacy displayed between marriage partners. Most traditional cultures demand shyness, restraint, even avoidance between a man and wife when others are present. In a l966 study, 37 out of 48 societies prohibited spouses from showing affection. But this shyness was not necessarily part of a general prudery. Some groups sang graphic songs or allowed sexual joking. Some groups were relatively permissive about premarital and extramarital relationships. **CE**

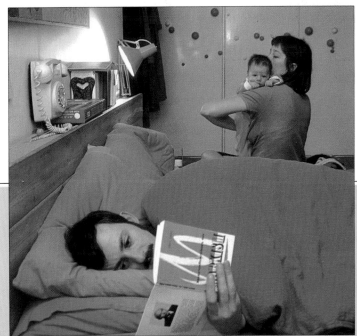

▲ **Providing a base for nurturing children** *is a central purpose of marriage. However, the majority of marriages become less satisfying when children are born. Wives become less involved with husbands, and intimacy declines. Marital satisfaction usually increases when children leave home.*

◄ **Marriage breakdown,** *one of the most shattering experiences of a lifetime, is reflected in the complete loss of communication between a couple waiting outside the divorce courts in Moscow. Contrary to common stereotypes men are not more likely than women to want to end a marriage.*

shocked to hear that his wife wants a divorce, feeling that he was not aware that they were having problems – while his lack of awareness is what has been frustrating his wife most.

Women have traditionally been encouraged to be concerned about relationships, and are often more sensitive to any changes in them. In addition, as more women have become concerned about meeting their own needs in marriage, and not just the needs of their husband and children, their expectations for marriage have increased.

At the same time, it is not always clear who is "really" responsible for ending a marriage. One study of divorce concluded that even in cases where it was the wife who filed for divorce, it was the husbands who wanted the divorce and drove their wives to end the marriage. On the other

hand, the husbands may have driven their wives to seek a divorce without intending to do so. Or perhaps the wives' expectations were unrealistic.

Usually conflict involves both partners failing to give in. Each feels justified in this and tends to blame the other for causing the conflict. At the same time, there is a desire to claim responsibility for ending the relationship – "I wanted it to end, because he/she drove me to it." As with premarital break-ups, both ex-partners usually say "I" wanted it to end, or it was "mutual" instead of saying "my partner" wanted it to end. This helps preserve their self-esteem and their sense of control. Those who do say their partner ended it report feeling more depressed and lonely than those who say it was at least partly their own choice.

It has been found that no matter who files for divorce, or who "really" wanted the marriage to end, both parties have a great deal of emotional upheaval and ambivalence following the separation. They feel angry, depressed, lonely, guilty and at the same time relieved. They hate their former partners, yet still love them too. They remember the good times, the reasons for loving and marrying, as well as the bad times and the reasons for the divorce. Often they telephone or visit for no apparent reason. "I was just in the neighborhood so I stopped by." Sometimes they go out on a date, or even have sex after the divorce is finalized. They still like some things about each other – even if they can no longer bear to live together.

Of course if they have children, there is usually a need to continue to be in contact, but this does not necessarily help their relationship. People feel that having children will give a couple something in common, to keep them together. Yet children very often create added stresses in a marriage.

▲ **Sharing experiences** *keeps a marriage vital, and one of the most binding is the event of a child's birth. It is only relatively recently that fathers in Western societies have been interested in taking part and encouraged to do so. In other cultures, it is almost entirely a female affair.*

◀ **Balancing two lives,** *a pair of tightrope walkers set out across the Colorado River below Hoover Dam to be married by a minister who will conduct the service by radio from the ground. Traditional marriage roles direct husbands and wives toward separate interests and activities, but some are able to pursue joint careers and joint hobbies.*

Divorcees remember the good times, the reasons for loving and marrying, as well as the bad ones and the reasons for divorce. Often they visit or telephone for no apparent reason. "I was just in the neighborhood so I stopped by."

Marital satisfaction tends to be highest right after the honeymoon, decreases through the child-rearing years, then increases after the children have left home. Children often become the focus of their parents' conflict, even if disagreement on how to raise the children is not the initial cause of the conflict. As a result, the children sometimes feel as if they are the trophy symbolizing who won in the battle of the divorce.

After a divorce, most people remarry. This is slightly more common for men (about five-sixths) than it is for women (about three-quarters), at least in the United States. They have not given up on the idea of marriage, but feel it will be better with a different partner. About half of all remarriages occur within three years of the divorce.

Since divorcees often have children when they remarry, their marriage becomes complicated by "his" and "her" children, as well as "theirs." This is one reason why husbands and wives sometimes even disagree on questions like "How many children do you have?" It is not that they cannot count, but rather that in this too each person views the marriage from a different perspective.

Is marriage better for men?

Research has found that married men score higher on measures of mental health than unmarried men, while unmarried women score higher than married women. Does marriage affect mental health or does mental health affect who gets married? It could be that marriage improves a man's health by providing someone to do his cooking and cleaning and to provide emotional support. At the same time, marriage may be detrimental to a woman's mental health if she is constantly putting her husband's and children's needs ahead of her own. On the other hand, it could be that men who are mentally healthy can more easily attract a mate. For a woman to succeed as a single career woman she must have good mental health, while those who marry may include some women with poor mental health who seek refuge in marriage. Hence at least some of the differences may exist before marriage. **CTH**

AGE PATTERNS IN MARRIAGE

■ *Husbands tend to be somewhat older than their wives. As a result, fewer young men are married than young women, and fewer older women are married than older men. The problem for spinsters is compounded by the fact that women tend to live longer than men, so that there are fewer men available to marry in later life. Why would a woman want to marry an older man? Older men tend to have more power, status and income than younger men. Why would a man want to marry a younger woman? Younger women tend to be more physically attractive and capable of bearing children. In many couples, however, the age differences are not great, because the more similar they are in age, the more experiences they have in common and the easier it is to communicate.*

▶ **The joys of a fulfilling relationship** *are not reserved for the young alone. It is very common for those who have lost their partners to remarry.*

165

Who Looks After the Children?

HOW SHOULD wives and husbands divide the task of looking after their children? As women's participation in the workforce increases, so does discussion of the changing roles of mothers and fathers. Some governments now have programs to encourage or support working parents, and to help men take an active role in child care. A study of personal letters and popular literature written over a period of 200 years has revealed four phases in the American father's evolving image, from "moral teacher," to "breadwinner," to "sex-role model," to "the new nurturant father" of today. There is no one standard way in which men and women approach their responsibilities as fathers and mothers, and there never has been.

Cultural patterns

How much similarity is there worldwide in parents' roles? Parents everywhere share three essential goals – to protect the health and survival of their children; to teach them how to support themselves when they grow up; to help them develop in terms of the central values of their culture (achievement, prestige, morality, etc). These essential goals, combined with common patterns in the way that children mature and develop, lead to similar stages in the development of the child-parent relationship, with the children moving from utter dependence to increasing self-reliance. But the common pattern leaves much room for variation.

Mothers are usually the principal (though not exclusive) carers of their infants, with more delegation of responsibility as the child grows older. In a 1988 report using observations collected in 12 communities on four continents, infants were found everywhere eliciting the same kinds of positive, nurturant behavior from whoever cared for them. Apart from mothers, the chief carers were older children. There are few cultural differences – mainly they are in how much carrying or face to face interaction infants receive.

As the child grows older, cultural contrasts become more important. There are sharp differences in the social behavior considered acceptable or praiseworthy for boys and girls of a given age. Children need to learn the skills of a particular culture as they grow up, and so variations are closely related to each community's way of life, its economy, household composition and division of labor.

In sub-Saharan Africa, where women have very heavy workloads that they do not regularly share with other women, they tend to assume what has been called the "Training Mother" profile. A woman's most common interactions with her 3- to 12-year-old children consist of suggestions and instructions about manual work.

In contrast, in upper-caste groups in northern India, where women are confined by *purdah* to crowded courtyards, and are less involved in subsistence work, the mother tends to assume the "Controlling Mother" profile. Her chief concern is to reprimand and correct her children's behavior and command them to do something to meet her own needs (for example, not to bother her).

Finally, in cultural communities (such as those of the

A striking feature of all cultures is that it is the child's mother who mainly cares for it, while the father is more distant. Yet extensive cultural variations in the paternal role indicate that it need not be a limited one.

United States of the 1950s) where the mother is often isolated and at home all day with children who are not expected to do many chores, she tends to assume the "Sociable Mother" profile. The mother treats her children, at times, as if they were her equals in status and her companions; sociability and the exchange of information then dominate the mother-child relationship.

Fathering, too, shows considerable cultural variation. In fact, there is perhaps even more variation here between the cultures than there is with mothering, in terms of the sheer extent of direct involvement. It varies from very distant to very intimate. In nonindustrial, subsistence cultures the fathers take little care of very young children. However, they do assist their wives considerably in those groups where the relations between husband and wife are closer and more interdependent.

In all cultures, however, fathers become increasingly involved with the children's upbringing from the age of two. It is evident also that fathers in many cultures take on other roles with their children besides care-giving. These roles – including resource provider, protector, playmate, work supervisor, teacher, disciplinarian – depend on the age and sex of children and the demands of the situation. Since these are also dimensions of the maternal role, we can conclude that men and women show similar capacities for parenting, even though the mothering role usually shows greater closeness and responsibility for the children. **CE**

Swedish parental leave

How well have the similar capacities of men and women displayed themselves in the world's most advanced experiment in fatherly involvement with children? In the 1960s Sweden had an expanding economy, eager to employ women, and an ideal of equality between the sexes that motivated legislators to seek ways of helping women to realize their personal potentials as easily as men. There

◄ A bath with mother and grandmother *in India. Three main styles of mothering emerge as infants grow into children. The "Training Mother" has a heavy workload and spends much time telling her 3- to 12-year-olds how to help her. The "Controlling Mother" mainly supervises her children's behavior. The "Social Mother," most common in countries where the mother is at home alone with her children, seeks companionship from them.*

▲ The "ideal father" *has changed dramatically in Western societies since the days of the strict Victorian breadwinner. Now, men are encouraged to be present at the birth of their children and to take part in their upbringing from the very first. In most countries, however, paternal involvement mainly means play – particularly with sons. Mother's responsibilities for children's basic needs have not greatly diminished.*

▲ A bath with father *for son and daughter in a Dinka family of the southern Sudan. After infancy, men around the world become more involved with their children. They may help with the intimate care of their children, but more usually teach them skills.*

were no domestic servants to look after the children and homes of working mothers, and it was apparent that equality would mean involving men in family responsibilities. Not only were daycare programs increased but the provisions for maternal leave following the birth of a child were broadened to "parental leave," which could be shared between the newborn's parents.

When parental leave was introduced in 1974, Sweden already had important maternity benefits. Since the 1950s, employed mothers had enjoyed six months paid maternity leave. Compared with some other countries, the rules were generous. A mother could start a new position when she was already pregnant and still qualify for leave. The money was paid even if she did not return to work, and if she wanted to return, her previous job was guaranteed. In practice, the leave provisions meant that women left work for at least six months following childbirth.

When fathers were first allowed equal rights in this respect, the leave period of six months per child remained the same. Thus the father could only use his right if the mother went back to work uncommonly soon. In 1980, the period was extended to one year. For nine months, the payment is closely related to a parent's regular income, for the remaining three, the payment is at a low, fixed level. Part of the period can be deferred for some years, although this option is not use extensively. The principle of counting one leave per child has been retained, and the parents decide between them how much time each will take.

For obvious reasons, fathers may not take parental leave before the birth of the child, and mothers must take the first month. However, in recognizing the need for paternal involvement from the very first, 10 special days leave, the "new dad days" were introduced in 1980, to be taken by fathers at the time of childbirth. Fathers display a great inter-

168

■ **Mothers' direct involvement with infants** *varies little from one culture to another. In an African village* LEFT *and industrial England* TOP, *women are primarily responsible for the care of their children. The charts below represent some of the findings of a study that compared 186 cultures, from hunters and gatherers to indus-* *trial societies.* BELOW LEFT *In 92 percent of cultures, mothers are the sole or principal carers of infants up to the age of two. Substitutes are usually female relatives: either adults (eg grandmothers) or child nurses (sisters).* BELOW RIGHT *There is more variation in how much time fathers spend with their children. In 20 percent of the* *cultures studied, fathers are rarely or never in the close proximity of infants, and in only 4 percent do they have a regular close relationship. However in the remaining 76 percent, varying degrees of proximity occur.*

CARE OF INFANTS
Proportion of societies studied

- Exclusively mother
- Mainly mother
- Mother and others
- Mainly others

PROXIMITY OF FATHERS

- Regular
- Frequent
- Occasional
- Rare
- None

About 25 percent of Swedish fathers take up some leave of absence from work when a child is born. Mothers, however, take most of the 12 months allowed each family – for the sake of breast-feeding and because they lose less pay.

est in this, with 85 percent taking advantage. Many of the other 15 percent would probably do so as well, were their children not born during holiday periods.

The leave program is financed by the National Insurance Board. This government-controlled body has actively promoted paternal leave through advertisements, a promotion that was supported by the media through very favorable coverage of pioneering fathers-on-parental-leave.

How much leave do fathers take?

Most mothers take the full 12 months, most fathers none. Between 20 and 25 percent of fathers take at least some parental leave, usually about two months. What stops fathers from participating in the program?

National opinion polls show only 8 percent of women and 24 percent of men clearly against the idea of men taking parental leave, and men of an age to be starting families are more in favor. However, only women breast-feed and since couples value breast-feeding highly this determines the issue for the first half year in many families. For the last three months, the fact that the wife's salary is usually lower makes her staying home more advantageous for most families. In addition, the couple must decide who most enjoys being home and whose career will suffer most. The

frequency of fathers taking leave rises to about 50 percent when the wife earns a salary in the range of a full-time professional woman. An important factor is how interesting and rewarding the mother finds her job.

The sharp difference in numbers of fathers and mothers taking leave does not necessarily mean that fathers are not usually involved in child care. In a representative sample, Swedish fathers were found to spend an average of 11 hours a week caring for their one-year-old, while mothers spent an average of 35 hours. Individual variation above and below the average for fathers was great.

How well do fathers on leave perform?

When fathers do take parental leave, this means that they act as the primary care-giving parents. It is regularly observed that they find caring for a baby unexpectedly demanding. However, most find the experience rewarding, except when they have been pressured into it. Fathers who take parental leave, particularly those who take more than one month, show a higher-than-average involvement in child care when the child is older. They take more responsibility for care and spend somewhat fewer hours in their paid work than other men.

One of the motivations for enabling fathers to take parental leave was to improve father-child relationships. American studies during the 1970s found that infants display increasing preferences for their fathers in their second year. This

169

▶ **Swedish fathering** *is actively encouraged – by government agencies and public opinion. Although most Swedish men do not take advantage of the generous provisions for parental leave following the birth of a baby, they do take more responsibility for child care than men in other countries. As a result, fathers become a familiar fixture in their children's lives, and Swedish infants tend to prefer their mothers. In the United States, studies have found two-year-olds preferring their fathers, who have more novelty.*

In any given year, about 35 percent of Swedish fathers and 45 percent of Swedish mothers take time off work to care for sick children. American and Swedish couples divide their household tasks in almost the same proportions.

was especially true for boys, and seemed more marked when a father was more involved with a child. Seeking an opportunity to study very involved fathers, researchers turned to Sweden. The results were surprising: regardless of infants' age or sex, and whether or not fathers took parental leave, Swedish infants with few exceptions preferred their mothers. Searching for explanations for the finding, the researchers noted several national differences in parental style. Overall, Swedish parents have a lower rate of interaction with their babies than Americans. Swedish fathers (including those not taking parental leave) are more involved in child care than their American counterparts, but do not engage in nearly as much vigorous physical play with their babies. Instead, they generally play like the mothers. Although other factors might also be involved, it seems that

American babies in their second year prefer their fathers for the excitement and novelty they provide, while Swedish fathers offer less of a contrast.

Equality after infancy

After the child's first year, the vast majority of Swedish parents have paid work. For married men, the employment rate is 97 percent, for mothers 86 percent. However, mothers often work less than full-time. The most important differences are in the nature of their work. Women do caring, teaching and secretarial work, while men work in industry, engineering and transport.

There is a great deal of equality between fathers and mothers when it comes to taking leave from work to care for sick children. In any given year, about 35 percent of fathers and 45 percent of mothers with children under 12 do this.

Time spent in direct care drops sharply after infancy, but time spent in indirect child care (usually classified as "housework" – for example, washing children's clothes and providing family meals) does not diminish. Although mothers continue to do most housework, Swedish fathers' involvement has shown an important increase over the course of one generation. In 1957, only 14 percent of them helped with the dishes. In 1977, the figure was 50 percent. For cooking, a more time-consuming task, the percentages are 4 and 37. In families with a mother working full-time, the father's involvement was higher both in 1957 and 1977, but the increase was about the same.

There is a much higher employment rate for Swedish mothers than American mothers, and, as we have seen, surveys have shown important increases in the involvement of

▼ **Children between the ages of 2 and 5** *are more involved with their fathers than younger infants are, according to the study of 186 cultures, described on p168.* BELOW LEFT *The mother's role as principal carer is found dramatically less frequently – occurring in only 26.5 percent of cultures – as she delegates more of the care of her children to others.* BELOW RIGHT *The closeness of the* *father-child relationship increases. Although men in only 9 percent of cultures ever achieve a really close relationship with children of this age, a greater increase in proximity is seen: in 79 percent of cultures, fathers are either occasionally or frequently near their children.*

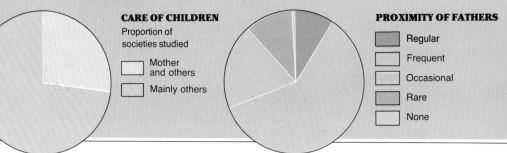

▲ **Younger fathers** *are more likely to be involved with the care of their children than older ones. While this may reflect cultural change, it could also be due to the fact that older men are under more pressure in their careers.*

CARE OF CHILDREN
Proportion of societies studied

☐ Mother and others
☐ Mainly others

PROXIMITY OF FATHERS

☐ Regular
☐ Frequent
☐ Occasional
☐ Rare
☐ None

170

Swedish fathers in household tasks. However, a study in 1982 found the division of household tasks between mother and father virtually identical in Sweden and the United States. The same study observed that American fathers continue – past the infant stage – to play more actively with their children than Swedes do, while Swedish fathers are more engaged in their children's intimate care. American mothers did not value their husbands' play, although all other child care activity was appreciated. The Swedish mothers valued their husbands' caring *and* playing.

In both countries, but especially Sweden, younger fathers are more involved than older ones in child care (regardless of the age of their children). The more a mother works outside the home, the more a father takes responsibility for the children and household, but the trend is that less housework gets done overall and the wife still does more of it.

Despite progress toward equality there continues to be a sharp division between the interests of young Swedish men and women when choosing a career. Different roles for men and women are still a strong feature of Swedish culture. Perhaps this culture is not really abandoning sex roles, but rather emphasizing different aspects of masculinity and femininity than some other cultures do. In Sweden, a "real man" is characterized by emotional control and objective competence rather than by dominance and daring, a "real woman" by interpersonal sensitivity and caring for others rather than by sex appeal and dependency on men. Still, it seems as if parenting increasingly places similar demands upon fathers and mothers in Sweden. **KS**

171

■ **In industrial societies** *during the past few decades, the role of the father has changed.* TOP *Men frequently play with their children, although this father demonstrating his prowess on a computer is also acting as teacher – a more traditional role.* ABOVE *While "househusbands" such as this man are not common, children are now much more likely to see their fathers performing at least some housework.* RIGHT *Despite all these changes, a mother continues to be the central person in a young child's life.*

Violence Between the Sexes

VIOLENCE at the hands of a stranger, in spite of public concern about increasing crime, is remarkably rare. In the United States, widely considered to be an extremely violent country, your chance of being the victim of a recorded criminal assault in a given year is one in 440. In almost any country the chances are considerably higher, however, that members of a family or partners in another close relationship will perpetrate unrecorded assaults on each other.

Domestic violence makes us all uncomfortable. We tend to distance ourselves from it by insisting that abusers are deranged, that the victims are masochistic (otherwise why would they put up with it?) and that the causes lie hidden in the childhood experiences of the abuser and abused. We want to believe that it cannot happen to anyone *we* know, but it can.

Of all those who are arrested for violent crimes, 90 percent are male. Domestic violence too occurs mainly at the hands of men. What sort of men are they and what sort of women are their victims?

Sex differences in aggression

Research with adults suggests that there are no important sex differences in the average number of anxiety-producing events in a given year, and women's ability to handle stress seems to be no better or worse than men's. Studies of anger, in which men and women are asked about the kinds of

events which spark it and what the emotion feels like, also throw up very few sex differences. Men and women are, for example, similar in being most likely to get angry with someone they love, because the other person has willfully violated their expectations or wishes, or has not behaved "properly."

However, women seem to control their aggression better, in spite of feeling just as much anger as men. Women experience more guilt and anxiety about aggressive behavior than men do. Lashing out does not make them feel better. In one study, subjects were provoked to real anger by a "plant" whom the experimenter put among them. They were then given the opportunity to get their revenge and express their anger by giving electric shocks to their tormentor. As they were doing so, the experimenter measured their heart rate and blood pressure. In men it went down, indicating that revenge was having a calming effect on their anger. In women, the readings actually went up. They became more tense and anxious when they retaliated than when they were

SEX DIFFERENCES IN AGGRESSIVE BEHAVIOR

■ In experiments, researchers have found that men are much more aggressive than women in certain distinctive circumstances, while sex differences are very small in others. In order of increasing difference, aggressive behavior is especially more characteristic of men than women when:

the aggressor has traditional attitudes about sex roles, especially the belief that men are aggressive and women are not.

the target of aggression is of the same sex as the attacker (men are more aggressive toward men than women are toward women).

the victim expresses pain (women are deterred more easily than men from continuing).

the aggressor has been exposed to television violence and male models of aggression.

the aggression is directly physical.

the aggressor's parents were uncaring, punished frequently and made their child feel rejected.

In order of increasing difference, men are only slightly more aggressive than women when:

the aggressor feels justified.

anonymity is assured (women are more likely than men to fear that they are creating a bad impression of themselves by showing aggression).

the aggressor is provoked and angry.

the aggressor does not have rigidly traditional sex-role attitudes.

the aggressor has not been exposed to much television violence.

the aggressor's parents were caring and punished infrequently. AC

In domestic situations women are far more likely than men to be the victims of physical violence. Fights usually reflect conflicts of control, and while women are as verbally aggressive as men, men may beat their wives to assert dominance.

suffering in silence. Society's expectations are clearly expressed through the reactions of both men and women to the "ugliness" of female aggression.

Consider two situations where, from laboratory tests, we know that women are likely to behave aggressively: first, when a supportive female observer is watching her, and second, when the person on the receiving end is her husband. In the first case, the observer's smile is telling her that the actions are "okay," that no one is shocked or upset by what she is doing. In the second, she knows her husband well enough and is sufficiently secure in his affection to risk behaving in a way society at large would condemn. It seems, then, that men and women may see aggression in different ways.

Women believe that yelling, screaming and hitting makes them look unattractive, and their regret afterward is not only concerned with what people think of them but also involves their belief that aggression is a loss of control and losing control is bad. **AC**

An astounding fact uncovered in an American survey of domestic conflicts was that wives actually appeared to use physical aggression more frequently than their husbands (4.6 percent against 3.9 percent). On the strength of these figures, husband abuse has been called the most "underreported crime in America." Clearly women do behave aggressively just as often as men do, at least at home. But the essential question here is whether aggression – even when it is physically expressed – should be equated with the kind of violence employed when women and children are the targets.

There are in fact several major problems with this survey. It lists threats, pushes, slapping etc as "violent behavior," although many people would accept them as normal aspects of family conflict. The survey disregards motive. Yet, while there are as many homicides by wives as there are by husbands in the United States, 60 percent of the male victims provoke their own deaths by abusing their wives. Only 10 percent of the women victims do.

◄ **Aggression in private** – *an angry exchange between husband and wife. Most women feel anxious and guilty when they show aggression in public, but they can be as aggressive as men in domestic situations. They are more likely to use verbal aggression than physical violence, however, and much less likely than men to inflict serious physical injuries on their partner.*

▲ **Aggression in public** *by rioting soccer fans. In public situations men are much more likely to show violence toward other men than toward women. In the home, however, nearly 4 percent of wives claim to be victims of physical abuse by their husbands.*

The survey also fails to take into account the very different ways in which men and women regard such violence. It is significant that the National Crime Survey, which only measures attacks considered criminal by their victims, found 3.8 percent of women claiming that they had been assaulted by their husbands but only 0.3 percent of husbands claiming assaults by their wives. Men rate women's aggressive acts as assaults only in those rare instances when weapons are involved (and the probability of injury is great). In contrast, women equate the physical force that men use with criminal assault – and with good reason. A review of 3,000 medical records has shown assault by domestic partners to be the most common cause of injury for which women seek medical attention, more common than car accidents, mugging and rape combined.

Which sex is responsible for battered children? Unfortunately, the statistics all too often lump together cases of physical abuse with cases of neglect. In 1983, for instance, 1.5 million American children were reported as abused or neglected, and in 62 percent of the cases the mother was to blame – hardly surprising in view of men's common absence from the home. Only 3.2 percent of the cases, however, involved allegations of major physical injuries, and here the surveys estimate that fathers or father substitutes

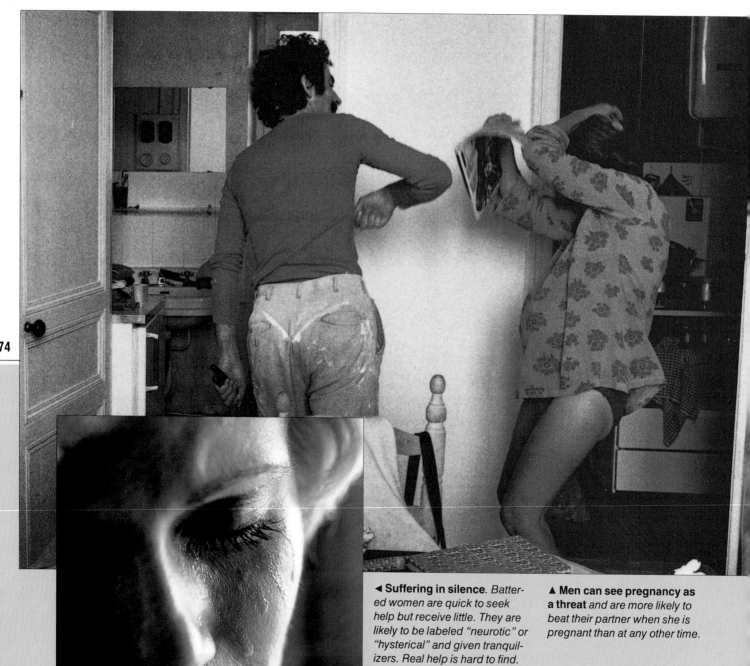

◀ **Suffering in silence.** *Battered women are quick to seek help but receive little. They are likely to be labeled "neurotic" or "hysterical" and given tranquilizers. Real help is hard to find.*

▲ **Men can see pregnancy as a threat** *and are more likely to beat their partner when she is pregnant than at any other time.*

Homes in which women are battered are often ones where children also suffer abuse. Women and men both beat children but it is the male batterer rather than the battered mother who is typically the child-abuser.

comprise up to 55 percent of all assailants and 75 percent of all assailants in families where fathers or father substitutes are present. Even more significantly, in the records of child-abuse cases in 1981-83 fully 80 percent of the fatal cases are attributed to men, and 20 percent are "unknown." None is attributed to a woman.

Tragically, child-beating and wife-battering often occur together. From the medical records of 116 mothers of abused children, it appears that 45 percent of these mothers were themselves being battered. The common belief is "husband beats wife, wife beats child." But the male batterer was the typical child-abuser, not the battered mother.

Are some women born to be victims?

Battered wives often display a complex mix of personal and social problems, including homelessness, poverty, unemployment and lack of education, as well as physical or mental illness.

They may also have had an array of childhood problems. Erin Pizzey, the founder of the Chiswick House, a pioneering refuge for battered women in Britain, believed that violence is transmitted from one generation to another, and that some women have a hormonal need for violence. She

was supported by the psychiatrist J J Gayford who interviewed 100 Chiswick residents. Finding that many of the women were divorced, alcoholic, had illegitimate children and reported that their children were abused, Gayford portrayed the typical battered woman as a pathetic, almost childlike individual. "Such women," he concluded, "need protection against their own stimulus-seeking activities. Though they flinch from violence like other people, they have the ability to seek violent men or by their behavior to provoke attack from the opposite sex."

American researchers at first followed the same route as Gayford, identifying "violence-prone" families as rare exceptions to normal behavior. However, this was difficult to sustain when 16 percent of the 2,143 couples in a national survey reported violence in their marriage. Careful comparisons were then made between 600 battered and 600 non-battered women. As Gayford had claimed, an exceptional number of abused women were alcoholic, had been raped, had attempted suicide and had children who had been abused. But Gayford and Pizzey were found to be wrong in one vital respect. The studies showed that battered women only experience these problems disproportionately *after* the onset of violence, indicating that violence was the cause of the problems, not the result.

American researchers also discovered another important fact. Battered women went for help early and often. But they

175

▶ **Goodbye to all that**. *For many, the only way to end violence is to end the relationship. Often, however, there is nowhere to go. Many wives are so dependent on their husbands for a home and financial support for themselves and their children that they endure many years of physical abuse. Some authorities suggest that certain women need and even invite violence. Others have rejected this view after careful study.*

were repeatedly frustrated. They received tranquilizers, were given stereotyped female labels (such as "hysteric") and were punished, sometimes by having their children removed to foster care. This treatment increased their sense of isolation, added to their fears that they could never escape from their situation, and aggravated the development of self-destructive behavior such as alcoholism and attempted suicide. The "helpers" themselves were thus contributing to the problems of those they were helping.

The studies also failed to identify any personality disturbance that might predispose some women to provoke abuse. Battered women appear more aggressive, hostile and dominant than most, but they are also more sociable and sympathetic, and they exhibit more self-assurance and independence than women in nonviolent relationships. Battered women admitted to mental hospitals may tend to blame

■ **Men in control**. *The family is traditionally dominated by men. In strict Moslem societies, women like these in Morocco* TOP *are kept in purdah, hidden from the eyes of men and strangers, and they control only a carefully restricted area of their lives. Where dominance is not so clearly stated and control is contested, violence can be a man's way of maintaining his superiority. Younger members of the family may also be dominated in this way. A father, seconded by the mother,* RIGHT, *physically threatens a boy,* *blocking his escape routes. The mere threat of physical injury is enough. Domestic violence is historically conditioned. It is used in virtually all cultures to maintain the family hierarchy and, in this context, receives social support in many.*

Some authorities have claimed that women who are abused have an emotional need for violence and actively provoke attack. Research with "violence-prone" families in the United States has failed to substantiate this suggestion.

themselves and lack self-esteem, but women in shelters do not. This suggests that much depends on whether being battered is treated as an illness or as a political issue.

Are some men born to batter?

There is even less evidence for a "violence-prone" personality among batterers than among their victims. Batterers have no less self-esteem than nonviolent men in distressed relationships. Both groups feel a mix of helplessness, powerlessness or inadequacy. They feel internal conflicts over being dependent on others. They have traditional attitudes, particularly about sex. They are pathologically jealous, fear abandonment and desire to control their women and children. They also find it difficult to communicate feelings or to identify with other people, and they suffer from difficulty in asserting themselves. Why are only some such men violent? There are three common explanations. In each of them is a grain of truth, but certainly no more.

One explanation, popular in the United States, is that both victims and abusers are predisposed to violence, because they are poor, black, unemployed or young. However, a difference of only 3 percent separates the incidence of violence against low-income women (11 percent) from that against women with family income of $25,000 or above (8 percent), while couples with the lowest educational level (a frequent indicator of poverty) are less prone to violence than those who attended high school. Certainly, violence at the hands of a male partner is a leading cause of death

WHAT LEADS SOME MEN TO VIOLENCE?

177

■ Men expect to dominate domestic partnerships, as the postures and expressions of the men TOP LEFT and BOTTOM LEFT clearly show. Unemployed men and those in lower income groups are likely to feel their status and authority threatened, especially if their wife has a higher status in her job. But violence is not restricted to them. It is almost as common in families in high income groups and is typically perpetrated by professional men who feel that their wives hold them back and undermine their status. Alcohol abuse is strongly linked to violent behavior, and men with alcohol problems are four times as likely as others to beat their wives.

among black women under 35. But whether this is a function of race, income or other factors is unclear. Among most groups with similar incomes, black women are less likely to be battered than white women.

There is little evidence that being without a job in itself increases violence. Housewives are actually less likely to be hit by their husbands than employed women, and unemployed men are likely to hit only when they have a strong belief in male superiority and they see the loss of their job as a damaging loss of prestige.

As for the dangers of youth, while 44 percent of the injuries to women under 35 are caused by their husbands, so are 18 percent of the injuries to women over 60, a clear indication that violence is a problem for every age group.

A second suggestion is that alcohol is the villain of the piece, as it removes inhibitions over the use of violence: end alcoholism and the violence will end. Violent behavior and the abuse of alcohol are certainly associated. For example, among male factory workers, those with an alcohol problem are nearly four times as likely to admit to fighting with their wives as are those without a problem. Still, alcohol and violence must be treated separately. Violence generally continues at the same level after batterers have completed alcohol treatment. In fact, both batterers and their wives are more likely to blame the woman for the violence after alcohol treatment than before.

As many as 90 percent of boys from violent homes do not grow up to beat their wives. One study has indicated that 80 percent of battered children do not abuse their own in adult life. They grow up with a wish to eliminate violence.

The third, and most common, suggestion is that those who beat their wives were themselves beaten as children: father beats mother, mother beats child, then child grows up to beat his wife. You would think so popular a belief to have been subjected to many rigorous studies. However, there have been few real tests of this proposition. Interestingly, the only survey bearing directly on the theory shows that 90 percent of the children from "violent" homes and even 80 percent of the children from homes where weapons were used (the "most violent" homes) do not grow up to beat their wives. Indeed, for every wife-beater who was actually hit as a teenager, two wife-beaters were not hit.

In another study, it was shown that more than 80 percent of those families where a parent was beaten as a child did not abuse their children. These nonabusing parents generally had a strong social network, good child-care arrangements, were optimistic and could cope with stress. Indeed adults who were abused as children often grow up to avoid violence and do their best to eliminate it.

There is an even stronger belief that battered wives must have been exposed to violence as a child. Again the statistics tell a different story. It is probable that about 85 percent were not victims of violence in childhood.

RAPE

■ *More than 60,000 rapes are reported to the police in the United States each year, and it is estimated that 600,000 may go unreported. In many of the unreported cases, victims are anxious to avoid the embarrassment and stress of a police inquiry. They are often pessimistic about being taken seriously and about the effectiveness of the police.*

Rape occurs frequently enough to be an aspect of human reproduction. During the Bangladesh war in 1971, it is estimated that as many as 400,000 women were raped and about 25,000 became pregnant as a result. Hundreds of conceptions by rape victims were recorded in Germany between 1945 and 1947. In violent conflicts between communities and in their immediate

aftermath, male hostility is high, and so is female vulnerability. These are circumstances that, by no one's choice, have probably occurred frequently during human evolution. Some authorities have speculated that most men have therefore inherited, as one of their many natural adaptations for the continuation of their genes, the capacity to be rapists in situations that present riskless opportunities. (Their main adaptation would

be instinctively to prefer to bring up their children in stable societies that do not permit riskless opportunities for rape to occur.)

Most rapes, however, cannot be construed as instinct-driven reproductive opportunities. A major obstacle to reporting them is that, in the great majority of cases, the victim has an established relationship with the rapist. When the victim is an adult, society tends to view this event as a private matter,

and the rapist may furthermore be a figure of authority whom the victim finds it difficult to go against. The authority of the rapist is especially an obstacle to seeking help when the victim is the rapist's own child.

The most important psychological factor in rape seems to be the urge to assert power over another. Many rapists report no sexual pleasure but say that they have enjoyed dominating their victims.

In anthropological surveys, rape has not been found universally, and attitudes toward it have varied widely. LEFT *Out of 40 societies, rape was accepted or ignored in 10, ridiculed in four, mildly disapproved in eight and strongly disapproved in 18.* RIGHT *Out of 34 societies, rape was absent in eight, rare in 12 and common in 14.*

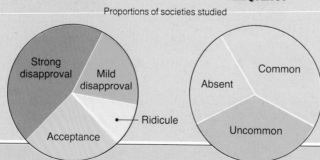

ATTITUDES
Proportions of societies studied

Strong disapproval
Mild disapproval
 Ridicule
Acceptance

FREQUENCY

Common
Absent
Uncommon

Challenges to male status

A number of facts suggest that domestic violence is in fact a response to real or perceived threats to male authority. A woman's body takes the blows, but they are aimed at her independence.

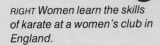

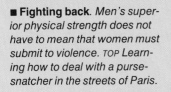

■ **Fighting back.** *Men's superior physical strength does not have to mean that women must submit to violence.* TOP *Learning how to deal with a purse-snatcher in the streets of Paris.*

RIGHT *Women learn the skills of karate at a women's club in England.*

The threats that men perceive may take various forms, but a recent study has identified the highest rates of violence among two types of families. In the first, the male is working-class, believes strongly in male superiority, and is married to a wife who has a relatively better job. The husband feels that his dominance is threatened. In the second type of family, which has the highest rates of violence, the husband is typically a professional man who sets an exceptional high value on social status and feels that he is being held back by his wife. Fully 40 percent of the women in this group are battered. Apparently, while the working-class males use violence to enforce control over their higher-status wives, the professional men become violent in response to their feeling that their higher position has not been appropriately rewarded.

Women who are separated or divorced – states that are effectively declarations of female independence – are also frequently victims of violence. The National Crime Survey in the USA indicates that separated women are the most vulnerable group, with divorced women next and married women last. Violence in casual relationships is almost as common (and as serious) as violence among traditional couples, indicating again that the family is only one setting in which women are battered.

Many men also perceive pregnancy as a threat. Studies in the USA indicate that up to 25 percent of all pregnant

179

women may be living with a man who abuses them, and for them the risk of battering is greatest during pregnancy. Battered women have no more children than nonbattered women, but they are pregnant nearly twice as often (often because they have been raped by the batterer) and are significantly more likely to have had a miscarriage or abortion.

The issues which lead to violence and the pattern of abusive injuries also point to sexual politics. One study in Britain reveals that domestic violence typically involves "Who's boss?" and begins in fights over money, housework, child care or sex. These are subjects in which sex stereotypes are most rigid. Injuries are typically concentrated on the face, breast or stomach, areas that symbolize female sexuality to men. In the United States, it is suggested that battering may be the single most common context for rape, accounting for a third of all rapes and for half of all rapes if a woman is over 30.

Although childhood abuse, poverty, alcohol and unemployment all contribute to domestic violence, their influence is small compared to the inequalities inherent between men and women and the struggles involving their relative status, authority and power.

Aggression and the family system

Aggression, anger, rage, hate and hostility are all too frequently lumped together as expressions of a "violence-prone" or otherwise disturbed personality. However, each of these states has a definite place in normal life. Aggression springs from an innate desire to grow and to master life. Mature adults attempt actively to shape or reshape their environment, to satisfy personal goals and desires. Only when

this process is obstructed does it lead to anger, rage and hate, and, eventually, ruthless, perhaps even homicidal, violence.

In a study tracing the experiences of 393 couples from the period just before they were married, 42 percent of the women and 33 percent of the men reported that over the past year they had in some way attacked their partner. What is especially interesting is that even the more aggressive

■ **Champions of battered women**. *The only real help and support for many abused women and their children is to be found in refuges like Chiswick House in England, founded by Erin Pizzey* ABOVE. *The face of the child sitting next to her cannot be shown because of an impending court case about her custody.* LEFT *Workers at a women's refuge in South London where local government authorities provide some of the funding for their activities.*

180

The family is typically a male-dominated system and some men react violently if their dominance is threatened. There have always been battered wives and the growing independence of women may be a new contributing factor.

couples had high scores on a marital adjustment test, indicating that they were relatively satisfied with their relationships. Indeed, many couples reporting aggressive behavior had very high marital satisfaction scores.

Are these aggressive relationships "violent" or "abusive?" Some probably are. These young couples may simply be naive about the consequences if physical aggression escalates. But the majority of aggressive couples are satisfied because they recognize that fulfilling relationships are possible only where individuals openly and aggressively negotiate for their basic rights and needs.

The family as a system is often characterized by inequality, conflict and contradiction. As a structure traditionally dominated by males, it requires all the members of the family to assume roles that may correspond very poorly to their real needs. All of them need control over their own lives, and the chance to support other members of the family and receive support from them, but this is impossible to attain in a structure dominated by men and from which men benefit more than do women or children. Thus, it is inevitable that women and children will struggle to expand their options.

Unfortunately, many men respond violently, seeking to obstruct these aggressive struggles for autonomy by sub-jugating the women and children. Violence typically arises in the attempt to obstruct or suppress someone's aggressive attempt to resist the family's status quo. Whether the domestic partner who initiates violence is male or female, once violence occurs, the woman, because of her lack of strength and legal rights, is always the one to suffer most, and, ironically, is the one least able to leave the violent situation.

Domestic violence is both historically conditioned and socially supported. Men typically become violent because they believe it "works." They have learned that one way to gain control in the home is to lose control physically (an option they do not even consider at work). Some men first pick up this message from watching their own fathers or brothers. Drugs, alcohol or psychological problems do sometimes contribute to the problem, but in virtually all cultures men resort to violence simply to get their way. The rewards may be tangible, such as control over money, domestic labor and sexual favors, or intangible, such as the status associated with "possessing" a woman. To this extent, violence is rational behavior, no matter how damaging it is, psychologically or otherwise.

There is no evidence that violence against women and children is more common today than a century ago. However, women's growing independence, and the decline of the traditional view of male superiority, may be encouraging men to resort to violence to maintain their privileges. **ES**

181

◄ **Helpless against the tide of male aggression**. *Police prepare to confront anti-government demonstrators in South Korea and a woman lays her head against a riot shield in a desperate pleading gesture. Women are often the helpless victims when men use violence against men to settle questions of dominance. Although many countries employ female police officers in a wide range of duties, and armies recruit women soldiers, it is rare for them to be used in armed combat.*

Emotions and Adjustment

THERE IS a common view of women as emotional, anxious and irrational. They are supposed to be volatile in their moods, and at the mercy of a monthly cycle that plays havoc with their mental state. Men are seen as independent, logical and less prone to emotional outbursts but more aggressive, less sympathetic and with less appreciation of art and literature. In one study , psychiatrists asked to describe the well-adjusted woman, pictured her as dependent, unambitious and less objective. They saw men as less emotional and largely unable to appreciate the feelings of others or to express tender feelings of their own. How accurate are these impressions which are held even by professional therapists? Are women's emotions really more easily aroused than men's? Do men really have calmer temperaments, and lower fear and anxiety levels?

Are women more fearful?

A common belief is that women are more fearful and timid than men. This would, on the face of it, seem to be borne out by an American study that aimed to try out different ways of curing people of snake-phobia. To find subjects, researchers advertised in the local newspaper for people who were afraid of snakes and were willing to join the study. Far more women than men answered the advertisement (43 women and five men were included in the experiment). However, this does not necessarily tell us that women are more *afraid* of snakes, but only that they are willing to *admit* to such fear.

There are many indications that fear, or at any rate the willingness to express it, is something males and females learn to control in different ways during their early lives. In small children no sex difference in fearful behavior is seen. Parents of those under six, asked to record when and in what circumstances their children show fear give remarkably similar reports for boys and girls. However, when children are old enough to report on their own fears, they begin to show researchers a different pattern, and it is girls who report more fear.

Teachers also say that girls are more timid than boys. Many psychologists believe that this is because boys learn, in response to adult expectation, not to show or admit to fear. "Big boys are not afraid. Men don't cry."

▲ **Showing emotion by hiding it**. *Men's feelings may go as deep as women's, but they are more likely to try to hide them. Ironically, covering his face with his hands shows us how much emotion this rugby player must be experiencing.*

▶ **Expressing the fear she has been hiding**. *Denial of fear may help us to control it. Research has found novice parachutists to feel increasing fear as the day of the jump approaches, but they do not admit to it. This probably helps them keep up the courage they need in order to go through with their commitment. Men more than women are taught as children not to show or admit to fear.*

Popular opinion is that women are more emotional and so less rational than men. Research shows that men conceal their emotions but not that they feel less. Men cope by hiding fears. Women cope by expressing anxieties.

It seems that boys use just such bravado on questionnaires. In addition to fear-related questions, some researchers add other questions designed to test for fake bravery – for example, "When one of your friends won't play with you, do you feel badly?" Boys are less likely to say they feel badly and are almost certainly being untruthful.

The general picture is that whether or not women actually feel more fear than men, they undoubtedly show and admit to more.

Are men more angry?

Anger is an emotion that seems to be very closely related to fear. Both involve similar bodily changes. When we are afraid or angry, our heart beats more rapidly, our breathing rate changes, and there is an increase in muscle tone and secretions from sweat glands. We equip ourselves for "fight or flight" – offensive or defensive action. These changes are brought about by an increase in the levels of two hormones – adrenaline and noradrenaline.

There may be a difference in male and female emotional response linked with the relative level of these two hormones. Early research showed that injecting only noradrenaline into an experimental subject produces a set of "fear-type" bodily responses, while injecting adrenaline and noradrenaline together induces a slightly different "anger-type" set of bodily changes. (In anger, the increase in muscle tone is greater, and there are more fluctuations in blood pressure and heart rate. In fear, there is a greater increase in respiration and more fluctuations occur in muscle tension and sweat gland secretions.) Interestingly, in a number of studies of men and women under stress such as being in an examination, women have shown a tendency to produce higher levels of noradrenaline but not higher levels of adrenaline than normal, while in men both noradrenaline and adrenaline increase. This could fit with the idea that women are more likely to show fear and defensive behavior when men feel anger and show aggressive behavior.

The limbic system, a region of the mid-brain, is heavily involved in the experience of emotion. Experimental stimulation of different parts of the limbic system (by applying tiny electric shocks during neurosurgery) can produce feelings of hunger, pain or thirst, or feelings of fear, sadness, anger or possessiveness or a desire for solitude. Not only does the limbic system affect hormone levels, but hormones themselves, including the sex hormones, can have an effect on the limbic system. Emotional arousal in men and women is a result of this complex interplay.

To see whether there are any differences in anger in

STEREOTYPES OF OUR EMOTIONS

■ *In reality, individual men and women are not uniformly "male" and uniformly "female" in their emotional responses, but* *researchers have found that we commonly think of the following patterns as characteristic of the sexes:*

MALE	FEMALE
Aggressive	*Unaggressive*
Independent	*Dependent*
Unemotional	*Very emotional*
Hides emotions	*Does not hide emotions*
Not excitable	*Excitable in a minor crisis*
Active	*Passive*
Feelings not easily hurt	*Feelings easily hurt*
Not aware of feelings of others	*Aware of feelings of others*
Very little need for security	*Strong need for security*
Does not cry very easily	*Cries very easily*
Ambitious	*Unambitious*
Able to keep feelings separate from ideas	*Unable to separate feelings from ideas*

males and females, researchers in the past have often looked at behavior, taking aggressive behavior as indicative of angry feelings. Men show more aggressive behavior than women, but more recent studies which have focused on self-reported anger indicate that there are few sex differences. Women do, however, show more anxiety about angry feelings and are likely to respond to "upsetting" events with tears rather than aggression. It is clear that we learn to interpret internal bodily states (changes in heart rate, sweating and shaking) from clues in the social environment. While girls learn to read these signals as distress, boys learn to label them as anger. Once we have attached a name to the emotion, we know the appropriate behavior – tears or blows.

Life events and our emotions

Women are far more likely than men to consult a psychiatrist about depression. Is this another manifestation of their readiness to admit to their mental state or do they really become seriously depressed more often than men? Many psychologists have studied the effects of stressful life events on people's emotional state, and some of this research has focused on sex differences. In one study, men and women from a variety of social and economical groups and of different races in the United States were asked to say how "upsetting" they thought 61 typical life events are to the

people experiencing them. These events ranged from minor ones like a temporary illness or moving house to major traumas such as a jail sentence, business failure or the death of a close relative. There was no significant difference between men and women in the relative order in which they placed these events on the "upsettingness scale." There was a difference, however, in the *amount* of emotional upset

---

EMOTIONS AND THE MALE MENOPAUSE

■ *Men experience a slower and more gradual change in their reproductive life with aging than do women. Levels of the male hormone, testosterone, do not usually decline significantly until the age of 70. However some men in their 50s and 60s experience many of the same symptoms that women experience during their menopausal years. Of 62 middle-aged men seeking medical help for symptoms of a male "menopause" 13 had hot flushes and 32 had sleep problems, depression or anxiety problems.*

For most men, though, aging is not accompanied by these adverse effects. There are well-studied changes in sexuality, but these need not be unwelcome ones. Older men may take longer to attain an erection, but the erection persists for longer and they are better able to control ejaculation. Older men are reported to derive more pleasure from an orgasm and may welcome a decrease in sexual tension.

A healthy and positive emotional attitude to aging can be encouraged by being informed about and prepared for changes, accepting them and keeping alive a happy and active sex life where possible. Many men are able to welcome the shift in emphasis of their relationships away from the more urgent sexual needs of their earlier years and enjoy their later years fully.

EMOTIONS AND THE FEMALE MENOPAUSE

■ *Unlike men, women experience a relatively sudden end to their reproductive lives – one that is clearly and inescapably identified by the cessation of their monthly periods. This usually happens between the ages of 45 and 55 and may be accompanied by a number of physical and emotional disturbances that vary in their intensity between individuals. Some women experience only mild symptoms. Others go through a period of severe emotional and bodily disturbances – hot flushes, headaches, insomnia, bone pains, irritability and depression.*

There are dramatic changes in hormone levels at menopause, but researchers have failed to discover any clear link between the extent of these and the severity of symptoms. Hormone replacement therapy is effective in some cases but of equal importance is a woman's attitude to the menopause. This

event can be seen as signifying the onset of old age, loss of attractiveness and sexuality and declining powers. Women who are dependent, anxious and depressive tend to have a more difficult time at menopause. The physical symptoms can be alleviated by a good diet and exercise; to combat the emotion

problems one needs the support of family and friends and a thorough understanding of and acceptance of the menopause. Women who are employed outside the home usually find that having a job helps them cope.

Women need not fear the menopause or be pessimistic about life after it. Very many

◄ **Emotional balance in middle age**. *Hormonal upsets marking the end of our reproductive lives need not interfere with the enjoyment of happy, harmonious relationships.*

women find that their 40s and 50s are the most enjoyable and rewarding years of their lives. They become free from the demands of young children, and equipped with the maturity and self-confidence of their years, are able to lead full and vigorous lives. Loss of reproductive capacity does not have to mean a decline in sexual feelings or an end to active sex. For many it removes anxieties and makes sex more enjoyable.

Women rate life crises as more upsetting than men do. They are also more likely to suffer from depression. This has been linked to feelings of powerlessness in their everyday lives, rather than the stress of having multiple roles.

they thought each event would cause. On average, women rated most life events 25 percent more upsetting than men did, and this was true of events experienced just as commonly by men as by women.

Why should women expect events in people's lives to have more impact on emotions than men would expect? Psychologists think that it may be because they are already heavily burdened with stress in their own lives. However, it is not, as might be expected, the women who are juggling the dual roles of mother and worker who are most likely to experience stress, but housewives at home. Compared to employed wives, housewives feel more anxious, lonely and worthless. They also often feel powerless to control many aspects of their lives because of the needs and demands of their families. This makes the effects of sudden changes in their lives more acute. But, even if women have a greater emotional response to their environments than men, it does not necessarily affect their performance. Physical stress like noise and high or low temperature affect men and women equally, as judged by their performance of mental and physical tasks. Overcrowded conditions upset men more.

The positive emotions

Positive emotions like joy, happiness, love and empathy are expressed in activities like caring, nurturing and help-

ing. These warm, interpersonal behaviors are all thought of as more feminine than masculine. Men are usually seen as competitive, less caring and less likely to express tenderness. Perhaps women have evolved a greater capacity to show love and empathy because of their role in caring for their young. There is, as we shall see, evidence that they do have such a tendency but it is not marked and could as easily be a result as much of social conditioning as any inborn quality.

Several studies have focused on nurturing and parenting behavior. One group of researchers looked at female animals who had never given birth to discover whether they would show maternal behavior when presented with another's litter. They did, but took a longer time to show caring behavior. This adjustment time could be dramatically shortened by giving the animal an injection of blood serum taken from a newly delivered mother, suggesting that the serum contained hormones that triggered a maternal response. The longer the time since the donor mother had given birth the less effective the serum was, so even though hormones may prepare a mother to care for her newborn infant, this effect is probably limited to a very short period.

Animal studies like this may not tell us very much about humans. Observations on fathers allowed time alone with their newborn infants show that they are likely to spend, if anything, more time touching, rocking, cuddling and looking at their babies than mothers do. This is true of all races and income groups studied regardless of whether or not the

▲ **Emotions and life crises.** *Major disturbances in our lives can arouse a strong emotional response. In psychological questionnaires, women identify typical life crises as more upsetting than men do. It is impossible to measure objectively whether women feel more emotion on such occasions, but it is clear that part of their coping strategy is to express their emotions more than men do. These women at a funeral for tornado victims in Texas are giving full expression to their grief.*

▲ **An emotional moment.** *For this couple a new life is beginning as the man returns home from a rehabilitation center for drug addicts. He shares the emotions of the event with his partner. Sharing emotions and feeling empathy are characteristics attributed more to women than to men but this does not mean men are unfeeling or lacking in emotions. They are more likely to share their feelings in a private situation than make them public.*

Men are more likely than women to become drug and alcohol abusers, while women are more prone to depression and anxiety. Women, compared with men, are more likely to admit to mental problems and seek professional advice.

father was present at the delivery. In other studies, men have proved slower than women to show caring behavior but just as responsive once the behavior has been established.

What of empathy? Partly, empathy means understanding how another feels. Researchers have studied this in men, boys, women and girls by showing them pictures of people showing various emotions. Both sexes were quite successful in identifying the emotions. However, empathy also means being moved by another's emotions. Some experiments suggest that women are more affected by another's plight than men. The subjects in one of these were instructed to administer an electric shock to someone learning a task, every time the person made an error. Women gave milder shocks than men and this difference became even more pronounced if the women had met the person per-

forming the learning task at the beginning of the experiment. Empathy is also shown in helping, comforting and sharing. Small girls are slightly more likely than boys to offer help, sympathy, comfort and to share toys.

Biorhythms and emotions

Men and women alike go through a daily cycle of change in body temperature and mental state that can be related to performance. There is some evidence that their are sex differences in this cycle. For both sexes, body temperature changes, ability at mental arithmetic, long-term memory and reaction times follow the same pattern of change with time of day, but there are slight sex differences in patterns of sleeping and in fatigue and arousal patterns. In studies of volunteers who occupied underground chambers for a month or more without knowing the time, it was found that we tend to stray from our usual 24-hour cycle – adopting, for example, a 25-hour cycle. Although individuals vary, women tend on average toward a cycle that is one half-hour shorter than men's and on average 18 percent longer than men's in these conditions. Cyclical changes in anxiety, extroversion, stress and depression are the same for men and women.

The monthly menstrual cycle has been recognized for at least 50 years as having an effect in women's emotional state. Statistics suggest that women are more likely to have road accidents and commit suicide in the few days of each month before menstruation begins – the premens. There are

---

MENSTRUATION AND MOODS

■ A number of physical and emotional functuations are related to stages of the menstrual cycle. The physical changes are well understood but none of them has been shown to cause the changes in emotional states which many women experience. Research suggests that the degree of mood change depends partly on whether a woman expects to experience them. Public discussion of premenstrual tension and the unpleasant aspects of the menstrual cycle may actually cause some of them. From 2 to 3 percent of women experience severely distressing premenstrual symptoms; 70 percent report moderate emotional and physical changes.

■ Feelings of physical and emotional well-being typically characterize the middle of the cycle and tend to decline after ovulation.

■ During the few days preceding menstruation many women report that they often feel irritable, depressed and sometimes aggressive. Physical conditions such as breast tenderness, a feeling of bloatedness and fatigue are well-documented and may contribute to these emotional states.

■ Levels of four hormones, estrogen, progesterone, follicle-stimulating hormone (FSH) and luteinizing hormone (LH) control the development of an egg in the ovary, its release at midcycle (ovulation) and the preparation of the uterus lining to receive it if it is fertilized.

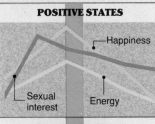

POSITIVE STATES

Happiness

Sexual interest   Energy

NEGATIVE STATES

Irritability   Physical complaints
Unhappiness

HORMONE LEVELS

LH   Progesterone
FSH
Estradiol

Ovulation
Menstruation   Premens
28 day cycle

► **Showing their positive emotions.** *TOP A couple who have won 10 million dollars show their joy and excitement in almost identical facial expressions. TOP RIGHT A mother and daughter share an affectionate exchange as part of the happiness of a loving relationship. BOTTOM RIGHT French Pentecostals offer their children to God. Their faces express the full emotion of this intensely spiritual occasion. BOTTOM LEFT The woman in this picture is making a conventionally female social display that causes her to appear more emotional than the men, but there is not necessarily any real difference in pleasure felt.*

also suggestions that at this time they are more likely to fail at interviews, beat their children and fail examinations, but these findings are not universal. There are certainly well-studied and clearly recognized physical changes during the menstrual cycle and there is some degree of physical discomfort and irritability in the few days during and, especially, preceding menstruation (see box).

Recent research suggests that some of the more extreme symptoms of premenstrual tension are partly brought on by women's expectation that they will occur. Most studies in the past involved women who were aware that their moods were being recorded in relation to their menstrual cycle. In studies involving women who are unaware that the research is about the menstrual cycle, there is less correlation between stage of the cycle and moods or activities.

Several studies which have sought a relationship between specific hormone levels and changes in mood and intellectual performance have found none. In the light of these findings one group of psychologists designed an experiment to discover whether moods experienced during menstruation could actually be manipulated by suggestion. They showed one group of women a film emphasizing the stresses and

187

discomforts of menstruation and another a film designed to give a positive and reasoning attitude to the menstrual cycle. The first group experienced far more unpleasant symptoms, during their subsequent two cycles, than the second. Women who expect to have unpleasant experiences related to menstruation are more likely to have them than those who do not.

Whatever the reason, some women do report real cycle-related discomforts and for some it evidently affects their everyday lives. But what of their performance in, for example, intellectual tasks? Where academic performance has been carefully measured, as in the case of a large group of female medical students who were followed through a year of their medical program, the menstrual cycle was not shown to have any effect even when the women reported physical discomfort.

What of men? Are their moods affected by hormone levels, and are there any cyclic changes in them? Researchers have found that, in some men, specific mood changes accompany changes in the amount of the male sex hormone, testosterone, in their blood. Strangely, the nature of the effect is different from one individual to another – some men feel more depressed, some more interested in sex and some more aggressive when testosterone levels are high.

In all men the levels of testosterone and other hormones fluctuate, and in some this may happen in regular cycles. However, these are not of a standard length or as predictable as the menstrual cycle in a women. In one group of men whose moods and hormones were monitored over a 60 day period, over half experienced cyclic changes but in cycles that varied from eight to 30 days. Research on cyclic variations in male hormones has only recently begun and there are no answers yet to questions about how widespread they are or why they happen.

188

ANOREXIA NERVOSA – A "FEMALE" ILLNESS?

■ *Anorexia nervosa is an eating disorder that mainly affects girls and women in their teens and early twenties. Only about 10 percent of anorexics are men. It is characterized by obsessive dieting that leads to excessive and sometimes fatal weight loss. The victim sees herself as fat even when reduced to a near skeleton. Anorexics tend to be high achievers and perfectionists. One theory is that they feel a sense of control when they succeed in losing weight – adolescents are at a stage in their lives when they feel a great deal of conflict about control in their lives. One reason why women are more prone to the condition than men is that they feel more pressure from society and the mass-media to be thin. Research shows that 85 percent of adolescent girls want to be thinner. That is not the whole story, however, since 45 percent of young men also want to be thinner. The difference is that men take exercise rather than dieting to lose weight. Some authorities have drawn parallels between women anorexics and men who indulge obsessively in physical exercise.*

CORONARY HEART DISEASE - A "MALE" ILLNESS?

■ *Cardiovascular disease, the leading cause of death in most industrial countries affects about twice as many men as women. It has been linked to the type-A behavior patterns characterized by:*
    eating and talking rapidly
    impatience
    tendency to think about more than one thing at once
    guilt about relaxing
    constant feeling of urgency
    loud and explosive speech, loud stressing of key words
    feelings of hostility
    suppressed anger
    Of all these characteristics, the ones scientists have been able to correlate directly with the build-up of fatty deposits in blood vessels (which causes coronary heart disease) are suppressed anger and feelings of hostility. Hostile feelings often result from disguised fear.

    Researchers suggest that if feelings of anger and fear could be reduced, the risk of heart disease would diminish. Studies have shown that men who admit they are afraid and can take their problems to their mates have lower levels of cholesterol (a factor also linked to heart disease) in their blood. They also have higher success in their jobs.

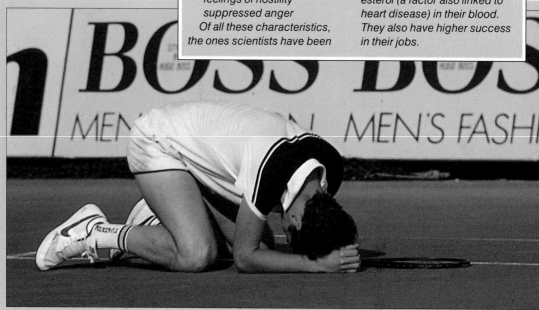

► **Coping with masculine emotions.** *Unlike this tennis player, giving vent to his frustration, men usually try to cope with their emotions by suppressing them. While hiding fear may have a positive value, studies of people experiencing grief, fear and guilt suggest that admitting and giving expression to their feelings helps them to cope physically and emotionally. Families whose members are able to discuss sadness and fear with one another have a lower rate of physical illness. Men may benefit by sharing their emotions more.*

Men are, on average, not as good at recognizing emotions and they show less caring behavior than women. But the difference is not marked and is probably a result of social conditioning. The sexes can be equally nurturant.

Our emotions can affect both our mental and physical health and men and women seem prone to different anxiety and stress-related illnesses. Men are more likely than women to suffer from coronary heart disease (see box), alcoholism and ulcers. They are also more likely to commit suicide. Women suffer more depression, phobias and eating disorders and are more likely than men to attempt suicide. Men and women are both likely to be victims of stress, so why should this lead to different kinds of mental and physical disorders? Is there some difference in the kinds of stress that men and women face or do they cope in different ways? The answer is probably yes to both of these possibilities.

Ulcers, typically a man's disease, are common in people in jobs with a high level of responsibility. One interesting experiment on monkeys looked at their susceptibility to ulcers in relation to responsibilities they were given. Pairs of monkeys were given mild but unpleasant electric shocks and one animal in each pair had the responsibility of pressing a lever to prevent the shock both for itself and its partner. Monkeys with this responsibility – the "executive monkeys" – were the most likely to get ulcers. But it was not only having the responsibility of pressing the lever that caused the ulcers. There were individual differences in the speed with which they hit the button. The more readily aroused ones who acted quickly were more likely to develop ulcers.

We are all familiar with the link between type A behavior patterns and coronary heart disease. Type A people are characteristically high-achievers who fight their way into top jobs. It is their personality and behavior which make them prone to heart disease, and the particular aspect of that personality which seems to be to blame is the tendency to hide anger and hostility – both male-type responses to the emotions of anger and fear.

Women's emotional makeup probably has little to do with their high rates of depression – this is more likely a result of lack of control in their lives – but the fact that they seek medical help rather than turning to alcohol is characteristic of women's readiness to admit to their emotions. The fact that women are more likely only to attempt suicide suggests that this is a desperate way of drawing attention to their needs for comfort and support.

What conclusion can be drawn then about men, women and their emotions? There may be small but real differences in the emotions they experience but the greatest difference is in the ways they express them.

It must be emphasized that these are *average* differences. Many men are more fearful, anxious or expressive than many women. Many women are more aggressive, competitive and stoic than many men. What we can gain from looking at sex differences is pointers about how the sexes cope with their emotions, how to make the most of the positive emotion like happiness, joy and trust and how best to handle the negative ones like fear and anger. **AC**

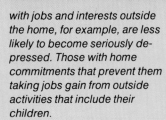

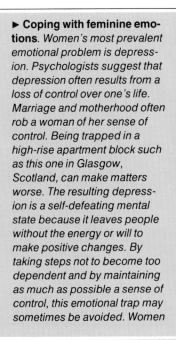

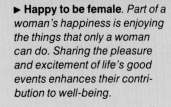

189

► **Coping with feminine emotions**. *Women's most prevalent emotional problem is depression. Psychologists suggest that depression often results from a loss of control over one's life. Marriage and motherhood often rob a woman of her sense of control. Being trapped in a high-rise apartment block such as this one in Glasgow, Scotland, can make matters worse. The resulting depression is a self-defeating mental state because it leaves people without the energy or will to make positive changes. By taking steps not to become too dependent and by maintaining as much as possible a sense of control, this emotional trap may sometimes be avoided. Women*

with jobs and interests outside the home, for example, are less likely to become seriously depressed. Those with home commitments that prevent them taking jobs gain from outside activities that include their children.

► **Happy to be female**. *Part of a woman's happiness is enjoying the things that only a woman can do. Sharing the pleasure and excitement of life's good events enhances their contribution to well-being.*

In the Workplace

ALTHOUGH every culture, from the simplest tribal communities to complex, stratified ones, makes sex distinctions in how it divides working roles, modern industrial societies have increasingly attempted to open the same employment opportunities to women as to men. Statistics show that women's role in the workplace has vastly expanded. However, men are still economically at an advantage and women at a disadvantage – they do not have the same opportunities and do not receive equal pay for equal work. Why is this so? Painstaking research has shown that no one type of person (such as the type called male or the type called female) is to blame for the inequality that persists so stubbornly. To blame are certain specific practices common to all employment, coupled with enduring features of our human nature.

Traditional divisions of labor

Anthropologists have found a generally consistent division of tasks between the men and women in subsistence cultures. In some groups, sex roles are more rigid than in others, and, in many, people sometimes cross sex divisions to perform work that must be done. However, activities that are more strenuous, cooperative and involve long-distance travel are usually carried out by men. Activities that are more solitary, interruptible and close to home are performed by women, generally with the help of their daughters and young sons.

A typically consistent division of work occurs in crafts. In most cultures, men do the work involved in manufacturing objects of metal, wood, stone, bone and shell. Women usually do the spinning, weaving, potting, basket-making and clothes-making. When men do these tasks, it is usually where they become a specialized commercial activity.

In hunter-gatherer societies, men are the hunters and usually also the fishers and women do most of the gathering. This means that for Eskimos, who eat almost nothing but meat and fish, men supply almost all the food, while for Kalahari Bushmen in southern Africa, whose diet is heavily balanced toward plants, women supply up to three-quarters of what people eat. In societies that combine hunting and gathering with some agriculture, the crops are usually the sole concern of women. (Probably it was women who first developed this revolutionary food supply – the plant- and seed-gathering women of those hunter-gatherer groups in the Middle East, some 10,000 years ago, who were the first people to derive part of their subsistence from cultivated crops.) Among settled people who live mainly from agriculture, the work of growing food tends to be shared, in some fashion, by the sexes.

A worldwide survey in 1937 found about the same number of cultures where women prepare the soil and do the planting as ones where men do this. The number of societies where women tend and harvest the crops outnumber those where men do, but there are many cultures where either sex may do these jobs. Throughout sub-Saharan Africa, women traditionally have done most of the weeding

▶ Bearing burdens. In 78 percent of subsistence cultures surveyed, it is usually women who gather and carry home fuel – mainly firewood, as here in Nepal. In 15 percent, men usually do this work, and only 7 percent of subsistence cultures do not regard it as a special task of one sex. Women are the usual water-carriers in 89 percent, and they usually carry the other burdens in 59 percent. Most other work is also sex-typed.

Modern industrial societies attempt to open the same employment opportunities to women as to men. However, women still achieve promotions less easily, and receive less pay for the same work. Neither men nor women are "to blame."

and cultivating, using the wooden digging-stick. In Europe and Asia, where plow and draft animals are used, men have the major agricultural responsibilities. The one job most usually defined as male is clearing land.

In many cultures there are distinctive men's and women's crops. For example, in the West African forest belt, it is mostly women who cultivate cassava, corn, beans and small "cocoa" yams. They do this near and within the village. Men travel farther from home to clear and burn patches in the forest where they scoop up soil with broad iron hoes to make high mounds where they grow white yams.

Why is there a general division of subsistence work by sex? First, some of the differences seem to be best explained by the fact that women usually do tasks compatible with infant care. For instance, household tasks are relatively in-

terruptible, take place close to home and pose little danger to nearby children. Second, some differences appear to be related to men's greater physical strength (especially shoulder and upper arm strength) and their capacity for quick bursts of energy. For instance, hunting often calls for running, throwing and lifting heavy carcasses. Third, some work seems to fall to men or women simply because it is close in the production sequence to other tasks for which they are responsible. For instance, men make nets and rope, used in fishing, while women make thread and spin cloth, used to make clothes. **CE**

Working for employers

In the United States and most of western Europe, women are a large proportion of the work force. For instance, they hold 44 percent of the paid jobs in the United States, approximately double the rate immediately following World War II. The most dramatic increase has been among the mothers of young children. Over one-half of married American women with preschool children are employed at least part-time. In the 1970s, only a third of such women worked outside the home.

Some change has also occurred in the structure of the labor market. At the end of World War II, fewer than 13 percent of the American female labor force held professional or managerial positions. Since then, increasing numbers of women have begun to enter the professions, through law schools, medical schools and schools of business administration. In the United States, for example, some analysts

▲ **"Men and women at work"** *increasingly means working together at the same tasks. Here currency dealers share a desk in Beirut. Women still face barriers to promotion and seldom receive equal pay for equal work.*

▶ **Man's work.** *Hard, physical, outdoor work in industrial cities, such as this window cleaning in Dallas, Texas, is almost always a man's job. Equal opportunity legislation, however, has guaranteed that women are represented in almost every area of employment.*

191

claim that in the late 1980s women constituted nearly a quarter of the nation's law students – a 400 percent increase over the previous two decades.

Not everything has changed, however. In some ways, the position of women in the work force is the same today as it was in the 1940s. More women than men are out of work and seeking work. More women than men work fewer hours than they would like. Only one category of male worker in the United States fares worse than the women – the black teenager.

Also, once women do obtain employment, they tend to cluster in particular sectors of the economy, while men cluster in others. Within the legal profession, for instance, women most often handle family law or public-interest law, while men more often work as highly paid corporation lawyers. Almost one-half of British medical students are women, but only 2 percent win out in the fierce competition for appointments as surgeons. Partly, this is parallel to the division of labor in subsistence cultures – women tend to cluster in jobs that can be interrupted in order to have a baby or to stay at home on days when a child is ill. Also they find it harder to compete for attractive jobs, because their husbands may be transferred, or they are themselves unable to move to take up distant posts. However, researchers have observed a new trend in the United States – large corporations have lowered their expectation that the most talented male employees will agree to be transferred. Talented men are likely to be married to talented women whose careers cannot be disrupted.

Even when women and men do perform the same work, men earn a great deal more money. This was especially well illustrated by the results of an employment survey in a suburb of Boston. The researchers took particular care to match women and men in terms of their ages, training,

seniority and the prestige attached to their jobs. The 162 employed women in the survey were matched to the 183 employed men on job attitudes (such as commitment) as well as on objective criteria (such as job title). There was only one difference between the samples, and that difference involved salary. The men earned 40 percent a year more, on average, than the exactly comparable women.

This survey, while meticulously conducted, included only

■ **Power and status in the workplace** *usually goes to men. Research shows that men in highly prestigious positions are more aware of and sympathetic about sex discrimination and other problems of women at work than men in lower positions are. The prestigious jobs continue, however, to be held predominantly by men. TOP LEFT Members of the London Metal Exchange pose with a selection of the commodities they deal in. TOP RIGHT A sea-faring man captains his ship. Women are more successful at being promoted to positions of authority when the organizations that employ them have a higher proportion of women in such roles.*

Overwhelmingly in the industrial world women fill jobs that use their traditional nurturant qualities – teaching, nursing, caring for children – or they supply cheap labor. BOTTOM LEFT A childminder in England. BOTTOM RIGHT Workers in a pineapple cannery in Thailand.

Women tend to cluster in female jobs, men in male ones. When both are represented within a single profession, such as medicine or law, men tend to dominate the most prestigious and best-paid specializations.

345 people, but economists have conducted national surveys throughout the United States and Britain, including large numbers of employed women and men. In these surveys the researchers examine the wage structure among male workers and then assign points for various characteristics, both of workers and of jobs, according to how much each characteristic influences earning among the men. Points are assigned, for example, to years of education, years of on-the-job experience, and level of job responsibility. If earnings relate statistically more to the employee's years of training than to his education, then training receives more points than education.

The next step is to apply the points system to female workers. This step invariably reveals that females earn significantly less money than the males. Increasing years of experience, for instance, spell large increases in earnings for men, but only small increases for women.

Why do inequalities persist?

How can we explain these persistent inequalities? Given the rapid increase in the number of women at work, why has there not been an equally swift fall in the rates of female unemployment, in the segregation of the labor force by sex and in the wage differentials?

Pressure groups, on both the political right and the political left, have approached the puzzle by blaming people. Feminists have pointed the accusing finger at men, and especially at men in positions of authority. Scoffers at feminism, on the other hand, have labeled female workers

193

WHY WOMEN DO NOT COMPLAIN

■ In view of the obvious inequalities that persist in the workplace, why do women not complain? The answer is that most women, most of the time, imagine themselves to be immune. They recognize that, generally speaking, women are at a disadvantage, but each believes she is the exception to the rule. This phenomenon, known as "the denial of personal disadvantage," was first documented in a study conducted in Massachusetts. The employed women in that study earned 60 percent of what the men earned even though the two groups were identical in terms of their qualifications and, theoretically, in terms of their jobs. Without question, the women in the survey suffered from inequality. When questioned, the women showed that they were well aware of the extent of inequality in the economy. They even estimated correctly the differential earning power of women and men in, for example, white collar jobs, and they expressed resentment about sex discrimination in general. Yet, the very same group of women declared themselves content with their own jobs. They displayed virtually no awareness that they themselves earned only six-tenths of what they would have earned if they were men. What accounts for this? One factor is people's reluctance to see themselves as mere statistics. Figures can apply to other people, preferably people we have not and will never meet. But it is hard – even distasteful – to think of them applying to us. We also have a naive assumption that all injustices are caused by malicious people. If we assume that every injustice is really the fault of some person or persons, then the lack of malicious people in our own environment leads us to conclude that we could not possibly be the victims of injustice. The assumption that wrongs only come from villains is, of course, incorrect. Injustices can exist even when everyone we know has good intentions. **FJC**

Inertia causes organizations that are mainly male to delay the readjustments that women employees will necessitate. Once they have enough women managers, however, hiring women no longer seems out of the ordinary.

as inferior, or at least as lacking in ambition and leadership skills. Neither extreme is correct.

The majority of men do not now overtly distrust women in working roles. Public opinion surveys, conducted with great frequency in the United States, have shown that over the years support for working women has increased dramatically. In the 1930s, the public thought the only acceptable motive for a woman going out to work was dire economic need, and no one then felt self-conscious about claiming that women were best suited to routine tasks. Managerial decisions, they said then, should be left to the men. Even in the 1960s only a minute percentage of the population recognized sex discrimination as a serious problem. Today, the public are in favor of equal opportunities, and the majority

of men and women are worried that the economy places women at a disadvantage.

Attitudes have changed just as rapidly and as much among the men in power as among other men. In fact, those men whose work carries the most prestige tend to be even more favorably disposed toward female workers than are men in less prestigious occupations. Their attitude toward working women, furthermore, does not depend on whether they had an employed mother or have an employed wife.

However, while most men and women are no longer overtly opposed to the employment of women, some sex stereotypes still operate at an unconscious level. One study in particular reveals how unconscious stereotypes can perpetuate imbalances. Researchers looked at the promotions that had been recommended and granted in one office of the Army over a period of a few years. When they found that women obtained promotions less frequently than men, the researchers scrutinized the letters of recommendation.

A high proportion of the letters about male candidates referred to leadership skills, and a high proportion of the letters about female candidates referred to neat appearance. Promotions were granted, rightly enough, on the basis of leadership and not on the basis of appearance. The

▲ **Socializing after work** is an essential aspect of building the acquaintanceships that can help you to advance a career, but family responsibilities are more likely to call a woman away urgently after work than a man. Business contacts are becoming more accessible to some women as court rulings require traditional men's service clubs to change their male-only membership rules.

▲ **Sexual harassment** led this woman fire fighter in England to give up her job. Here it involves being the butt of a joke about "bunny girls." By conservative estimates, about 20 percent of American women employees experience unwelcome verbal or physical expressions of male sexuality at work. Sexual harassment occurs most frequently in occupations that stress the physical appearance of women workers, and airline stewardesses are frequent targets.

In one survey, fewer than 20 percent of women but nearly 75 percent of men said that they would feel flattered by a sexual proposal at work. About 10 percent of American male employees complain of unwanted attention, mainly from young unattached women.

194

question then arose: did the people who wrote the letters of reference – mostly male officers – feel that the women lacked leadership abilities? They did not. They felt that the women were very capable and deserved promotion, and they saw no significant differences between the female and male candidates. They were surprised and dismayed when the researchers pointed out the unconscious bias they had introduced into their letters.

This study of promotion letters provides an important clue to the mystery of persistent inequalities between the sexes. Clearly, there are similarly subtle factors, of which most of us are quite unconscious, that place female workers at a considerable disadvantage. First, people sometimes know that a woman could do the job as well as a man, but are reluctant to turn an organization upside down, simply to assure equality. Second, people sometimes miscalculate the true qualities of a woman, just because they imagine that her conduct in her present job results from her personality rather than from the requirements of the job itself. Finally, companies systematically undervalue females by persisting with criteria for job selection that distinguish accurately between male candidates, but put female candidates at a disadvantage.

The force of inertia

Inertia is a powerful force in every organization. Any sort of tinkering runs the risk of causing deterioration rather than improvement, and for this reason alone we are often reluctant to introduce change into systems that seem to function well. Let us suppose, for example, that a male applicant for a typist vacancy is clearly slightly better than a female applicant, but that the women secretaries all say they would feel uncomfortable with a man working in their midst. In such a case, is not the female applicant likely to get the job?

Now let us suppose the open position is not clerical but executive. If a female applicant appears slightly better qualified than a male applicant, the organization might still select the male. Why? In this case, the slight superiority of the female candidate might not assure enough organizational gain to offset the potential loss in organizational efficiency arising from the discomfort of the company's officers at the thought of sharing the executive washroom with a woman!

Each organization acts in isolation. Few organizations try to exclude men altogether from the typing pool, nor women altogether from executive positions. But the individual, isolated decisions are bound to have a cumulative effect.

▲ **Forming first impressions**, we are bound to be heavily influenced by a small sample of information. Psychologists say that we are "susceptible to salient cues." The most salient cue in this picture is that the man left of center is doing the talking and counting off points on his fingers in an authoritative way. He seems more important and more in command than the others. Another salient cue is that he is a man. We are likely to associate this with drive and competence, because we so much more often see men recognized for these qualities.

MUST ASSISTANTS STAY ASSISTANTS?

■ *We all have a tendency to imagine that behavior springs from people's personalities rather than from the requirements of their role in a system. We ascribe to the person the behavior that the situation brings out in them, and consider that they would behave in the same way more or less always. Unless we become very self-conscious about how we reason, we all commit this error. Everybody falls into the same trap. The trap has special relevance for women in the workplace, because they tend to be assistants. The role of assistant allows for some behavior that would be inappropriate in a leader – for example, waiting for other people to make decisions rather than taking important initiatives yourself. Since we usually see women in subordinate roles and usually see them shouldering no more than the responsibilities of a subordinate we tend to stereotype them as not having executive ability, one of the many hurdles that an individual woman faces when seeking promotion.* **FJC**

One aspect of inertia is the tendency of like to hire like. Of course, people resemble or differ from each other in a great number of ways. In some situations, however, sex is a salient characteristic, and in any organization it is likely to be a major factor in the recruitment of staff, unless there is a critical mass of women in its upper reaches. Once there is a critical mass, however, hiring more women will no longer seem out of the ordinary. Inertia itself will then operate to maintain a balance.

Why do women seem less able?

The examples about hiring a male typist or a female executive presuppose that organizations can gauge ability, and it is here that we find the second factor that subtly perpetuates imbalance. The more concrete or technical a job, the easier it is to assess ability. The more abstract, complex and managerial the job, the harder it is. We can say with some assurance whether or not someone will make a good typist. How are we to predict whether someone will make a good supervisor?

Imagine that you are seeking to hire a supervisor. You wish the person to possess good administrative skills and to display self-assurance. You have noticed a secretary who seems to be a paragon administratively (she keeps track of everything, and never loses anything) but she seems a little too meek for the post of supervisor. Many people, in such a situation, would not promote the secretary because they would assume that her meek behavior in the office stemmed from her personality.

Such an assumption is very likely to be wrong. To a degree that we rarely recognize, our behavior depends on our situation as much as, or even more than, it does on our personality. To behave meekly and perhaps overpolitely as a secretary is simply to behave in role. The person who behaves "appropriately" as a secretary – that is, nonassertively – usually also behaves appropriately as a supervisor – that is, assertively.

Because most female employees occupy subordinate positions, it is often assumed that women lack the necessary ambition and assertiveness to be effective in the middle and upper reaches of organizations. Women are said, for example, to suffer from "fear of success." Women's motives for seeking and keeping employment are commonly believ-

▲ **Police work** *is viewed more and more as an appropriate career for women. Their role has been expanded from care of female detainees to include community-relations, patrol, crowd-control and detection duties.*

▶ **High technology.** *Male and female silhouettes poised together over the precise design of an intricate circuit that eventually will be reduced to microchip proportions.*

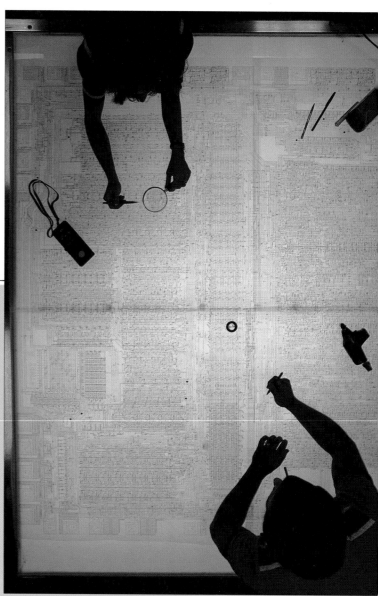

In most organizations, those at the top watch for promising subordinates and informally reserve for them an inner track in the race for promotion. Promising women are at a disadvantage, because there are so few at the top to help them.

ed to be different from those of men. Some people claim, for instance, that females work outside the home because they enjoy the companionship, while men are motivated by their enjoyment of autonomy and power. In fact, research shows that women and men are equally unafraid of success and work for very similar reasons.

The third factor that works to the disadvantage of women at work – and to the disadvantage of their employers – is the failure of employers to take context into account. Many organizations have standard means for predicting future performance. If, for instance, a large computer company finds that its most successful supervisors are those with a good mathematical ability, it is likely to use a mathematics test when selecting supervisors.

The problem is that a test that has differentiated well among one set of people may not differentiate well among another. The criteria used by the computer company, which were based on its experience with male candidates when it first began, could well rule out otherwise excellent female candidates. Compare, for example, the Scholastic Aptitude Tests that American high school students take when they apply to enter university. Scores give a fair indication of how well white middle-class students will do at university. The scores of black Americans, however, are a poor indicator of university performance. Should these tests then be used as a criterion for admission to university? Among whites, perhaps yes; but certainly not among blacks.

Standards such as these can also be misapplied when they are poorly specified. If I want to give the prize money to the horse that wins the race, I must have some unambiguous description of what it means to "win the race." Does it

mean crossing the line first or running faster than the other horses? The horse on the outside track might run faster than the others, and still not be the first to break the ribbon.

How does all this apply to the sexes? In most organizations, those at the top watch for promising subordinates and informally reserve for them an inner track. Promising women are at a disadvantage here, simply because there have been, and are still, so few women at the top to give them a helping hand. The promising young woman often has to scramble for a place at the starting line and must content herself with the outer track. No one discriminates consciously against her. Yet, unless the organization takes into account that she has had an outside track, she may never win. If the organization does take her starting position into account, it may lay itself open to cries of "reverse discrimination."

The first steps toward enhancing the position of women in the workplace have already been taken. The next step in the process is to recognize how many problems remain, despite good will on all sides. Very few of the disadvantages under which women still suffer can be accounted for by anti-female hostility. Nor is the real reason for their disadvantage lack of ability or ambition on the part of women workers. The real reasons for inequality between the sexes are more subtle and more complex. But even subtle factors can be changed. **FJC**

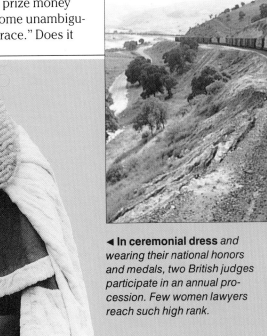

197

◄ **In ceremonial dress** *and wearing their national honors and medals, two British judges participate in an annual procession. Few women lawyers reach such high rank.*

▲ **Every boy's dream** *is to grow up to be a locomotive engineer, and this woman has realized it. For her living, Tonda Kennedy drives 150-car freight trains along the West Coast of the United States.*

FAMILY OR CAREER?

■ *"A career or a family – or both?"* This is the choice set before an increasing number of women. For the majority of working-class and rural women in the world, the question does not arise. Yet the seemingly enviable choice often becomes, for women in affluent societies, a soul-searching dilemma.

Modern women receive the same education as men and are brought up to expect the same rewards of job satisfaction, self-respect, independence and financial gain. However, today's standards of baby and child care are very high, and we expect our children to be stimulated and guided through their early years with a high degree of commitment and involvement. If a woman wants to combine a job with a family – and there are many strong reasons for wanting to do this – she still wants to make sure that her children receive this high quality of care. Affluent societies also have high ideals about the relationship between marriage partners, and women want to have loving relationships with their husbands in spite of being under pressure of work to give less time to them.

Common sense suggests that the strain of filling three demanding roles – wife, mother and worker – would make a woman worse off. But what does research show?

COSTS AND REWARDS

A large body of research shows that women today benefit psychologically and materially from combining roles. One study, conducted in Massachusetts, divided women into different categories reflecting the combinations of major life roles they played. Women who played three life roles – mother, worker and wife – were more satisfied with their lives and felt better about themselves than did women who played only two roles. Least happy were those with one role. Paid em-

ployment gave women a sense of competence. Motherhood and wifehood enhanced their sense of pleasure in life.

Numerous studies have confirmed this. For black women and white women, older women and younger women, women in high-prestige jobs and those in lower-level jobs, mothers of grown children and mothers of young children, there is, by and large, a strong positive association between the number of life roles and health. Unless the role burdens are too heavy (as, for example, is true of the wife role when the husband is violently abusive – see Ch21), women are happier, less depressed, physically healthier, more satisfied and more self-assured when they combine participation in the paid labor force with domestic responsibilities. Having important roles to play away from work (as, say, a wife, mother or volunteer worker) enhances job satisfaction. Working outside the family – either for pay or in volunteer projects – enhances satisfaction with home life.

Men benefit as much as women do when they fulfill different life roles. In fact, what originally led researchers to investigate the effects of multiple life roles among women was the observation that men, who have always combined family and work roles, evidence greater mental health than women.

It is perhaps a little surprising that women should benefit as much as men from the combination of paid work and home life. Women are, after all, at a disadvantage in the paid labor market. Many women feel they have to work harder (and prove themselves better)than a man to reap the same occupational rewards. At home, a woman bears the major part of the burden. Many studies have recorded that women who work even full-time in the paid labor market also work full-time at home. When a woman goes out

▲ **Intruding on home life**? Women who combine a career with marriage inevitably have less time to spend with their husbands who can easily feel neglected and undervalued.

▼ **Sharing a career** by starting a business together is the way that some couples prevent their jobs from coming into conflict.

Women who take work outside the home experience the stress of conflict between three roles – it is difficult to reconcile the duties of a wife with those of a mother and employee. The effect of this stress, however, seems to be positive.

of the house to work, her hours of housework and child care decline, but never as much as her hours of labor outside the home increase. Women who balance roles as wife, parent and worker surrender their leisure time. They typically experience great time conflicts too.

How can we explain the evident benefits that women derive from balancing different life roles? First, variety enlivens us. Work and home roles can each relieve the monotony of the other. Similarly, positive events and successes in one role may not only buffer negative events in the other but make us cope more effectively with them. The extent to which adequate performance in one role can buffer both men and women against severe disappointments in others was illustrated in a study

involving middle managers who had gone through a divorce. Having success in a responsible position gave many the self-esteem and self-confidence to face abuse and criticism from their marriage partners.

CAN THE FAMILY COPE?

What about the woman's family? It may be that the woman benefits from balancing work and home life, but at the expense of her family. The question of maternal employment has concerned social scientists for a long time, and numerous studies have now been conducted. Taken together they show that children do, indeed, need stable and loving attention, but that it need not be the biological mother who provides that attention 24 hours a day. Relatives and non-relatives alike can give a child love. And children grow emotionally and intellectually from being in contact with other adults and other children. By putting the child in a well-run daycare center or a well-organized after-school program, the parent can share responsibility for the child's development without abdicating.

Though many studies have dispelled fears about the consequences of maternal employment, other research has confirmed the conviction that female employment outside the home leads to a renegotiation of marriage. The more money a woman brings into a marriage the more power she has over decisions at home. And when a woman changes from having a job to having a career, her husband can feel confused, and even betrayed. However, research shows that it can benefit a man as much as a woman to share the burdens as well as the privileges of the provider role. Being flexible about sex roles can cause initial confusion but successful adjustment can have rewards for both partners. **FJC**

▲ **The rewards**. The work is done and the couple can relax and enjoy each other's company in a marriage that has been adjusted to accommodate both partners' roles outside the home. The wife can contribute to the marriage in new ways – materially by the money she brings home and psychologically by being happier, enlivened and self-assured. If her husband can avoid feeling threatened they can both enjoy these rewards.

Influence and Persuasion

WOMEN are stereotyped as more receptive to other people's views than men, more easily persuaded, more dependent, less dominant and less able to act as leaders. Men are typically seen as resistant to influence. When *exerting* influence, men are stereotyped as more likely to threaten, to mention that they have the right to expect compliance, to claim superior knowledge and to provide reasons. They are expected to be open and direct, implying that they are competent and have authority. In contrast, women are commonly thought more likely to plead, to manipulate and to offer personal favors, such as promises to like and admire others and to provide sexual rewards.

Research has examined whether these sex differences do exist. Although the majority of studies have not found women easier to influence, some have. It has been found that stereotypes reflect reality in at least some degree when it comes to strategies for winning influence.

How different are we?

In studies of how easy it is to influence them, men and women are presented with information that challenges their opinions. The critical question is whether they resist the presenter's attempt to influence them, or adopt this person's views. Experiments are usually designed with a view to balancing topics or avoiding those that favor one sex's typical interests over the other. This has to be done because in everyday life, the topic under discussion is often an important determinant of sex differences. When you are very interested in a topic, and know a great deal about it, your opinion should be relatively difficult to change. In discussions on football, for example, about which men report a greater interest and display more knowledge than women, men should be relatively resistant to influence. However, when the topic reflects women's interests and expertise, such as daycare for children, their opinions should presumably be more resistant to change than men's.

Even when precautions are taken to avoid a male bias in topics, the results suggest that women are slightly more amenable to persuasive argument than men, and even more susceptible when someone simply states an opinion without arguing and expects listeners to conform to it. Women conform more than men especially when the opinion-giver will *know* whether the opinion has been accepted.

The majority of research on sex differences in influence strategies rely on people's reports of what they do. Among dating couples, men report that they are indeed relatively direct in discussing how the couple should organize their activities and their relationship. They present logical arguments, for instance, or bargain. Women report that they are relatively indirect – becoming silent and withdrawn when their view is not accepted, or going off on their own.

Interestingly, these results may depend as much on the sex of the person being influenced as on the sex of the person exerting influence. In one study, which included

► **Setting the mood.** *Sharing a joke with a friend and associate lightens the atmosphere at a social occasion. Men in particular are skilled at using humor as a technique to create a relaxed mood, establishing a rapport that lowers resistance to influence. Boys learn more humor skills than girls while still at school. They feel freer about telling jokes and doing funny things, while girls are more restrained. One study observed that girls tend to check the reactions of others before laughing at cartoons.*

Men and women tend to use different strategies to influence people; and women seem to be less resistant to influence than men. Differences in social roles and social status are the likeliest causes of these sex differences.

both homosexual and heterosexual couples, partners of men (both men and women) reported using the tactics typically associated with women, such as manipulating others and pleading.

Self-reports may not be accurate, because some people may be unwilling to tell the truth, or because their memory lets them down. A few studies have been attempted, therefore, that directly observe the way men and women exert influence. These are almost always simulations, in which men and women have to act out what they would do when attempting to influence others, such as a fellow employee at work. Perhaps the most important finding in these direct observations is that there is not always a difference in style between the men and women. However, when sex differences do appear, they seem to be consistent with the self-report findings. Women attempt to exert influence less often than the men, and employ a more limited range of strategies. When they do exert influence they offer rewards less frequently and they threaten punishment more often.

Personality and influence

As they grow into men, boys are taught to develop the masculine attributes of dominance, competence and assertiveness. Girls become oriented toward the more feminine attributes of selflessness, concern for others and emotional expressiveness. These different personality styles could explain why women are more easily influenced than men – it might be particularly difficult to change the opinions of dominant, assertive people, and a concern for other people's feelings could be expressed through a readiness to agree with them. Personality scales have been devised to measure masculinity and femininity (see *Ch30*), and so we can examine how easily each personality type, regardless of sex, can be influenced. Although some studies have found that highly masculine people are more resistant to influence than people who score high on femininity, most have identified no relation between personality and resistance to influence.

There are few direct research tests of personality as an explanation for differences in style of *achieving* influence, but it remains a plausible account. The relatively direct strategies employed by men might indeed be an expression of high levels of competence and dominance. Strategies attributed to women, such as indirect methods and independent action, might be an expression of their concern for others.

What is the effect of social roles?

The different social roles of men and women provide another way of explaining women's poorer showing in the world of influence. According to Role Theory, our expectations of others are based largely on the social roles in which

201

◀ **Making his point**. *Having made his joke, the story-teller takes the opportunity to make a persuasive point. Wives smile, but are not participants in the exchange. The laughing and gesturing serve also to inform others at this gathering about the men's relationship. Studies of persuasion show that humorous people are perceived as more likable, and this enables them to have greater influence generally.*

we encounter them. These expectations are communicated to others through both words and body language, and reinforced when others conform to them. The typical high school athlete may act like one because his fellow students expect him to. They are responsive to his athletic prowess while disregarding any other balancing or interesting intellectual qualities he may have. He responds by playing his role. A few years after graduation, which marks the end of his athletic career, those same students report with astonishment that he has turned into a complex, multi-faceted individual. According to Role Theory, they have not observed a transformation, just an individual whose current situation no longer requires him to conform to their limited expectations.

From this perspective, sex differences in social behavior occur, not because of deep-seated personality traits, but because most of the time men and women tend to behave according to other people's expectations. One important difference between typical social roles is that men's tend to be higher in status and authority. In the workplace (see *Ch 23*), men fill a disproportionate number of high-status positions. In the family, the woman is almost always the homemaker. Of course, men's and women's roles are changing. For example, many more women are now in the workforce than was true a few years ago. However, the status differences between men and women persist. Women continue to earn less than men and continue to hold low-prestige jobs.

Because of this distribution of men and women into different social roles, someone's sex serves as a general cue to their status. This means that when you know little about others apart from their sex, you are likely to accord the men who are present a higher status. Your expectations for men's and women's behavior may differ even in settings where

men and women supposedly have almost identical roles.

Status is linked to influence. Higher-status people are perceived to be more dominant and assertive than lower-status people. They are perceived as more powerful and believed to exert influence more successfully and to be less easily influenced. Those with low status are not typically expected to be influential. They need to justify any attempt they might make to influence others. One way to do this is to show that

■ **Female stereotypes of influence strategies**. *Women have more scope than men to influence a situation by using in-direct, emotional cues, for this lower-status, more child-like style is not compatible with male standards of dignity. Women may have less scope to exercise influence directly.* TOP *A woman enhances the effect of her words by using facial expression and other body language to appeal to a man's feelings.* BOTTOM LEFT *The shy-child pose influences mood – arousing affection – by signaling vulnerability.* BOTTOM RIGHT *A woman speaks her mind. The reaction of her man is embarrassment. In general, both husbands and wives lose social standing when their partner criticizes them in public, but the bossy wife is a more widespread negative stereotype.*

Regardless of their sex, people in positions of authority use direct, rational arguments. Those with little power, or who have low self-esteem, attempt to manipulate people's feelings in order to make their influence felt.

the attempt is motivated by a concern for the other's interests. Low-status people need to make themselves agreeable. A readiness to agree is, therefore, one way for low-status people to justify their attempts at influence.

Men's relatively high status enhances their resistance to influence. Women's relatively lower status promotes their willingness to agree with others. It also helps to explain the finding that women conform more than men when they are aware that other people can observe whether or not they conform. Low-status people are inclined to make themselves agreeable to high-status people.

Those in powerful positions, regardless of their sex, report they do use direct, rational strategies to influence others, while those in less powerful positions say that they use indirect strategies such as manipulation. These self-reports include those of couples. The amount of power you have within the relationship affects the method that you use. If you believe you have more power than your partner, then you are likely to report using the strategies typically associated with men. If you believe that you have less power than your partner, you are likely to report using strategies typically associated with women. In simulated encounters between fellow employees, few sex differences in influence style appear when men and women have comparable access to power and comparable status.

At the most basic level, people conform to others' expectations because they will be rewarded if they do so and disadvantaged if they do not. Thus, men typically act like rela-

tively powerful individuals and women less powerful ones, because other people expect them to do so. What happens when a man adopts a strategy usually associated with a low-power person, such as presenting himself as helpless? What happens when a woman employs a strategy usually associated with a powerful person, such as presenting herself as an expert? Although their persuasiveness may not be diminished, such people are liked less – thus reinforced less in their way of doing things – than individuals who use strategies that correspond to common expectations.

Sex differences in practice

The status that women are actually accorded in two strikingly different social settings involving influence can serve to illustrate these points in practice.

First, exerting influence over others and being influenced by them are very important processes in work groups. In order to function efficiently, many work groups identify one or more people as leaders and the rest of the group as followers. Research in this area has shown that women are less likely than men to be identified as group leaders.

How do groups select leaders? One view is that they choose the individual who is most likely to succeed. That is, the person who is the most competent, or who seems to possess the skills necessary to get the job done. Because men typically fill higher-status positions than women, maleness is associated in most people's minds with competence, and men are more likely to be chosen.

Men, and others judged highly competent, are also likely to be given many opportunities to speak in group discussion. When they speak, their suggestions are likely to be

203

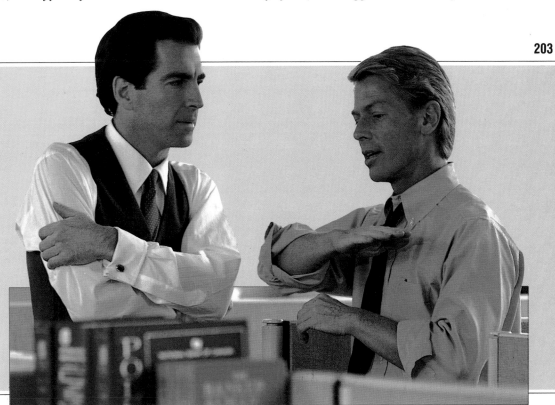

► **Direct influence**. *People in high-status positions, regardless of their sex, use a direct, rational approach to influence the opinions of others. Here facial expression, voice and gesture all signal that the speaker expects his words to be taken seriously and weighed for their logical worth. The forearm slicing air is not an appeal to emotions but a way of emphasizing the power of his point. The listener stands with folded arms, signaling that he has not been won over, but he watches intently, indicating that he will not ignore arguments reasonably made.*

HOW WOMEN CAN INCREASE THEIR INFLUENCE

■ *How can women increase their influence and fill leadership positions?*

1 *They should draw attention to their own strengths. Being male is only one among many ways of having status. A woman's special expertise or educational qualifications can identify her as highly competent. Research suggests that women tend to minimize their achievements while men emphasize attributes at which they excel. Do not wait for others to discover your talents – this may never happen.*

2 *Show that you are better than, not merely equal to others. Women and other low-status people may need to demonstrate that they are better qualified than others in order to be equally influential.*

3 *Even women with strong qualifications are often passed over if they do not demonstrate assertive qualities. Getting your point across without alienating others is a learned skill that women need to acquire in order to be taken seriously.*

4 *Be agreeable and show that you care about the organization. Its lower-status members will not be thought to have much right to make suggestions and offer opinions, but by being agreeable is one way to increase the legitimacy of low-status attempts to exert influence. It signals that you are motivated by a concern for the group, rather than a need for personal point-scoring. It can be a stepping stone to higher status by increasing future opportunities to be influential.*

▲ **An equal exchange**. *These business associates demonstrate not only similar facial expressions and body language, but also similar styles of dress. Studies show that maintaining a touch of femininity helps businesswomen to make a positive impression.*

▼ **Paying attention**. *These men have all adopted an open posture, indicating a willingness to be influenced by what their colleague says. Their forward leans signal interest, and one has tilted his head in thoughtful consideration of what is being said.*

It may not be enough for low-status members of the group to be equal in competence to others. They may have to demonstrate that they are more skilled and agreeable if their contributions are to be recognized as equal in merit.

given careful attention by the rest of the group. Women, and others judged less competent, are not likely to be given as many chances to contribute to the discussion and their contributions are not likely to receive as careful consideration from the rest of the group.

On average, men's ideas are more influential in group discussion. Influencing others is an important attribute of leadership. When you successfully convince others that your opinions are correct you are increasing your own power and prestige. When others convince you that they are correct you are allowing them to have power over you.

To take another situation, every day on television we are subjected to a barrage of attempts to influence us. People try to persuade us to buy a product or to do something new. How are women depicted in such advertisements? What kinds of power do they seem to have? In television commercials, women are most often depicted using products in

a domestic context, taking care of their families. However, women talk about the product in only about one-third of television commercials. In most of them, a male "voice-over" is used, in which a man describes to the viewers the product's technical properties, and explains how it works. Thus, in most commercials, the mother and housekeeper is presented simply as a product user.

Women play a major role in one other kind of television commercial. This is in the advertising of products designed to increase women's well-being or sexual attractiveness. In this area, women typically are not only portrayed as using the product but also invited to talk about its qualities. In less than half of such commercials is a male announcer used.

This link between women and beauty is, of course, used in other ways in commercials. Physical attractiveness is sometimes used as a marketing technique to sell products that actually have little to do with beautifying the body. A common example of this is the beautiful driver in many of the advertisements for cars. However, that is scarcely an example of influence through expertise. **WW**

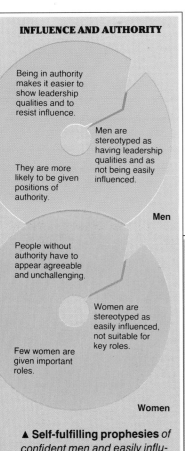

INFLUENCE AND AUTHORITY

Being in authority makes it easier to show leadership qualities and to resist influence.

They are more likely to be given positions of authority.

Men are stereotyped as having leadership qualities and as not being easily influenced.

Men

People without authority have to appear agreeable and unchallenging.

Few women are given important roles.

Women are stereotyped as easily influenced, not suitable for key roles.

Women

▲ **Self-fulfilling prophesies** *of confident men and easily influenced, agreeable women. To achieve greater status and influence, women need to overcome these stereotypes.*

▲ **The ideal of equality** *in male-female relationships prompts couples to strive for a balance of influence over the life they lead together. Achieving this is far from easy – and researchers find it difficult to* measure how successful we are – since ideas about the importance of an issue in the relationship may vary between the partners (see Ch19). What seems clear is that in happy couples, each partner has the *right amount of control over issues which are important to them.*

205

Ambition and Leadership

IT IS A TRUTH universally acknowledged that there are fewer women than men in positions of power and authority – in the business world, in the professions, in the arts, in politics. Women are not the anomaly in the corporate boardroom that they once were, but they are not represented in proportion to their numbers or their talents. For example, in the United States women hold only 3 to 4 percent of the directorships of the top 1000 firms, and only 25 percent of those companies with women directors have more than one token woman. Why this is so remains a matter of some controversy, and two very different routes have been taken by those who would explain the situation. On the one hand, "person-centered explanations" try to discover what there might be in the "female personality" that would make women less ambitious, or otherwise less suited for leadership roles. "Environmental explanations," on the other hand, emphasize the psychological barriers to female advancement found in the makeup of those who select and encourage new leaders – not just personnel officers, but all of us – for example, as voters and as patrons of arts.

Do women fear success?

One person-centered explanation – taken as demonstrated, until quite recently –is that women simply lack the motivation to compete. A number of studies have compared how much difference there is in the achievement of men and women at set tasks, when given "relaxed instruction" and "competitive instruction." When giving competitive instruction researchers tell those who have volunteered for the experiment such things as that the results will be used to measure their "intellectual and leadership capacities." Men's rate of achievement tends to increase substantially when this element of competition is introduced, whereas women's does not. However, close scrutiny of the findings has revealed that although competition fails to increase the women's achievement, this is already much higher than the men's under relaxed instruction. What is revealed is not female absence of a desire to achieve but lower male achievement when men are not given a special motivation.

Researchers have also suggested that women are frightened of success, especially if they see it as incompatible with femininity. According to this theory, fear of success is aroused in those situations in which the emphasis is on competitive success, and the woman feels anxious about the aggressive overtones of competitiveness. It is assumed to be especially acute for women if the competition is against males. For example, a bright young woman who aspires to be a lawyer might settle for a career as a legal secretary because she fears that success as a lawyer might diminish her image as a desirable woman and wife.

A high female fear of success was first recorded in an experiment in which women university students were asked to write completions to the following statement: "After first term finals, Anne finds herself at the top of her medical school class." The completions were analyzed for the presence or absence of imagery implying that success seems a frightening prospect. The following are typical of those regarded as expressing such fear:

"No one will marry her. She has lots of friends but no dates."

"Unfortunately, Anne suddenly no longer feels so certain that she really wants to be a doctor. She wonders if perhaps it is not normal."

"Anne is a code name for a nonexistent person created by a group of medical students."

"She starts proclaiming her surprise and joy. Her fellow

▶ **A male physique** *is no longer a necessary qualification for a career in fire fighting. Women the world over are discovering that their ambitions need not be thwarted by imagined physical capacity. Although the physical prowess of the top few percent of male athletes may never be rivaled by women, there are now very, very few traditionally male occupations in which strength and endurance play a part where women have not shown that they can hold their own with the vast majority of men.*

classmates are so disgusted with her behavior that they jump on her body and beat her. She is maimed for life."

Male students wrote responses to the same statement, but for them the central character was named John instead of Anne. The difference between the responses of males and those of females was dramatic. In contrast to the females' 65 percent, fewer than 10 percent of the male respondents wrote stories implying fear of success.

This study was conducted in the 1960s, but strong evidence soon emerged that this male-female difference reflected the mood of the times rather than nature. Several American surveys conducted in the early 1970s found the fear of success among males to be as high or higher than that of females. This was a time when the rejection by young men of traditional American values – a trend which had only begun in the mid-1960s – had reached its climax. In particular, large numbers of young American men of the early 1970s had come to see a drive for success (especially success in the business world) as making a person seem insensitive to issues ranging from egalitarianism to international peace.

Now that success is back in fashion, male fear-of-success scores are once again lower, although not so much lower, than women's. It seems that women are not naturally less motivated than men, but in our present social climate some may be less likely to appear hungry for success in situations in which they view competitive success as incompatible with femininity.

Another person-centered explanation, based on research in 1977, is that women have not been brought up to compete or to play on teams. Because of this, they lack the requisite managerial skills or traits necessary for success in the corporate jungle. According to this theory, men more optimistically balance the chances of success against the possibility of failure, whereas for women the consequences of failure loom larger. However, since this view was put forward there has been a dramatic increase in the number of women starting their own businesses. Starting a business on your own has long been regarded as a high risk because of the high rate of failure (80 percent). Yet, contemporary American women are three to five times more likely than men to go into business for themselves. Women may be less likely than men to learn to play on teams, but that does not seem to provide an adequate explanation for their absence from high-status positions.

A good environment for ambition?

A common environmental explanation for the small numbers of women business executives is that the distribution of opportunity and power, and the social composition of groups at work, result in boundaries that inhibit women

207

◄ **A "male" mind** *is no longer an essential attribute even in a national leader. When Norway elected its first woman Prime Minister – shown here in her office – it joined a growing number of nations, among them Britain, Iceland, India, Israel and Sri Lanka, in which women of great character have risen to fill the supreme political post in the public life of their country. In view of traditional biases in favor of males, their successes under democratic electoral systems have been all the more striking.*

WOMEN WHO ARE BREAKING THE MOLD

■ These are a few of the many thousands of women who have shown themselves in terms of drive, temperament and intellect to be more than equal to the demands of some of the most taxing jobs traditionally monopolized by men.

▼ **Conducting a performance** at one of the world's great opera houses, Covent Garden, London, is female "maestro" Sian Edwards, the first woman to conduct a full-length opera at this world center of the art.

▶ **Guardian of the Constitution** Sandra Day O'Connor, first woman to sit on the bench of the Supreme Court of the United States, noted for her "meticulous legal mind" and for being "tough but fair."

▲ **The president** of a large business corporation today is sometimes a woman who has worked her way up through the echelons in free and equal competition with her male colleagues. Francine Gomez, French president of the Waterman Society in Paris, is just one impressive example.

▶ **Unflappability** is a quality all three of these British Airways airline pilots have in abundance. In training, they have proved themselves to be just as cool, calm and collected in emergencies as their male counterparts. Women are even being trained as fighter pilots in some of the world's airforces.

208

> *There is now no responsible job category in which some woman has not proved herself outstandingly competent. The success stories of women suggest that any idea that they are "natural subordinates" is misconceived.*

▼ **Entrepreneurial flair** *and drive leading to big time business success is now the trademark of an ever increasing number of women. In fact, women are no strangers to the adventure of starting up a business. In the United States, for instance, they are several times more likely than men to make the effort to go into business for themselves. The successful entrepreneur here is Diane von Furstenberg, of the New York fashion world.*

from succeeding. According to this view, a critical factor holding women back is the fact that there are far fewer women than men in full-time work. As a minority of the workforce, women are consequently scrutinized more closely, are under pressure to prove that they are not partisan to feminist views and are expected to conform both to their traditional social position and the prevailing sex-role stereotypes. The same is true of many other kinds of organizations, such as political parties and government agencies.

Women's social position, in comparison to men's, is secondary. This means that, without knowing anything else about two individuals, we tend to accord a higher status to the one simply because he is a man, and a lower status to the other simply because she is a woman. Women are stereotyped as more emotional, nurturant, passive and sens-

WOMEN'S INTUITION?

■ *As we all know, women are stereotyped as more emotional, nurturant, passive and sensitive than men, but could it be that these characteristics are not typical so much of women as of those who are called to play a subordinate role in society?*

In one study, both women and men were asked to play the roles of leaders or followers (teachers and learners, respectively.) Overall, the women displayed no greater sensitivity than the men. However, indivi-

duals (female or male) assigned the subordinate role were more sensitive to the other person (leader) than those in the leader role. Perhaps women's intuition might more aptly be labeled subordinates' intuition.

Undoubtedly, subordinates have greater need to be aware of the feelings and reactions of others to them in order to respond to their needs and to earn their favor.

itive than men. Secretaries therefore are implicitly expected to "understand" their bosses (usually male) by responding to moods, whims, needs and personal quirks much as a wife would.

As a result, managers tend to assume that a secretary's nurturant and submissive behavior reflects her personality rather than requirements of her job, and they are unlikely to recommend her for promotion to positions of greater responsibility on the assumption that she lacks the necessary traits to succeed (see *Ch 23*).

One very subtle form of sex discrimination at work lies in the very different ways in which the performance of men and women is assessed and rewarded. Experiments and interviews have indicated that in business a man's successful

performance of a task is generally attributed to his skill, whereas a woman's successful performance of the same task is attributed either to luck or exceptional effort. On the other hand, a man's failure is attributed to bad luck, a woman's failure to low ability.

It has also been found that such distinctions can have a dramatic impact on personnel decisions. Business students were asked what recommendations they would make on a number of equally successful employees. Four different causes – skill, effort, luck and task ease – were offered to account for different employees' successes. The only ones the students recommended for promotion were those whose success was attributed to skill. Competence was in every case viewed more favorably than a reputation for hard work. These findings imply that women who are assumed more often than men to be successful because of effort are apt to be bypassed when the most favored organizational rewards – promotions – are distributed.

In view of this it is hardly surprising that any employer interested in maximizing productivity will believe that it is far more cost-effective to encourage the men rather than the women with generous pay rises and promotion. Why waste valuable resources trying to increase the output of the women, who are already apparently working as hard as they can to compensate for their lack of ability?

The fact is that despite the persistence of this belief that male and female behavior differs in the workplace, there is little evidence that it really does. The bulk of evidence on sex differences in managerial behavior indicates that, as in-

210

▲ Too attractive to succeed? *Unless they are their own boss, disturbingly pretty women may find their looks a hindrance rather than a help in the race for the boardroom. Very "sexy" women are liable to be taken even less seriously by men – and by women too!*

▶ Dedicated employees *or time-servers dreaming of a future dominated by marriage and family life? Male employers often find it difficult to shake off a suspicion that their younger female employees, however hard-working, see themselves as birds of passage.*

Women embarking on careers in the business world or the professions still have to contend with the fact that women in full-time and in managerial positions are heavily outnumbered by men. Despite this, the imbalance is gradually lessening.

dividuals, executive men and women seem to be virtually identical psychologically, intellectually and emotionally. In one study of men and women ecologists, a difference was found in the scientific productivity of the male group and the female group – more of the men's research was published and later referred to by other researchers in their publications. However, a meager 4 percent of the men in the study accounted for this difference; 96 percent were no more productive than the average woman ecologist. Many of the women had heavier family responsibilities than any of the men, and their lower average productivity probably reflects this.

Why women opt out of competition

Misunderstandings in the workplace help to preserve the status quo. Women have made inroads into lower and middle management, but the difficulties they face are themselves a deterrent to ambition. The "glass ceiling" beyond which they have difficulty ascending has led many women to opt out altogether. Some seek to pursue power and influence through entrepreneurial channels, others to redirect the motherhood-work balance in favor of motherhood. For it is motherhood that, for most women, ultimately takes priority over their other ambitions.

Men, of course, want to be fathers, but our cultural outlook is only gradually shifting the expectation that although this should create no career conflicts for them, a woman must choose between a serious commitment to her job and serious commitment to her family. Employers ask prospective female employees what their husbands' work is and whether the husband is likely to be transferred, and they want to assess whether a new employee is likely to start having babies. If there are children, it is expected that the mother rather than the father will stay with them when they are ill and be the first one home in the evening to relieve the nanny or the childminder. All of this ties one hand behind a woman's back when she is competing to get ahead in the corporate world, in scientific research or in the professions. Many a "supermom" drops out exhausted. Others redefine their roles to exclude goals that are incompatible with family responsibilities. Not because they are unable to meet the challenge, but because they are unwilling to pay the high price of traditionally defined success.

In spite of the barriers, women can be expected to arrive in increasingly greater numbers in positions of power. As they do, we may also expect to see changes in the environment in which men and women pursue their ambitions. There is no consistent picture of what happens when women are in power, but in Norway, where the Prime Minister is a woman, as are seven of seventeen members of the Cabinet, and over 40 percent of the members of the Parliament, child-care subsidies have increased, as well as the number of weeks in the paid parental leave scheme resembling Sweden's (see p168). **VOL**

"SHALL I RISK GIVING HER THE JOB?"

■ *Male employers increasingly find themselves in situations where they have to balance the claims of female job-applicants against those of similarly qualified males for the same highly responsible job. When they do, they are typically prey to certain doubts which, if not resisted, can often unfairly disadvantage the women candidates concerned. Here are some of the male interviewer's more familiar worries:*

"How long will she stay with the firm? Is she likely to marry in the near future, and then perhaps leave? Or – if already married – will she fall pregnant and disappear for months, perhaps forever? And if she has family responsibilities, to what extent will these intrude into the working day?"

"Does she have a husband whose job takes priority? How likely is he to have to move to another area?"

"Aren't women more prone than men to illness and absence? Haven't I heard that women tend to visit their doctor two or three times as often as men?"

"And what about the menstrual cycle? Some women are briefly incapacitated by their period. And then there is PMS (Pre-Menstrual Syndrome): will she make objective decisions every day of the month?"

"Women have a reputation for emotional instability? Don't they suffer more than men from self-doubt, stress and depression?"

"Don't women more often run into difficulties when they try to motivate and discipline subordinate men – or, for that matter, subordinate women?"

In fact, women in responsible positions in companies are no more likely than men to change jobs, to take leave of absence, to suffer ill health, to show effects of stress or depression, or to be ineffectual in their management style.

Creativity

ASK a friend or your family to name five famous women and five famous men who are creative artists. They will find it much easier to name five men – indeed, numerous male composers, painters, film-makers and dramatists will come to mind. It is much more difficult to think of prominent women in the arts – famous names emerge only with a certain amount of thought and prompting, except perhaps for novelists: George Eliot and George Sand were already prominent in the mid-1800s, even if they took men's names. Are women somehow less creative than men, or does society not recognize their talents? Or is their creative productivity somehow stifled?

What is creativity?

Defining creativity is a problem that has intrigued philosophers, psychologists and educators. It is of direct practical concern to government planning bodies, advertising agencies and industrial firms, which need to understand how to find and effectively manage creative personnel.

Many would think of "the creative person" as someone who has achieved distinction in a particular field, but having special gifts is not necessarily the same thing as creativity – drive and determination are more closely related with greatness. And in one sense, *everyone* is creative; a 7-year-old's painting may be just as creative for that child as a Picasso masterpiece is to the art world. We need to think carefully about what is the best defining attribute for creativity in any given sphere of activity.

We meet the term "creative" in a bewildering variety of contexts. We go to evening classes to learn creative writing. In business we look for creative solutions to problems. When we are rearranging the furniture, magazines on interior decorating tell us to make creative use of space. We even hear of "creative accounting" and "creative divorce." The uses of the word are so diverse that it is important to be clear about what exactly it *does* mean.

There are two main ways in which psychologists have tried to go about this. The first has been to study creative *products*: to look at scientific inventions and publications, works of art, children's school achievements and so on. The advantage of this is that we can look at creativity as it occurs in the real world, in response to real demands – but

▲ **Equal creativity – equal work**. Creativity occurs equally in both sexes, but jobs demanding creative input are not usually as evenly distributed between the sexes as they are in this Australian design studio. Men are perceived (by both men and women) as more serious and more likely to be well qualified. More men than women seek creative careers and people have higher expectations of them when they do.

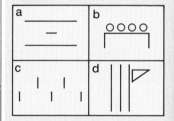

TEST YOUR CREATIVITY

■ To test your creativity:
1 think of all the things that each of these patterns might be.

2 List as many uses as you can think of for:
   a brick
   a paper clip
   a blanket
   a jam jar.
3 List all the ways in which the following are alike:
   an apple and a pear
   a radio and a telephone
   a violin and a piano
   a cat and a mouse.
   You can compare your answers with a friend's and score them for "fluency" by simply counting the number of responses you come up with. If your answers were scored by a professional researcher, their originality could be assessed by working out statistically their unusualness in comparison with the answers of other people who have been tested. By comparing your own answers with those of a wide circle of friends, however, you can at least form an impression

Women perform as well or better than men in tests of creativity. But very few become famous for creative achievements. Is this because creativity tests do not measure the qualities that great artists need or is it because female talent is overlooked?

the disadvantage is that our understanding will lack generality. Such an assessment of creativity applies in a different way to each particular class of products under investigation.

The other approach has been to look at *people* rather than products: to try to identify the general aspects of their behavior that underlie creativity. A good deal of effort has been devoted especially to the study of *creative thinking* and its measurement by means of "creativity tests."

Originality or practicality?

By far the most common creativity tests are those of "divergent," or "lateral" thinking. Whereas *convergent* thinking focuses narrowly on the one correct solution to a problem, *divergent* thinking means generating a number of different approaches to an open-ended question. Some of the more common divergent tests include thinking of unusual uses for everyday objects, doing a variety of drawings all based on one simple outline, and thinking of different

213

of who among you is more original. Nothing in this test measures the degree of ingenuity you might have at finding practical solutions to problems. This form of creativity involves not only fluency and originality but also the ability to analyze a problem and apply ideas to it.

▲ **What is creativity?** *It means finding not just original solutions, but ones that are satisfying. Brought up to be more independent than women, men are more likely to do things whose creative value is controversial, such as this man on Vancouver Island building his home from bottles.*

▲ **Preparing food is an everyday activity,** *but it can reach artistic heights.* TOP *When men cook, this is exceptional, and their efforts are often considered exceptional too. The role of a great chef is almost always taken by a man.* BOTTOM *The less creative catering jobs are usually performed by women.*

Their labor is inexpensive and they welcome opportunities to work part-time, as in this kitchen preparing school meals, so that they can be home to cook the family dinner.

Creativity is about thinking of new solutions to old problems, yet people associate creative ability much more with arts than with science. Children whose play is not sex-typed have better creativity scores than their peers.

interpretations of ambiguous figures. These tests are designed to measure *fluency* – the number of different responses you can come up with – and *originality* – the unusualness of the responses. A creative person is someone who can produce a lot of ideas which have not been seen before. But this is only an indicator, not a guarantee, of creative potential. To find out whether the tests really do measure this, we need to see whether high scores produce creative accomplishments in real life.

Unfortunately, the evidence for this is rather disappointing. Studies comparing children's performance on creativity tests with their creative achievements at school, for example, have shown few clear relationships. Real-life creativity entails not only fluent and original thinking, but also the ability to tailor such thinking to practical problems. It would be easy to design clothes or furniture, for example, that are so bizarre and unusual that they could without hesitation be described as original. But they may be at the same time be completely impractical – too clumsy, too expensive or too uncomfortable. A truly creative designer is one who produces garments that are original *and* also meet practical demands. This is one reason why psychologists are now paying more attention to creative products, rather than trying to assess creativity in terms of people's abstract qualities.

Androgyny and creativity

Psychologists ought to be able to throw some light on the puzzle of female creativity by looking for sex differences in the results of tests for divergent thinking. Several attempts have been made to do this, but, in fact, males and females typically obtain very similar scores. If anything, women may score slightly higher on the tests of fluency and originality with words. This is in keeping with their higher scores

generally in tests of verbal ability (see *Ch10*). We clearly cannot say that any measured difference in *ability* explains why there are fewer famous women than men in the arts. There should actually be more women than men who are renowned for doing creative things with words. This, in fact, *is* an area where women are better known than in others. However, as a group, women writers are still not as important as male writers.

Another explanation might be in terms of masculine and feminine *personality*. Male artists are stereotyped as being more effeminate than men in other occupations: Oscar Wilde, Richard Wagner and Frederic Chopin are three names that spring readily to mind. And it is much more difficult to think of famous creative females who are noted for their masculinity. In one study (see box), British secondary schoolboys associated femininity with artists, regardless of sex. At school, art, literature and music are seen as more likely subjects for girls than mathematical and scientific ones. They involve such feminine qualities as emotionality, sensitivity and expressiveness. We should expect the more feminine sex to be artistically more successful than the more masculine one, but it is not.

Perhaps creativity is enhanced by sex-role versatility – after all creativity requires flexible thinking – and perhaps men have more of this versatility. A link between *androgyny* (see *Ch30*) and creativity has been suggested by several psychologists. Androgynous people are those who are

THE ARTIST AND THE SCIENTIST

■ *In study of stereotypes, British secondary schoolboys were asked to choose between pairs of adjectives such as "exciting" and "dull," "dependable" and "undependable," to typify mathematicians, poets and several other kinds of people. The results showed that the typical scientist and the typical artist were seen with quite distinct personal qualities.*

For example, here are the 10 qualities most often attributed to the novelist and to the physicist. They are listed in order of how consistently they were chosen.

Although not all boys thought novelists feminine and physicists manly, most did.

NOVELIST	PHYSICIST
imaginative	valuable
warm	intelligent
intelligent	hard-working
exciting	dull
valuable	dependable
undependable	cold
smooth	hard
soft	manly
feminine	rough
lazy	unimaginative

capable of feminine or masculine behavior, whichever is appropriate to the situation. It has been proposed that they are able to use the opposite-sex side of their makeup in the service of their creativity. Uncreative people, correspondingly, are seen as feminine females and masculine males who *inhibit* the opposite-sex sides of their personalities.

Some experimental evidence supports this view, and the findings are clearer for males than for females. Studies in California of the personalities of architects, for example, have found that male architects acknowledged as creative by their peers have distinct styles of personality as compared with their less creative colleagues, including

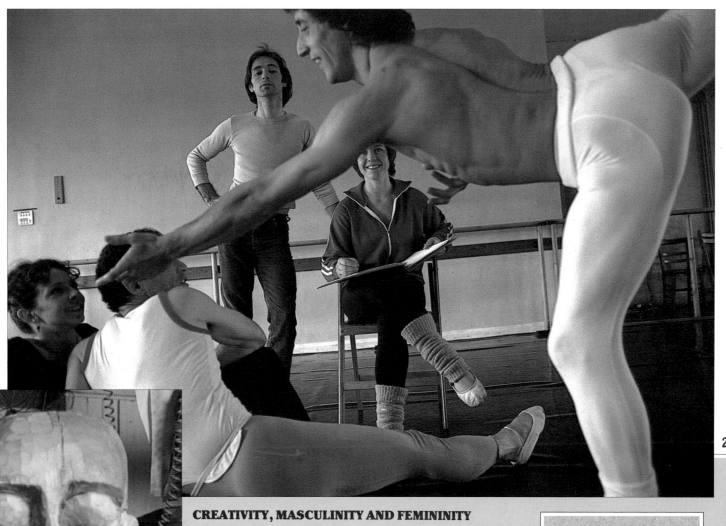

215

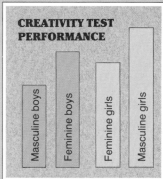

CREATIVITY, MASCULINITY AND FEMININITY

■ The creativity of professional dancers TOP and other male artists is commonly thought to benefit from a "feminine" emotional sensitivity. Do women artists, such as the sculptor BOTTOM, benefit from masculine traits? At least one study suggests that they might, making role versatility rather than femininity the key factor. 52 children aged 10 to 11 were asked to say how they preferred to play. On the basis of their answers they were rated as masculine or feminine by comparison with results from previ-

ous surveys. Four groups were distinguished: masculine boys, masculine girls, feminine boys and feminine girls. The graph shows how the four groups then performed on a creativity test in which they had to think of as many uses as they could for a variety of objects. The androgynous groups (feminine boys and masculine girls) scored significantly higher than their "sextyped" counterparts (masculine boys and feminine girls). The "masculine girls" obtained the highest scores overall.

The averaged findings of

CREATIVITY TEST PERFORMANCE

(bar graph with bars labeled: Masculine boys, Feminine boys, Feminine girls, Masculine girls)

creativity studies show no male-female differences, but studies with children sometimes reflect earlier development in girls. **DJH**

higher than average scores on measures of femininity.

Such occupational research, however, provides inadequate opportunities to compare male and female potential, because a preponderance of males already fill creative roles. Women, in fact, are more likely to be androgynous than men (about 30 percent of women as opposed to about 20 percent of men in most surveys), and at least one study has found androgynous females more creative than androgynous males. A study of 10- to 11-year-old schoolchildren (see box) found significantly more creative thinking among androgynous children of *both* sexes, and the highest scores belonged to masculine girls. Greater male versatility seems an unlikely explanation for greater male success.

Fulfilling a sex role

Famous women artists are "clumped" in certain fields. This provides a clue to why there is inequality of artistic recognition. The most obvious examples of famous women are to be found in literary writing. There are many well-known female novelists. In music there are numerous world-famous female performers (Jacqueline du Pré, Kyung-Wha Chung, Kiri Te Kanawa), but not composers or conductors.

Female composers *do* exist, but their names are unfamiliar. Even in the exceptional case of jazz, where improvised performance is essentially creative, the most famous female artists (eg Billie Holiday, Ella Fitzgerald, Sarah Vaughan) have all been vocalists rather than instrumentalists.

These groupings are probably best explained in terms of what is possible for women living women's roles. Writing and musical performance, at least in Western society, have long been considered to be acceptable "ladylike" domestic pursuits.

It was part of the traditional upbringing of well-bred, well-educated ladies that they should play perhaps the harpsichord and write refined letters to each other and their hus-

216

▲ **Equal numbers** of boys and girls have been recruited for this youth orchestra. At school and in out-of-school lessons more girls than boys learn to play the piano or another instrument. But, usually, many fewer women than men are found in an adult orchestra. Male musicians are perceived by audiences as making an orchestra more serious and more competent, and orchestras attempt to recruit more of them.

If the artistic establishment is not inclined to pay a good deal of attention to the composer Luise Adolpha Le Beau, the painter Mary Cassatt or the photographer Dorothea Lange, girls are unlikely to hear of or be inspired by them.

bands, who might often be away at war or colonizing distant lands. As education spread, it was considered suitable, on this model, that girls of a wider and wider class should develop literary and musical skills.

Young ladies were not, however, introduced as quickly to drawing, painting and sculpting – skills that aristocrats of neither sex had modeled as personal refinements: these had been activities for male artisans to pursue for profit in studios shut away from the distracting domestic world of their wives and children.

Besides educational bias, there is the fact that most women take on traditional female responsibilities in the home and cannot pursue an outside career with the same commitment as men. Today writing continues to be a livelier possibility for a creative woman than many other pursuits. It is interruptible work that can be performed in the home, and you do not have to get out to galleries and other people's studios to be aware of what is happening in your field.

To be a concert performer competes more disruptively than writing with family concerns, and there are fewer female concert performers than women novelists. However it competes less disruptively than being a conductor, who works with and coordinates a schedule with a more complex array of other musicians, and there are even fewer women conductors and composers.

Sex divisions partly arise, as well, from the public's perception of the roles of men and women in art. Women soloists are often positively selected to provide female charm for the benefit of a male audience. Jazz promoters often hire female vocalists in order to add glamour to otherwise all-male bands.

Organizers of classical music concerts report that audiences still sometimes react against "too many" women in the orchestra – it seems to undermine their estimation of how seriously the music is being performed.

Finally, artistic standards and values are set and maintained by many different male-dominated institutions in the world of education (art colleges, conservatories and academies), in broadcasting and the media (radio, television and the press), in commerce and advertising and in arts promotion itself (concert halls, art galleries, festival programming).

All of these constitute the "artistic establishment." If they are not inclined to take a good deal of notice of the composer Luise Adolpha Le Beau, the visual artist Mary Cassatt or the photographer Dorothea Lange, young girls are not likely to ever hear of them or be inspired to follow in their footsteps. **DJH**

▲ **Jazz vocalization** *is a creative role often associated with women, although they are hardly ever found as jazz instrumentalists. Men predominate in jazz bands for the same reasons as they do in symphony orchestras. They are seen as exercising more power and control over instruments. However, a good female vocalist extends the band's range and enhances audience appeal. Her special ability to interpret female emotions is not questioned.*

▲ **A male establishment.** *Art is big business and it is a business that is dominated by men. Artistic standards and values are influenced by the events that occur in auction rooms such as this. Many institutions exist to shield the arts from commercial pressures, but these institutions as well – art galleries, art colleges, arts-funding bodies – are also usually headed by men.*

217

Styles of Communication

HAVE YOU ever found yourself talking to someone and feeling unsure about which sex they are? This can happen because of a bad telephone connection, or because the person's clothing or build leaves room for doubt. In the 1960s, many people complained that they were often unsure of a person's sex because of the fashion of long hair and similar clothes for men and women. Yet, although this uncertainty has probably befallen most of us at some time, it is, in fact, very rare. In experiments, people can usually tell another person's sex from the smallest of clues, even from a tiny light attached to the body of someone moving about in a darkened room. We can almost always recognize a male or female voice within the first one or two words of a telephone conversation.

When people are asked to describe themselves, one of the very first pieces of information they give is which sex they are. It seems that knowledge of another person's sex is so necessary for normal social interaction that we try to establish it immediately. When we are in doubt about another's sex, we feel acutely uncomfortable, and it becomes difficult to pay attention to what that person is saying. One reason for this need to know is that we employ very different styles of communication, depending on whether we are interacting with members of our own or of the opposite sex.

In same-sex interactions, the differences can be seen at their most extreme. Men in conversation look at each other much less than women do, whereas women are much more intimate when they are together, standing closer and touching more often. However, in interactions with the opposite sex, people moderate their behavior to make their nonverbal style more like their partner's – they try to meet each other half way. A man will seek eye contact a little more than usual, for instance, while a woman will do so a little less. Why do we behave like this? Why are meetings with the opposite sex like encounters with a different culture?

Decoding body language

In everyday encounters, people often convey more information by facial expression and other body language than by what they actually say. We form important impressions of others just by the way they look at us, from how close they stand to us and how often they smile or touch us. In this

◀ **Infant-like postures** of supplication are typically assumed by women who are "acting up" to, entreating or otherwise attempting to manipulate their menfolk.

▲ **Conflicting signals**. The backward-leaning posture and hand position of the young man exchanging a mouth-to-mouth kiss clearly reveal that his heart is not in it.

ATTRACTIVE EYES

■ One form of nonverbal communication over which we have very little control is the way our pupils widen, or dilate. This is associated with sexual and emotional arousal. How pupil dilation is perceived has been demonstrated by research. A young woman was photographed twice: once with her pupils at normal size, and then with her pupils dilated. These photographs were shown to preadolescent and adult males and females, who were asked to choose which photograph they preferred. Only adult males showed a distinct preference for the photograph with dilated pupils, indicating that it is the arousal signal that makes wide pupils so attractive. Interestingly, these men were unable to explain their choice.

How you behave in the company of another depends both on your own sex and on that of the other person. Your sex may also determine which aspects of body language you chiefly notice and how well you interpret their meaning.

way, we discover not only if we are liked or disliked but whether we are being patronized, lied to, flattered or supported.

One reason why we take these nonverbal cues so seriously is that the sender is not normally aware of them. Nonverbal communication is important precisely because it is largely unconscious. We convey our feelings without intending to, and it is their honesty that makes them vital sources of information.

We are conscious of some communication channels more than others. When we speak, we are usually aware of and control our facial expressions, but we pay much less attention to our bodies and voices and to the meshing of signals from these different sources. The biggest clues to whether a person is insincere are "interchannel discrepancies" – the contradictions between the face (which we control most easily) and the body, which may be "leaking" opposite signals. For example, someone may greet you warmly and their face may carry a welcoming smile, but other cues – such as restlessness and moving away – may tell you that they are really not pleased to see you.

Most studies have found women more accurate than men in "decoding" the emotional messages that can be read from body language. One way of measuring this talent is by use of the PONS (Profile of Nonverbal Sensitivity) test. Male and female volunteers are shown a series of film clips of an

actress conveying emotions in a variety of situations, such as criticizing someone for being late, asking forgiveness or talking about a divorce. The sound track is treated electronically so that volunteers cannot tell what is actually being said, but they can distinguish the tone of voice. They are also exposed to different communication "channels" in isolation – voice alone, the face, the body minus the face and both together. The volunteers are scored on how well they identify the emotions portrayed.

Hundreds of males and females of different ages and from different countries have taken the PONS test, and the results show women better at interpreting emotions. Is this because an actress rather than an actor was used? Apparently not, since further studies have revealed that women can equally decode male emotions better than men. It may even be that "feminine intuition" is much less mysterious than has been supposed: sensing or knowing things that have not yet been said may be the unconscious use of decoding skill. In one test, however, the Communication of Affect Receiving Ability Test (CARAT), in which volunteers watch videos of 25 different people, men do better. Researchers believe that in some way PONS and CARAT measure different decoding skills, but they have not been able to analyze the difference.

While women may be more successful than men at reading other people's undisguised emotions, they do not spot deceptions as well. They tend to concentrate more on the face (which liars find easiest to control), followed by the body, then the voice and only then interchannel discrepancies. Women's seemingly inherent politeness is nowhere

◄ **Are women more accurate** *than men in their reading of the emotional messages conveyed nonverbally by body language? Most studies have found that they are. Women are particularly sensitive to the emotions of children; and they are better than men at interpreting even men's emotional states – but only if these are candidly expressed and undisguised.*

more subtly expressed than in their refraining to check the "leaky" channels. Knowing that people do not appreciate having their unintended messages received and understood, women seem politely to ignore the tell-tale rise in voice pitch that may accompany insincerity, and the slower, more careful rate of speech that is another sign. They are less attentive to the liar's uncertain hands movements. (When we attempt to deceive, tension makes us want to touch ourselves, even hug ourselves, as though to steady our nerves. Consciousness that this may give us away can in turn make us give ourselves away by trying to keep our hands uncommonly still, even sitting on them.) The fact that women do not watch the leaky channels as much as men indicates a less suspicious nature. In general, when people of either sex are warned in experiments that they are about to watch someone who may be lying, they pay more attention to voice characteristics and to body and hand movements. Men seem to do this more readily than women in situations where they have *not* been warned.

Sending nonverbal messages

Women are more accurate *conveyers* of emotion than men, and it has been suggested that this also is part of women's politeness: demonstrating emotion opens up an interaction by including the other person in the private feelings of the speaker.

Women's openness is also reflected in the fact that they do not excel at deceit: when asked to suppress an emotion, more feminine people "leak" their true feelings to a greater extent than do masculine personality types.

▲ **It falls to the man** to pour the champagne. Men are traditionally expected to be masterful, to take the initiative...and, in the end, to suit themselves. To the extent that men seek to live up to the stereotype, they are perhaps aided by the fact that women are the more likely to be taken in by disguised emotions.

Women are more unerring than men in their reading of freely expressed emotions, are more inclined than men to express their own emotions freely and are more sociable than men. But men are better spotters of emotional duplicity.

The openness of women also seems to be evident in the clear sex differences in smiling. People of both sexes smile more at women than at men, and women themselves smile more. Of course, they are careful about where and to whom: they smile noticeably more than men in conversations with people they know, but they are less likely than men to smile in more fleeting public encounters – for example, with strangers on the street – when their smiling could be misconstrued.

While smiling is commonly thought to indicate a relaxed and happy mood, women's smiling actually seems to be linked sometimes to nervousness. Women score higher than men on scales of social anxiety, and in one study the amount of smiling they did during an interaction was directly related to how nervous they reported they had felt when interviewed afterward. In another study, it was discovered that, as conversations became more relaxed over time, women smiled less and less.

So although a woman's smile may seem to signal open-

ness, it is more closely related to her need to be liked and her fear that she will not be. Women even smile when conveying bad news, and in fact, they smile so much that they may actually defeat their own goal. We are so used to women smiling that the smile has all but lost its impact. When viewing videotapes of people and rating them for positivity, both men and women give higher ratings to men when they smile but not to women. Presumably we discount their smile because they use it so indiscriminately.

In some cultures, people stand closer to each other, touch more and exchange more eye contact than in others. In conversation, Mediterranean people and Latin Americans

SPACE, TOUCH AND STATUS

■ Men take up more space than women in social encounters. They are more likely to point their elbows out from their bodies, as they stand with legs apart and hands on hips or lounge with legs outstretched and arms resting across the backs of furniture. Women sit and stand in postures that take up a minimum of space. They move out of the way more quickly than men in crowded streets and turn their bodies away from men when both are passing through narrow doorways. Studies have shown that men find it harder than women to cope when space is limited — for example, in crowds. Men in all-male crowds show more physiological signs of stress than women do in all-female crowds. Men also take the liberty of touching women more often than women take the liberty of touching men. But whereas women record on average a drop in blood pressure on receiving a reassuring touch from a woman, men record on average a rise in

blood pressure. At least part of the social reality that these differences reflect is the unequal status of men and women. Regardless of sex, people make themselves look bigger when acting out higher-status roles. They make themselves smaller (men hold their hands behind their backs, for example) when they want to avoid challenging a superior. In many situations, a reassuring or friendly touch signals equality, but if there are no special marks of equality in the situation, experiments show that people assume the toucher to be of superior status to the one who only receives the touch. It is possible that men are more anxious in crowded situations and as recipients of touches because of the sex role they are expected to live up to. Being in these positions conflicts with their greater need to assert themselves socially, and (in the case of touches of reassurance) to rely on their own emotional resources and avoid being patronized.

221

◀ **In crowded places**, *women generally feel more at ease than men. They look more relaxed and more cheerful. Men feel more comfortable with space around them. Even in situations in which men and women are equally at ease, or in which women but not men are nervous, women tend to smile more readily than men. The contrasting expressions in this photograph, however, may also reflect a difference in what men and women find humorous.*

■ **Dominant and protective postures**. *In their social encounters with women — especially women whom they do not know well and wish to impress with their masculinity, or cow into an "appropriate" state of submissiveness — most men unconsciously try to make themselves look bigger and taller. They do this by assuming postures that are higher and take up more lateral space than those assumed by women. "And that's how it should be" is the conventional message reflected in the poster* RIGHT.

are warmer and more intimate, in just these ways, than northern Europeans and North Americans. In all cultures, however, the women seem to outdo the men. Italian women touch each other and stand closer even than Italian men. American women greet each other with kisses and hugs and touch during conversation. American men sometimes shake hands at greeting, but after that they keep their distance. They rarely touch their sons after adolescence.

Communicating in words

Contrary to popular opinion, women and men talk equally as much when they are together in groups. However, it is true that women talk more among themselves than men in pairs or groups do. The fact that men manage to corner their share of the speaking time in mixed-sex groups may be due

to their more rapid rate of speech, their louder voices and their tendency to interrupt more often. A man is more likely to talk over the top of what a woman is saying. In addition, when men are uncertain about what to say next but are determined not to yield the floor, they are more likely to use what is called the "filled pause" – that is, "ums" and "ahs." This can be irritating when it prevents others from saying anything without appearing rude, or introduces an awkward delay into the proceedings.

Another type of conversational disturbance more common in men is the speech error – repetitions, omissions, slips of the tongue, sentence corrections, incompletions and stuttering. It seems likely that these male weaknesses are related to their generally lower verbal skills in both writing and speaking. They may also reflect men's anxiety in social situations, and could be the masculine counterpart to the nervous smiling of women.

A man is more likely to change the topic of conversation and to resist when a woman tries to change the topic. Men also reveal more about themselves in conversation with women than the women do.

Why there are differences

Taken together, the evidence seems to suggest that women do have a greater sensitivity to nonverbal signals than men, but why this should be so is still the subject of controversy.

Is sensitivity to other people's messages a part of what you have to have to meet the standards of femininity conventionally laid down by society? Studies that have examined how people think each sex will and should behave –

 In conversation, *women typically stand closer together, touch each other more and exchange more eye contact than men. The difference is much less marked, however, in countries in which demonstrative rather than reserved interaction with new acquaintances is the male norm.*

Men who feel tense or anxious in conversation are prone to make common speech errors. This may be the male counterpart of the nervous smiling to which women tend to resort under similar circumstances.

that is, sex stereotypes – have certainly suggested that this is true. Boys soon learn that society perceives men as more concerned with getting things done than with getting along with others, whereas society tends to reward girls when they are skilled at attuning themselves to other people's feelings.

However, if this explanation were true, one would expect more feminine people of either sex to do better on the PONS test. To discover if this was the case, the test was carried out with people whose degree of masculinity or femininity had been measured by a standard questionnaire. The results showed that being very feminine does not make people better decoders. In fact, the reverse is true: not only are women in general better decoders than men in general but also women and men with highly masculine personalities are better than men in general.

Perhaps it all has to do with empathy. Do women read emotions better because they share other people's moods more easily and more often than men? Apparently not. People who score high on tests measuring empathy do not do any better on the PONS test than low scorers.

It could be that women learn to pay more attention to others than men do. In mixed-sex groups, where men dominate the conversation, women are denied the opportunity to participate equally. They may while away the time by watching others. Obviously, we do better at a task when we pay attention to it, and research has indicated that this may be the key to women's superiority in this area. There is a

223

▲ **Glancing up** *at her partner's face to check that her suggestion accords with his appreciation of what is required, this woman's own face may reflect a tendency on the part of women in general to attune their feelings with those of others.*

▶ **Women talk more among themselves** *and reveal more to each other about their private lives than men do. In mixed gatherings, however, men are just as talkative; and in conversation with women, men tend to reveal more about themselves than women reveal in conversing with men.*

positive relationship between the amount of looking at people's faces and the accuracy of emotional recognition.

A controversial explanation has also been suggested: the oppression of women has led to their increased attentiveness and sensitivity to social messages. People with little social power need to be able to detect the moods and feelings of superiors so that they can adapt their own behavior as necessary and maximize their chances of placating their oppressors.

In fact, the evidence for this view is quite weak. Women holding traditional views of a woman's place, who presumably have lives of greater powerlessness and are more accepting of male domination, actually do worse on the PONS test than those with more liberated views. In addition, women from countries where there is much occupational, cultural and educational discrimination against women show no greater advantage over men than women from more emancipated societies. And according to this suggestion, not only women but also black people – another historically oppressed group – should be more accurate at nonverbal decoding, but they are not.

Alternatively, there may be a physical explanation. The two halves of the brain differ in the kinds of tasks they perform best. The left hemisphere is responsible for language and verbal skills, while the right hemisphere deals with spatial and abstract tasks (see p90). Women have superior skills in those tasks controlled by the left hemisphere. Could the decoding of emotions be related to a difference of brain function in men and women?

Men tend to process information about faces more strongly through the right hemisphere than women, who show a more equal involvement of both sides of the brain. Although processing of the facial image is a spatial, right-hemisphere task, it may be that the ability to apply accurate descriptions to what has been seen belongs to the left hemisphere.

What may be crucial, however, is the communication between the two halves of the brain. Indeed, the nerve structure connecting the two – the *corpus callosum* – is bulkier in women than in men (see p90). This may explain why women are particularly successful at recognizing faces they have seen before and naming them. In tasks where social naming is not important – such as the capacity to recognize previously seen snowflakes or inkblot patterns – women perform no better than men.

How women's skills reflect their social role

If we accept the fact that there are specific differences in brain function – and even differences in brain structure – between men and women, it may be that women's non-

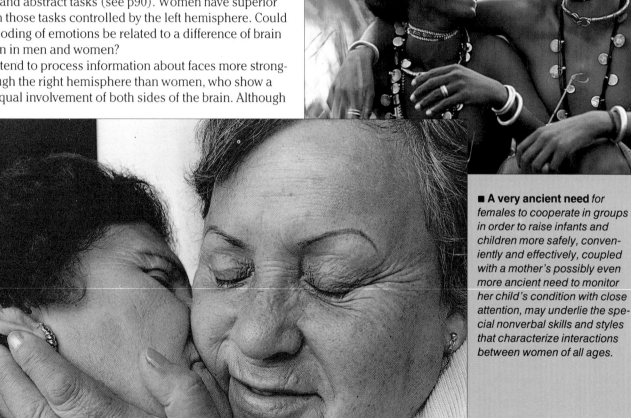

■ **A very ancient need** *for females to cooperate in groups in order to raise infants and children more safely, conveniently and effectively, coupled with a mother's possibly even more ancient need to monitor her child's condition with close attention, may underlie the special nonverbal skills and styles that characterize interactions between women of all ages.*

Women's superior skills in decoding facially expressed emotions may ultimately be based on small differences in the structure of the female brain, an evolutionary adaptation favored by women's role in the early nurture of children.

verbal skill was laid down eons ago. Why should the two sexes have evolved so differently?

Women have always taken primary responsibility for the care and socializing of children. Groups of prehistoric women would have been alone with their children for long periods while the men were out on hunting trips – a situation that is little changed today. A newborn or toddler without the capacity to communicate in words surely must make the heaviest demands on our decoding skills. Is the baby normally sleepy or abnormally lethargic? Does that way of crying mean hunger, pain or fear? The subtle transition in a child's face from excitement to overstimulation can make the difference between happiness and tears. Mothers learn to spot it.

With all this practice in decoding, women could only have become more and more accurate. It may also be that a genetic predisposition was encouraged by evolution, since mothers with such a sensitivity would be more likely to produce surviving offspring than those who did not. How-

ever, while this is an appealing idea, it is one that we can never put to the test.

There is little doubt that the advantage women have in interpersonal communication was also fostered by social convention. The fact that their nonverbal style is particularly evident when they are with other women rather than with men suggests that their openness and intimacy may not have evolved to attract men, as has been sometimes suggested, but more likely was encouraged by those early groups of women who cooperated closely in the raising of children.

Yet women's nonverbal style can be seen in a negative light. Their openness and accommodation to others is sometimes interpreted as naivety and obsequiousness. If women want to succeed in a man's world, it has been argued, they should learn from men and develop a more distant and insensitive style. By aspiring to power, they may have to sacrifice intimacy, become more reserved and interrupt and dominate conversations. However, male behavior may not be the criterion by which everyone should measure themselves. Perhaps women should be helping men to be more effective communicators. **AC**

In the Media

MOST people spend about five hours a day taking in information from the mass media – television, magazines, newspapers and books. This is more time than we spend eating or talking to friends, and – at 35 hours per week – it is about as much time as we spend at work. We consciously choose what will stimulate our emotions or teach us new skills and ideas, but this happens within a cultural context – the stimulation and learning we receive carry with them many indirect messages not consciously chosen but habitually accepted. We are constantly reminded, for example, of how our culture conceives of the roles of men and women. Imagine that you have amnesia as the result of a serious accident. You are lying in hospital, trying to reconstruct your life. You search the world around you for answers: "Who am I?" "What's important?" "How should I behave?" Your major contact with life outside the hospital is by means of the mass media. Research has in fact analyzed what you would learn about men's and women's places in the world.

Why television programs are so much alike

The nurse turns on your television set. The programs are produced daily at great expense, and they aim at mass appeal in order to recover their costs. Conservative, traditional images of men and women are what have this appeal, and they are the images you will see.

There are four significant differences in the way men and women are shown on television. First, men are seen more often. In all types of programs, there are more male than female leads, and women appear on the screen for less time. Second, men are shown in a wider range of roles. They are more often depicted as employed and their range of occupations is much broader. If both men and women are portrayed as employed, the men are more likely than the women to be shown at their jobs. The pattern is very much the same in television commercials. Third, there are male-female differences in the importance of the family and of personal relationships. Women are more often shown in family roles than men. A woman's marital status is more likely to be included in the script than is a man's. The majority of female characters are married, about to be married or in a serious relationship with a man; the majority of male characters are single. A woman's domain, then, is portrayed as largely in the emotional realm. Her power lies in her ability to express emotions, and in her ability to arouse a man's emotions. Her physical appearance is a key element in this power. She must be young and above average in her beauty, but her hero can be fat, bald, crude and uneducated. Fourth, men are much more likely to dominate women than women are to dominate men. In a television show, the figure in authority is more likely to be a man. Even when men and women have equal status, men are more likely than women to assume control. Male dominance is most exaggerated in crime dramas and least obvious in situation comedies. Male dominance is portrayed in both the physical and emotional realms. When men and women are involved in violence, the woman is much more likely to be the victim than the aggressor. Women are depicted as inferior even in programs catering specifically to them. For example, in female-oriented soap operas, a man typically presents the solution to a

◀ **Ready to transmit the ultimate image** *of the girl who got her man, photo-journalists assemble from around the world for a royal wedding in London. Daily, between 80 and 95 percent of news stories are about men. When a woman appears in the news, it is usually because of her special physical beauty, because her accomplishments are unusual for a female, or because she has established a relationship with an important man.*

▶ **A parody of physical power and aggression,** *created for the television screen by professional wrestlers. These men are comic because they display artificial emotions that are incongruous with the male role. In general it is their lack of expressed feeling that gives men on television more powerful personalities than the women. Men are seen more often than women on television, in a wider range of roles. Women are more often shown in family situations – but when they are not, their marital status is usually still part of the script. The majority of female characters are married. The majority of male characters are single.*

> *By appealing to the widest possible audience the entertainment and advertising media reinforce the most common ideals of how each sex should behave. They present powerful models for men, submissive and dependent models for women.*

woman's emotional crisis. Similarly, a female character trained in self-defense, such as a police officer or private detective, is rescued by a male colleague more often than she rescues him.

During the program intervals, all of these messages will be reinforced in the commercials. Guess the sex of the characters in these commercials:

1 This executive thinks all brands of paper towels are the same.
2 This adult washes clothes and toilets.
3 This parent drives on family outings.
4 This person likes to be very clean.
5 This adult does not know how to cook.

It is easy to score 100 percent on such a quiz, because, although men and women appear in equal numbers in primetime commercials, their ages, activities, roles and authority follow a predictable pattern.

Women are young, and their primary concerns are their appearance and their families. They want their families and bodies to be clean – very clean. Their most common role is as a family member. They are much less often portrayed as employed than men are, and when they are employed, their jobs are typically low-status ones. Television commercials depict men in their middle years (35-45) and employed. The majority of men are portrayed as working outside the home in a wide range of occupations, and they occupy positions of high status more often than women. In family settings, men are the drivers, and the recipients of women's work (cleaning and cooking). They are typically the authorities on product virtues, as seen in endorsements, and as heard in 90 percent of the off-camera voices.

So, what have you learned about men and women while lying in your hospital bed? Men are the movers and shakers of the world. Men earn the money; women are responsible for the well-being of families. We judge men by what they

do; we judge women by their relationships with men. She is his sex object; he is her success object. Men dominate women both physically and mentally; women are passive physically and mentally.

Why magazines are different

You turn off the television, and read a few magazines. The nurse has brought you both men's magazines and women's magazines. Do you see a difference? The articles and advertisements in women's magazines are not the same as the articles and advertisements in men's. Women are exhorted to find and keep their man. Men are exhorted to become successful. A "successful" man earns a large salary or has a prestigious job – and ideally he has both.

Magazines ensure their survival by focusing on a narrow audience. In this way, the articles and advertisements can be kept easily on target both for the readers and for the advertisers. The readers are given the articles they want, and the advertisers are given the audience they need.

Women's magazines tend to focus on fashion, food and home. And most of the articles in these magazines are self-improvement articles. "How to Lose Five Pounds in Five Days." "Nineteen Ways to Glitter This Christmas Season." "Dazzle Your Family with Holiday Treats." "Make Your Husband Sing Your Praises with Pasta." Clearly, a successful woman is one who has a man. If you do not have a man, or if you have one and do not want to lose him, the responsibility is totally yours. If you look better, or cook better,

228

PICTURES OF POWER

■ *It is usually the picture that draws our eyes to advertisements in newspapers and in magazines. In these, images of men and women are really images of power and lack of power. This power statement is made in several ways. One of the most important of these is that men are shown actively employed in high-status positions more often than women are. Women are often depicted in childlike positions, clothing or activities, sometimes with their hands in or near their mouths, like young children who suck their thumbs.*

POSTURE
■ *The person with authority in an advertisement is usually shown as taller than subordinates. A man is usually taller than a woman. The exception occurs when a picture is designed to be humorous, showing, for example, a tall, overweight woman with a small man. In many photographs the man is in an elevated position, perhaps standing above a seated or reclining woman. Often the woman is seductively posed, showing cleavage*

or shapely legs in her half-reclining position. Her eyes are looking up to his. Women's submissiveness is also shown in the tilted head, the bent knee and the crossed legs. These positions communicate passivity. But power is relative to the situation. In the household, the woman is more powerful: higher than, and more active than, the man. In family scenes the man is often pictured seated and the woman is standing (and usually cooking and cleaning).

TOUCH
■ *The powerful person in an advertisement may touch the subordinate. A man touches a woman's arm to give her directions, or to show her how to hold a golf club. As a couple, the man's touch is more engulfing than the woman's: his arm encircles her shoulder, while her finger-tips rest lightly on his arm. As with any baby, the person held is less powerful than the person holding.*

EXPRESSION
■ *Eye-contact patterns and smiling are two key facial ex-*

pressions of the power relations shown in advertisements. Smiling is a signal of friendliness, but also of powerlessness; women smile more often and more broadly than men. Direct eye contact is a signal of power; women are often shown gazing away from the camera; women display a broader range of emotions than men – rage, joy, grief, sadness and contentment. The most common emotional expression for men is also the most powerful – the absence of emotion.

▲ **Posture, expression and touch** *all advertise male dominance as well as a product in this image. In order for the coats to appeal to intended customers, the man assumes a superior posture, the woman a fawning one. His face expresses power through direct gaze and lack of expression; hers expresses dependence. She touches him submissively – his hand lies over hers in a gesture of control.*

Eye-contact patterns and smiling often indicate the power relations between men and women in advertisements. Women are represented as creatures of emotion in contrast to men, whose expressions suggest powerful equanimity.

your man will stay. Even articles that appear to address professional women are couched in similar terms: "Using Business Buzzwords," "How to Succeed in Business Without Working Your Way Up the Ladder." The image painted for women is that success does not require work. Instead, the right phrase spoken at the right time is the key to success. These articles rarely provide genuine help, such as financial or educational counseling. They suggest quick, no-work solutions.

Even for a professional woman, the primary measure of success is still apparently a relationship with a man. For example, "Making the Business Conference Pay" is the title of an article that actually discusses how to flirt discreetly at meetings, how to pick out the married men and how to present your ideas in feminine (meaning passive) ways.

Some magazines aim at the nontraditional female audience. Their focus is in marked contrast to the traditional self-improvement emphasis in other women's magazines. Articles highlight the achievements of women and the possibilities open to them. The readership runs below

10 percent of the circulation of traditional magazines.

Men's magazines display a variety of masculine interests, from sports and finance to photography and pornography. The best-selling women's magazines use pictures of the home and family; the best-selling men's magazines use pictures of beautiful (and naked) women. But men need to succeed before they can confidently approach women. Therefore, popular men's magazines also show men how to succeed. And wherever a man chooses to perform, whether in sports, business or war, there is a magazine that specializes in his field.

At this point, if you are a woman, you may be turning to the nurse to ask her opinion about how you could improve yourself. If you are a man, perhaps you will be asking – no – *telling* the nurse to summon the doctor. You need to get out into the world and start succeeding!

229

▲ **Parody of the female form**. *An exaggerated cut-out figure announces the swimsuit rack in a Chicago clothing store. The image that it is hoped women customers will identify with accentuates techniques for attracting and flattering men.*

The posture is extremely open to male advance. Sunglasses mute the power of the eyes, but the direction of gaze is selective and inviting. The smile is a display of undemanding submission. Traditional pin-up and calendar art for men uses all of

these devices and also exaggerates the length of the model's legs, for, during the growth spurt at puberty, girl's legs become disproportionately long at just about the time when men begin to find them sexually attractive.

▲ **Parody of female cooperation**. *At a photo call at the Cannes Film Festival in France, an aspiring movie starlet performs the annual ritual of the as-yet-unknowns making themselves known to the photographic press. In a satirical gesture, she enhances the contours of her breast. Although normally on a beach in France few women would wear a top, the fact that this covered one has become a media event is enough to draw the attention of passers-by.*

The men who are in the news

Once you settle down again, you discard the magazines and look at the newspapers. You reason, "Because newspapers are published daily, they might reflect a more dynamic view of men's and women's roles." And so, as you read, you begin searching. But, in section after section, you ask: "Where are the women?" They are missing even from the obituary section. Women are rarely written about, and rarely too are they the writers. News articles are typically about men (80-95 percent). The photographs are of men. The editorial pages are filled with the actions and ideas of men.

Even the articles on the "women's" pages are more likely to be about men than about women, and to be written by men. The overwhelming majority (75-90 percent) of by-lined journalists are men.

When a woman appears in the spotlight, it is most likely because of her unique physical beauty or the fact that she is a woman in a nontraditional role. For example, a recent article on "The First Woman Director To Be Nominated," focused on the film maker's unique position of being a woman director rather than on her talent.

In the cartoon pages, as well, male characters significantly outnumber female characters. Women are more likely to be drawn at home; men are at work or outside the home. Men and women are shown in stereotyped divisions of household work – men read newspapers or mow the lawn, for instance, while women cook and clean. Female characters are more passive about solving problems than are male characters. We are back in the world of mass appeal. While most magazines are specialized for particular audiences – golfers, gourmet cooks, computer enthusiasts – and therefore can cater to the unique views of their readers, newspapers jeopardize their survival by specializing.

Men and women in books

Does the equation "mass appeal equals traditional sex roles" hold true for books as well? The nurse brings you a few examples of the best-selling fiction for adults and children. You scan both types of books for lessons on how men and women should behave. You will observe that male and female characters populate adult fiction in almost equal numbers. They are both likely to be under 30. The physical descriptions of women are much more detailed. The men are more likely than the women to be wage-earners, and the men have more managerial jobs than the women have.

READING HABITS

■ **Male and female reading habits** in the United Kingdom RIGHT. Almost all romantic novels are bought by women, but so are the majority of serious novels. Men like to read stories of crime, war and science fiction more than women do. Women read less nonfiction than men. BELOW A growing category of mass-market women's fiction reflects a trend away from the traditional romance, in which a young woman is swept off her feet by a superior male. Clockwise from the top in this selection of covers, a woman gazes at us with direct and even greater force than her man, a ruthless woman triumphs over several men, an ambitious and passionate woman rules a business empire.

MEN	WOMEN
Crime	Romance
War/adventure	Serious novels
Occult	
Science fiction	
Humor	
Other fiction	Historical
History	
Other non-fiction	Biography

Romantic novels tell and retell the same story: a young, inexperienced woman meets an older, more experienced – and wealthy – man who appears to dislike her at first. Although the path of romance is not smooth, love triumphs.

But one category of adult fiction out-sells all others: romance novels. No one title sells more than a fraction of the copies that a bestseller does, but the number of titles available is enormous. Women of all ages in most countries buy them. They are inexpensive, short and repetitive. Characters and plots follow a formula, retelling the same story: a young, inexperienced woman meets an older, experienced, wealthy man who appears to dislike her at first. He is cynical or aloof or indifferent. Although the path of romance is not smooth, once his love is revealed, she reciprocates. A happy ending is always guaranteed.

Romance novels are criticized for being nonfeminist, but at least the woman wins. It has been suggested that their appeal depends on giving women a romantic interpretation of the inequalities created by a male-dominated culture. The man appears cruel and indifferent, but really he is in love and wants to avoid showing his emotions. The woman appears passive and sometimes manipulative, but really she is young, inexperienced...and in love. The woman reader wins because she can identify with both the hero and the damsel in distress; the damsel wins because she ends up as lady of the manor.

And what do you find in the children's books? Do we give

■ **Powerful action, female support**. *ABOVE Women cheerleaders provide the half-time entertainment at a bruising exhibition football match between the Chicago Bears and the Dallas Cowboys. In advertisements, too, men play, women* *cheer – or, as in this picture LEFT created for the advertising industry, a woman stands helplessly by as a man saves her by fighting off a wild beast. In other typical images, men pay while women watch, or men teach and women learn* *from them. Men are more often shown talking, women listening. Even in television advertisements where a smiling woman stands next to a washing machine that women will buy and use, a male voice on the soundtrack explains the technical* *virtues of the product. Women often serve a purely decorative function. They do not do anything, but simply stand near the object advertised.*

our children the same messages about women's and men's roles? Yes. Here too, with remarkable consistency, women are both misrepresented and underrepresented. The majority of the characters are male. This is true whether the book is fiction or nonfiction, about animals or people, for pre-school or high school.

Women are generally shown within the home, where their primary skills of cleaning, cooking and caretaking shine. Women are not the farmers counting their bushels of peas nor are they often famous enough to be included in the bio-graphies. Men are clever, competent problem-solvers who succeed due to their own cunning, adventurous spirit. Women usually end up crying about their problems rather than solving them. In one reader for 10-year-olds, a child climbs too far into a tree. Instead of his mother carrying the ladder from the garage, the boy remains in the tree for three hours until his father comes home to help.

What truly is the influence of the media?

Your eyes hurt from reading all afternoon. But you are satisfied that you are beginning to remember. Women are passive, inexperienced, incompetent and happiest when they are home taking care of everyone else. Men are active, experienced, competent and happiest when they are challenged by a difficult task.

By now you are feeling much better. Your bruises are disappearing. You are ready to leave the hospital, confident that you know how to behave. The mass media have taught you how to be a "natural" man or woman. As a man, you will probably stride confidently out the door of the hospital, eager to succeed and to make love to a woman. As a woman, you will probably leave the hospital smiling at everyone and hoping to find a man who will love you.

But, of course, you are not *really* in the hospital with amnesia. You are living within a particular culture, remembering attitudes and messages from your entire life. Do the media's images of men and women have an impact on you? Probably. But it is impossible to devise any experiment that will isolate the effect. People who participated in such an experiment would come to the research situation with years of personal history. There is no way to wipe the slate clean for them before the experiment, to test *just* the effect of the media.

The clearest information we have deals with the effect of

◀ **Advertisements for movies** promise revealing glimpses of girls TOP in France and BOTTOM in Thailand. A night out at the movies in France will feature female bondage and an unrestrained male power. A night at the movies in Thailand will feature very aggressive female fighters, but they will not be dressed in a very practical way for combat. Girls of Thailand's Muslim minority pass by, heavily garbed to protect their chastity.

POWERFUL CLOTHING

■ *In advertising men are typically shown in business suits or casual wear. Women are shown in everything from formal dresses to nightgowns. For example, in two promotions for the same breakfast cereal, one showed a man, dressed in jeans and wool shirt, enjoying his cereal on a mountain top. The other showed a woman, dressed in a very brief nightgown, enjoying her cereal on a windy patio near the beach.*

Revealing clothing – or no clothing at all – indicates vulnerability, and this is not the typical male image conveyed. Men dress powerfully.

Do the media affect our attitudes and behavior? One study found that men were more critical and less supportive of their wives after television programs showing violence than they were after they had watched nature films.

the media on children. Most of this research has been done to evaluate educational television and the effects of television violence. The findings are clear that television can teach both intentional and unintentional lessons. By changing the content of their television programs, researchers have shown that children became less aggressive, more helpful, more generous and more knowledgeable than other children who did not watch the altered programs. Some television programs make children less fearful, less prejudiced against minorities and less angry.

Experiments show that both boys and girls pay more attention to television characters of their own sex. Boys, for instance, are more successful in doing a task after watching a male television character try the same task and succeed; girls are more successful doing the task after watching a female television character try it and succeed. It has also been shown that both boys and girls base their views of which careers are appropriate for men and women on the careers held by men and women in television programs.

Another study, this time on adults, showed that men were more critical and less supportive of their wives after watching violent television programs than they were after watching nature films.

Boys and girls absorb sex-role messages from television, and adults are reinforced in the sex-role images they have already learned. But it is simplistic to claim that television is *responsible* for this or that change of attitude. Television alone would have little impact on our attitudes if it were the single medium delivering the messages. All forms of the mass media give very consistent images of men and women, and these messages are compounded by what happens generally in the world around us, where men drive while women ride, where men go out to work while women stay at home. When the messages from friends, family and the media are in such harmony, it is tempting to believe that the sex roles spring forth "naturally."

The vital question is: do the media *reflect* or *create* the values of the society? Since the main goal of the media is commercial success, the media must appeal to the largest audience in order to survive. And that appeal is maximized when the media *reflect* the values of the dominant group in society. Clearly then the media reflect rather than create those values. However, the media certainly also *reinforce* society's values, because it is largely through the media that our culture communicates its messages to its young – and old – on how they should behave. **EC**

◄ **A cosmetics advertisement** *in a street in Okinawa, Japan. The advertising media surround us with constant reminders that women are expected to dress and groom themselves with extra attention to the effect they are creating on the opposite sex. Men generally need to attend only to the minimum requirements of neatness and cleanliness. When a man is presented as sexually attractive, he usually looks aloof, not interested in becoming a rewarding companion.*

Sex Stereotypes

PEOPLE like to *know* about the opposite sex. We want to know how to behave together and what to expect of each other. We also like to know about our own sex, not least because we believe that this helps us better to understand ourselves. We reach for this knowledge all of our lives, observing men and women, noticing how they appear in the news and entertainment media and listening to the opinions of friends and acquaintances. The impressions we form in this way are *sex stereotypes* – images of the "typical" man or woman, and also images of who is typical of particular subcategories, such as businesswomen, housewives, working men.

The images often mislead us when we form impressions of individual people and decide how to behave with them. Stereotypes exaggerate similarities between members of the *same* social group and differences between members of *different* groups. They sometimes contain erroneous elements, and they are sometimes self-fulfilling prophesies – by the fact that they are widely accepted and influence people's behavior, they help to *create* the realities they *seem* only to reflect.

While being sensitive to these problems, however, it is important to recognize that forming stereotypes is something natural and necessary. It is not something done only by foolish and unsophisticated people.

How stereotypes work

The Greek root *stereo* means "solid." Before the term "stereotype" was introduced into the social sciences in the 1920s, it had been used in printing, where it meant a plate cast in metal from a mold. This older meaning provided a perfect analogy for the group images that researchers wanted to investigate – they saw them as inflexible pictures stamped into our minds by the society that shapes us. More

recently, researchers have given attention to the fact that we each construct stereotypes for ourselves. At the heart of any stereotype is a generalization about a category of people. This is not necessarily a distortion. Putting people and things into categories is natural and inevitable. The world is complex and we make it manageable by treating each new object or person as a particular *kind* of person or thing. Can you even imagine yourself without thinking of your sex, for example, or perhaps instead your nationality or cultural identity? A category, in turn, is of no use to us unless we organize information around it. We each have a personal set of ideas, for example, about different kinds of dogs and different kinds of television sets. These help us to decide which dogs to pet and which to avoid, which television set to buy and which not to. To take another example, friends announce that they are bringing their ten- and eight-year-old

234

■ **Mind and body** *can be made to reflect, and exaggerate, the typical expectations that we have of men and women.* RIGHT *A champion body builder displays the extreme in hard, masculine physical development.* FAR RIGHT *A chess champion, hard-faced, competitive and ruthlessly logical, displays the behavioral counterpart of masculine physique.* CENTER *A Hollywood sex idol, physically soft, emotionally warm and yielding, symbolically offers herself to the troops she is entertaining. Men and women receive fame and admiration for developing and presenting their bodies and their personalities in these ways, because the images they create give* vivid form to social standards of how males and females should present themselves – men are expected to be tough and capable of controlling themselves and others, while women are expected to be cooperative and appealing. The extreme role for women is to be a sex object, valued for submissive sensuality alone.

We all form mental pictures of the typical man and the typical woman. They help us to predict how people will behave and also give us models to live up to. However, these pictures usually do not represent real sex differences.

sons when they call by for a visit this afternoon. On putting down the telephone, you try to imagine from your general knowledge of boys of that age what will entertain them.

In fact, when researchers record sex stereotypes, they do no more than measure the generalizations we make about social groups that we identify by sex. Most often measured are generalizations about adult males and adult females. Researchers ask people to think of the average man or woman and to mark a point along a scale between opposites – such as "very aggressive" and "not at all aggressive." When a person thinks that men and women differ significantly on a particular trait, the trait is then counted as part of that person's male or female stereotype. A single character-

istic may also be called a stereotype – for example, being aggressive is a male stereotype for people who think of men as typically aggressive and of women as not.

Stereotypes help us to form impressions of people and decide how to behave. But they are often inaccurate. This is so especially when people's wishes and needs cloud their judgment. When we identify with a group, we tend to form an exaggeratedly positive mental picture of it. This boosts morale and helps to release positive energies in us. However, we almost never achieve this without downgrading other groups. Seeing your own nationality as more hard-working, more rational, more inventive and more discerning than others gives you a positive image to live up to, but it also gives you a motive for seeing laziness, irrationality and a lack of imagination and sophistication when you look abroad for confirmation of your view.

Often, a negative view of others goes no further than bolstering your self-esteem. The fun we make of foreigners, for example, is sometimes innocuous. To their own separate benefit, the French and the English enjoy funny stories at each other's expense, which cannot always be successfully translated – because you need the right picture of an Englishman or a Frenchman in your mind in order to see the joke. Even the translation of language itself is affected. The French phrase *filer à l'anglaise* (to go away without permission or without paying your bill) becomes "to take French leave" in England. English speakers associate sexual oddity with the French, and when condoms were still an under-the-counter item they acquired the name "French safes" or "French letters." French-speakers think the English are sexually odd and refer to condoms as *les capotes anglaises* (English jackets).

When different categories of people live together, however, but with different roles, the established general-

izations about each category can arise out of and act as justifications and reinforcements for the way the roles have been shared out. When one group has more influence than others the distortions it creates can even become accepted by others. This can result in low-status groups adopting an unflattering self-image because people they respect have a low opinion of them.

An extreme example of this kind of stereotype was the "Black Sambo" image of a simple-minded slave on southern plantations before the American Civil War. Trans-Atlantic slave traders drew Africans of all personality types and levels of intelligence from a striking variety of cultures and language groups, and from different classes and ranks within their cultures. However, most learned to adopt a uniformly ingratiating and simple manner, and this became a typical slave personality. It allowed the slaves to appease the power of their masters. Successive generations of plantation owners and slaves alike came to see simple and dependent behavior as "natural" to black people.

The stereotypes for master and slave had separate lists of good and bad qualities for each, representing the virtues and faults that were possible within the roles they played. A good master was wise and gentlemanly. He might be humane and loving but had to be demanding. A bad master was cruel or neglectful, but he was still acting like a master,

and his neighbors were not nearly as likely to shake their heads over these faults as they were if he lost control over his slaves. A good slave was loyal, hardworking and grateful to his master for looking after him. In general, however, it was to be expected that slaves would be lazy and foolish. This fitted in with their status and their supposed nature. What was not to be expected, or tolerated, was that they should be proud, rebellious or smart.

Although some slaves tried to escape and many attempts succeeded, most behaved in a submissive way that was consistent with their own self-image and with their own conception of their interests. Both master and slave were rewarded with social approval for holding and teaching the established stereotypes and punished with social disapproval and worse for undermining them. But usually it did not take much effort to see white masters and black slaves in the way you were supposed to. You only had to look at the way they actually behaved. Racial and ethnic stereotypes have, of course, influenced much more complex and subtle social patterns, and continue to do so today.

How do we stereotype the sexes?

The average person's picture of a typical man has been found to contain adjectives such as "active," "courageous" and rational"; women are generally described as "kind" and

236

USING STEREOTYPES

■ *Imagine that you have just walked into an office. Very quickly, and usually without being aware of it, you make different guesses about the roles, abilities and personalities of the people you see there. "Who is the middle-aged, neatly dressed woman? Probably the secretary. And who is the man in the three-piece suit? The manager." Having made these guesses, you may expect the woman to be friendly, and the man to be aggressive, and you may decide on strategies – to try to charm the woman, but to convince the man by the force of your arguments.*

This imaginary situation illu- *strates our use of sex-typed categories – the way we divide up the social world on the basis of sex (first into men and women, and then into types of men and types of women), the* *way we use such categories to help us guess what people may be like, and the way we use the guesses to guide our behavior.*

When a stranger we meet is not clearly labeled – for *instance, like the woman ABOVE, with a mixture of feminine and masculine style – we may feel less sure how to react until better acquainted.*

Underlying the male stereotype is a self-reliant achiever, while the female image is of someone who is emotionally expressive and cares about people. Men may also seem cruel, severe, tact-less, women fickle, helpless and weak.

"sensitive" as well as "gentle." These sample items share a theme. Underlying the male image is a self-reliant achiever, while the female image is an emotionally expressive person who cares about other people. There is also a negative side to these pictures. For men, typical negative adjectives are "cruel," "severe" and "tactless"; for women they are "fickle," "helpless" and "weak." The male image, including both its positive and negative elements, suggests a hard approach to life committed both to self-control and control of others, whereas the female image implies softness and a readiness to be controlled by other people and one's own emotions.

The positive part of your image of women is your ideal of *femininity*. The positive part of your image of men is an ideal of *masculinity*. The qualities you consider feminine are the ones you consider desirable, appropriate and attractive in women precisely because of their suitability to a woman's role as you conceive it. And masculine qualities are the ones you see as helping a man to live up to his role. In courtship, for example, whatever attracts a typical man to a woman is typically feminine. This may include showing a readiness to be dependent on the man, for in family life it is traditionally the woman who will take the caring, nurturant

role and it is the man who will compete in the world for material needs, using his masculine determination and toughness.

Negative aspects of the male and female pictures, meanwhile, are still *appropriate* qualities. Women are supposed to be bad drivers – underlining that competence at things mechanical is a masculine trait. Men are supposed to be uncaring, thoughtless, untidy. They can be like this because they are supposed to leave nurturance, concern for other's feelings and neatness to women.

Some of our male and female stereotypes are accurate. On average, women *are* gentler, more nurturant, more emotionally expressive than men. Men *are* more aggressive and competitive than women. Is this because our stereotypes reflect "natural" differences? Evidence exists that some behavioral differences between the sexes may have a basis in biology. An obvious candidate, of course, is the fact that men by and large are attracted sexually to women and women to men, but other differences have also been linked

▲ **Unexpected images** *leave us puzzled, unable to predict how others will behave or to decide how we should react. This is due to the fact that when we first meet we rely on generalizations about how people typically look and behave. We only gradually come to know and understand each other as individuals.*

KNOWING WHAT THE OTHER IS THINKING

■ *In dealing with the opposite sex, it is useful to know what stereotypes the person you are with is being guided by. For example, research has shown that personnel officers who, on the one hand, would feel comfortable about hiring a very feminine-looking woman as a receptionist do not, on the other hand, respond favorably to businesswomen unless they dress in a somewhat masculine (but not too masculine) way. Women presenting themselves at job interviews make profitable use of this kind of information about female stereotypes.*

In forming a more personal relationship with another, knowing how they expect your sex to behave is again a crucial piece of information. Sound relationships are based on similarity (see Ch 18) but when it comes to selecting a romantic partner, one of the similarities that matters most, ironically, is how closely you share a view of the ways men and women should be different. Initial mutual interest suggests that you look right to each other – the degree to which the man emphasizes his masculine physical traits strikes a chord in the woman and the way she physically presents her femininity strikes a chord in the man. If both are strongly sex-typed and feel that they need the opposite sex truly to be opposite sex, then strongly masculine and feminine clothing and grooming will advertise this attitude and help to create a sense of attraction. However, another couple might be attracted because the outward styles of both convey the preference for a partner who will not make an insistent point of being treated like a man, or like a woman.

As with any first impression, the implicit exchange of promises lying behind these messages needs to be verified and reinterpreted through a process of getting to know each other better. Each partner needs to learn in more precise detail how the other will want them to behave.

To some extent, partners will re-educate each other in what to expect of the opposite sex, but mainly the courtship process will be one of discovery, and since people's needs and preconceptions seldom match closely enough, a majority of romances do not last.

237

at least partly to biology. Studies of brain structure and of the influence of sex hormones (see *Chs 1, 7, 10*) have hinted at physiological explanations for greater female verbal skill, greater male mathematical skill and higher levels of male activity. It has been suggested that such differences may be among numerous subtle influences on learning and behavior that have evolved as natural adaptations to help us fit into our sex roles. It would not be surprising if this were to

some extent true, since in so many other species, males and females are adapted for different social behavior. No one has ever proven that human sex roles are "natural" in this way, but for an up-to-date review of the evidence see *Ch 16*.

Whatever truth there may be in the evolutionary story, however, it is clear that male and female roles vary in some respects from culture to culture and that many of our male and female images are kept alive without a factual basis. People seem to believe many of them because they fit a traditional pattern. Some are straightforwardly inaccurate – for example – "Women are bad drivers." The statistics in many countries suggest the opposite. Women drivers in the United States, to take just one of many instances, cause fewer accidents than men.

More subtly, when we distinguish the male category from the female, we tend to underestimate the differences *within* and overestimate the differences *between* them. This reflects something that happens when we compare any two overlapping groups. In one experiment two sets of volunteers were asked to estimate the lengths of eight lines. For one group (those placed in the "classification condition") the four shortest and four longest lines were grouped, and the groups were labeled A and B. Compared with people who judged the line lengths without these labels, volunteers in the classification condition saw the lines within groups as more similar in length, and they saw the A lines as more different from the B lines. Experiments tend to show that we exaggerate the differences between groups *more* than we exaggerate the similarities within them.

In reality, men as individuals are more unlike each other in abilities and personality than men and women are as groups. Yet we fail to see and appreciate the diversity between individuals and the similarities between the sexes. The average male is taller than the average female, but we

238

◄ **The stereotype of the woman driver** *says that she has poor control and low confidence, and this is how she is* *supposed to be with all things mechanical. In reality, women cause fewer traffic accidents than men but in many situations feign or exaggerate mechanical incompetence, because they think that it makes them more feminine.*

► **A beauty contestant's personality** *is one of the attributes on which she is supposed to be judged, but in most contests she will be expected to say very little about herself that could reveal a genuine individuality of character.*

NARROWING THE GAP

■ *The average man is 30 percent stronger than the average woman, but when men and women both try hard, differences in physical powers shrink. Between 1939 and 1981, the* women's 800m world record in running improved by more than 18 seconds, the men's by only 4.9 – the gap was cut from 25 to less than 12 seconds. Between 1956 and 1981, the difference between male and female running records in general narrowed by 36 percent. Today's women's 400m free-style swimming record would have won the men's 1972 Olympic gold medal. Women are actually faster at swimming the English Channel.

▼ **World long-jump records.** *In 1948, the women's record was still a third of a meter short of the men's 1896 record. By 1986 it exceeded the 1896 record by more than a meter.*

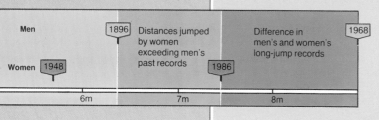

Men			
	1896	Distances jumped by women exceeding men's past records	Difference in men's and women's long-jump records	1968
Women 1948		1986	
	6m	7m	8m

Some stereotypes are straightforwardly false – for example, "Women are bad drivers" – others may reflect reality, but in an exaggerated way. Many sex stereotypes are prophesies that fulfill themselves by guiding our behavior.

all know many women who are taller than many men, and this overlap is even greater for verbal and mathematical abilities and for interests and personality traits than it is for physical attributes. Men and women are stereotyped, however, as psychological opposites. Contradictory though it may appear, people assess *others* in just this way, although they can and often do see *themselves* as possessing both masculine and feminine traits (see *Ch30*).

Self-fulfilling prophesies

In many cases, when a stereotype and a scientifically verified sex difference match in some degree, the real sex difference can be explained plausibly as the *result* of a social arrangement that, ironically, the stereotype helps to keep alive. For example, women are stereotyped as – and on average really are slightly – easier to influence than men. The impression this creates of women helps to sort them into lower-status roles in society. People sometimes refer to women's lower resistance to influence as a justification for reserving important roles for men. Not seeing women in important roles, furthermore, men and women alike think of

the status of women as a lower one than that of men. And people who see themselves as lower in status than others are inclined by the very fact of their low status to be more agreeable and less challenging (see *Ch24*). There is thus a vicious cycle, and in at least some degree the stereotype is a self-fulfilling and self-reinforcing prophesy.

Men are commonly stereotyped as having leadership ability. As a consequence, they are more likely to be given positions of authority. And, because we have greater confidence in male leaders, we are more likely to comply with their demands than with similar requests made by women. This behavior can effect a self-fulfilling prophesy by making the male's job far easier, so that he does, in fact, outperform his female counterpart. It is, however, worth noting that when women are given clear and unambiguous positions of leadership, whether of a business – or even of a country – they are as effective as male managers.

Many men feel incompetent at looking after babies, all the more so when they see with what confidence women handle infants, but most women have little competence either until they have been thrown in at the deep end. Men do not usually see or understand a first-time mother's initial shock at having a helpless being utterly dependent on her.

Prior generalizations in themselves and the experience of

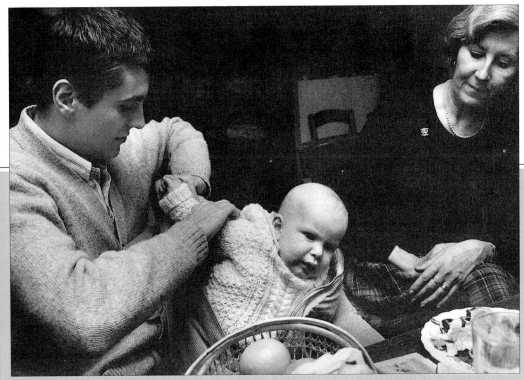

▲ **Sex stereotyping in the division of child care** *can leave men feeling awkward when they have to perform tasks they see as requiring female expertise. In fact, the sexes often start from an equal position of competence in infant care. In today's small families, most girls have little opportunity to learn about babies at first hand and only begin when they become mothers. Interviewed before their first child's birth, fathers-to-be who consider themselves competent to handle a baby are more likely to play an active role when the baby arrives.*

seeing men and women in characteristic roles create in us certain expectations. In everyday encounters, these affect what we notice about people, how we interpret their actions, and, later, what we remember about them. We are all the more predisposed to pay attention to and to recall later any behavior that fits a pattern we *approve* of. Anything that at first conflicts with the pattern may be unconsciously reinterpreted so that it can made to fit. For example, when a mother goes out to work, she is less likely to be seen as doing so out of a need for self-fulfillment as out of a need for extra family income, because this neatly fits the image of women as self-sacrificing.

Can we avoid stereotypes?

Governments concerned to promote equality of opportunity have legislated against sex discrimination. This means that in a number of situations, including most decisions about who to employ, it is illegal to deal with an individual on the basis of a generalization about their sex. In practice, such laws are impossible to enforce with any precision – personnel officers often unconsciously frame interview questions in a way that prompts a candidate to reinforce a first impression, and our first impressions are powerfully influenced by group images – knowing little about a person as an individual, we fall back on what we think we know about people *like* them.

The greatest impact on stereotyped thinking – the most genuine opportunity to make general impressions of the sexes less rigid and less inaccurate – is probably to be made at the personal level. Even without a conscious awareness of the distorting influence of stereotypes, we normally do limit their power. In most situations, our impressions about and behavior toward other people are determined by sex *in combination with* other factors. An individual woman's businesslike manner can make a man (or a fellow

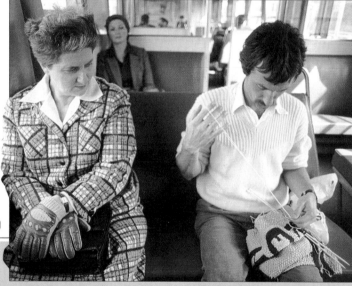

■ **Breaking the male stereotype**. *A woman fellow passenger TOP cannot help looking with fascination at a man knitting. A man with a baby hangs out the washing RIGHT. People who act out of role make us search unconsciously for a new set of generalizations to make sense of what we see – the knitter must be pursuing a creative career that involves artistry with wool; the man at the washing line must be one of those who allow themselves to be bossed by their wives. If the usual stereotype will not fit, we find another.*

■ **Breaking the female stereotype**. *TOP Women body-builders at Madison Square Garden in New York City display their muscles. Both male and female body builders use diet, grueling exercise – and, often, steroid drugs – to distort the human form. Many people are repelled by the unnatural appearance that results, but the effect is more readily tolerated, and even admired, in men than in women. The female distortions seem more disturbingly unnatural because the aspects of the human form that they exaggerate belong to our ideal of physical masculinity. This makes it seem to many women,*

240

Even without being consciously aware of how far stereotypes distort reality, we normally limit their power. The more we know about individual interests, strengths and weaknesses of another, the less we judge them by preconceptions.

woman) temporarily put aside preconceptions about scatterbrained females. In some situations we are guided less by the stereotype than in others. A young female receptionist greeting a male visitor, for example, is in a more sex-stereotyped situation than when she is dissecting a rat with a fellow student on return to university after her working holiday. During her summer job, she may find herself acting in a more typically feminine way just because it fits the role she is playing. In general, the more we know about another person's individual interests, strengths and weaknesses, the less likely we are to rely on stereotypes when we are making judgments about them.

Rooting out rigid and oversimplified ways of thinking can

make your own personal experience of the opposite sex more rewarding, by making it easier to understand individuals on their own terms and deal with them under a richer, more flexible, more accurate and therefore more useful set of expectations. For example, overcoming typical misconceptions about male and female sexuality can lead to a more satisfying sexual experience (see *Ch 17*). Men or women who are constantly baffled or disappointed by the opposite sex typically fail to treat them as much like individuals as they would members of their own sex. Often the responses that this elicits reinforce the negative aspects of a sex stereotype: women seem all the more irrational, or men all the more hostile.

Avoiding excessively stereotyped thinking can be very liberating in terms of your own self-image. You probably have, in addition to all of the qualities that suit you to your traditional sex role, some that a member of the opposite sex would find useful in their traditional role as well. If your conception of yourself as a man or a woman is flexible enough, you can release more of this potential.

The secret of avoiding rigidity in our stereotypes is, of course, to keep an open mind, to deal with individuals – as much as possible – as individuals, and to accept diversity within groups. It is important to be skeptical about statements about the sexes. What is the evidence for them, and how great, on average, is the alleged difference? We will never, of course, dispense with the need to form impressions quickly, and first impressions will inevitably overlook most of a person's individual qualities, but we can practice caution about the way we act on them.

241

who find it difficult to identify with them, that female body builders reject their sex. The attitudes and sex orientations of body builders, in fact, vary with the individual. RIGHT A woman cameraman and her male assistant break the stereotypes for their sexes simply by going about their work.

Role Versatility

IF YOU TRY to classify yourself or people you know as *either* masculine *or* feminine, you will probably have some difficulty. Most people, to some degree at least, combine traits that we would think of as masculine with traits we would consider feminine. Whether male or female, they may be assertive when dealing with people at work, yet sympathetic when comforting a distressed friend.

Many people, however, still set great store by being a very "feminine" woman or a very "masculine" man, actively avoiding behavior that they would think inappropriate to their sex. As we shall see, these attitudes can be very deep-rooted in some people while others are much more flexible in their sex roles. Psychologists are now beginning to look at some of the drawbacks of rigid sex-typing and at the benefit of role flexibility.

Masculine and feminine traits

Before the early 1970s, psychologists tended to classify people as masculine or feminine at opposite ends of a single scale. This approach emerged from a deeply rooted network of largely unexamined beliefs which governed not only research in psychology, but also the general public's view of sex roles and personality. There was a basic belief that masculine and feminine personalities are, by their very nature, opposites.

Two further assumptions strongly influenced the direction of traditional research. First, psychologists assumed that people must be either appropriately sex-typed (masculine males or feminine females) or reversed (feminine males and masculine females). Second, they assumed that being a totally masculine male or a totally feminine female was the most desirable and healthy condition.

Psychologists therefore, as well as the general public, held that it was good for girls to inhibit any masculine characteristics and to develop only feminine ones; not to be, for example, independent and analytic but to be tender and soft-spoken.

Correspondingly, traditional psychology as well as traditional culture held that it was good for boys and men to inhibit any feminine characteristics and to develop only masculine ones; not to be yielding and sympathetic, for example, but to be competitive and forceful. Those who deviated were expected to encounter social pressures and to suffer psychological problems.

These ideas went largely unchallenged until the social climate of the 1960s and 1970s brought increasing suggestions that men and women should resist the constraints imposed upon them by traditional sex roles. Psychological research reflected these concerns, suggesting that masculinity and femininity, in themselves of equal value, could be combined in the same person. In other words, well-adjusted people do not necessarily conform to rigid sex types but

► **Emotional versatility** *permits people to express or hide emotions as appropriate, without considering whether they are men or women. Here members of an alcoholic rehabilitation group try to establish a bond as part of their therapy. Although expressions of emotional dependence between members of the same sex are more characteristic of women, even in many traditionally masculine situations, such as war, men rely intensely on each other, and they express feelings freely.*

Are you masculine, feminine or both? Some traits traditionally identified with the opposite sex are included in everyone's makeup, and about 25 percent of people are "androgynous," combining high degrees of masculinity and femininity.

may be *androgynous* (masculine and feminine to more or less equal degrees) and that it is actually the androgynous person who shows the most satisfactory psychological and social adjustment.

Testing for androgyny

There was an immediate practical problem in exploring this idea. This was that the existing sex-role tests provided no way to identify or study androgynous personalities. A new test was needed, one that assessed masculinity and femininity separately.

The first of these tests to appear was the Bem Sex Role Inventory, and it is still the most widely used modern test. It differs from earlier tests not only by having independent masculinity and femininity scales but also by incorporating only *socially desirable* traits.

To design her test, the American psychologist Sandra Bem chose 400 personality traits and selected from these 40 which were rated as definitely more desirable in one sex but not the other by two groups of university students. Bem now had an instrument with which to measure masculinity and femininity and to identify as androgynous those people whose personalities incorporated socially valued masculine and feminine qualities.

Bem gave this test to large samples of students and derived each student's masculinity and femininity scores. Students with a high masculinity score and a low femininity score were defined as masculine sex-typed and those with high femininity and low masculinity scores as feminine sex-typed. If both scores were high, the student was classified as androgynous, and if both were low the student was not classified as any of those three.

One-quarter of the students were androgynous (29 males and 21 females), one-quarter feminine (16 males and 34

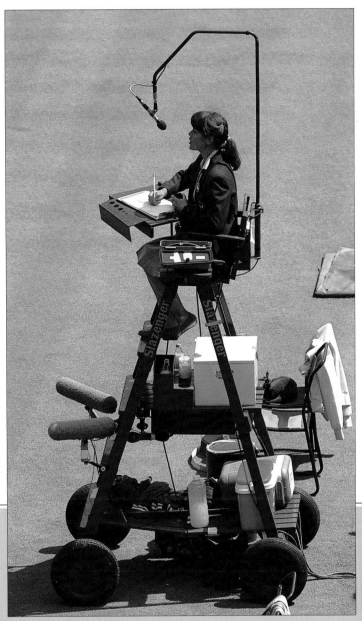

▲ **Assertiveness**, *traditionally considered a masculine trait, goes with the job of being a tennis umpire, and it is a useful personality adaptation for anyone in everyday life. When people understand what you want them to understand about your needs and wishes, they can interact more effectively with you. Getting the message across (both what you mean and the fact that you really mean it) involves a definite tone of voice and a posture that accentuates the size of your body.*

▶ **The feminine touch** *does not have to be abandoned if you work as a mechanical engineer. Feminine dress can be combined with hard hats, and a pleasant smile can go with giving instructions.*

females) and one-quarter masculine (37 males and 16 females). Several other researchers also compiled similar inventories, and with these new measuring instruments psychologists set out to test the claims that had been made in favor of androgyny.

How flexible are we?

The earliest studies focused specifically upon the issue of whether or not androgynous people display a greater flexibility than others in coping with day-to-day problems. Do feminine women perform well only in situations calling for traditionally feminine behavior, and are masculine men restricted to performing well only in masculine situations? Are androgynous people able to perform in both masculine and feminine ways, depending upon the demands of the situation? To test these ideas, Bem and her colleagues carried out a series of laboratory studies.

In one, individual students were left alone for 10 minutes with a five-month-old infant. They were told that the researchers would be observing, through a one-way mirror, how the baby responded to them as a stranger. In fact, the researchers measured how the student responded to the baby. They assessed how much the student talked to and smiled at the baby, nuzzled, kissed and held it, and played with it in ways that involved touching. Both feminine and androgynous students were significantly more at ease with the baby than were the masculine students, whether they were men or women.

In another study, researchers assessed the degree to which volunteers for an experiment were sympathetic and supportive when listening to a lonely peer. Volunteers were told that the study was about the "acquaintance process" and were introduced to a person of the same sex as themselves who was assigned the role of talker, while the subject was labeled "listener." As conversation progressed, the talker (actually one of the researchers) began to describe emotional and love-life problems, and researchers behind a one-way mirror noted the facial expressions of the listener, how many times they nodded and how many comments they made. Again, feminine and androgynous subjects showed the more "feminine" behavior.

Another study was designed to test independence, usually considered a masculine trait. Groups of four students, all of the same sex, were asked to rate a series of cartoons for funniness. (Only one of these was an experimental subject. Unknown to them the other three "students" were actually experimental assistants. Also unknown to the student, judges had previously rated half of the cartoons as very funny and the other half as very unfunny.) In the study, the three experimental assistants all stated their judgments aloud before the student was called upon, and all three gave a prearranged false response. The measure of the student's independence was the number of times he or she resisted the group pressure by not conforming to the false responses. Both masculine and androgynous students were significantly more independent than feminine subjects. Again this pattern held for both men and women.

A further study found that masculine males and feminine females actively resisting behavior traditionally thought appropriate for the other sex, even when such resistance

---

TEST YOUR PERSONALITY

■ Below are 28 positive self-descriptions that could all be true of one person. Most of us could not honestly claim to be so well-rounded, but some of these statements are probably very true of you. Note the numbers of those that are and score 5 points beside each. Rate yourself out of 5 on all of the other statements too, all the way down to 1 for those that are very untrue of you.

1 I know the ways of the world.
2 I express my feelings easily.
3 My judgments are objective.
4 I am a cheerful person.
5 I am affectionate.
6 I am self-confident.
7 I find it easy to make up my mind.

8 I make up my own mind.
9 I am gentle with others.
10 I find it easy to tell people what I think.
11 I am a good listener.
12 I am interested in my appearance.
13 I am aware of the feelings of others.
14 I take charge when things have to be done.

15 My feelings are not easily hurt.
16 I am logical.
17 I like to win.
18 I am loyal.
19 I understand people's needs.
20 I have a warm and caring personality.
21 I am cooperative.
22 I have a lot of drive.

23 I like to make people feel secure.
24 I appreciate being complimented.
25 I have a sense of adventure.
26 I appreciate what people do for me.
27 I keep my feelings and my ideas separate.
28 I like to take the initiative in social encounters.

SCORING

Statements 1, 3, 6, 7, 8, 10, 14, 15, 16, 17, 22, 25, 27 and 28 all report characteristics that are typically viewed as enhancing a man's masculinity. The total of your self-ratings on these statements is your masculinity score. The remaining statements report characteristics that are typically viewed as enhancing a woman's femininity. The total of your self-ratings here is your femininity score. The positive aspects of your personality may be mainly masculine, mainly feminine or "androgynous" – combining both.

In experiments, androgynous volunteers are more at ease with babies and more sympathetic and supportive with new acquaintances than masculine ones. They are more independent than feminine volunteers.

cost them money. Volunteer students were told that researchers needed photographs of the same person engaging in different activities. Each student was given a list of pairs of activities and was asked to select one activity from each pair which he or she would prefer to perform. In each pair on the list, the student could earn more money by

selecting one of the two activities, and in each case it was the less sex-appropriate that paid more. The masculine males and feminine females were significantly more likely that androgynous people to avoid activities traditionally thought inappropriate for their sex, even where such choices cost them money. Androgynous people were much more likely to base their choices simply on the payment schedule. They also reported feeling less discomfort after actually performing sex-inappropriate activities.

245

▲ **Emotional support by touching** *is regarded as a feminine gesture in most situations, but it does not seem unnatural to these male team members to emphasize their solidarity in the face of defeat by holding hands. Sport is an area in which men exchange touches freely. Studies have found that they pat each other in encouragement and give consoling touches at at least as high a rate as women friends do in everyday conversation. The majority of touches are directed to neutral parts of the body, where they are less likely to be misunderstood as overpersonal or sexual. About 60 percent are to the hand, and only 10 percent are to the head or buttocks. Members of women's teams show the same behavior. Observations of mixed teams have revealed an equal absence of sex differences in touching.*

◀ **Practical solutions to practical problems** *often involve crossing the boundaries between what appears masculine and what appears feminine. However, research has found that highly sex-typed people will sacrifice material advantages in order to avoid being associated with activities or objects that seem sex-inappropriate. Some studies have found the effect only with highly masculine people, other with highly feminine people as well.*

Some other studies have had slightly different findings from this. Although masculine men preferred sex-appropriate activities, this trend was not seen in women. However, all studies agree on the behavioral flexibility of the androgynous person.

Self-esteem and well-being

Having established the concept of androgyny, researchers began to broaden their idea of its likely psychological advantages beyond the narrow issue of behavioral flexibility.

First they focused on the relationship between sex roles and self-esteem. Self-esteem is of particular importance because high self-esteem has been shown to be related to psychological well-being generally, while low self-esteem is related to depression, anxiety and poor adjustment. After analyzing the results of extensive studies of feelings of worth and adequacy, however, researchers had concluded that it is psychological masculinity, high for both androgynous and masculine people – not androgyny as such that contributes to self-esteem.

This basic pattern seems to hold good also for other measures of psychological well-being. Two recent analyses examined studies on general adjustment and depression. In both of these, healthy psychological functioning showed a relatively large and consistent relationship with masculinity, and only a small relationship with femininity. Thus, men and women high in masculinity (masculine and androgynous individuals) are relatively high in general adjustment and low in depression.

So the traditional view that appropriately sex-typed people are the most socially and psychologically well-adjusted seems to be wrong. But equally the idea that it is the androgynous individual who is the best-adjusted has not been substantiated. It is clear instead that psychological health is fostered by masculinity in both sexes. Androgynous people exhibit superior flexibility or adaptability and, largely because of their high level of masculinity, tend to be psychologically well-adjusted. This is possibly

246

▲ **Grooming one another** *is usually something that girl-friends do, but here a young couple make it part of their own pattern of cross-sex intimacy.*

▶ **Learning how to act out their sex roles.** *Will these boys develop strongly masculine personalities, while their sister develops a strongly feminine one, or will they be role-flexible? It depends of the parental example, but also on the influence of playmates and society at large (see Ch 3).*

Both androgynous and masculine people enjoy more self-esteem than feminine people. Studies of adjustment and depression show a large and consistent relationship between psychological health and masculinity, whether in men or women.

because society as a whole values and rewards the traits we think of as masculine more than those we traditionally think of as feminine.

A deep-rooted dichotomy

Bem has carried out studies which emphasize how deep an impact the concept of their sex has on every aspect of many people's lives. Children grow up learning to classify a wide variety of ideas, characteristics and objects, from clothing to occupations and behavior, according to a sex-related schema (see *Ch 3*). Experiments have indicated that sex-typed people remember lists of everyday things by associating objects with sex roles. Androgynous people do not do this to a very strong degree,

Some researchers criticize the use of the terms "masculine" and "feminine" to label traits of personality since these attributions are based on stereotypes which they will likely perpetuate. They agree that there is nothing intrinsically masculine or feminine about specific aspects of behavior or personality and that what we really should be focusing on is the way important individual characteristics like assertiveness, self-reliance, tenderness and sensitivity are related to levels of self-adjustment and psychological well-being.

This is an appealing view. However, research has shown that many deeply ingrained associations will have to be overcome if we are to achieve this. One thing we have learned is that either women should allow themselves to be more masculine or society should place more value on "feminine" traits. **EL**

▲ **Sharing life with a member of the opposite sex**, *what do we need to understand about femininity and masculinity? Often, their membership in the* male and female social categories will have an important impact on how a couple interacts, how they organize their daily lives and what they expect of each other – men and women who attach importance to their masculinity and femininity tend to attract each other. However, those who are not strongly sex-typed are attracted more by the similarity of their personalities and interests.

247

FURTHER READING
AND CONTRIBUTORS' SOURCES

READERS of *The Opposite Sex* may want information about other aspects of a subject it has discussed, or detail on particular topics that have aroused their interest. With this in mind, some generally available books and periodicals suggested for further reading are listed below. The main published sources consulted by the contributors to this book follow the further reading suggestions.

1 Before Birth
Durden-Smith, J and Desimone, D 1983 *Sex and the Brain* Arbor House, New York; Goy, R W and McEwen, B S 1980 *Sexual Differentiation of the Brain* MIT Press, Cambridge, MA; Money, J and Ehrhardt, A A 1972 *Man and Woman, Boy and Girl* Johns Hopkins University Press, Baltimore, MD; Ounsted, M 1972 "Gender and Intrauterine Growth" in Ounsted C and Taylor, D C (eds) *Gender Differences: Their Ontogeny and Significance* Churchill Livingstone, London; Trivers, R and Willard, D 1973 "Natural Selection of Parental Ability to Vary the Sex Ratio of Offspring" *Science* 179, pp90-2.

2 Early Infancy
Archer, J and Lloyd B 1982 *Sex and Gender* Penguin, Harmondsworth; Hargreaves, D and Colley, A 1986 *The Psychology of Sex Roles* Harper and Row, London; Lewis, C 1986 "Early Sex Role Socialization" in Hargreaves, D J and Colley, A (eds) *The Psychology of Sex Roles* Open University Press, Milton Keynes; Power, T 1981 "Sex-Typing in Infancy: the Role of the Father" *Infant Mental Health Journal* 2, pp226-40; Ruble, D 1984 "Sex-Role Development" in Bornstein, M and Lamb, M (eds) *Developmental Psychology: An Advanced Textbook* Erlbaum, Hillsdale, NJ.

3 Adopting a Sex Role
Bem, S L 1983 "Gender Schema Theory and its Implications for Child Development: Raising Gender-Aschematic Children in a Gender-Schematic Society" *Signs* 8, pp598-616; Fagot, B I 1985 "Beyond the Reinforcement Principle: Another Step Toward Understanding Sex Role Development" *Developmental Psychology* 21, 6, pp1097-1104; Klein, N 1973 *Girls Can Be Anything* Dutton, New York; Maccoby, E E 1980 *Social Development* Harcourt Brace Jovanovich, New York, pp203-50; Serbin, L A, O'Leary, D, Kent, R N and Tonick, I J 1973 "A Comparison of Teacher Response to the Preacademic and Problem Behavior of Boys and Girls" *Child Development* 44, pp796-804; Waxman, S 1976 *What is a Girl, What is a Boy?* Peace Press, Culver City, CA.

4 The Freudian View
Lerman, H 1986 "From Freud to Feminist Personality Theory: Getting Here From There" *Psychology of Women Quarterly* 10, pp1-18; Lorber, J, Coser, R L, Rossi, A S and Chodorow, N 1981 "On the Reproduction of Mothering: A Methodological Debate" *Signs* 6, 3, pp482-514.

5 Brothers and Sisters
Dunn, J and Kendrick, C 1982 *Siblings, Love, Envy, and Understanding* Harvard University Press, Cambridge, MA; Lamb, M E and Sutton-Smith, B (eds) 1982 *Sibling Relationships: Their Nature and Significance Across the Lifespan* Erlbaum, Hillsdale, NJ; Sutton-Smith, B and Rosenberg, B 1970 *The Sibling* Holt, Rinehart and Winston, New York.

6 When Mother Goes to Work
Borman, K M, Quarm, D and Gideonese, S (eds) 1984 *Women in the Workplace: Effects on Families*

Ablex, Norwood, NJ; Clarke-Stewart, A 1982 *Daycare* Harvard University Press, Cambridge, MA; Gottfried, A E and Gottfried, A W (eds) 1988 *Maternal Employment and Children's Development: Longitudinal Research* Plenum, New York; Kamerman, S B and Hayes, C D (eds) 1982 *Families that Work: Children in a Changing World* National Academy Press, Washington, DC; Scarr, S 1984 *Mother Care, Other Care* Basic Books, New York.

7 The Roots of Aggression
Averill, J R 1982 *Anger and Aggression: An Essay on Emotion* Springer-Verlag, New York; Bandura, A 1973 *Aggression: A Social Learning Analysis* Prentice Hall, Englewood Cliffs, NJ; Tavris, C 1980 *Anger: The Misunderstood Emotion* Simon and Schuster, New York.

8 Toys and Play
Brown, C C and Gottfried, A W 1985 *Play Interactions: The Role of Toys and Parental Involvement in Children's Development* Johnson and Johnson, New York; Block, J H 1984 *Sex Role Identity and Ego Development* Jossey-Bass, San Francisco, CA; Chance, P 1979 *Learning Through Play* Johnson and Johnson, New York; Johnson, J E, Christie, J F and Yawkey, T D 1987 *Play and Early Childhood Development* Scott, Foresman, London; Laosa, L M and Sigel, I E 1983 *Families as Learning Environments for Children* Plenum; Pitcher, E G and Schultz, L H 1983 *Boys and Girls at Play: the Development of Sex Roles* Praeger, New York.

9 Friendship
Rubin, Z 1980 *Children's Friendships* Harvard University Press, Cambridge, MA.

10 Skills and Aptitudes
Durden-Smith, J and Desimone, D 1983 *Sex and the Brain* Arbor House, New York; Hall, J A 1984 *Nonverbal Sex Differences: Communication Accuracy and Expressive Style* Johns Hopkins University Press, Baltimore, MD; Hall, R L, Draper, P, Hamilton, M E, McGuinness, D, Otten, C M and Roth, E A 1985 *Male-Female Differences: A Bio-Cultural Perspective* Praeger, New York; Nicholson, J 1984 *Men and Women: How Different Are They?* Oxford University Press, Oxford; Springer, S P and Deutsch, G 1985 *Left Brain: Right Brain* Freeman, New York.

11 At School
Deem, R 1984 *Coeducation Reconsidered* Open University Press, Milton Keynes; Eddowes, M 1983 *Humble Pie: The Mathematics Education of Girls*; Mahoney, P 1985 *Schools for the Boys? Coeducation Reassessed* Hutchinson, London; Stanworth, M 1983 *Gender and Schooling* Hutchinson, London; Wilkinson, L C and Marrett, C B 1985 *Gender Influences in Classroom Interaction* Academic Press, New York.

12 When Parents Split Up
Bowlby, J 1969 *Attachment and Loss: 1 Attachment* Basic Books, New York; Bowlby, J 1973 *Attachment and Loss: 2 Separation* Basic Books, New York; Rutter, M 1972 *The Quality of Mothering: Maternal Depriviation Reassessed* Penguin, Harmondsworth; Tessman, L H 1978 *Children of Parting Parents* Aronson, New York.

13 Moral Development
Damon, W 1988 *Children's Morality* Free Press, New York; Piaget, J 1934/65 *The Moral Judgment of the Child* Free Press, New York.

14 Getting Into Trouble
Adler, F 1975 *Sisters in Crime* McGraw-Hill, New York; Campbell, A 1984 *The Girls in the Gang* Basil Blackwell, New York; Mann, C R 1984 *Female Crime and Delinquency* University of Alabama Press, Birmingham, AL.

15 Puberty
Brooks-Gunn, J and Matthews, W 1979 *He and She: How Children Develop Their Sex-Role Identity* Prentice-Hall, Englewood Cliffs, NJ; Brooks-Gunn, J and Petersen, A C (eds) 1983 *Girls at Puberty: Biological and Psychological Perspectives* Plenum, New York; Erikson, E 1958 *Identity: Youth and Crisis* Norton, New York; Gaddis, A and Brooks-Gunn, J 1985 "The Male Experience of Pubertal Change" *J of Youth and Adolescence* 14, 1, pp61-9; Gilligan, C 1982 *In a Different Voice* Harvard University Press, Cambridge, MA; McAnarney, E R and Levine, M (eds) 1987 *Early Adolescent Transitions* Heath Publications, New York.

16 Evolution
Fedigan, L M 1982 *Primate Paradigms: Sex Roles and Social Bonds* Eden Press, Montreal; Kinzev, W G 1987 *The Evolution of Human Behavior: Primate Models* Suny Press, Albany, NY.

17 Sexuality
Farrell, W 1987 *Why Men Are The Way They Are* McGraw-Hill, New York; Masters, W H and Johnson, V E 1976 *The Pleasure Bond* Bantam Books, New York.

18 Attitudes to Love
Hill, C T, Rubin, Z and Peplau, L A "Breakups Before Marriage: The End of 103 Affairs" *J of Social Issues* 32, 1, pp147-68; Peplau, L A, Rubin, Z and Hill, C T 1977 "Sexual Intimacy in Dating Couples" *J of Social Issues* 33(2), pp86-109; Rubin, Z 1973 *Liking and Loving: An Invitation to Social Psychology* Holt, Rinehart and Winston, New York; Walster, E and Walster, G W 1978 *A New Look at Love* Addison-Wesley, Reading, MA.

19 Marriage
Brehm, S S 1985 *Intimate Relationships* Random House, New York; Cherlin, A J 1981 *Marriage, Divorce, Remarriage* Harvard University Press, Cambridge, MA; Doyle, J A 1985 *Sex and Gender: The Human Experience* Wm C Brown, Dubuque, IA; *Journal of Marriage and The Family* Special Issue: Decade Review, 42, 4, 1980; Weiss, R S 1975 *Marital Separation* Basic Books, New York.

20 Who Looks After the Children?
Lamb, M E 1987 *The Father's Role: Cross-Cultural Perspectives* Erlbaum, Hillsdale, NJ; Lewis, C and O'Brien, M (eds) 1987 *Reassessing Fatherhood: New Observations on Fathers and the Modern Family* Sage, London; Wistrand, B 1981 *Swedish Women on the Move* The Swedish Institute, Stockholm.

21 Violence Between the Sexes
Dobash, R E and Dobash, R P 1979 *Violence Against Wives: A Case Against the Patriarchy* Free Press, New York; Marsden, D 1978 "Sociological Perspectives on Family Violence" in Martin, J M (ed) *Violence in the Family* Wiley, New York; Stark, E and Flitcraft, A 1988 "Personal Power and Institutional Victimization: Treating the Dual Trauma of Woman Battering" in Ochberg, F M (ed) *Post-Traumatic Therapy and Victims of Violence* Brunner/Mazel, New York; Straus, M, Gelles, R and Steinmetz, S K 1980 *Behind Closed Doors: A Survey of Family Violence in America* Doubleday, New York.

22 Emotions and Adjustment

Friedman, M and Ullmer, D 1978 *Treating Type-A Behavior and Your Heart* Fawcett Crest, New York; Gazzaniga, M S 1985 *The Social Brain: Discovering the Networks of the Mind* Basic Books, New York; Justice, B 1987 *Who Gets Sick: Thinking and Health* Peak Press, Houston, TX; Lynch, J *The Broken Heart: The Medical Consequences of Loneliness* Basic Books, New York; Ornstein, R 1987 *The Healing Brain* Simon and Schuster, New York; Pettler, P 1986 *The Joy of Stress* Quill, New York.

23 In the Workplace

Friedl, E 1975 *Women and Men: An Anthropologist's View* Holt, Rinehart and Winston, New York; MacKinnon, C 1979 *Sexual Harassment of Working Women* Yale University Press, New Haven, CT; Nieva, V F and Gutek, B A 1981 *Women and Work* Praeger, New York; Tavris, C and Wade, C 1984 2nd edn *The Longest War* Harcourt, Brace, Jovanovich, New York.

24 Influence and Persuasion

Courtney, A E 1983 *Sex Stereotyping in Advertising* D C Heath, Lexington, MA; Eagly, A H 1987 *Sex Differences in Social Behavior: A Social Role Interpretation* Erlbaum, Hillsdale, NJ; Meeker, B F

and Weitzel-O'Neill, P A 1977 "Sex Roles and Interpersonal Behavior in Task-Oriented Groups" *American Sociological Review* 42, pp92-105.

25 Ambition and Leadership

Kanter, R M 1977 *Men and Women of the Corporation* Basic Books, New York; O'Leary, V E and Hansen, R D 1985 "Sex as an Attributional Fact" in Sonderegger, T (ed) *Nebraska Symposium on Motivation* 32, University of Nebraska Press, Lincoln, NE; Tresemer, D 1974 "Fear of Success: Popular but Unproven" *Psychology Today* April.

26 Creativity

Hargreaves, D and Colley, A 1986 *The Psychology of Sex Roles* Harper and Row, London; Winner, E 1982 *Invented Worlds: The Psychology of the Arts* Harvard University Press, Cambridge, MA.

27 Styles of Communication

Argyle, M and Cook, P 1976 *Gaze and Mutual Gaze* Cambridge University Press, Cambridge; Bull, P 1983 *Body Movement and Interpersonal Communication* Wiley, New York; Knapp, M L 1980 *Essentials of Nonverbal Communication* Holt, Rinehart and Winston, New York.

28 In the Media

Farrell, W 1987 *Why Men Are the Way They Are* McGraw-Hill, New York; Goffman, E 1979 *Gender Advertisements* Harper and Row, New York; Tuchman, G, Daniels, K A and Benet, J (eds) 1978 *Hearth and Home: Images of Women in the Mass Media* Oxford University Press, New York.

29 Sex Stereotypes

Ashmore, R D, Del Boca, F K and Wohlers, A J 1986 "Gender Stereotypes" in Ashmore, R D and Del Boca, F K (eds) *The Social Psychology of Female-Male Reactions: A Critical Analysis of Central Concepts* Academic Press, New York; Deaux, K and Kite, M E in Hess, B B and Feree, M M (eds) *Women and Society: Social Science Research Perspectives* Sage, New York; Ruble, D N and Ruble, T L 1982 "Sex Stereotypes" in Miller, A G (ed) *In the Eye of the Beholder: Contemporary Issues in Stereotyping* Praeger, New York.

30 Role Versatility

Heilbrun, C G 1973 *Toward a Recognition of Androgyny* Harper and Row, New York; Kaplan, A and Sedney, M 1980 *Psychology and Sex Roles: An Androgynous Perspective* Little, Brown, Boston, MA; Singer, J 1977 *Androgyny: Toward a New Theory of Sexuality* Anchor Books, Garden City, New York.

CONTRIBUTORS' SOURCES

1 Before Birth Aase, J, Laestadius, N and Smith, D 1970 "Children of Mothers Who Took LSD in Pregnancy" *Lancet* 2, p100; Bar-Anon, R and Robertson, A 1975 "Variations in Sex Ratio Between Progeny Groups in Dairy Cattle" *Theoretical and Applied Genetics* 46, pp63-5; Breen, D 1975 *The Birth of a First Child* Tavistock, London; Butler, N R and Alberman, E D 1969 *Perinatal Problems* Livingstone, Edinburgh; Chagnon, N 1979 "Is Reproductive Success Equal in Egalitarian Societies?" in Chagnon, N and Irons, W (eds) *Evolutionary Biology and Human Social Behavior* Duxbury, MA; Dohler, K D, Coquelin, A, Davis, F C, Hines, M, Shryne, J E and Gorski, R A 1984 "Pre- and Postnatal Influence of Testosterone Propionate and Diethylstilbestrol on Differentiation of the Sexually Dimorphic Nucleus of the Preoptic Area in Male and Female Rats" *Brain Research* 302, pp291-5; Ehrhardt, A A, Meyer-Bahlburg, H F L, Rosen, R L, Feldman, J F, Veridiano, N P, Zimmerman, I and McEwen, B S 1985 "Sexual Orientation after Prenatal Exposure to Exogenous Estrogen" *Archives of Sexual Behavior* 14, pp57-77; Hines, M 1982 "Prenatal Gonadal Hormones and Sex Differences in Human Behavior" *Psychological Bulletin* 92, pp56-80; Hytten, F E and Leitch, I 1971 2nd edn *The Physiology of Human Pregnancy* Blackwell, Oxford; James, W H 1971 "Cycle Day of Insemination, Coital Rate and Sex Ratio" *Lancet* 1, p112; James, W H 1985 "The Sex Ratio of Infants Born After Hormonal Induction of Ovulation" *British J of Obstetrics and Gynecology* 42, pp229-301; Kang, Y S and Cho, W K "The Sex Ratio at Birth and Other Attributes of the Newborn From Maternity Hospitals in Korea" *Human Biology* 34, pp38-48; Kinsey, A C et al 1948 and 1953 *Sexual Behavior in the Human Male and Sexual Behavior in the Human Female* Saunders, Philadelphia, PA; Lyster, W R 1968 "The Sex Ratio of Live Births in Integrated but Racially Different Populations, USA and Fiji" *Human Biology* 40, p63; Lyster, W R and Bishop, M W H 1965 "An Association Between Rainfall and Sex Ratio in Man" *J of Reproductive Fertility* 10, pp35-47; Maccoby, E E and Jacklin, C N 1974 *The Psychology of Sex Differences* Stanford University Press, Stanford, CA; Meisel, R L and Ward, I L 1981 "Fetal Female Rats are Masculinized by Male Littermates Located Caudally in the Uterus" *Science* 213, pp239-42; Middleton Hyatt, H 1935 *Folk Lore From Adams County, Illinois* Alma Egon Hyatt Foundation, Illinois; Mittwoch, U 1985 "Erroneous Theories of Sex Determination" *J of Medical Genetics* 22, pp164-70; Resnick, S M, Berenbaum, S A, Gottesman, I I and Bouchard Jr, T J 1986 "Early Hormonal Influences on Cognitive Functioning in Congenital Adrenal Hyperplasia"

Developmental Psychology 22, pp191-8; Snyder, R G 1961 "The Sex Ratio of Offspring of Pilots of High Performance Military Aircraft" *Human Biology* 33, pp1-10; Trivers, R and Willard, D 1973 "Natural Selection of Parental Ability to Vary the Sex Ratio of Offspring" *Science* 179, pp90-2.

2 Early Infancy Gunnar, M 1978 "Changing a Frightening Toy into a Pleasant Toy by Allowing the Infant to Control its Actions" *Developmental Psychology* 14, pp157-252; Lamb, M E 1977 "The Development of Mother-Infant and Father-Infant Attachments in the Second Year of Life" *Developmental Psychology* 13, pp637-48; Lewis, C 1986 "Early Sex-Role Socialization" in Hargreaves, D J, and Colley, A (eds) *The Psychology of the Sexes* Open University Press, Milton Keynes; Power, T 1981 "Sex-Typing in Infancy: the Role of the Father" *Infant Mental Health Journal* 2, pp226-40; Rosenthal, M K 1983 "State Variations in the Newborn and Mother-Infant Interaction During Breast Feeding: Some Sex Differences" *Developmental Psychology* 19, pp740-5; Ruble, D 1984 "Sex-Role Development" in Bornstein, M and Lamb, M (eds) *Developmental Psychology: An Advanced Textbook* Erlbaum, Hillsdale, NJ.

3 Adopting a Sex Role Bandura, A 1977 *Social Learning Theory* Prentice Hall, Englewood Cliffs, NJ; Bem, S L 1981 "Gender Schema Theory: A Cognitive Account of Sex-typing" *Psychological Review* 88, pp354-64; Bem, S L 1984 "Androgyny and Gender Schema Theory: A Conceptual and Empirical Integration" *Nebraska Symposium on Motivation* University of Nebraska Press, Lincoln, NE; Emmerich, W 1977 "Structure and Development of Personal-Social Behaviors in Economically Disadvantaged Preschool Children" *Genetic Psychology Monograph* 95, pp191-245; Fagot, B I 1985 "Changes in Thinking About Early Sex-Role Development" *Developmental Review* 5, pp83-98; Kail, R V and Levine, L E 1976 "Encoding Processes and Sex-Role Processes" *J of Experimental Child Psychology* 21, pp256-63; Kohlberg, L A "A Cognitive Developmental Analysis of Children's Sex-Role Concepts and Attitudes" in Maccoby, E E (ed) *The Development of Sex Differences* Stanford University Press, Stanford, CA, pp82-173; McArthur, L Z and Eisen, S V 1976 "Achievements of Male and Female Story Book Characters as Determinants of Achieving Behavior by Boys and Girls" *J of Personality and Social Psychology* 33, pp467-73; Maccoby, E E (ed) *The Development of Sex Differences* Stanford University Press, Stanford, CA; Perry, D G and Bessey, K "The Social Learning Theory of Sex Differences: Imitation is Alive and

Well" *J of Personality and Social Psychology* 37, 10, pp1699-712; Perry, D G and Perry, L C 1975 "Observational Learning in Children: Effects of Sex of Model and Subject's Sex Role Behavior" *J of Personality and Social Psychology* 31, pp1083-8; Slaby, R G and Frey, K S 1975 "Development of Gender Constancy and Selective Attention to Same-Sex Models" *Child Development* 46, pp849-56.

4 The Freudian View Chodorow, N 1978 *The Reproduction of Mothering: Psychoanalysis and the Sociology of Gender* University of California Press, Berkeley, CA; Freud, S 1910 *Three Contributions to Sexual Theory* (Brill, A A, trans) J of Nervous and Mental Diseases Publishing Co, New York; Freud, S 1949 (originally published 1940) *An Outline of Psychoanalysis* Norton, New York; Horney, K 1935 "The Problem of Female Masochism" *Psychoanalytic Review* 22.

5 Brothers and Sisters Adler, A 1958 *What Life Should Mean To You* Capricorn Books, New York; Altus, W D 1966 "Birth Order and Its Sequelae" *Science* 151, pp44-9; Brim, O G 1958 "Family Structure and Sex Role Learning by Children: A Further Analysis of Helen Koch's Data" *Sociometry* 21, pp1-16; Dunn, J 1983 "Sibling Relations in Early Childhood" *Child Development* 54, pp787-811; Galton, F 1974 *English Men of Science: Their Nature and Nurture* Macmillan, London; Irish, D P 1964 "Sibling Interaction: a Neglected Aspect of Family Life Research" *Social Forces* 42, pp279-88; Leventhal, G S 1970 "Influence of Brothers and Sisters on Sex-Role Behavior" *J of Personality and Social Psychology* 16, pp452-65; Schachter, F 1982 "Birth Order and Sibling Status Effects" in Lamb, M E and Sutton-Smith, B (eds) *Sibling Relationships: Their Nature and Significance Across the Lifespan* Erlbaum, Hillsdale, NJ, pp153-8; Sutton-Smith, B and Rosenberg, B 1970 *The Sibling* Holt, Rinehart and Winston, New York.

6 When Mother Goes to Work Belsky, J 1988 "Risks of Infant Day Care Reconsidered" *Early Childhood Research Quarterly*; Bronfenbrenner, U and Crouter, A C 1982 "Work and Family Through Time and Space" in Kamerman, S B and Hayes, C D (eds) *Families that Work: Children in a Changing World* National Academy Press, Washington, DC, pp39-83; Gottfried, A E and Gottfried, A W 1988 *Maternal Employment and Children's Development: Longitudinal Research* Plenum, New York; Heijns, B 1982 "The Influence of Parents' Work on Children's School Achievement" in Kamerman, S B and Hayes, C D (eds) *Families that Work: Children in a Changing World* National Academy Press, Washington, DC, pp229-

CONTRIBUTORS' SOURCES CONTINUED

67; Hoffman, L W 1986 "Work, Family, and the Child" in Pallak, M S and Perloff, R O (eds) *Psychology and Work: Productivity, Change and Employment* American Psychological Association, Washington, DC, pp173-220.

7 The Roots of Aggression Campbell, A and Muncer, S 1987 "Models of Anger and Aggression in the Social Talk of Women and Men" *J for the Theory of Social Behavior* 17, pp489-512; Eron, L D 1980 "Prescription for Reduction of Aggression" *American Psychologist* 25, pp244-52; Kreuz, L E and Rose, R M 1972 "Assessment of Aggressive Behavior and Plasma Testosterone in a Young Criminal Population" *Psychosomatic Medicine* 34, pp321-32; Money, J and Erhardt, A A 1972 *Man, Woman, Boy and Girl* Johns Hopkins Press, Baltimore, MD; White, L W 1983 "Sex and Gender Issues in Aggression Research" In Geen, R and Donnerstein, E (eds) *Aggression: Theoretical and Empirical Reviews 2* Academic Press, New York; Whiting, B and Pope, C P 1973 "A Cross-Cultural Analysis of Sex Differences in the Behavior of Children Aged Three to Eleven" *J of Social Psychology* 91, pp171-88.

8 Toys and Play Carpenter, C J, Huston, A C and Spera, L "Children's Use of Time in Their Everyday Activities During Middle Childhood" in Bloch, M and Pellegrini, A (eds) *The Ecological Context of Children's Play* Ablex, Norwood, NJ; Carpenter, C J 1987 "Boys and Girls: Why They Behave Differently" *Health and Medical Horizons* Macmillan Education Company, New York; Carpenter, C J and Huston-Stein, A C 1980 "Activity Structure and Sex-Typed Behavior in Preschool Children" *Child Development* 51, pp862-72; Carpenter, C J, Huston A C and Holt, W 1986 "Modification of Preschool Sex-Typed Behaviors by Participation in Adult-Structured Activities" *Sex Roles* 14, 11-12, pp603-15; Fagot, B I 1974 "Sex Differences in Toddler's Behavior and Parental Reaction" *Developmental Psychology* 10, pp554-8; Fein, G, Johnson, D, Kosson, N, Stork, L and Wasserman, L 1975 "Sex Stereotypes and Preferences in the Toy Choices of 20-Month-Old Boys and Girls" *Developmental Psychology* 11, pp527-8; Huston, A C, Carpenter, C J, Atwater, J and Johnson, L 1986 "Gender, Adult Structuring of Activities, and Social Behavior in Middle Childhood" *Child Development* 57, pp1200-9; Lever, J 1978 "Sex Differences in the Complexity of Children's Play and Games" *American Sociological Review* 43, pp471-83; Serbin, L A and Connor, J M 1979 "Sex-Typing of Children's Play Preferences and Patterns of Cognitive Performance" *J of Genetic Psychology* 134, pp315-16; Serbin, L A and Sprafkin, C 1982 "Measurement of Sex-Typed Play: A Comparison Between Laboratory and Naturalistic Observation Procedures" *Behavioral Assessment* 4, pp225-35.

9 Friendship Berndt, T J 1986 "Sharing Between Friends: Contexts and Consequences" in Mueller E C and Cooper, C R (eds) *Process and Outcome in Peer Relationships* Academic Press Inc, Orlando, FL, pp105-27; Fischer, K W and Lazerson, A 1984 *Human Development: From Conception Through Adolescence* Freeman, New York, p517; Himadi, W G, Arkowitz, H, Hinton, R and Perl, J 1980 "Minimal Dating and Its Relationship to Other Social Problems and General Adjustment" *Behavior Therapy* 11, pp345-52; Lever, J 1976 "Sex Differences in the Games Children Play" *Social Problems* 23, pp478-87.

10 Skills and Aptitudes Baker, M A (ed) 1987 *Sex Differences in Human Performance* Wiley, New York; Halpern, D F 1986 *Sex Differences in Cognitive Abilities* Erlbaum, Hillsdale, NJ; Hyde, J S and Linn, M C (eds) 1986 *The Psychology of Gender: Advantages Through Meta-Analysis* Johns Hopkins University Press, Baltimore, MD; Maccoby, E E and Jacklin, C N 1974 *The Psychology of Sex Differences* Stanford University Press, Stanford, CA; Wittig, M A and Peterson, A C 1979 *Sex-Related Differences in Cognitive Functioning* Academic Press, New York.

11 At School Davies, L 1984 *Pupil Power: Deviance and Gender in School* Falmer Press, Falmer; Dweck, C S and Bush, E G 1976 "Sex Differences in Learned Helplessness: Differential Debilitation with Peer and Adult Evaluators" *Developmental Psychology* 12, pp147-56; Fenema, E and Peterson, P 1985 "Autonomous Learning Behavior: A Possible Explanation of Gender-Related Differences in Mathematics" in Wilkinson, L C and Marrett, C B (eds) *Gender Influences in Classroom Interaction* Academic Press, New York; Kelly, A 1978 *Girls and Science* Almqvist and Wiksell, Stockholm; Marland, M (ed) 1983 *Sex Differentiation and Schooling* Heinemann Educational Books, London; Mortimore, P, Sammons, P, Stoll, L, Lewis, D and Ecob, R 1988 *School Matters* Open Books, London; Rosenthal, R and Jacobson, L 1967 *Pygmalion in the Classroom* Holt, Rinehart and Winston, New York; Rutter, M, Maughan, B, Mortimore, P and Ousten, J 1979 *15,000 Hours* Open Books, London.

12 When Parents Split Up Borduin, C and Henggeler, S 1982 "Psycho-Social Development of Father-Absent Children" in Henggeler, S (ed) *Delinquency and Adolescent Psychopathology* John Wright, Littleton, MA; Emery, R E 1982 "Interparental Conflict and the Children of Discord and Divorce" *Psychological Bulletin* 92, pp310-30; Hetherington, E M 1979 "Divorce: A Child's Perspective" *American Psychologist* 34, pp851-58; Rutter, M 1979 "Maternal Depriviation 1972-1978: New Findings, New Concepts, New Approaches" *Child Development* 50, pp283-305; Wells, E and Rankin, J H 1985 "Broken Homes and Juvenile Delinquency: An Empirical Review" *Criminal Justice Abstracts* 17, pp249-72.

13 Moral Development Colby, A, Kohlberg, L et al 1987 *The Measurement of Moral Judgment* 1, Cambridge University Press, New York; Damon, W 1988 *Children's Morality* Free Press, New York; Eisenberg, N (ed) 1982 *The Development of Prosocial Behavior* Academic Press, New York; Gilligan, C 1982 *In a Different Voice* Harvard University Press, Cambridge, MA; Walker, L 1984 "Sex Differences in the Development of Moral Reasoning: A Critical Review" *Child Development* 55, pp677-91.

14 Getting Into Trouble Canter, R J 1982 "Family Correlates of Male and Female Delinquency" *Criminology* 20, pp149-67; Cernkovich, S A and Giordano, P C 1979 "Delinquency, Opportunity and Gender" *J of Criminal Law and Criminology* 70, pp145-51; Datesman, S K, Scarpitti, F R and Stephenson, R M 1975 "Female Delinquency: An Application of Self and Opportunity Theories" *J of Research in Crime and Delinquency* 12, pp107-21; Hindelang, M J, Hirschi, T and Weis, J G 1981 *Measuring Delinquency* Sage, Beverly Hills, CA; Jensen, G J and Eve, R 1976 "Sex Differences in Delinquency: An Examination of Popular Sociological Explanations" *Criminology* 13, pp427-48.

15 Puberty Attie, I and Brooks-Gunn, J 1988 "The Emergence of Eating Disorders and Eating Problems in Adolescence: A Developmental Perspective" *J of Child Psychology and Psychiatry*; Brooks-Gunn, J 1988 "Antecedents and Consequences of Variations in Girls' Maturational Timing" *J of Adolescent Health Care* 9, 5, pp1-9; Brooks-Gunn, J and Warren, M P 1988 "The Psychological Significance of Secondary Sexual Characteristics in 9- to 11-year-old Girls" *Child Development* 59; Gaddis, A and Brooks-Gunn, J 1985 "The Male Experience of Pubertal Change" *J of Youth and Adolescence* 14, 1, pp61-9; Hill, J P 1982 Introduction to Special Issue on Early Adolescence *Child Development* 53, pp1409-12; Hill, J P 1988 "Adapting to Menarche: Familial Control and Conflict" in Gunnar, M R and Collins, W A (eds) *Development During the Transition to Adolescence: Minnesota Symposia on Child Psychology* 21, Erlbaum, Hillsdale, NJ, pp43-77; Hill, J P and Lynch, M E 1983 "The Intensification of Gender-Related Role Expectations During Early Adolescence" in Brooks-Gunn, J and Petersen, A C (eds) *Girls at Puberty: Biological and Psychological Perspectives* Plenum, New York, pp201-28; Lauersen, N and Whitney, S 1977 *It's Your Body: A Woman's Guide to Gynecology* Grosset and Dunlap, New York; Mead, M 1935 *Sex and Temperament* Morrow, New York; Tanner, J M 1962 *Growth and Adolescence* Lippincott, New York; Weideger, P 1975 *Menstruation and Menopause* Knopf, New York.

16 Evolution Blumenschine, R J 1987 "Characteristics of an Early Hominid Scavenging Niche" *Current Anthropology* 28, pp383-407; Bunn, H T and Kroll, E M 1986 "Systematic Butchery by Plio/Pleistocene Hominids at Olduvai Gorge, Tanzania" *Current Anthropology* 27, pp431-52; Fedigan, L M 1986 "The Changing Role of Women in Models of Human Evolution" *Annual Review of Anthropology* 15, pp25-66; Potts, R 1984 "Home Bases and Early Hominids" *American Scientist* 72, pp338-47; Smith, R L (ed) 1984 *Sperm Competition and the Evolution of Animal Mating Systems* Academic Press, New York; Snipman, P and Rose, J 1983 "Early Hominid Hunting, Butchering, and Carcass-Processing Behaviors: Approaches to the Fossil Record" *J of Anthropological Archeology* 2, pp57-98; Wrangham, R W 1987 "The Significance of African Apes for Reconstructing Human Social Evolution" in Kinzey, W G (ed) *The Evolution of Human Behavior: Primate Models* Suny Press, Albany, NY.

17 Sexuality Farrell, W 1987 *Why Men Are the Way They Are* McGraw-Hill, New York; Masters, W H, Johnson, E and Kolodny, R C 1985 2nd edn *Human Sexuality* Little Brown, Boston, MA; Masters, W H and Johnson, V E 1966 *Human Sexual Response* Little Brown, Boston, MA; Tavris, C and Offir, C 1983 2nd edn *The Longest War: Sex Differences in Perspective* Harcourt Brace Jovanovich, New York.

18 Attitudes to Love Blau, P 1964 *Exchange and Power in Social Life* Wiley, New York; Hunt, M 1959 *The Natural History of Love* Knopf, New York; Levinger, G and Moles, O C (eds) 1979 *Divorce and Separation* Basic Books, New York; Weiss, R 1975 *Marital Separation* Basic Books, New York.

19 Marriage Bernard, J 1972 *The Future of Marriage* World, New York; Blau, P 1964 *Exchange and Power in Social Life* Wiley, New York; Falbo, T and Peplau, A 1980 "Power Strategies in Intimate Relationships" *J of Personality and Social Psychology* 38, pp618-28; Goode, W 1956 *After Divorce* Free Press, Glencoe, IL; Gottman, J 1979 *Marital Interaction* Academic Press, New York; Hill, C T, Peplau, L A and Rubin, Z 1981 "Differing Perceptions in Dating Couples" *Psychology of Women Quarterly* 5(3), pp418-34; Johnson, P 1976 "Women and Power: Toward a Theory of Effectiveness" *J of Social Issues* 32, pp99-110; Parsons, T and Free Bales, R 1955 *Family Socialization and Interaction Process* Free Press, Glencoe, IL; Peplau, L A, Rubin, Z and Hill, C T 1976 "The Sexual Balance of Power" *Psychology Today* November; Rubin, Z, Hill, C T, Peplau, L A and Dunkel-Schetter, C 1980 "Self-Disclosure in Dating Couples: Sex Roles and the Ethic of Openness" *J of Marriage and the Family* 42(2), pp305-18; Waller, W W and Hill, R 1951 *The Family* Dryden, New York.

20 Who Looks After the Children? Barry III, H and Paxson, L 1971 "Infancy and Early Childhood: Cross-Cultural Codes 2" *Ethnology* 10, pp466-506; Haas, L 1987 "The Effects of Fathers' Participation in Parental Leave on Sexual Equality in the Family" in *Nordic Intimate Couples: Love, Children and Work* Report From an International Symposium at Hässelby Castle, Stockholm (JÄMFO); Hwang, C P, Eldén, G and Fransson, C 1984 *Attitudes of Employers and Colleagues to Paternal Leave* 1, Psychological Institute, University of Göteburg; Katz, M M and Konner, M J 1981 "The Role of the Father: An Anthropological Perspective" in Lamb, M E (ed) *The Role of the Father in Child Development* pp155-86, Wiley, New York; Lamb, M E, Hwang, C P, Broberg, A, Booksetin, F L, Hult, G and Frodi, M 1987 "The Determinants of Paternal Involvement in a Representative Sample of Swedish Families" *International Journal of Behavioral Development*; Lamb, M E, Frodi, A M, Hwang, C P and Frodi, M 1983 "Effects of Paternal Involvement on Infant Preferences for Mothers and Fathers" *Child Development* 54, pp450-9; LeVine, R A 1980 "A Cross-Cultural Perspective on Parenting" in Fantini, M D and Cardenas, R (eds) *Parenting in a Multi-Cultural Society* pp17-26, Longman, New York; Sandqvist, K 1987 *Fathers and Family Work in Two Cultures: Antecedents and Concomitants of Fathers' Participation in Child Care and Household Work* Almqvist and Wiksell, Stockholm; Stephens, W N 1963 *The Family in Cross-Cultural Perspective* Holt, Rinehart and Winston, New York; Whiting, B B and Edwards, C P 1988 *Children of Different Worlds: The Formation of Social Behavior* Harvard University Press, Cambridge, MA.

21 Violence Between the Sexes Atkins, S and Hoggett, B 1984 *Women and the Law* Blackwell, London, p125; Dobash, R E and Dobash, R P 1979 *Violence Against Wives: A Case Against the Patriarchy* Free Press, New York; Gayford, J 1975 "Wife Battering: a Preliminary Summary of 100 Cases" *British Medical Journal* 25, pp194-7; Marsden, D 1978 "Sociological Perspectives on Family Violence" in Martin, J M (ed) *Violence in the Family* Wiley, New York; O'Leary, K D 1988 "Physical Aggression between Spouses: A Social Learning Theory Perspective" in Van Hasselt, V B et al (eds) *Handbook of Family Violence* Plenum, New York; Stark, E and Flitcraft, A 1985 "Woman Abuse, Child Abuse and Social Heredity: What is the Relationship?" in Johnson, N (ed) "Marital Violence" *Soc Review Monograph* 31, Routledge and Kegan Paul, London; Stark, E and Flitcraft, A 1988 "Personal Power and Institutional Victimization: Treating the Dual Trauma of Woman Battering" in Ochberg, F M (ed) *Post-Traumatic Therapy and Victims of Violence* Brunner/Mazel, New York; Starr Jr, R H 1988 "Physical Abuse of Children" in Van Hasselt, V B et al (eds) *Handbook of Family Violence* Plenum, New York; Straus, M, Gelles, R and Steinmetz, S K 1980 *Behind Closed Doors: A Survey of Family Violence in America* Doubleday, New York; Van Hasselt, V B, et al (eds) 1988 *Handbook of Family Violence* Plenum, New York, p93.

22 Emotions and Adjustment Baker, M A (ed) 1987 *Sex Differences in Human Performance* Wiley, New York; Benjamin Jr, L T, Hopkins, R J and Nation, J R 1987 *Psychology* Macmillan, New York; Blackstrom, T, et al 1983 "Mood, Sexuality, Hormones and the Menstrual Cycle: II Hormone Levels and Their Relationship to the Premenstrual Syndrome" *Psychosomatic Medicine* 45 (6); Donovan, B T 1985 *Hormones and Human Behavior* Cambridge University Press, Cambridge; Guttentag, M, Salasin, S and Belle, D 1980 *The Mental Health of Women* Academic Press, New York; Maccoby, E E and Jacklin, C N 1974 *The Psychology of Sex Differences* Stanford University Press, Stanford, CA; Zimbardo, P G and Ruch, F L 1975 *Psychology and Life* Scott, Foresman and Company, New York.

23 The Workplace Crosby, F 1982 *Relative Deprivation and Working Women* Oxford University Press, New York; Crosby, F 1984 "The Denial of Personal Discrimination" *American Behavioral Scientist* 27, pp371-86; Crosby, F, Clayton, S, Hemker, K and Alksnis, O 1986 "Cognitive Biases in the Failure to Perceive Discrimination" *Sex Roles* 14, pp637-46; D'Andrade, R G 1966 "Sex Differences and Cultural Institutions" in Maccoby, E E (ed) *The Development of Sex Differences* Stanford University Press, Stanford, CA, pp174-204; Ember, C R 1981 "A Cross-Cultural Perspective on Sex Differences" in Munroe, R H, Munroe, R L and Whiting, B B (eds) *Handbook of Cross-Cultural Human Development* pp531-80, Garland Press, New York; Golding, J, Resnick, A and Crosby, F 1983 "Work Satisfaction as a Function of Gender and Job Status" *Psychology of Woman Quarterly* 7, pp286-90; Gutek, B A 1985 *Sex and the Workplace: The Impact of Sexual Behavior and Harassment on Women, Men and Organizations* Jossey-Bass, San Francisco, CA; Kahn, W and Crosby, F 1985 "Change and Stasis: Discriminating Between Attitudes and Discriminatory Behavior" in Larwood, L, Gutek, B A and Stromberg, H A (eds) *Women and Work, An Annual Review* 1, Sage, Beverly Hills, CA, pp215-38; Kanter, R M 1977 *Men and Women of the Corporation* Basic Books, New York; MacKinnon, C 1979 *Sexual Harassment of Working Women* Yale University Press, New Haven, CT; Murdock, G P 1937 "Comparative Data on the Division of Labor by Sex" *Social Forces* 15, pp551-3; Nieva, V F and Gutek, B A 1981 *Women and Work* Praeger, New York; *Statistical Abstracts of the United States* 1987 US Government Printing Office, Washington, DC; Thomas, P J 1987 "Appraising the Performance of Women: Gender and the Naval Officer" in Gutek, B A and Larwood, L (eds) *Women's Career Development* Sage, Beverly Hills, CA, pp86-109.

24 Influence and Persuasion Berger, J and Zelditch, M 1985 *Status, Rewards and Influence* Jossey-Bass, San Francisco, CA; Eagly, A H and Carli, L L 1981 "Sex of Researchers and Sex-typed Communications as Determinants of Sex Differences in Influenceability: A Meta-Analysis of Social Influence Studies" *Psychological Bulletin* 90, pp1-20; Eagly, A H and Wood, W 1985 "Gender and Influenceability: Stereotype vs Behavior" in O'Leary, V E, Unger, R K and Wallston, B S (eds) *Women, Gender, and Social Psychology* pp225-56, Erlbaum, Hillsdale, NJ; Falbo, T and Peplau, A 1980 "Power Strategies in Intimate Relationships" *J of Personality and Social Psychology* 38, pp618-28; Instone, D, Major, B and Bunker, B 1983 "Gender, Self-Confidence, and Social Influence Strategies: An Organizational Simulation" *J of Personality and Social Psychology* 44, pp322-33; Mamay, P D and Simpson, R L 1981 "Three Female Roles in Television Commercials" *Sex Roles* 7, pp1223-32; Ridgeway, C L 1978 "Conformity, Group-Oriented Motivation, and Status Attainment in Small Groups" *Social Psychology Quarterly* 41, pp175-88; Wood, W and Karten, S J 1986 "Sex Differences in Interaction Style as a Product of Perceived Sex Differences in Competence" *J of Personality and Social Psychology* 50, pp341-7.

25 Ambition and Leadership Eagly, A H 1986 *Sex Differences in Social Behavior* Erlbaum, Hillsdale, NJ; Heilman, M and Guzzo, R A 1978 "The Perceived Cause of Work Success as a Mediator of Sex Discrimination in Organizations" *Organizational Behavior and Human Performance* 21, pp347-57; Horner, M S 1968 "Sex Differences in Achievement Motivation and Performance in Competitive and Noncompetitive Situations" unpublished doctoral dissertation, University of Michigan; Hennig, M and Jardim, A 1977 *The Managerial Woman* Wiley, New York; Kanter, R M 1977 *Men and Women of the Corporation* Basic Books, New York; Morrison, A, White, R and Velsor, E 1987 "Executive Women: Substance Plus Style" *Psychology Today* August, pp18-21; O'Leary, V E and Hansen, R D 1985 "Sex As an Attributional Fact" in Sonderegger, T (ed) *Nebraska Symposium on Motivation* 32, University of Nebraska Press, Lincoln, NE; Schein, V E "Would Women Lead Differently?" in Rosenbach W and Taylor R (eds) *Contemporary Issues in Leadership* Westview, Boulder, CO; Snodgrass, S E 1985 "Women's Intuition: The Effect of Subordinate Role on Interpersonal Sensitivity" *J of Personality and Social Psychology* 49, pp146-55.

26 Creativity Hargreaves, D J 1977 "Sex Roles in Divergent Thinking" *British J of Educational Psychology* 47, pp25-32; Hudson, L 1968 *Frames of Mind* Methuen, London; Kogan, N 1974 "Creativity and Sex Differences" *J of Creative Behavior* 8, pp1-14; MacKinnon, D W 1962 "The Nature and Nurture of Creative Talent" *American Psychologist* 17, pp484-95; Torrance, E P 1962 *Guiding Creative Talent* Prentice Hall, Englewood Cliffs, NJ.

27 Styles of Communication Birdwhistell, R L 1971 *Kinesics in Context* Allen Lane, London; Duncan S and Fiske D W 1977 *Face to Face Interaction* Erlbaum, Hillsdale, NJ; Exline, R V 1972 "Visual Interaction: The Glances of Power and Preference" *Nebraska Symposium on Motivation* 1971, University of Nebraska Press, Lincoln, NE, pp163-206; Hall, J A 1978 "Gender Effects in Decoding Nonverbal Cues" *Psychological Bulletin* 85, pp845-57; Hoffman, M L 1977 "Sex Differences in Empathy and Related Behaviors" *Psychological Bulletin* 84 pp712-22; Lipps, R 1977 "The Naive Perception of Masculinity-Femininity on the Basis of Expressive Cues" *J of Research in Personality* 12, pp1-14.

28 In the Media Butler, M and Paisley, W 1980 *Women and the Mass Media: Sourcebook for Research and Action* Human Sciences Press, New York; Farrell, W 1987 *Why Men Are the Way They Are* McGraw-Hill, New York; Goffman, E 1979 *Gender Advertisements* Harper and Row, New York; Key, W B 1973 *Subliminal Seduction* New American Library, New York; Mischel, W 1966 "A Social-Learning View of Sex Differences in Behavior" in Modleski, T 1984 *Loving With a Vengeance: Mass-Produced Fantasies for Women* Methuen, New York; Tuchman, G, Daniels, A K and Benet, J 1978 *Hearth and Home: Images of Women in the Mass Media* Oxford University Press, New York.

29 Sex Stereotypes Ashmore, R D 1981 "Sex Stereotypes and Implicit Personality Theory" in Hamilton, D L (ed) *Cognitive Processes in Stereotyping and Intergroup Behavior* Erlbaum, Hillsdale, NJ; Broverman, I K, Vogel, S R, Broverman, D M, Clarkson, F E and Rosenkranz, P S 1972 "Sex-Role Stereotypes: A Current Appraisal" *J of Social Issues* 28, pp59-78; Tajfel, H and Wilkes, A L 1963 "Classification and Quantative Judgment" *British J of Psychology* 54, pp101-14.

30 Role Versatility Bem, S L 1974 "The Measurement of Psychological Androgyny" *J of Consulting and Clinical Psychology* 42, pp155-62; Bem, S L 1975 "Sex Role Adaptability: One Consequence of Psychological Androgyny" *J of Personality and Social Psychology* 31, pp634-43; Bem, S L 1977 "On the Utility of Alternative Procedures for Assessing Psychological Androgyny" *J of Consulting and Clinical Psychology* 45, pp196-205; Bem, S L 1985 "Androgyny and Gender Schema Theory: A Conceptual and Empirical Integration" in Sonderegger, T B (ed) *Nebraska Symposium on Motivation, 1984: Psychology and Gender* University of Nebraska Press, Lincoln, NE, pp179-226; Helmreich, R L, Spence, J T and Holahan, C K 1979 "Psychological Androgyny and Sex Role Flexibility: A Test of Two Hypotheses" *J of Personality and Social Psychology* 37, pp1631-44; Lott, B E 1981 *Becoming a Woman: The Socialization of Gender* Charles C Thomas,

Springfield, IL; Orlovsky, J D 1981 "Relationship Between Sex Role Attitudes and Personality Traits and the Sex Role Behavior Scale: 1 A New Measure of Masculine and Feminine Role Behaviors and Interests" *J of Personality and Social Psychology* 40, pp927-40; Spence, J T, Helmreich, R L and Holahan, C K 1979 "Negative and Positive Components of Psychological Masculinity and Femininity and Their Relationships to Self-Reports of Neurotic and Acting Out Behaviors" *J of Personality and Social Psychology* 37, pp1673-82; Spence, J T, Helmreich. R L and Stapp, J 1975 "Ratings of Self and Peers on Sex Role Attributes and Their Relation to Self-Esteem and Conceptions of Masculinity and Femininity" *J of Personality and Social Psychology* 32, pp29-39; Spence, J T 1984 "Masculinity, Femininity and Gender-Related Traits: A Conceptual Analysis and Critique of Current Research" in Maher, B A and Maher, W D (eds) *Progress in Experimental Personality Research, 13: Normal Personality Processes* pp1-97, Academic Press, Orlando, FL; Taylor, M C and Hall, J A 1982 "Psychological Androgyny: A Review and Reformulation of Theories, Methods and Conclusion" *Psychological Bulletin* 92, pp347-66; Whitley, B E 1983 "Sex Role Orientation and Self-Esteem: A Critical Meta-Analytic Review" *J of Personality and Social Psychology* 44, pp765-78; Whitley, B E 1974 "Sex Role Orientation and Psychological Well-Being: Two Meta Analyses" *Sex Roles* 12, pp207-25.

ACKNOWLEDGMENTS

PICTURE AGENCIES/SOURCES

AB Anthony Blake, London.
ASp Allsport UK Ltd.
BC Bruce Coleman Ltd, Uxbridge, Middx.
C Colorific Photo Library Ltd, London, New York.
CJ Camilla Jessel, Twickenham, Middx.
DP Dominic Photography, London
F Format Photographers, London.
FSP Frank Spooner Pictures, London.
GF Genesis Films, Oxford.
H The Hutchison Library, London.
HS Homer Sykes, London.
I Impact Photos, London.
JB Jo Bond Words Pictures, Oxford.
MG Magnum Photos Ltd, London, Paris.
N Network Photographers, London.
PF Petit Format, Paris.
PS Photo Source, London.
R Rex Features Ltd, London.
RHPL Robert Harding Picture Library Ltd, London.
SGA Susan Griggs Agency, London.
SPL Science Photo Library, London.
SRG Sally and Richard Greenhill, London.
T Topham Picture Library, Kent.
TCL The Telegraph Colour Library, London.
TIB The Image Bank, London.
TN The Times Newspapers Ltd, London.
TPL The Photographers' Library, London.
TS Tony Stone Associates, London.
V Viewfinder Colour Photo Library, Bristol.
VI Vision International, London.
WP Wheeler Pictures.
Z Zefa, London.

PICTURE LIST

Page number in **bold** type. Photographer's initials in parentheses.

Frontmatter
2 Couple on beach (LD) TIB. **3** Argument (MBa) MG. Woman making face (Za) MG. **4** Girl in sea (SB) C. **5** Beach scene (JB) R. **6** Bouncing tent (HS) Ascot races (HS). **7** Royal wedding, Marrakesh (BB) MG. Japanese sex show (MMI) H. **8** Breast feeding (AS) VI. **9** Boy and doll, CJ. **10** Christian Lacroix (A) MG. **11** 3 day eventing (PS) TIB. **12** Girl at mirror (KP) Motorcycle rider (KP). **13** Boy in car (KP) Boy and girl on sofa, (ST). **14** Couple at Ascot (BRy) I, Mary Decker at Olympics (TD) ASp. **15** Couple on bed (NDMcK) A. Elderly couple (WM) MG.

Part title Childhood: Girls and Boys **16/17** Boy kissing girl (SZ) TIB.

1 Before Birth
18 Sperm meets egg, FSP/Gamma. **19** Pregnant woman (AS) Z. Embryo, PF/Nestlé/SPL. **21** Fetus (LN). Male genitalia (NB) GF. **22** Fetus PF/Nestlé/SPL. **23** Talking to unborn (K) Liaison/FSP. Birth (SRG) SRG. **25** Woman having scan (NCH) V. Ultrasound images courtesy of West London Hospital, England.

2 Early Infancy
26 Gripping (JdaC) PF. **26/7** Baby on bed (AS) Z. **27** Mother and baby (BF) Z. Child crying (EAr) **28** Father and baby (JS) N. Seaside R. **29** In the air, Novosti FSP/Gamma. **30** Breast-feeding (AS) Z. **31** Study of different walking styles courtesy of Dr Charles Lewis.

3 Adopting a Sex Role
32 At birth (SRG) SRG. Beauty parlor (DS) MG. **33** Fishing (CB) R. Demonstration, Iran (A) MG. **34** Parade (GC) RHPL. Playing nurses, R/SIPA. **35** Masked wrestler (AWe) MG. **36** Baseball (RLa) SGA. **37** Shaving (SRG) SRG. Dolls (JM) C. Go-karts

(SFe) I. **38** Babies (ES) RHPL. Dressing up, R. **38-39** Girl's bedroom (JMcN) WP/C. **39** Boy's bedroom WP/C. **40** Stunt, R. **41** Cookery class (JMa) F. Cleaning windows (BGl) MG. In bath (NDMcK) H.

4 The Freudian View
42 Underwater, R. **43** Potty training, R. **44** Child with red boots (AS) VI. Father-son rivalry (KP). **45** Girl with mother (E) Z. **46** Empty cradle (SLo) SGA. Birth (NDMcK) H. **47** Feeding boys (RK) MG.

5 Brothers and Sisters
48 Seaside, R. **49** Mother reading story (AS) VI. Carrying brother (AS) VI. **50** Brothers with clock (SLo) SGA. **51** Sisters (MBo) SGA. **52** Kibbutz dormitory (PT) C. Girl with baby (AS) VI. Children with baby (JS) N. **53** Rural school children, N Ireland (JOB) F.

6 When Mother Goes to Work
54 Mother going to work (EL) TIB. **54/5** Father going to work (KB) Z. **55** Playing with puppet (RN) Z. **56** Father and daughter, Janeart Ltd/TIB. Telephoning father with baby (MGo) TIB. **57** Mathematics lesson (BP) F. Washing car (DBr) TIB. **58** Going to work (CJ) CJ. **59** Minder and children (SRG) SRG. Mother and son (EA) MG. **60** Paddling pool (RF) C. Playing doctors (AU) TIB. Children painting (ST). **61** Boys cooking (WBi) TIB. **62** Baby in cot (CJ) CJ. Baby (SRG) SRG. Latch key child (KP). **63** Mother and baby (AS) VI.

7 The Roots of Aggression
64 Children playing (SRG) SRG. **66** Girls playing, R. **67** Children wrestling, Japan R. On tree trunk (MA) N. **68** Watching television (JCo) N. **69** Boy with bottle, R. In gymnasium (LS) N.

8 Toys and Play
70 Hide and seek (MK) TIB. Fancy dress (SDC) RHPL. **70/1** Jumping from boat (CJ) CJ. **71** Playing with blocks (PT) C. **72** Boy on telephone (SRG) SRG. **73** Father and son at breakfast (CJ) CJ. Girls and dolls, Marshall/Liaison/FSP. Playing baseball (RK) MG. **74** Miss America Jr (BL) N. Mother and

KEY TO PHOTOGRAPHERS

A Abbas. **AC** Anita Corbin. **AH** Alan Hutchison. **AS** Anthea Sieveking. **ASe** Art Seitz. **AU** Alvis Upitis. **AW** Adam Woolfitt. **AWe** Alex Webb. **B** Berretty. **Bo** Bourseiller. **BB** Bruno Barbey. **BC** Babette Cooper. **BE** Ben Edwards. **BF** Bruce Fleming. **BG** Bruce Glinn. **BH** Brian Harris. **BHo** Bill Holden. **BL** Barry Lewis. **BP** Brenda Prince. **BR** Bernard Régent. **BRy** Brian Rybolt. **CA** Catherine Ashmore. **CB** Catherine Blackie. **CE** C Edinger. **CF** Cliff Feulner. **CJ** Camilla Jessel. **CJo** Carol Jopp. **CL** Cédric Laur· **CSP** Chris Steele - Perkins. **CW** Cary W_..nsky. **DB** David Burnett. **DBr** David Brownell. **DC** David Cannon. **DHt** Diana Hunt. **DK** Don Klumpp. **DL** David Levenson. **DMS** D M Simonet. **DR** Dick Rowan. **DRd** David Reed. **DS** Dennis Stock. **DT** Denny Tillman. **DV** David Vance. **DWH** David W Hamilton. **E** Edgeworth. **EA** Eve Arnold. **EAr** E Arnone. **EE** Elliott Erwitt. **EG** Edna Gladny. **EH** Eric Hartmann. **EL** Elyse Lewin. **ER** Eli Reed. **ERi** Eugene Richards. **ES** Erika Stone. **F** Ferorelli. **FL** Francois Lochon. **G** Gurlitt. **GC** Gina Corrigan. **GF** Geoff Franklin. **GG** G Granham. **GGu** Gilles Guittard. **GK** Geoff Katz. **GLQ** Guy Le Querrec. **GPe** Gilles Peress. **GS** Geray Sweeney. **HS** Homer Sykes.

HT Hanbury-Tenison. **IL** Ian Lloyd. **JA** Jacques Alexandre. **JAz** Jose Azel. **JB** Jacques Bourboulon. **JCa** Julian Calder. **JCo** John Cole. **JCF** Jean Claude Francolon. **JD** J Dimaggio. **JdaC** Jérôme da Cunha. **JDo** Joe Doherty. **JDr** John Drysdale. **JFB** J F Bauret. **JH** Jim Howard. **JK** Josef Kondelka. **JA** Kalish. **JL** Jerry Lodriguss. **JM** John Moss. **JMa** Jenny Matthews. **JMcG** John McGrail. **JMcN** Joe McNally. **JMe** Joel Meyerowitz. **JN** Jeremy Nicholl. **JOB** Joanne O'Brien. **JP** Judah Passow. **JS** John Sturrock. **JU** Jay Ullal. **JW** Jenny Woodcock. **K** Kermani. **Ke** Kennerly. **K** Benser. **KP** Kate Pattullo. **LB** Lee E Battaglia. **LD** Larry Dale Gordon. **LE** Liane Enkelis. **LF** Leonard Freed. **LIT** Luca Invernizzi Tettoni. **LN** Lennart Nilsson. **LS** Laurie Sparham. **M** Mazziotta et al. **MA** Mike Abrahams. **MBa** Michael Bar'Am. **MBo** Michael Boys. **MC** Mark Cator. **MF** Melanie Friend. **MG** Mike Goldwater. **MGo** Michael Going. **MJ** Monique Jacot. **MK** M Kriegelstein. **MM** Maggie Murray. **MMI** Michael MacIntyre. **MR** Mark Richards. **MRo** Martin Rogers. **NB** Nancy Brown. **NCH** Nigel Cheffers-Heard. **NDMcK** Nancy Durrell McKenna. **NM** Nadia Mackenzie. **NS** N Schaeffer. **PD** Peter

Davey. **PF** Paul Freestone. **PFu** Paul Fusco. **PH** Phillip Hayson. **PI** Peter Ibbotson. **PS** Paul Slaughter. **PT** Pennie Tweedie. **PTr** Peter Trievnor. **PW** Patrick Ward. **PZ** Patrick Zachmann. **RA** Robin Adshead. **RB** René Burri. **RBd** Rodney Bond. **RC** Robert Cundy. **RD** Raymond Depardon. **RDM** Raul De Molina. **RF** Rick Friedman. **RFr** Richard Francis. **RH** Robert Harding. **RK** Richard Kalvar. **RLa** Richard Laird. **RLo** Romilly Lockyer. **RM** Robert McFarlane. **RMo** Richard Moll. **RN** Richard Nicholas. **RP** Raissa Page. **RPe** Roger Perry. **RW** R Woldendorp. **RWa** Robert Wallis. **SB** Susanna Burton. **SDC** S H and D H Cavanaugh. **SF** Stuart Franklin. **SFe** Sally Fear. **SH** Scott Henry. **SK** Sebastian Keep. **SN** Steve Niedorf. **S/ L** Schmid/Langsfeld. **SLo** Sandra Lousada. **SM** Steve Mayes. **SRG** Sally and Richard Greenhill. **SSa** Sebastiao Salgado Jr. **ST** Sue Turvey. **SV** Santi Visalli. **SZ** San Zarember. **TD** Tony Duffy. **TE** Tijas Earp. **TSt** Tom Stoddart. **TSv** T Svav. **TV** T Voigt. **V** Vandystadt. **VP** Van Pariser. **WB** Werner Bokelberg. **WBi** Walter Bibikow. **WH** Wally Herbert. **WM** Wayne Miller. **Za** Zachmann. **ZG** Zao Grimberg. **ZL** Zao Longfield.

children (AS) VI. Computers, Minneapolis (DB) Contact Press Images/C. **75** Bicycle race (RFr) C. **76** Boys playing chess (SSa) MG. Water play on Lake Okanogan (RH) RHPL. **77** Playing school (PH) C.

9 Friendship
78 Little girls by pool (SRG) SRG. Fighting over toy (CJ) CJ. **79** Primary education (SLo) SGA. **80** Tree house (DHt) C. Boys diving (B) C. Children playing, China (AH) H. Music for youth, R. **82** Venice, Los Angeles (MMI) H. **82/3** Garden Temple, Japan (BR) DIAF/H. **83** In grass (AS) VI.

10 Skills and Aptitudes
84 Children on slope (AW) SGA. Girls preparing tea party (AS) VI. **85** Catching ball (JM) C. Playing football (AS) VI. **86** Reading to teddy (AS) VI. Learning reading and writing (AS) VI. Dolls' party, Marshall/Liaison/FSP. **87** Making model with straws (MM) F. Lego, R. **88** Painting (CB) R. **89** Computer fair, France (RK) MG. **91** Brain scan (M) SPL. Boy at blackboard (KP).

11 At School
92 Eton metalwork class (SF) V. **92/3** Color coding (JMa) F. **93** Girl working alone (AS) VI. Boy reading (MF) F. **95** Learning with computer (JMcN) WP/C. Boy with mathematics teacher (F) WP/C. **96** Painting faces (MM) F. Boy and girl writing (SRG) SRG. **97** Welders (JDo) Mega/FSP. **98** Boys' primary school, N Ireland (JOB) F. **99** Girls' science class (BP) F.

12 When Parents Split Up
100 Divorce court, France (PZ) MG. **101** Moving house (CJ) CJ. Children, mother and lover (NB) TIB. **102** Father and son (CL) FSP. Worried mother (DT) TIB. **103** Pancake day (BP) F. **104** Family fight (KP). **105** Bunk beds (EA) MG. Meal in the garden (SSa) MG. **106** Father and child (MA) N. On the beach (BC) V. **107** Boy smoking (RK) MG. **108** Looking at photographs (GF) N. **109** Football advice (DK) TIB.

13 Moral Development
110 African children (PF). Children on rocks (GS) I. **111** Broken plate (KP). **112** Squabble (CJ) CJ. Football argument (CB) R. Playground dispute (SRG) SRG. **113** Chess (ST) I. **114** College meeting (EE) MG. **115** Bar mitzvah (AS) VI.

14 Getting Into Trouble
116 Police and boy (LF) MG. **117** Pregnant teenager (JFB/EG) FSP/Gamma. Homework (SRG) SRG. **118** Strangeways prison (CSP) MG. Parisian children (GLQ) MG. **119** Girl with bottle (PFu) MG. **120** Girls in bedroom (TV) Z. Teenagers on motorbikes (RW) SGA. **121** Boys and policeman (HS) I. Boys in bowler hats (SM). **122** Street gang funeral (MR) C. **123** Girls in pub (JCa) I.

15 Puberty
124 Sports day (SRG) SRG. Bedroom (SRG) SRG. Girl and mirror (VP) TS. **126** Eating and chatting (JA) TIB. **127** Girls at window (LF) MG. On beach (EL) TIB. **128** Bicycles (SRG) SRG. **128/9** By the river, Kotoh/Z. **129** Makeup (LS) N.

Part title Adulthood: Men and Women
130/1 Couple in bed (ZG) TIB.

16 Evolution
132 Eskimo capturing seal (WH) RHPL. Yanomamo woman, Brazil (HT) RHPL. **133** Computer development (JMcG) C. **134** Skull (RBd) JB. Mary Leaky (RBd) JB. **135** Picket line (RP) F. Chimpanzee (PD) BC. **136** Skinning bear (WH)

RHPL. **137** Farm labor (MG) N. Yanomamo women in river (HT) RHPL. Mother and baby (NDMcK) H. **138** Film Festival (RD) MG. **139** Couple (RC) RHPL. Computer (MRo) C. **140** Couple, Berlin (RB) MG. **141** Mother and child, Namibia (CJo) RHPL. Yanomamo father and son (HT) RHPL.

17 Sexuality
142 Lovers, Spain (SK) RHPL. **142/3** Nude couple (RM) SGA. **143** The golden years (PFu) MG. **145** Nude couple (RM) SGA. **146** Bottoms up, Hong Kong (IL) H. **147** Beach (G) FSP/Gamma. Male stripper (FL) FSP/Gamma. **148** Young Conservatives dinner, England (HS) HS. At the Ritz, New York (ER) MG. **149** Party brush off (RK) MG. **150** Couple (DWH) TIB. **151** Couple (DV) TIB.

18 Attitudes to Love
152 Couple (WB) G&J Images/TIB. **153** Couple in sea, R. Couple in field, R. **154** Couple in grass (JM) C. **155** Couple in bed (ZG) TIB. **156** Couple in park (NDMcK) H. Couple in car (NB) TIB. **157** Pop concert (MG) N. On the beach (SRG) SRG.

19 Marriage
158 Family hike (AS) VI. Wedding, E Germany (LF) MG. **159** Bride and father (NM) V. **160** Denja Akuku with wives in field (AWe) MG. Couple with donkey (CJ) CJ. Purdah (EA) MG. **161** Indian wedding (HS) I. **162** Sunning on bench (BH) I. Couple laughing (NDMcK) H. **163** Divorce, Moscow (EA) MG. Feeding time (SRG) SRG. **164** Birth (SRG) SRG. Wedding on tightrope (SH) Liaison/FSP. **165** Newlyweds (DMS) FSP/Gamma.

20 Who Looks After the Children?
166 Women and baby bathing (JU) G&J/TIB Images. **167** Parents playing with child (AS) VI. Father washing children, Sudan (PI) RHPL. **168** Mother and child (GGu) TIB. Breast-feeding (NDMcK) H. **169** Swedish father (DR) SGA. **170** Joyful father (JW) V. **171** Computer family (JMcN) WP/C. Househusband (LE) Stock/C. Mother and child on bicycle (NS) Z.

21 Violence Between the Sexes
172 Couple arguing (AS) VI. **173** Football riot, Brussels (DC) ASp. **174** Man hitting woman (GLQ) MG. Woman crying (SN) TIB. **175** Woman leaving home (GK) C. **176** Women in purdah (BB) MG. Family argument (RK) MG. **177** Man and woman (RP) F. Man on telephone (RMo) FSP/Gamma. **179** Self-defense (V) ASp. Women's karate club (AC) I. **180** Women's refuge workers (MM) F. Erin Pizzey and masked child (SRG) SRG. **181** South Korea (TSv) C.

22 Emotions and Adjustment
182 Rugby player (GG) TCL. **182/3** Jumping from plane (Bo) FSP/Gamma. **184** Gardening (AS) VI. **185** Funeral, Texas, T. Former drug addict at rehabilitation centre, Arizona (ER) MG. **186/7** Royal London Yacht Club (HS) HS. **187** Lottery winners (CE) FSP/Gamma. Mother and daughter (MJ) SGA. Pentecostals with babies (JK) MG. **188** John McEnroe (ASe) FSP/Gamma. **189** Mother and baby, Scotland (MA) N. 7 months pregnant (NDMcK) H.

23 In the Workplace
190 Carrying firewood, Nepal (RA) V. **191** Dealing room (TE) TPL. Window cleaner, Dallas, Texas (BL) N. **192** London Metal Exchange (PW) TCL. Childminder (SRG) SRG. **193** Ship's captain (BHo) TPL. Pineapple industry, Thailand (LIT) Photobank BKK/RHPL. **194** Socializing (BL) N. Firewoman teased by colleagues (JDo) Mega/FSP. **195** Geneticists (EH) MG. **196** Police work (JDo)

Mega/FSP. Circuit on light box (LB) C. **197** Judges, procession England (SRG) SRG. Locomotive engineer (JDo) Mega/FSP. **198** Couple doing woodwork (SRG) SRG. **198/9** Doing accounts (CW) C. **199** Paying the bill (CW) C.

24 Influence and Persuasion
200 Nightclub, Miami (AWe) MG. **201** Nightclub, Miami (AWe) MG. **202** Little-girl pose (MMI) H. Golfing couple (S/L) TIB. Having words (AS) VI. **203** Business office (WBi) TIB. **204** Businessman and businesswoman (WBi) TIB. Architects (JCa) PS. **205** Couple (JH) C.

25 Ambition and Leadership
206 Woman firefighter (TSt) FSP. **207** Norwegian Prime Minister, Gro Harlem Bruntland, T. **208** Conductor Sian Edwards at Covent Garden (CA) DP. Waterman's Director, Francine Gomez (JCF) FSP/Gamma. **208/9** Judge Sandra Day O'Connor (Ke) FSP/ Gamma. **209** Airline pilots (PTr) TN. Diane Von Furstenberg (EE) MG. **210** Business people, TS. **210/11** Designers in studio, TS.

26 Creativity
212 Australian designers (PT) I. **212/ 3** Bottle house, Canada (JDr) C. **213** Chef, AB. Dinner ladies (HS) I. **214/5** Sculptor (HS) HS. **215** Dancers (RPe) I. **216** Music for youth R. **217** Jazz, New York (AWe) MG. Christie's auction (BE) TS.

27 Styles of Communication
218 Couple with ball (ZL) TIB. Young couple kissing (HS) HS. **219** Family center, England (MA) N. **220** Drinking champagne (JS) N. Crowd (JP) N. **221** Couple on porch (JD/JA) TIB. Poster, FSP. **222** Women talking (RK) MG. Men talking (RK) MG. **223** Buying antiques, Rainbird/RHPL. Women talking (LF) MG. **224** Two women (ERi) MG. Girls giggling (JU) G&J Images/TIB. **225** Massage (JU) G&J Images/TIB.

28 In the Media
226 Photographers at Royal wedding, England (MC) I. **227** Wrestlers (RDM) Blackstar/C. **228** Sylvester Stallone, Visages/C. **229** Swimwear department (RB) MG. **230/1** Cannes Festival, France, 1980 (GLQ) MG. **230** Book covers courtesy of Worldwide publishers. Leopard attack (CF) TIB. **231** Cheerleader (JN) I. **232** French movie poster (GPe) MG. Thai movie poster (A) MG. **233** Cosmetics poster, Okinawa (ER) MG.

29 Sex Stereotypes
234 Body building (DRd) I. **235** Monroe entertains Army, Chapman Collection/SNAP PHOTO/C. Karpov playing chess (JN) I. **236** Business people (ZL) TIB. **237** Father with scythe (MM) F. **238** Woman driver (JMe) TIB. **239** Beauty contest (RLo) TIB. Father dressing baby (RK) M. **240** Man knitting (PZ) MG. Hanging out washing (SRG) SRG. **240/1** Body building competition (BGl) MG. **241** Camerawoman (EA) MG.

30 Role Versatility
242 Men embracing T. **243** Wimbledon umpire (DL) C. Mechanical engineers (BP) F. **245** Man with umbrella (JAz) Contact Press Images/ C. Footballers (JL) Sports Illustrated/ W. **246** Japanese couple (RWa) JB Pictures/C. Family in park (BHo) TPL. **247** Couple, R.

253